Fathers' Involvement in their Children's Education

Rebecca Goldman

A review of research and practice

National
**Family &
Parenting**
Institute

The National Family and Parenting Institute is an independent charity set up to enhance the quality of family life, by encouraging families and parents to ask for help when they need it, by ensuring they can find the right information and advice and by influencing public policy to make society more family friendly.

Visit our website at www.nfpi.org for information about our publications and research.

The NFPI would like to thank the Families Division at the DfES.

Rebecca Goldman is a social policy and educational researcher who completed this research whilst on secondment to the National Family and Parenting Institute in 2004-05. She has been advising Ministers and policymakers, and commissioning and managing research, for several years in central government departments, currently in the Department for Education and Skills (DfES). Her focus in DfES has been extended schools, parental involvement, childcare and early years intervention.

Series Editor: Clem Henricson, Head of Research & Policy at the National family and Parenting Institute. She was formerly a social policy consultant with a variety of family policy organisations and has published widely in the field of family research.

© NFPI 2005

Published by
National Family and Parenting Institute
430 Highgate Studios
53–79 Highgate Road
London NW5 1TL

Tel: 020 7424 3460
Fax: 020 7485 3590
Email: info@nfpi.org
www.nfpi.org

Design and print: www.intertype.com
ISBN 1 903615 38 0
Registered charity no. 1077444

Contents

Acknowledgements

The author would especially like to thank the project managers and practitioners from the case study programmes in this report, who all spent much time telling me about their initiatives and commenting on drafts of the written case studies; and also everyone else who responded to my consultation about projects and research.

Thanks also to Clem Henricson, Carolyn Unsted, Adrienne Burgess, Helen Barrett, John Clawley, Juliette Collier, Richard Fletcher, Marcia Gibbs, John Gibson, Tessa Hall, Fatima Husain, Veronica McGivney, Andrea Mearing, Alwyn Morgan, Margaret O'Brien, Roger Olley, Vicki Stewart, Sheila Wolfendale, and members of the DfES Fathers Advisory Group for their invaluable comments on my draft report and/or advice and information throughout the research. Very many thanks also to Mariska van der Linden, who worked as a research assistant in August 2004, enthusiastically conducting rigorous searches of bibliographic databases, and to Ruth Lawrence at NFPI for taking this report through the publication process.

The National Family and Parenting Institute would like to thank the Department of Education and Skills for funding Rebecca's secondment.

The Author

Rebecca Goldman carried out this research on fathers' involvement in their children's education whilst on a secondment in 2003-04 to the National Family and Parenting Institute from the Department for Education and Skills. Rebecca has been advising ministers and policymakers, and commissioning research projects, for several years in central government departments; initially in the Department of Social Security, and more recently in the DfES; on extended schools, childcare, nursery education and early years intervention.

The evidence in this report is based on the author's interpretation of home-school and family learning initiatives, research papers, website information and other literature at the time of writing. The views expressed are those of the author.

Executive summary

Introduction

The demographic and policy context

- One aspect of changing families in recent years is greater involvement by fathers in their children's lives. Many initiatives to promote involved fatherhood have emerged.

- There have also been renewed emphases in education on building strong school–home partnerships and on family learning. The Green Paper *Every Child Matters* makes recommendations for family learning programmes, better communication between parents and schools, and involving fathers in school life.

- There is strong research evidence showing that parents' involvement in their children's learning has a substantial impact on children's educational attainment. In light of a gender achievement gap in schools, many experts propose the importance of positive male role models for boys' learning and reading.

- Much of the research published on the relationship between parents and their children's learning uses the term 'parent' but focuses almost entirely on mothers. Fathers are also absent in many family learning programmes and their evaluations.

The research in this report

- This report takes a comprehensive look at fathers' involvement in their school-aged children's[1] learning and education, and in schools and family learning programmes.[2]

- The research was carried out in 2003-04 in partnership with a Department for Education and Skills (DfES) Fathers Advisory Group of local policymakers, voluntary organisations and practitioners, which looked at how best to involve fathers in their children's learning and in schools.

- The term 'father' is used broadly in this report, including both biological/adoptive fathers (resident and non-resident) and a range of other male carers and 'father figures' (such as older brothers, grandfathers, uncles, foster fathers and step-fathers).

---

1   Children aged 4-16.

2   The following definition is used to define family learning programmes: "They should include opportunities for intergenerational learning and, wherever possible, lead both adults and children to pursue further learning...Usually the 'family' should include at least one adult member...and at least one child member." (LSC, 2004).

- Part One of the report looks in detail at the research evidence on the extent of fathers' involvement in their children's learning, schools and family learning programmes; why their involvement is important and the relationships with children's educational outcomes; and the barriers to their involvement.

- Part Two of the report consists of a guide to effective practice in schools and family learning programmes; and 13 in-depth case studies of schools and family learning providers in England and Wales which successfully engage fathers.

- Part Three of the report draws conclusions and assesses the implications of the research findings for central government, local policymakers, and other national and local organisations with a strategic role in schools and family learning.

- An extensive review of research evidence and other literature (published or carried out between 1997 and 2004 in the UK, USA, Australia, New Zealand, Canada and Europe) and projects and practice on fathers' involvement in their children's learning and education was conducted for this report. Extensive searches of bibliographic databases were carried out, and requests for information were made over various practitioner and organisational networks, in summer 2003.

How involved are fathers in their children's learning and education?

Extent of fathers' involvement in their children's learning and education

- Resident fathers are less likely than resident mothers to be involved in many aspects of their children's out-of-school learning and in their children's schools.

- Fathers contribute substantially to specific areas of their children's out-of-school learning: building and repairing, hobbies, IT, maths, science, sports, physical play, outdoor activities and family trips. There is a focus on play, leisure, practical activities and fun. Their involvement in these areas of learning is (in some research studies) at higher rates or more frequent than mothers' participation.

- Considerable proportions of fathers also read with their children, help with homework, and give praise and support to their children for their schoolwork, but at lower rates or less frequently than do mothers. When fathers read with their children, they often use non-fiction, environmental print and recreational materials.

- Additionally, considerable proportions of resident fathers attend parents evenings and general school meetings, and drop off and pick their children up at school, but at lower rates or less frequently than do mothers.

- Fathers are especially unlikely to be volunteers in the classroom, or participants in organised family learning programmes which take place during the daytime and are not targeted at men. A greater proportion of adult learners in wider family learning programmes are men than in family language, literacy and numeracy programmes.

- There are many examples of home–school and family learning programmes which specifically target and successfully engage fathers, including non-resident fathers, fathers in deprived areas, and black and minority ethnic fathers. Many of these are on stereotypically male themes such as sport, ICT and technology, but there are also programmes with learning in visual arts, music, reading and creative writing.

- Gaps in home–school and family learning programmes for fathers include work with teenagers, daughters, single-parent fathers, and children with special needs.

- Much less data was found on the involvement of non-resident fathers and single-parent fathers than on the involvement of resident fathers in two-parent families.

- Non-resident fathers are especially unlikely to be involved in their children's schools. Involvement with their children's out-of-school learning often (but not always) takes place at weekends and has a recreational focus. Schools and family learning programmes have the potential to be a neutral place where non-resident fathers and their children can have positive time together.

- Single-parent fathers tend to get more involved in their children's schools than do resident fathers in two-parent families.

Population groups of fathers who are more and less involved

- Fathers are more likely to be involved if their child's mother is involved in the child's learning and education, they have good relations with their child's mother, they or their child's mother have relatively high educational qualifications, they got involved in their child's life early on, their child is in primary school rather than secondary school, their child is doing well in secondary school, and their child's school is welcoming to parents. The strongest association is with the level of mother's involvement.

- Fathers are less likely to be involved if they are a manual worker, they work evenings, or their child has emotional or behavioural problems in primary school.

- There are mixed findings on whether there are any differences between fathers' involvement in boys' learning and in girls' learning. There is some evidence that fathers spend more time with their sons than their daughters in sports, hobbies, practical tasks, outings and leisure; and that fathers are more involved in secondary schools when they have a male child.

Black and minority ethnic fathers' involvement

- All the research studies accessed on black and ethnic minority fathers' involvement with their children's learning and education were small-scale and localised. Different black and minority ethnic groups differ greatly in their prevalent family structures, gender roles and religious and cultural orientations.

- There is a focus on religion and culture in some black and minority ethnic fathers' involvement in their children's learning. For some of these fathers, religious leaders and community workers are important sources of advice.

- In South Asian and African-Caribbean communities, children often have a range of 'father figures', for example older brothers, uncles and grandfathers, who are likely to live nearby or in the same household.

- Fathers in some families of South Asian origin are more likely than mothers to speak English, and so take on responsibility for communication with their children's schools.

Why involve fathers in their children's learning and education?

Impacts of fathers' overall involvement on children's educational outcomes

- There is consistent evidence that the quality and content of fathers' involvement matter much more for children's outcomes than the quantity of time for which a father and child are in contact or the frequency of contact and visits. This applies to both resident and non-resident fathers.

- In particular, fathers' affection, support and 'authoritative' parenting style are related to children's positive educational outcomes. Poor parenting by fathers is associated with children's decreased educational attainment.

- It is important for teachers to find out about fathers' involvement in the lives of the children in their class so that they can understand the successes and problems of these children much better, and work with these children in an appropriate way.

Impacts of fathers' involvement in their children's learning and education on children's educational outcomes

- Many research studies assessing the impact of fathers' involvement in their children's learning and education on children's educational outcomes are localised and small-scale. This report focused on five high-quality studies with large-scale, nationally representative samples of fathers and children.

- These five studies show that fathers' greater interest and involvement in their children's learning and in schools are statistically associated with better educational outcomes for children, including better exam results, better school attendance and behaviour, and higher educational expectations. There are also associations with better social and emotional outcomes for children.

- In one high-quality study, a father's interest in his child's education had a stronger association with the likelihood of that child having qualifications in adult life than did contact with the police, poverty, family type or the child's personality.

- These statistical associations with fathers' involvement are independent of mothers' involvement. They exist for primary school children and secondary school children; for children in two-parent families, single-mother families with non-resident fathers, and single-father families; and irrespective of the gender of the child.

- Mothers' involvement is no substitute for fathers' involvement. Psychologists write about a 'double dose' effect in which children are influenced by the active involvement of two parents or carers. This leads, not only to greater total parental involvement, but to a diversity of parental skills, interests, parenting styles and types of involvement.

- There are mixed findings on any differences in the strength of impact of fathers' involvement and mothers' involvement. There are also mixed findings on whether or not the strength of impact of fathers' involvement is greater for boys than for girls.

- There is very limited quantitative research evidence on the mechanisms of impact because of data and sample size limitations in research studies. It is rare for studies to isolate one specific mechanism from others.

- Proposed mechanisms include socialisation / role-modelling; direct acquisition of information, skills and learning styles; the formation of key social contacts such as a good relationship with the child's teacher; and enhancement of the father–child relationship. These mechanisms also apply to mothers.

- Small-scale evaluations of family learning programmes involving fathers consistently report many perceived benefits for children and fathers including skill acquisition, greater confidence, a better father–child relationship, and increased engagement with learning. Children much enjoy it when fathers are involved. Fathers develop a better understanding of learning activities and resources for their children, and become more comfortable in schools.

- However, no evaluations of family learning programmes were found that systematically measured outcomes for children, or had control / comparison groups.

Benefits of fathers' involvement for fathers and mothers

- There is the potential for family learning to be a 'progression route' to adult learning for fathers, as it is for mothers. Small-scale evaluations of family learning programmes involving fathers reported some progression on to accreditation for adult learning; mentoring of other men in family learning programmes; and voluntary and paid work in schools, family learning programmes and the community.

- However, no evaluations of family learning programmes were found that systematically measured outcomes for adults, or had control/comparison groups.

- Some writers argue that increased fathers' involvement matters because of a need for gender equity. Just as women are entitled to equality with men in the work and public spheres, so men are entitled to this in the spheres of the home, the school and family services. Additionally, greater father involvement can relieve the burden on mothers who combine work and family commitments.

- There are theories in the fatherhood literature, and evidence from small-scale evaluations of family learning programmes, that greater father involvement can lead to emotional and social benefits for fathers. However, as for working mothers, the juggle for involved fathers between work and family life may be a struggle.

- There are conflicting arguments in the literature, but little robust evidence, about whether or not greater fathers' involvement is beneficial for mothers.

What are the barriers to fathers' involvement?

Cultural belief systems relating to gender roles in families

- There are traditional cultural belief systems about fathers as economic providers, and mothers as childcarers. These beliefs contribute to several other barriers, including the attitudes of some fathers, mothers, children and teachers, the gender pay gap, fathers' long working hours, and 'feminised environments' in education.

Work, lack of time, and the gender pay gap

- Fathers in the UK are much more likely than mothers to work full time. When fathers work, they tend to work long hours (the longest working hours in Europe for fathers). Some fathers also have atypical working hours (i.e. outside the 9-5 working day).

- The gender pay gap, and employment which is insufficiently family-friendly, may both contribute to long working hours. Fathers may not know that family friendly policies exist or apply to them. Fathers may feel uncomfortable discussing family commitments in the workplace, and managers may not be understanding.

- It is widespread in some black and minority ethnic communities for fathers to be working long, unpredictable and atypical hours.

- Single-parent fathers may be especially challenged to combine work and family commitments.

Schools and family learning programmes as feminised environments

- Primary schools and family learning providers are often feminised environments with few male teachers, practitioners or other adults.

Funding issues

- Funding offering little sustainability and from multiple sources have been challenges for family learning programmes. There has been recent progress.

Fathers' beliefs and attitudes

- Many fathers see their family role as predominantly 'a breadwinner'. This view is exacerbated by a consumer culture amongst children. Some fathers feel that they have to work long hours to meet all their families' material expectations.

- Some men see schools, their own education, and involvement in their children's education as 'women's work'; and schools and family learning programmes as 'women's spaces'. This is exacerbated by a relatively high prevalence amongst fathers of bad experiences of school when they were children (higher prevalence than amongst mothers). There is an intergenerational cycle of these beliefs within some families, and a link with the gender achievement gap.

- Men tend to be much more reluctant than women to seek help from health and family services or to disclose about personal issues.

- Peer pressure can be an important factor in maintaining these beliefs and attitudes.

- Differences in how women and men interact may create communication difficulties between fathers and teachers in female-dominated educational settings. Some single-parent fathers say that they are excluded from school-based networks of local mothers. Some Muslim South Asian fathers see the mosque as their social space, and prefer to leave the school and its playground as mothers' social space.

- Fathers are less likely than mothers to think that children's education is equally or more parents' responsibility than that of schools. But quantitative evidence from the UK and

US suggests that fathers are similar to mothers in their levels of interest in and expectations for their children's education. Low-qualified fathers may have little confidence or interest in learning. Evidence is mixed on whether fathers' confidence in helping their children learn is lower than mothers' confidence.

- Some fathers do see it as their responsibility to help their children with their learning and education, and to join family learning programmes. Three common reasons for getting involved are because their children ask them to, to build a closer relationship with their children, and to support their children's educational achievements. Issues commonly discussed by involved black and minority ethnic fathers are wanting their children to do well in school, and the need to impart religious and cultural values. Evidence from small-scale research studies suggests that fathers are less likely to get involved in family learning programmes because they wish to learn new skills for their own benefit, or to gain accreditation, or to meet other adults for friendship. Some mothers see the limited involvement of fathers in their children's learning and education as unproblematic. They expect low involvement and do not question it. Other mothers value fathers' involvement and actively facilitate it.

Potential 'gatekeepers' to fathers' involvement: mothers, children and practitioners

- Mothers may want fathers to be more involved in family life, but on 'their own terms', so retaining control. Mothers may be most likely to act as a gatekeeper when they are not resident with their child's father.

- Some older children take active steps to prevent their parents' involvement in their education. In some research studies, children tend to have traditional views on fathering roles, seeing provision of a family income as central.

- Only limited research evidence has been found on teachers' attitudes towards father involvement. In one study, teachers expected the fathers to have very little involvement in their school and felt more comfortable talking to mothers.

- Some teachers fear possible aggression and child abuse from fathers, or alienating and upsetting mothers, especially when involving non-resident fathers.

Fathers' circumstances

- Individual fathers' circumstances (e.g. geographical distance from child, large family, poor health or disability) may be barriers. Some fathers have low literacy levels, and some minority ethnic fathers have limited English language skills.

Policy and practice in individual schools and family learning programmes

- There is inappropriate policy and practice in some schools and family learning programmes for engaging fathers including:
  - lack of information about children's fathers, particularly non-resident fathers
  - weekday/daytime timing of events and meetings
  - a female orientation to delivery and content of family learning programmes, and recruitment of fathers.

What is effective practice in engaging fathers in schools and family learning programmes?

- Some of the good practice recommendations in the report apply to working with mothers as well as fathers, but research suggests that they can be even more crucial for fathers because of traditional cultural belief systems about gender roles in families, fathers' greater likelihood of full-time work, fathers' greater likelihood to have had bad experiences at school, and so on.

General principles of good practice

- It appears easiest to engage fathers in home–school and family learning programmes developed especially for fathers, although practical family learning activities such as design and technology can engage both mothers and fathers when appropriately designed.

- There are some tried and tested ways of effectively involving fathers in schools and family learning programmes:
  - include non-resident fathers, and a range of male carers and 'father figures', not just resident biological/adoptive fathers
  - consult fathers, mothers, children and practitioners
  - welcome and appreciate fathers
  - recognise, respect and adapt to individual and cultural diversity
  - work in partnership with other organisations, and share good practice.

- In most cases, it is not sufficient to think about the details of specific programmes when engaging fathers. Headteachers and senior managers need to implement a 'whole school' or 'whole family learning provider' approach involving:
  - high-level strategy, planning and commitment with clear policies
  - obtaining sufficient funding
  - staff with appropriate skills and sufficient designated time
  - building positive attitudes amongst all teachers and practitioners (not just those working directly with fathers) towards fathers' involvement, using training and/or reflective practice
  - collecting information about children's fathers and male carers, including non-resident fathers, on school records
  - research and evaluation on working with fathers.

Curricular content, learning methods and information for involving fathers in family learning programmes

- The two most frequent messages on engaging fathers in family learning programmes are to have fun, and to use practical, dynamic, 'hands on' activities, rather than too much discussion. Outings, IT, audio, video, other technology and high-quality materials are popular with fathers. Discussions and workbooks can be used if fathers feel at ease and with skilled facilitation.

- The mapping found several examples of successful family literacy programmes specifically for fathers and children, oriented towards typical male interests, and using web pages and non-fiction.

- Incorporating religious and cultural traditions into family learning programmes can be very successful in engaging black and minority ethnic fathers.

Involving fathers in their children's schools

- Schools can involve fathers, including non-resident fathers, by regularly keeping in touch (by telephone and email where relevant), inviting them to school meetings and events, and working individually with fathers to help children's educational, emotional and social development, all of which many schools do with mothers.

- Schools can also ask fathers to support the school curriculum and to volunteer, for example with after-school sports and helping out with DIY. This can provide positive male role models for boys in schools which have few male teachers.

- Extended schools can involve children's fathers in the services that they offer the local community, for example sports, leisure and adult education. This can be a first step for 'school-phobic' fathers who wish to get more familiar with the school and then support their child's education.

- There are child protection issues to consider when involving fathers in schools and family learning programmes, as there are with any adults, but these should not prevent work with the great majority of fathers.

Practical matters and recruitment

- Professional sports clubs have become popular venues for family learning programmes.

- Ideally, family learning programmes for fathers should be free for the participants, and provide financial help with childcare and transport.

- Recruitment of fathers is often challenging and time-consuming. It requires persistence, creativity, patience, sensitivity and sufficient practitioner resource. A good recruitment message is to explicitly tell fathers how their involvement will help their children.

- 'Pupil post' (where children take school letters and information home to their parents) and school newsletters are generally unreliable methods to get invitations and other information to fathers, in particular non-resident fathers.

- Effective recruitment methods are through children, mothers and involved fathers, making use of peer group power, and imaginative outreach strategies. Offering fathers and their children incentives for their participation can also be very helpful.

More research needed

- There is more inconclusive or complex evidence on the following issues:
  - gender mix amongst teachers and practitioners – male teachers and practitioners may be helpful but are not vital
  - number of sessions in family learning programmes – this may depend on the fathers and programme content

- timing of sessions (daytime, evenings or weekends) – flexibility, taking account of local diversity, and consulting local fathers are all important – non-resident fathers who do not live locally or have limited access to their children may be able to come along with their child only on weekends

- degree of 'traditionally masculine' curricular content – many writers recommend being realistic about typical male interests, and this is often a good first step, but a much broader curricular content can successfully engage fathers, and may be needed for programmes for fathers and daughters

- venues – although school venues can be a barrier for some fathers, most of the case study programmes ran successfully in schools

- accreditation for fathers – this may be a facilitator or inhibitor of fathers' involvement

- more research on these practice issues would be helpful.

What are the policy implications?

The wider context: gender roles, work, childcare, and early fatherhood behaviours

- Fathers' non-economic involvement in their children's lives, and in their learning and education more specifically, would be greatly facilitated by the development of:

  - more flexible societal attitudes to masculinity and fatherhood, in which a greater number of fathers feel able to play non-economic roles in their children's lives, including their learning and education

  - pay equality between men and women in employment

  - more widespread family-friendly employment, including flexible working hours (shift swapping, compressed working hours, flexitime, and time-off-in-lieu schemes) and shorter working hours, for both mothers and fathers

  - a greater supply of quality, affordable childcare.

- The Government has implemented a number of policies and provided financial support to move closer to these goals. One possibility would be for larger employers to set up pilots of paid parental leave schemes, supported by central government, which give fathers and mothers with school-age children (up to the age of 16) some time off work each year to attend school meetings and events, and to help out on school trips and other occasional voluntary work in schools. Employees who are not parents could be given similar time off to carry out other forms of caring or voluntary work in their communities.

- There is the need for a greater emphasis on parenthood education in schools (with discussion of fatherhood and motherhood roles); and continued funding of parenting education targeting fathers, and also couples together, ante-natally, post-natally and in the early years.

Implications for educational policymakers and funders

- The new DfES good practice guide for schools *Engaging fathers – Involving parents, raising achievement,* which has drawn extensively from the research review and case studies in this report, is an important step in disseminating effective practice to LEAs, local LSCs, Ofsted inspectors, schools and family learning providers.

- It would be helpful if training modules for the benefit of headteachers, teachers, other school staff and family learning practitioners on working with fathers were developed for initial practitioner training and continuous professional development.

- Most official guidance for schools on working with parents, and most government communications with parents, use the gender-neutral term 'parents and carers'. However, as shown in this report, in our society at present, fathers and mothers tend to have different family roles, and some different strategies are needed when recruiting and engaging men and women in learning. This suggests the need for a return to some gendered language ('mothers/female carers' and 'fathers/male carers') in the medium term in the strategies, targets, policies, guidance, inspection frameworks, training modules, and communications with parents of key national and local educational organisations.

- Furthermore, some guidance could be revised to suggest examples of the different strategies and good practice often needed to engage fathers and mothers.

- Other policy options to facilitate fathers' involvement in their children's learning and education include:

  - developing and piloting approved family literacy, language and numeracy (FLLN) programmes targeted at fathers and male carers for national roll-out, building on evidence to be gained in Phase Two of the Skills for Families initiative

  - increasing the status of and funding for wider family learning programmes (without reducing the status or funding of FLLN programmes)

  - funding the development and piloting of home–school and family learning programmes specifically for or inclusive of fathers and daughters, fathers and teenagers, non-resident fathers, single-parent fathers, black and minority ethnic fathers, and children and fathers with special needs and disabilities

  - specific funding for recruitment and outreach by schools and family learning providers to engage hard-to-reach learners such as fathers

  - specific funding for LEAs and schools to recruit home–school liaison practitioners, fathers workers and other community workers, and to give some teachers some non-classroom time to work with fathers and mothers.

- Increased fathers' involvement in schools would also be facilitated by continued work by the DfES, the Teacher Training Agency, LEAs and schools to:

  - increase the number of male teachers and other staff in schools

  - pilot initiatives and subsequently make longer-term changes to make schools more attractive to current and future generations of boys, without disadvantaging girls.

1 | Introduction

> "We should recognise the vital role played by
> fathers as well as mothers."
>
> *Every Child Matters* (HM Treasury/DfES, 2003)

One aspect of changing families in recent years is greater involvement by fathers in their children's lives, and many initiatives to promote involved fatherhood have emerged. Over a similar period of time, there has been emphasis in education on building strong school-home partnerships and on family learning. There is strong research evidence showing that parents' involvement in their children's learning has a substantial impact on children's educational attainment. The Green Paper *Every Child Matters* makes recommendations for family learning programmes, better communication between parents and schools, and involving fathers in school life (HM Treasury/DfES, 2003).

Even so, much of the research published on the relationship between parents and their children's learning uses the term 'parent' but focuses almost entirely on mothers. Similarly, fathers are absent in many family learning programmes and their evaluations. An Ofsted report noted the "disturbing absence of men involved in family learning" (Ofsted, 2000), and an evaluation of family learning programmes recommended that research is carried out on how the recruitment, retention and progression of men can be improved (NIACE, 2003).

This report takes a comprehensive look at fathers'[1] involvement in their school-aged[2] children's learning and education. The research was carried out in 2003-04 in partnership with a Department for Education and Skills (DfES) Fathers Advisory Group of local policymakers, voluntary organisations and practitioners which looked at how best to involve fathers in their children's learning and in schools.

Following an Executive Summary, and then this Introduction to set the scene, the report is divided into three parts. Part One looks in detail at the research evidence on the extent of fathers' involvement in their children's education, schools and family learning programmes; why their involvement is important and the relationships with children's educational outcomes; and the barriers to their involvement. Part Two consists of a guide to effective practice in schools and family learning programmes (drawing on relevant research) and 13 in-depth case studies of schools and family learning providers in England and Wales which successfully engage fathers. Part Three draws conclusions and assesses the implications of the research findings for central government, local policymakers, and other national and local organisations with a strategic role in schools and family learning. Each chapter ends with a summary of the key findings. The following section outlines the research questions addressed in each chapter.

---

1 The term 'father' is used broadly in this report, to include biological/adoptive fathers (resident and non-resident) and a range of other male carers and 'father figures' (such as older brothers, grandfathers, uncles, foster fathers, step-fathers).

2 This research investigated fathers' involvement in school-aged children's education (aged 4-16). It did not look at research or practice relating to the early years (0-4 years) or pre-school education.

1.1 Research aims, questions and scope

The aims of the research were to examine, specifically in relation to fathers' involvement in their school-aged children's learning and education:

- types of fathers' involvement out of school, in school and in family learning programmes

- the relationship of this involvement to educational outcomes for children

- barriers to this involvement

- approaches to involving fathers, successful practice, and the evidence base for good practice.

There are many definitions of family learning programmes, but in this report, the following definition is used: "Family programmes aim to encourage family members to learn together. They are learning as or within a family. They should include opportunities for intergenerational learning and, wherever possible, lead both adults and children to pursue further learning...Usually the 'family' should include at least one adult member...and at least one child member" (Learning and Skills Council (LSC), 2004). A narrower definition is in an Ofsted report: "...learning which brings together different family members to work on a common theme for some, if not for the whole, of a planned programme" (Ofsted, 2000).

Family learning also takes place informally in families, for example in the home and during activities outside the home. In this report, informal family learning is referred to as 'parents' involvement in their children's learning', and the term 'family learning' is used to mean organised family learning programmes.

Part One of the report addresses questions such as:

- Are fathers involved in their school-aged children's learning and education, and in schools and family learning programmes? If so, how and do they play a distinctive role? What proportion of fathers get involved, and what level of involvement do they have? (Chapter 2)

- Which population groups of fathers are more – or less – involved? Who are the hard-to-reach fathers? What is known about the involvement of black and minority ethnic fathers? (Chapter 2)

- How does fathers' involvement in their children's learning and education relate to children's outcomes? (Chapter 3)

- What are the impacts of fathers' involvement on fathers, mothers and schools? (Chapter 3)

- What are the barriers to fathers' involvement in their children's learning and education, and in schools and family learning programmes? What are fathers' views and attitudes related to this kind of involvement?[3] What kinds of involvement do fathers want? Why do fathers get involved? (Chapter 4)

---

3   The terms 'involve' and 'involvement' in this report usually refer specifically to fathers' involvement in their children's learning and education, and in schools and family learning programmes. Where these terms refer more generally to fathers' overall involvement in their children's lives, this is noted in the text (for example in Section 3.2).

- What are the views and expectations of key stakeholders (children, mothers, teachers, family learning practitioners, educational authorities)? (Chapter 4)

Part Two of the report looks at questions such as:

- What approaches are people using to successfully involve fathers in schools and family learning programmes? What is the range of effective practice and models? (Chapters 5 and 6)
- What communication channels work for schools and family learning providers to engage fathers? (Chapters 5 and 6)

The research was restricted to fathers' involvement in the learning and education of school-aged children (aged 4-16 years). It did not investigate research or practice relating to the early years (0-3 years) and pre-school education (3-4 years) nor to parenting education and family and children's services more generally (see Levine et al., 1993; Lloyd et al., 2003; Ghate et al., 2000). There is a growing body of literature on guidelines for children's and family services working with fathers which complements this report, including *Working with Fathers: a Guide for Everyone Working with Families* (Burgess and Bartlett, 2004), *What Works with Fathers?* (Lloyd, 2001), and *Fathers and Families* (Burgess, 2002).

The focus of this report is mainly on fathers' involvement in their school-aged children's learning, but other types of fathers' involvement in schools are included too, for example volunteering in schools and participation in extended services in schools. Adult learning programmes[4] are one type of service in 'extended schools',[5] and these can be sometimes be a gateway for fathers' involvement in their children's learning by becoming more comfortable with the school environment.

The term 'father' is used broadly in this report, to include biological and adoptive fathers (resident and non-resident) and a range of other male carers and 'father figures' (such as older brothers, grandfathers, uncles, foster fathers and step-fathers).

It is important to take into account the great diversity of fathers. This report looks at the involvement of black and minority ethnic fathers, fathers in disadvantaged working class areas, unemployed fathers, single parent fathers, and fathers who work long or atypical hours. In some chapters, research findings on different groups of fathers are reported separately, but in other chapters, findings on different groups are integrated into the main text.

Finally, it is important to remember that each father is unique. Therefore, the research findings presented in this report on what is typical for fathers' involvement in their children's learning and education will not apply to every father.

---

4 The term 'adult learning' is used here to mean educational programmes just for adults, in which children do not participate, as distinguished from 'family learning', in which both adult family members and children participate.

5 These schools provide a range of services and activities often beyond the school day to help meet the needs of children and young people, their families and the wider community (www.teachernet.gov.uk).

1.2 Research methods

All three Parts of the report draw on three main sources of evidence:

- a review of research evidence and other literature (published or carried out between 1997 and 2004 in the UK, USA, Australia, New Zealand, Canada and Europe) on fathers' involvement in their children's learning and education

- a review of recent and current practice and projects in England and Wales that engage fathers in family learning and in schools

- 13 in-depth case studies of schools and family learning programmes in England and Wales which successfully engage fathers.

Extensive searches of educational and psychological bibliographic databases were carried out in summer 2003 to find published research; and requests were made over various practitioner and organisational networks in summer 2003 to locate other relevant research and literature (for example, unpublished project evaluations), projects and practice. A number of websites were also searched. The case studies were constructed in 2003-04 from information gained in telephone interviews with project managers and in examination of project documentation and evaluation reports. Further details of the methodology are presented in the Appendix.

All the Chapters in this report except for Chapter 3 are based on a full review of all the relevant research evidence and literature found in the searches. In Chapter 3, a more restricted range of literature is reported, as explained in that chapter.

Discussions of the DfES Fathers Advisory Group 2003-04[6] and a joint DfES/ National Family and Parenting Institute (NFPI) seminar on fathers' involvement in education and family services (in December 2003) also informed our work, particularly on good practice and policy implications.

1.3 The demographic and policy context

This section sets the scene for the rest of the report by summarising some recent changes in family structures, employment and gender roles in the UK, and also recent policy developments of relevance. The topic of this report, fathers' involvement in their children's learning and education, cuts across a number of policy areas: parents' involvement in their children's education and in schools; family learning programmes; reducing the gender achievement gap in schools; work-life balance and family-friendly employment; and fathers' roles in families.

Changing family structures and employment

There have been substantial changes in family structures in the UK and some other countries over the past 30 years which are associated with an increase in the proportion of children who have a non-resident father and/or a resident step-father or other male carer (Box 1). There have also been changes in employment which have increased the number of children a father working long or atypical hours or not working at all, and with a mother who works outside the home (Box 2). These changes have had an influence on fathers' overall relation-

---

6   The information from these meetings which is included in this report does not necessarily reflect the views of the DfES. The group included a range of policymakers, voluntary organisations and practitioners.

Box 1: Changing family structures

- **Less marriage and more cohabitation**, with the marriage rate for men marrying for the first time in 1997 being about a third of the rate in 1971 (Lewis, 2000b)

- **More divorce**, with a sharp increase in divorce rates during the 1960s and 1970s: about 40% of children born to married parents "will have experienced their parents' divorce by the time they are 16" (Lewis, 2000b)

- **More births outside marriage**, with almost 40%of babies born each year having parents who are cohabiting – the rate in the early 1970s was 8% (Lewis, 2000b): cohabitees' children are even more likely than married parents' children to experience their parents' separation

- **More single parent families and more non-resident fathers** - nearly a quarter of children live in one-parent families, mainly (90%) with the mother (Office for National Statistics, 2003)

- However, Lewis (2000b) notes that "despite the image of the absentee father and historically high levels of divorce, 7 out of 10 families consist of dependent children living with both their birth parents."

- **More children with a resident step-parent -** more than one-tenth of dependent children (Office for National Statistics, 2003)

Box 2: Changing employment

- **Longer working hours, especially for fathers:**

  - Fathers in the UK work the longest hours in the European Union, on average about 47 hours a week (O'Brien and Shemilt, 2003; Hatter et al., 2002). Around one in eight fathers work 60 hours a week or more, and almost 40% of fathers work 48 hours or more a week

  - "The volume of paid work undertaken by fathers remains two-thirds higher than that undertaken by mothers." (Hatter et al., 2002)

- **More shift work and work at atypical hours (the '24-hour society'):** About 40% of fathers in dual-income families working early mornings, 45% working evenings, 17% working night shifts and about a third working at least one Sunday a month (La Valle et al., 2002)

- **Greater long-term unemployment and decreased manual work**, with nearly one-fifth of households having no adult working

- **More mothers working:**

  - Two-thirds of mothers with dependent children are either working or actively seeking work, compared with fewer than half in the early 1970s (Lewis, 2000b)

  - Most of these mothers work part time (Equal Opportunities Commission, 2003)

- **More children being cared for by grandparents and in group childcare settings** whilst their mothers and fathers are working ships with their children, and more specifically on fathers' involvement in their children's learning and education, as seen throughout this report. They also mean that a wide range of male carers and 'father figures' may be involved in children's learning and education.

Changing gender roles in families

Despite changing gender relationships in society and increasing rates of mothers in employment, resident fathers still tend to have greater responsibilities as economic providers ('breadwinners') than resident mothers (see Box 2). They mostly spend less time with their children and are less likely than mothers to have responsibility for organising their children's daily lives and care (Clarke and O'Brien, 2004; Warin et al., 1999; Lewis, 2000b; Pleck and Masciadrelli, 2004; Burgess and Ruxton, 1996). These traditional gender roles are likely to limit fathers' potential involvement in their children's learning and education.

However, the fact that fathers generally play a less extensive role than mothers at home does not mean they play no role at all. A literature review commissioned by the Equal Opportunities Commission (EOC) reports that about one-third of active childcare by parents is carried out by fathers, often when mothers are working (EOC, 2003). Teenagers in research in a working class area of East London typically reported that, on weekdays, they spent about four and a half hours with their father, and just under six hours with their mother, increasing by about three hours with each parent at weekends (O'Brien and Jones, 1996). Boys in this study reported spending more time with fathers and slightly less time with their mothers than did girls.

Many writers say that fatherhood is in a time of change and negotiation (O'Brien and Jones, 1996), or even "confusion and disagreement" (Lewis, 2000b) (also see Burgess and Ruxton, 1996). Fathers are beginning to share childcare with mothers, especially where both parents work full time (Equal Opportunities Commission, 2003). Several authors remind us that the traditional roles of father as breadwinner and mother as non-earning carer emerged only during the 19th century with industrialisation and changes in men's working patterns (Lewis, 2000b).

In terms of resident fathers' time spent with their children, most sources show a rising amount of this time (although slowly) since the 1970s in both the UK and US (O'Brien, 2004). A small increase in fathers' involvement applies in the US in two-parent families where both the mother and father are in paid work (Pleck and Masciadrelli, 2004), although "even when both mothers and fathers are employed 30 or more hours per week...many fathers assume little responsibility for childcare" (Lamb and Tamis-Lemonda, 2004). Fathers' involvement in childcare has increased to a greater extent than their contribution to other work in the home (Gershuny, 2000), and they are now children's most frequent carers whilst mothers are working (Lewis and Warin, 2001; EOC, 2003).

Qualitative research commissioned by the EOC found four main categories of fathering role (Hatter et al., 2002). These ranged from 'enforcer dad' (not involved at all in the day-to-day care of children) to 'fully-involved dad' (equal sharing of responsibility for household tasks and childcare), but also included the most common two groups of 'entertainer dad' (entertains the children whilst the mother does household work, and is not involved in housework) and 'useful dad' (entertains the children, but also helps out with childcare and some household tasks, although the mother remains in charge of the household). Lewis and Warin (2001) remind us that "most men are neither 'superdads' nor 'absentee fathers'"; and O'Brien (2004) that "contemporary fathers are a diverse and somewhat polarised group".

In the context of potential barriers to fathers' involvement in their children's learning and education, Section 4.1 of this report discusses cultural belief systems relating to gender roles in families. Sections 4.5 and 4.6 discuss the corresponding beliefs of fathers, mothers, children and teachers.

Policy on parental involvement in children's education

In education in Britain (DfEE, 1998; HM Treasury/DfES, 2003) and some other countries (Desforges and Abouchaar, 2003; Fletcher and Dally, 2002; Nord et al., 1997), parents are seen as active partners with teachers in children's education, and schools are encouraged to build effective home-school relationships. There is strong research evidence showing that parents' involvement in their children's learning and education, as well as overall parenting styles, have more impact on children's educational attainment than do family background, family size and level of parental education (Desforges and Abouchaar, 2003; DfES, 2003d).

Therefore, engaging parents is seen as an essential element in improving the educational achievement of school children, so contributing to the Government's educational standards agenda. The DfES strategy for parental involvement has three main elements:

- communicating with parents, including providing printed information

- giving parents a more effective voice

- encouraging parental partnerships with schools.

Home–school agreements[7] between parents and schools have been introduced in England. Other DfES policies and programmes to involve parents in their children's education include: a requirement for schools to produce an Annual Report and School Prospectus and to hold an annual meeting for parents; developments in parent governors' roles in schools; parental involvement in Ofsted inspections; and a wide range of information for parents on education such as *Parents and Schools* magazine, *The Parent Centre* website, and booklets on the school curriculum, learning at home, and other educational issues (see www.standards. dfes.gov.uk/parentalinvolvement/ and www.teachernet.gov.uk/wholeschool/familyandcommuunity/workingwithparents/).

There have been a great number of parental involvement and home-school initiatives[8] in local education authorities (LEAs), schools, the media, and the voluntary sector (Desforges and Abouchaar, 2003). Some schools now employ home-school practitioners and other community workers to work with families on school issues.

Schools have also sought to involve parents in children's attendance and behaviour as part of the Government's Behaviour and Attendance Strategy. Recently, Parenting Contracts and Parenting Orders have been introduced to both support and sanction parents whose children do not attend school or who have been excluded from school.

---

7 A home–school agreement "is a statement explaining: the school's aims and values; the school's responsibilities towards its pupils who are of compulsory school age; the responsibilities of the pupil's parents; and what the school expects of its pupils" (The DfES Standards Site, October 2003).

8 For examples see www.teachernet.gov.uk; www.standards.dfes.gov.uk and www.dundee.ac.uk/fedsoc/ParentsinEducation

So how have parents responded to this direction in educational policy and practice? According to a summary of research published by the DfES:

- most parents in England believe that they share responsibility for their child's education with schools

- about 70% of these parents say that they want more involvement in their children's schools

- about one-third of these parents feel very involved in their child's school life

- parents in Britain spend about four times as much time doing homework or reading with their children as they did 35 years ago (DfES, 2003d citing Gershuny, 2000).

Although this looks promising, there are great variations both in children's educational achievement and in parental involvement, especially between different social classes (Desforges and Abouchaar, 2003). This has led to an inclusion agenda in education to make sure that all children benefit from a quality education.

More recently, policy in the DfES has gone one step beyond parental involvement in children's education, with support given to 'extended schools'. These schools provide a range of services and activities often beyond the school day, to help meet the needs of children and young people, their families and the wider community, for example adult education, ICT facilities and community sports programmes (www.teachernet.gov.uk/wholeschool/extendedschools).

Family learning programmes

A working definition of family learning programmes was given in Section 1.1. There are many different family learning providers including LEAs, schools, early years settings, primary health care trusts, social services, voluntary sector organisations, adult education colleges, libraries, museums, sports and leisure services, religious bodies, the private sector and the media (NIACE, 2003). In family learning programmes, teachers of children and teachers of adults (the latter are also referred to as adult education practitioners) often work together to share their knowledge and skills, involving partnership working between different sectors. There is a National Family Learning Network and an annual Family Learning Week (www.campaign-for-learning.org.uk).

The Government has set up the national Learning and Skills Council (LSC) and local LSCs to fund and support adult ("lifelong") learning, including adult and community learning and further education. There is a 'widening participation' agenda for increasing the engagement of adults from disadvantaged groups in education and training. As part of adult and community learning, the LSC funds and supports family learning programmes, calling them 'family programmes'. LEAs have family learning co-ordinators who plan, fund, co-ordinate and deliver family learning programmes in their local area, and develop local infrastructure for family learning, in partnership with their local LSC and other family learning providers. Requirements and guidelines for these programmes are set out in *Family Programmes: Guidance for Local Learning and Skills Councils and Local Education Authorities 2004/05* (LSC, 2004).

The LSC defines the objectives of family programmes that it funds: to "develop the skills or knowledge of both the adult and child participants", and "help parents/carers to be more active in the support of their children's learning and development and to understand the impact of that support" (LSC, 2004).

LSC-funded family programmes are divided for funding and organisational purposes into 'family literacy, language and numeracy' (FLLN) and 'wider family learning' (all other curricular areas). Wider family learning programmes are less prevalent than FLLN programmes, and their funding level is lower than for FLLN (Ofsted, 2000; NIACE, 2003). For 2004-05, the LSC received an allocation from the DfES of £23 million for FLLN and £12 million for wider family learning. This was a substantial increase from the 2002-03 figures of £15.3 million for FLLN and £7.5 million for wider family learning (NIACE, 2003).

The aims of FLLN programmes funded by the LSC are to "help parents and their children to improve their literacy, language and numeracy skills separately and together" (LSC, 2004). Details of approved FLLN programmes (developed and managed by the Basic Skills Agency) are given at www.familyprogrammes.org. These programmes are part of the Government's *Skills for Life* strategy, which has set national targets for improving adults' basic skills in literacy, language and numeracy (DfEE, 2001), and introduced national literacy and numeracy qualifications (www.dfes.gov.uk/readwriteplus/). In *Skills for Life*, parents are one of the national target groups, and some LEAs have separate FLLN co-ordinators.

Skills for Families, a joint initiative of the DfES and the LSC, started in 2003 with 12 local LEA/LSC pilot partnerships (www.skillsforfamilies.org) and has recently been extended into Phase Two with up to nine new projects (DfES/LSC, 2004a). It is managed by a consortium led by the Basic Skills Agency. Amongst other objectives, this initiative is developing and testing a range of delivery models for FLLN; and disseminating effective practice.

Wider family learning has a broader curriculum than FLLN, for example ICT, arts and crafts, sports and music, although programmes may also include elements of FLLN (LSC, 2004). This breadth can effectively engage hard-to-reach groups of learners including fathers (Ofsted, 2000; NIACE, 2003) and can "be central to community capacity building and to the regeneration or renewal of neighbourhoods and communities" (LSC, 2004). NIACE (2003) reported that nearly 70 per cent of LEAs "have a higher demand for wider family learning programmes than they are able to supply". Some work on increasing the status of wider family learning is underway, for example, the DfES is encouraging the funding of family learning programmes in a sporting context (NIACE, 2004; LSC, 2004).

NIACE (2003) and Ofsted (2000) reported that improvements to the infrastructure of family learning were needed, although this infrastructure has grown considerably over the past few years. For example, NIACE (2003) recommended: a single national framework for family learning; a longer-term, more sustainable funding framework; a national staff development and training strategy for practitioners; the development and extension of local and regional family learning networks; and the building of capacity in local LSCs to support LEAs and other family learning providers.

Good progress has already been made towards these goals, for example three-year funding allocations to LEAs by local LSCs (NIACE, 2003, 2004). National occupational standards are being developed for family learning practitioners (New Directions Consulting Ltd, 2004b) and a national FLLN Professional Development Programme for teachers of children and of adults has been introduced. FLLN practitioners have to attain qualifications in a *Skills for Life* Teaching Qualifications Framework. Prior to September 2001, there was no requirement for those teaching in adult or further education to possess a teaching qualification.

The gender achievement gap

The school achievement of boys is lower than that of girls in the UK and some other countries, and this is known as the 'gender achievement gap' (McGivney, 1999, 2004). According to Millard and Hunter (2001), "the gap in reading test scores between boys and girls aged 9 in England and Wales was more than twice that of the United States and Switzerland". The gap is now narrowing in some areas of the curriculum (e.g. reading), and "opinions differ on the magnitude and gravity of the gender gap", which varies in different ethnic groups (McGivney, 1999, 2004). Social class differences in achievement are much greater.

Boys are also substantially more likely than girls not to attend school and to be excluded from school, especially those from working-class families and African-Caribbean families. There are strong links between poor school achievement and school exclusion amongst boys and later unemployment and crime, especially with the reduction in unskilled jobs in recent times (McGivney, 1999). There has been much action nationally to reduce the gender achievement gap, and much research conducted into this issue (www.standards.dfes.gov.uk/genderandachievement).

Many experts propose the importance of fathers and 'father figures' acting as positive male role models for boys' learning and reading, as well as for their mental health and behaviour (e.g. Yeung et al., 2000; Bryant and Zimmerman, 2003). In fact, it is argued that having positive male role models could break intergenerational cycles of low school achievement and criminal behaviour among males in some families (McGivney, 1999; Home Office, 1998a).

Policy and initiatives on fatherhood

Responding to both demographic changes and changing societal attitudes about gender roles, there has been a rapid increase in policy and programme focus on fatherhood over the past decade, both in government and outside government (Clarke and O'Brien, 2004; McGivney, 2004; Lewis, 2000b). The initial policy direction in government was largely economic (Lewis, 2000b), with the formation of the Child Support Agency in 1991 to make sure that non-resident parents (then known as 'absent parents'), who were mainly fathers, contributed financially to their children, at the same time reducing the Income Support payments paid by the state to many single parent mothers.

Since 1997 the Government has widened this focus to support fathers' non-economic roles in family life. The Government document *Supporting Families* included a statement that "fathers have a crucial role to play in their children's upbringing" (Home Office, 1998b). The Family Support Grant,[9] which funds innovative voluntary sector projects which support parents, has had a focus on fathers for some of its funding rounds.

Since 1 December 2003, unmarried fathers can gain legal parental responsibility for their children by registering the birth together with the child's mother. On 21 July 2004, the Government published the Green Paper *Parental Separation: Children's Needs and Parents' Responsibilities* to improve the outcomes for children following parental separation and "better support fathers who are going through separation" (Department for Constitutional Affairs, Department for Education and Skills, and Department for Trade and Industry, 2004); this was out for consultation at the time of writing.

---

9 The Family Support Grant was originally administered by the Home Office. It has now been incorporated into the new Strengthening Families Grant programme at the DfES.

Following an influential publication on public policy and fatherhood (Burgess and Ruxton, 1996), there are now many national, regional and small-scale local initiatives promoting involved fatherhood (www.fathersdirect.com). A national voluntary organisation, Fathers Direct, provides information and support to both fathers and the practitioners who work with them, and it campaigns on fatherhood issues, taking the well-being of the child as its starting point. In 2004, a Fatherhood Forum of practitioners working with fathers was created, and in April 2004, Fathers Direct organised a national conference, 'Working With Fathers', with government ministers speaking.

It is important to note that interest in involved fatherhood is also growing in other countries. For example, in 1995 in the US, President Clinton issued a memorandum asking all executive agencies and departments to include fathers in their policies, programmes and research where appropriate and feasible (Nord, 1998).

Fathers and work-life balance

In 2000, the Government introduced a Work-Life Balance campaign to encourage and support work-life balance initiatives for mothers, fathers, and employees without children. The objectives of this campaign are to "help employers to recognize the benefits of adopting policies and procedures to enable employees to adopt flexible working patterns" (Department for Trade and Industry) (www.dti.gov.uk/work-lifebalance in October 2004).

The campaign involves persuading employers that work-life balance will benefit their business or service, generating and disseminating good practice and research on work-life balance, and working in partnership with employers on special initiatives. There has been some funding available to help employers meet costs, such as The Partnership Fund.

Originally, the impetus for this work was mothers' needs for family-friendly employment, but more recently, there has been a focus on fathers too.

> "Fathers are more likely to work long hours, and therefore it is generally they who miss out most on the opportunity to share in the upbringing of their children...Supporting greater participation of men in family responsibilities is important to the objective of gender equality, and as important as increasing women's ability to participate in the labour market"
>
> *Balancing work and family life: enhancing choice and support for parents*
> (HM Treasury and DTI, 2003)

Organisations outside government also play a major role in supporting family-friendly employment for both mothers and fathers: the Equal Opportunities Commission (EOC, 2003, 2004), and voluntary organisations such as Working Families (Working Families, 2004). The EOC has published research on fathers balancing work and family life (O'Brien and Shemilt, 2003; Hatter et al., 2002). Specifically in relation to fathers, Fathers Direct has launched a Charter for Father Friendly Britain to work with employers and public services to develop 'father-friendly workplaces', in partnership with the company BT (Fathers Direct, 2004b; Fisher, 2004). A network of 'Employers for Fathers' will disseminate good practice.

New legal measures have been introduced to create family-friendly employment (HM Treasury and Department for Trade and Industry (DTI), 2003). In the 2002 Employment Act (effective from April 2003), the DTI introduced new regulations on rights for employees[10] who are mothers, fathers, guardians or foster parents, or their partners, to apply to their employer for flexible, part-time and home working arrangements when their children are under six years old or under 18 years old if they have disabilities (www.dti.gov.uk/workingparents). Employers "have a statutory duty to consider these requests seriously" according to specific procedures, although "there will always be circumstances when the employer is unable to accommodate the employee's desired work pattern" (DTI, 2003a).

Additionally, since April 2003, mothers and fathers[11] who have completed at least one year's service with their employer are entitled to 13 weeks of unpaid parental leave to care for their children (www.dti.gov.uk/workingparents), but this applies only to children's first five years of life[12] (DTI, 2003b).

Other relatively new rights for all working adults (Warin et al., 1999) include the European Working Time Directive in 2000, and the introduction of the National Minimum Wage. However, fathers in the UK have the option to opt-out voluntarily from the Working Time Directive, which limits weekly work to 48 hours. At the time of writing this report, the DTI had recently issued a Consultation on Working Time to seek views on opt-out and other Directive issues.

Fathers, schools and family learning programmes

A prominent Government focus on fathers has been in the early years, childcare, education and family learning spheres. Fathers Direct, in their response to the Green Paper *Every Child Matters,* mention the "pioneering work" of the DfES in looking at engaging fathers in schools, and that "this is the most precisely and well-defined gender specific measure in the whole Green Paper" (Fathers Direct, 2003). Additionally, one element of the evaluation of Sure Start local programmes has been about father involvement (Lloyd et al., 2003), and the Sure Start Unit has had a target for more men amongst early years and childcare practitioners.

The initial drive for looking at fathers and schools was reducing the achievement gap between teenage boys and girls, and in 2002, the DfES ran a *Dads and Sons* campaign to raise awareness of the importance of fathers' involvement in their teenage sons' (11-14-year-olds) learning, and to increase fathers' involvement. The campaign comprised two booklets and a website (DfES, 2002a; see www.dfes.gov.uk/dadsandsons).

Last year, the Green Paper *Every Child Matters* included a statement that universal services for parents should ensure "better communication between parents and school...and especially fathers" (HM Treasury/DfES, 2003). In 2003, the DfES set up a Fathers Advisory Group of practitioners and policymakers to look at how best to involve fathers in their children's learning and in schools. This activity around fathers and children's education has recently resulted in a DfES good practice guide for teachers on how to engage fathers in schools: *Engaging fathers – Involving parents, raising achievement (*DFES, 2004a), which has drawn substantially from the evidence review and case studies in this report.

---

10 Those with a qualifying length of service, and excluding agency workers and members of the armed forces.

11 And others who have "obtained formal parental responsibility for a child".

12 Or, in the case of adopted children, the first five years after their placement; and, in the case of children with disabilities, 18 weeks parental leave up to the child's 18th birthday.

Additionally, the DfEE issued a guidance note[13] to maintained schools in 2000 about the legal requirements and good practice in involving all parents, (where possible) in their children's education including non-resident parents: *Schools, 'Parents' and 'Parental Responsibility'* (DfEE, 2000).

As mentioned earlier, in terms of fathers and family learning programmes, Ofsted (2000) wrote that "there is a disturbing absence of men involved in family learning". Three years later, the voluntary organisation NIACE recommended that there is "a need for "further research of successful programmes especially with regard to fathers and children...the curriculum should be broadened to include the arts, popular culture, sport and leisure...this would help appeal to under-represented groups such as men..." (NIACE, 2003).

Phase Two of the *Skills for Families* initiative requires new partnerships to develop new approaches to FLLN from a list that includes "promotion and content that brings in fathers, including non-resident fathers" and "programmes that use sport as a focus" (DfES/LSC, 2004a). Additionally, male family members are a priority group for LSC-funded wider family learning programmes (LSC, 2004). In the past year (2003-04), there have been several national and regional conferences looking at fathers, other male family members and family learning either as their prime focus or in workshops.

There have been also been several articles written in the specialist and general media in the UK and US about how to involve fathers in their children's learning and education (BBC News, 2003; Pendleton, 2003; DfES, 2003a; Wallace, 2000; Brookes, 2002; Mitchell, 1993; Reissman, 2001; De Nicola, 1997).

1.4 Summary

- One aspect of changing families in recent years is greater involvement by fathers in their children's lives. Many initiatives to promote involved fatherhood have emerged.

- There has been renewed emphasis in education on building strong school-home partnerships and on family learning. The Green Paper *Every Child Matters* makes recommendations for family learning programmes, better communication between parents and schools, and involving fathers in school life.

- There is strong research evidence showing that parents' involvement in their children's learning has a substantial impact on children's educational attainment. In light of a gender achievement gap in schools, many experts propose the importance of positive male role models for boys' learning and reading.

- Much of the research published on the relationship between parents and their children's learning uses the term 'parent' but focuses almost entirely on mothers. Fathers are also absent in many family learning programmes and their evaluations.

- This report takes a comprehensive look at fathers' involvement in their school-aged children's learning and education, and in schools and family learning programmes (children aged 4-16).

---

13 This guidance is not statutory guidance and does not provide a complete statement of the law in this area.

- The research was carried out in 2003-04 in partnership with a Department for Education and Skills (DfES) Fathers Advisory Group of local policymakers, voluntary organisations and practitioners which looked at how best to involve fathers in their children's learning and in schools.

- The term 'father' is used broadly in this report, to include both biological and adoptive fathers (resident and non-resident) and a range of other male carers and 'father figures' (such as older brothers, grandfathers, uncles, foster fathers and step-fathers).

- The following definition is used to define family learning programmes: "They should include opportunities for intergenerational learning and, wherever possible, lead both adults and children to pursue further learning...Usually the 'family' should include at least one adult member...and at least one child member" (LSC, 2004).

- Part One of the report looks in detail at the research evidence on the extent of fathers' involvement in their children's learning, schools and family learning programmes; why their involvement is important and the relationships with children's educational outcomes; and the barriers to their involvement.

- Part Two of the report consists of a guide to effective practice in schools and family learning programmes and 13 in-depth case studies of schools and family learning providers in England and Wales which successfully engage fathers.

- Part Three of the report draws conclusions and assesses the implications of the research findings for central government, local policymakers, and other national and local organisations with a strategic role in schools and family learning.

- A wide-ranging review of research evidence and other literature (published or carried out between 1997 and 2004 in the UK, USA, Australia, New Zealand, Canada and Europe) and projects and practice on fathers' involvement in their children's learning and education was conducted for this report. Extensive searches of bibliographic databases and websites were carried out, and requests for information were made over various practitioner and organisational networks, in summer 2003.

Part One

Research as context

2 | How involved are fathers?

> "...parent involvement in our schools...usually translates in actuality to Mom Power – as in class mother, mom chaperone, mother as volunteer, and so on. Where, oh where, has Dad disappeared to?"
>
> Reissman, 2001

> "There are fathers who read bedtime stories to their children
> And there are fathers who cannot read."
>
> A poem written at the International Fatherhood Summit, England, 2003 (Fathers Direct/Van Leer Foundation Fatherhood Summit Delegates, 2003, in Burgess and Bartlett, 2004)

Much research on parents' involvement in children's education and home–school relations uses the term 'parent' rather than 'mother' or 'father', which can be described as a "gender-neutral" approach (Turbiville et al., 2000). Some research studies collect information from both mothers and fathers, but then aggregate these two distinct groups into one group of 'parents' for analysis and reporting (as discussed in Flouri and Buchanan, 2004; Fletcher and Dally, 2002; Shumow and Miller, 2001). But, in other studies, the samples of 'parents' in the research are exclusively or mainly mothers, often because the 'parents' involved in home–school/family learning programmes are exclusively or mainly mothers, as seen later in this chapter (Brassett-Grundy, 2002; Fletcher and Dally, 2002; Clough et al., 2000; Ortiz, 2001; Stile and Ortiz, 1999; Turbiville et al., 2000; Caddell, 1996).

It is misleading to use the word 'parent' if research is based mainly or entirely on mothers; and research that aggregates fathers and mothers into a group of 'parents' offers a limited perspective. Fletcher and Dally (2002), writing about parents' involvement in literacy activities with their young children, argue that "using gender neutral language in studies...may mask important gender differences between mothers and fathers in their attitudes and approaches to participation".

So, returning to the quote at the beginning of this chapter, is 'Mum Power' dominating parents' involvement in children's learning and education, and has Dad disappeared? To help unpack this, the following questions are addressed in this chapter:

- **Section 2.1**

What is the range of ways in which fathers can get involved in their school-aged children's learning and education?

How do these types of involvement relate to key models in the parental involvement in children's education research literature, and in the fatherhood research literature?

- **Section 2.2**

What should be taken into account when interpreting research studies on fathers' involvement in their children's learning and education?

- **Section 2.3**

What proportion of fathers get involved, and what level of involvement do fathers have? In what types of learning and in what aspects of children's education are fathers most involved? How does this compare with mothers' involvement? Is there a distinctive 'fathers' role'?

- **Section 2.4**

Which population groups of fathers are more involved and which are less involved?

- **Section 2.5**

What is known about the involvement of black and minority ethnic fathers?

The answers to these questions are based on the evidence gained from comprehensive searches of educational and psychological bibliographic databases in summer 2003 (see Chapter 1 and the Appendix).

The focus in this chapter is on fathers' behaviours with regard to their children's learning and education, whereas fathers' beliefs and attitudes are discussed in Chapter 4.

2.1 Types of fathers' involvement in their children's learning and education

First, models in the research literature on parental involvement in children's education are examined. According to DfES (2003d), a key summary of research evidence, there are two broad types of such involvement:

- "Involvement in support of the individual child at home and at school", which is defined as comprising activities which primarily benefit the learning and education of parents' own children, such as reading together at home, going together on outings with a learning content, or attending parents evenings at school and talking informally to their children's teachers.

- "Involvement in the life of the school", which is defined as comprising activities benefiting the whole school, and not just the parent's own children, such as school governance and classroom volunteering.

Epstein (2002) has developed a more detailed model of home–school–community relationships, with six categories of partnership:

- 'Parenting', which relates to families' basic obligations

- 'Communication' between families and schools

- 'Volunteering' of parents in schools

- 'Learning at home' between parents and children (including family learning activities)

- Parents' participation in 'school decision making'

- 'Collaborating with the community', which relates to the idea of 'community schools' in which "programs and services for students, parents and others are offered before, during and after the regular school day", i.e. similar to the 'extended schools' currently being funded in England by the DfES.

In this model, school–family relationships are distinguished "at an institutional level (e.g. when a school invites all families to an event or sends the same communications to all families)" and "at an individual level (e.g. when a parent and a teacher meet in conference or talk by phone)".

Within the fatherhood research literature, a commonly used model of resident fathers' involvement was developed by American researchers (Lamb, Pleck, Charnov and Levine) in the 1980s (Pleck and Masciadrelli, 2004). There are three main categories:

- 'Engagement', which is fathers' direct interactions with their children, including joint father–child activities (this category has been most researched)

- 'Accessibility', which is fathers' availability for potential interaction with their children by being physically present (including elsewhere in the home), or otherwise available (e.g. by telephone)

- 'Responsibility' for childcare and other resources for their children (this category has been least researched)

and two types of 'responsibility':

- 'process', which is taking initiative, remembering, monitoring and planning for the children's care; asking for and managing contributions of other individuals (including fathers) to the children's care (deciding what needs to be done and when, "regardless of who actually ends up doing them"); processing relevant information

- 'indirect care', which comprises "activities conducted for the child but not with the child", such as arranging appointments, arranging non-parental childcare, organising children's time with friends, and shopping for children.

Other fatherhood researchers discuss the different 'roles' that fathers play in the lives of their children (Halle,1999; Palkovitz and Palm, 1998; Berger, 1998). There has been a relatively recent broadening of fathers' roles from the traditional 'breadwinner' and 'standard setter' (Berger, 1998).

References were found in the research literature to many different ways in which both fathers[1] and mothers can get involved in their children's learning and education and in schools. These are listed in Tables 1, 2 and 3, with an interpretation of how they might relate to the models just outlined.

---

1   A useful source is O'Brien (2004).

Table 1: Fathers' involvement in support of their children's out-of-school learning

Type of involvement	Epstein model	Lamb et al. model	Fathering roles
Communicates his interest in, and aspirations and expectations for, child's education	Parenting	-	
Support, praise and encouragement given to child for their learning/achievement/ talents and for their school attendance/behaviour	Parenting; Learning at home	Engagement	Friend, nurturer, caregiver
Modelling of own learning attitudes, learning behaviours, and educational achievement	Parenting	-	Caregiver, role model, moral teacher, guide
Making sure that child gets to school; transport to school and out-of-school activities	Parenting	Engagement/ Accessibility	Caregiver, monitor, disciplinarian
Monitoring child's use of time after school so that they do homework	Parenting; Learning at home	Accessibility	Monitor, guide, disciplinarian, caregiver
Being at home after school so that child can ask questions about their homework or talk about school day	Parenting; Learning at home	Accessibility	Adviser, teacher, friend, nurturer, caregiver
Conversations with child about learning, education, homework and school	Parenting; Learning at home	Engagement	Friend, adviser, guide, nurturer, caregiver
Conversations with child about educational and occupational choices	Parenting; Learning at home	Engagement	Friend, adviser, guide, nurturer, caregiver
Informal learning at home with child including play, games, reading, story-telling, writing, arts and crafts, music, construction/DIY, technology/ ICT, educational computer games and TV/internet, cookery, sport, other curricular subjects	Learning at home	Engagement	Teacher, guide, playmate, friend
Help with child's homework and other schoolwork	Learning at home	Engagement	Teacher, guide
Informal learning outside home with child including outdoor play, sports, visits to libraries, museums, etc, other outings, leisure and recreation	Learning at home	Engagement	Playmate, friend, teacher, guide
Planning child's out-of-school and recreational activities	Learning at home	Responsibility	Caregiver, guide, monitor
Conversations with mother about child's learning and education, and about mother's involvement in school/family learning; support to mother for her involvement	Parenting	Responsibility	Support to mother
Providing money for educational and learning resources including books, games, ICT/educational software, school trips and out-of-school activities, recreation, private tutoring, private schools, living in neighbourhoods with good schools	Parenting	Responsibility	Economic provider

Table 2: Fathers' involvement in support of their children at school

Type of involvement	Epstein model	Lamb et al. model	Fathering roles
Participation with child in organised family learning programmes	Parenting; Learning at home; Communication; Collaborating with the community	Engagement	Caregiver, teacher, playmate, friend, resource[2]
Participation in organised home–school programmes, with or without child	Communicating; Parenting; Learning at home; Collaborating with the community	Engagement/ Responsibility	Caregiver, teacher, playmate, friend, resource
Attending school events, induction events for parents, regular parents' evenings, ad hoc meetings with teachers etc (with or without child)	Communicating; Parenting	Responsibility	Advocate, caregiver, resource
Informal discussion with teachers (e.g. in school playground or by telephone) about child's progress at school/ educational decisions/ any attendance or behaviour problems/child's experiences at home	Communicating; Parenting	Responsibility	Advocate, caregiver, resource
Being available during working day for phone calls from school, e.g. if child is ill, or because of other issues such as child's school attendance or behaviour	Communicating; Parenting	Responsibility	Caregiver
Choice of school, and research into local schools (e.g. prospectuses) and educational issues (e.g. DfES and school information for parents on school curriculum)	Communicating; Parenting	Responsibility	Advocate, caregiver
Taking responsibility for parents' interaction with teachers (including home–school agreement), and for parents' attendance at school events	Communicating; Parenting	Responsibility	Caregiver
Reading and responding to school correspondence and information, including children's school reports and school newsletters	Communicating; Parenting	Responsibility	Advocate, caregiver

2   Halle (1999): "links to extended family and community resources...facilitate the transmission of family history and cultural knowledge to his child...can help to build the child's own social capital."

Table 3: Fathers' involvement in the life of their children's schools

Type of involvement	Epstein model	Lamb et al. model	Fathering roles
Voluntary work for school, e.g. in classroom, on school trips, out-of-school activities, fundraising, school security, practical help	Volunteering	-	Advocate, resource
Involvement in school and Ofsted consultations with parents	Communicating; Decision making	-	
Involvement in school governance and decision making, e.g. membership of PTA, and being parent governor	Decision making	-	Advocate, resource
Use of schools for activities without child such as adult learning, parenting education, family support health, and leisure – the 'extended school' (new DfES programme) or 'community school' (Epstein)	Collaborating with the community; Parenting	-	

2.2 Methodological considerations

When looking at the findings of any research study, it is vital to consider the characteristics and quality of its design and methods. There are some specific questions which should be asked when looking at research on fathers' involvement in their children's learning and education.

What type/s of fathers' involvement is the study investigating?

See Tables 1-3.

Who reports fathers' involvement?

Researchers measure fathers' involvement in different ways, for example by asking fathers directly; by asking teachers, mothers or children to report their perceptions of fathers' involvement; or through independent observation of fathers' behaviours. Resident fathers in two-parent families tend to report their involvement at higher levels than do mothers, but the differences are small (Pleck and Masciadrelli, 2004). Lamb and Lewis (2004) note that caution is required when using mothers' reports, as these could reflect issues like family harmony or the mother's psychological well-being; this point can also apply to fathers' and children's reports. Non-resident fathers report more frequent father–child contact than do mothers (Amato and Sobolewski, 2004), perhaps influenced by social desirability (Pleck and Masciadrelli, 2004). Paulson and Sputa (1996) found that "both mothers and fathers perceived themselves to be higher on all aspects of parenting than their adolescents perceived them to be". Raymond and Benbow (1986) argue, however, that children's perceptions of their parents' involvement are more important than the actual parental behaviours "because the child's interpretation determines his or her reaction" and, therefore, the child's outcomes.

Do quantitative studies report:

- the (average) level/frequency of involvement/amount of time, or

- the (average) quality/content of involvement (e.g. educational quality of time), or

- what proportion of fathers are involved on at least one occasion ('prevalence'), or

- fathers' involvement relative to mothers' involvement?

Nearly all the research studies found report the level or frequency of fathers' involvement, although Chapter 3 shows that it is the quality of involvement which is key to children's outcomes. There are different ways to collect data on the level or frequency of involvement: time diaries completed by fathers, mothers or children; estimates of total time given by fathers, which are much less precise than time diary measures; and reports by fathers, mothers and children of how frequently fathers engage in specific activities, which are the most common measures (Pleck and Masciadrelli, 2004). Pleck and Masciadrelli note that some researchers have combined quantity and quality measures into 'positive involvement' variables.

Do quantitative studies report fathers' involvement with a specific child, or with all their children (for fathers who have more than one child)?

What country is the research study conducted in?

In what year was the study conducted?

The level of fathers' involvement could be influenced by, for example, school structures, beliefs about education, and styles of parents' interactions with their children which are specific to a particular country, or to a specific time-period (Trent et al., 1996). O'Brien (2004) reminds us that fatherhood has had a much more prominent place in public policy in the US than in the UK. However, despite important cultural, educational and other contextual differences, it is important to look at the findings of research studies from other countries. Desforges and Abouchaar (2003) note that most of the large-scale, high-quality studies investigating the impact of parental involvement in children's education have taken place in the US.

What is the research population?

Are the fathers in the study resident or non-resident with their children, biological or non-biological, living in two-parent families or a one-parent family? Are step-fathers and other 'father figures' included? What are the fathers' characteristics in terms of location, social class, age, employment status, and ethnicity? How old and what gender are the children? Is the sample of schools representative?

What is the sample size, how was the sample selected, and how representative is it of the population?

In quantitative studies, what was the response rate? Pleck and Masciadrelli (2004) conclude that "self-selection bias among fathers participating in research...is likely [to be] a greater threat to validity than is self-report bias".

Where these methodological details were available from the research papers that were accessed, or from the websites of large-scale research studies, they are included in the tables that follow, or as footnotes.

2.3 Extent of fathers' involvement in their children's learning and education

Fathers in different family types

Most of the data found on the extent of fathers' involvement in their children's learning and education is about the involvement of resident fathers. There has been little research specifically on non-resident fathers' involvement with their children's education (Baker and McMurray, 1998). Most research on non-resident fathers has focused on formal child support or the frequency of father–child contact; and little research has been carried out on the different roles that fathers living apart from their children play in their lives (Le Menestrel, 1999). It is difficult for researchers to access a representative sample of non-resident fathers (Clarke and O'Brien, 2004).

The little research found on non-resident fathers' involvement in their children's learning and education is about fathers who are not resident with their children because of parental separation/divorce, or because of never having been in a relationship with the child's mother. But it is important to remember that fathers can also be non-resident with their children for long periods as a result of military service, imprisonment, long-term stays in hospitals and social care institutions, or work that requires travel or which is abroad (Frieman and Berkeley, 2002).

An assumption cannot be made that resident fathers are involved fathers, nor that non-resident fathers are not involved. Frieman and Berkeley write that "some fathers although physically present are emotionally absent from their children". Non-resident fathers are not all "deadbeat dads". There are several sources of data from the late 1990s that consistently report that between 70 and 80 per cent of non-resident fathers in the UK have contact with their children, although the frequency of contact varies widely (Lewis and Warin, 2001). In a more recent survey of resident and non-resident parents in England, 14 per cent of non-resident parents reported that they never saw their children, and 77 per cent said they saw their children either every day, or at least once a week, or at least once a month. Responses from resident parents indicated that only 60 per cent of their children's non-resident parents saw their saw their children either every day, or at least once a week, or at least once a month (Blackwell and Dawe, 2004).

Although most fathers spend less time with their children after parental separation, some fathers who were not that involved in their children's lives before divorce became more involved afterwards (Frieman, 1998). This increased involvement may result from non-resident fathers needing to actively maintain their relationships with their children to a greater extent than they did when they were sharing a home together. Amato and Sobolewski (2004), drawing on the work of Hetherington and Kelly (2002), call this group "divorce-activated fathers". Likewise, Lewis and Warin (2001) write that "many non-resident fathers offer an alternative home when the need arises" and that many fathers enjoy taking responsibility for their children during contact after divorce, which they may not have had any opportunity to do before.

Just under 10 per cent of all lone parents in England and Wales are men (Office for National Statistics, 2003) but very little research evidence has been found on their engagement with their children's learning and education. Gingerbread (2001), a voluntary organisation in Britain of single parent families, say that single parent fathers are "a neglected area of research".

No research was found that was specifically about the involvement of step-fathers and other resident 'father figures' in children's learning and education.

Fathers' involvement in support of their children's out-of-school learning

Table 4: Key statistics on fathers' involvement in their children's out-of-school learning

	Fathers	Mothers	Source
Praised or rewarded their children for good schoolwork	**8%** of fathers never, **42%** every day, **32%** once or twice a week	No data	National Center for Fathering (1999), using data from survey of nearly 900 adults in US (nationally representative)
Percentage of resident fathers/ mothers who reported that they read or looked at books with their children at least once a week	**39%** of resident fathers	**55%** of resident mothers	Brown et al. (2001), using data from US Panel Study of Income Dynamics (large-scale and nationally representative)
Percentage of children who said they played sports with their father/ mother	**49%** with father	**22%** with mother	Kids Club Network (2003), using data from survey of over 1,400 children between 4 and 13 years participated (average age of 8).
Percentage of father/mothers who said they helped with their children's homework "every time"	**24%** of resident fathers	**37%** of resident mothers	Williams et al. (2002), using data from 2001 survey[3] of parents in England (large-scale and nationally representative)

3   This key source on fathers' involvement in the UK was a telephone survey carried out for the DfES by the market research agency BMRB on parental involvement in their children's education, with an emphasis on in-school involvement (Williams et al., 2002). Much of the data is

Monitoring their children's time after school (Table 5)

Resident fathers commonly monitor their children's after-school activities and homework completion on a regular basis, although slightly less frequently than do mothers.

Table 5: Fathers' and mothers' monitoring of their children's time after school

	Fathers	Mothers	Source	Population
Percentage of resident fathers who often or very often set limits on what TV their child could watch	**61%** of resident fathers	**71%** of resident mothers	Brown et al. (2001), using data from US Panel Study of Income Dynamics[4] (large-scale and nationally representative)	US resident parents in 1997
Percentage of resident fathers who often or very often set limits on how much TV their children could watch in a day	**40%** of resident fathers	**48%** of resident mothers	Brown et al. (2001), using data from US Panel Study of Income Dynamics (large-scale and nationally representative)	US resident parents in 1997
Average number of days per week on which father/mother checked that child had done homework or other school assignments	**3.5** days per week for fathers	**4.3** days per week for mothers	Halle (2001), using data from 1992 US National Survey of Families and Households (large-scale and nationally representative)	US resident parents in 1992

Conversations with their children about learning and education, and educational and occupational choices (Table 6)

Research in the UK and US shows that, in general, children report being emotionally closer to their mother than their father (Warin et al., 1999; Katz, 2003; Halle, 2001; O'Brien and Jones, 1996; Raymond and Benbow,[5] 1986; Lamb and Lewis, 2004). Teenage children are much more likely in the UK to discuss their personal worries, their experiences and progress at school, and their homework with their mother than with their father (Warin et al., 1999; O'Brien and Jones, 1995, 1996; Katz, 2003). In O'Brien and Jones' research with working class teenagers in East London, the areas of discussion for which fathers were most likely to be named by adolescents as the main confidantes were money, sport and difficulties with mothers. The teenagers were most likely to talk with their fathers on Sundays, when talking was the most common shared activity with fathers.

---

presented for parents in aggregate, and not separately for mothers and fathers. The data on fathers' involvement was obtained from an interview with a resident parent, either the mother/step-mother (59 per cent of cases), or the father/step-father (41 per cent of cases). In two-parent households, the mother or father was randomly sampled. All data from this report is on resident fathers only.

4   Data on resident fathers' involvement for 3,600 children aged 0-12 years was obtained from either the mother or father (Brown et al., 2001). One adult per household was interviewed by telephone.

5   Raymond and Benbow (1986) carried out their research in the US with a group of "extremely mathematically and verbally talented young adolescents" (i.e. gifted children) and a comparison group of high achieving (but not extremely so) adolescents.

Yet, a considerable proportion of fathers do frequently praise or reward their children for good schoolwork, and talk with their children about school issues (Halle, 2001; National Center for Fathering, 1999). These are widespread ways in which fathers engage in their children's learning.

Warin et al.'s research showed that conversation between fathers and teenagers in this locality was often an incidental part of time together (a "secondary activity" – Pleck and Masciadrelli, 2004), rather than the purpose of the shared activity, for example, whilst in the car with daughters or during sports with sons. It is interesting that Pleck and Masciadrelli report a greater quantity of such secondary activities between US fathers and children in rural areas than in urban areas. We speculate that this could be connected with rural fathers giving their children lifts more often and for longer journeys.

Non-resident fathers are usually less likely than resident fathers to discuss schools and careers with their children (Barber, 1994 cited in Tucker et al., 2001).

Table 6: Fathers' and mothers' conversations with their children

	Fathers	Mothers	Source	Population
Closeness between parents and children				
Adolescents asked how close they feel towards their father/mother	Less close to fathers	Closer to mothers	Halle (2001), using data from US National Longitudinal Study of Adolescent Health (large-scale and nationally representative)	US adolescents in grades 7-12 in 1995, and in grades 8-12 in 1996
Percentage of teenage boys who said they would turn to their father/mother for emotional support	**23%** of boys with low self-esteem and **61%** of boys with high self-esteem would turn to father	**44%** of boys with low self-esteem and **76%** of boys with high self-esteem would turn to mother	Katz (2003), using data from 1998 survey[6] of about 1,350 teenage boys across Britain	Teenage boys in Britain in 1998
Conversations about learning, education, homework and school				
Percentage of teenagers who said that their father was their main confidante for discussing homework and progress at school	**23%** of children for homework **17%** of children for progress at school	Data not reported	O'Brien and Jones (1995, 1996), using data from survey of about 600 children in six state secondary schools in London	Teenagers (average age 14-15)[7] in "a predominantly working class urban East London locality"

6 The questionnaires were distributed in newspapers and to schools and youth clubs (Katz, 2003), so it is not known how representative the study is of teenage boys in Britain.

7 About 65 per cent were living with both their biological parents; the remainder in step-parent families, single-parent families, or with guardians/foster parents (O'Brien and Jones, 1995, 1996). Parents' educational qualification levels were relatively low, and many of the fathers were in manual occupations. Eighty-three per cent of the children were white British in ethnic origin.

	Fathers	Mothers	Source	Population
Percentage of fathers who had discussed school safety issues with their children	**45%** of fathers	No data	National Center for Fathering (1999), using data from survey of nearly 900 adults in US (nationally representative)	US fathers of primary and secondary school children in 1999
Percentage of fathers who praised or rewarded their children for good schoolwork	**8%** of fathers never, **42%** every day, **32%** once or twice a week, **11%** once or twice a month	No data	National Center for Fathering (1999), using data from survey of nearly 900 adults in US (nationally representative)	US fathers of primary and secondary school children in 1999
Average number of days a week on which father/mother talked with child about things he/ she has learned in school	**3.5 days** a week for fathers	**4.2 days** a week for mothers	Halle (2001), using data from 1992 US National Survey of Families and Households (large-scale and nationally representative)	US families in 1992
Conversations about educational and occupational choices				
Percentage of young people who said their (step)dad/ (step)mum was a source of information for their decisions about higher education	**39%** of young people said their father	**38%** of young people said their mother	MORI Social Research Institute (2003), using data from 2002 MORI Schools Omnibus (2,670 young people)	Young people in UK in 2002
Percentage of 11-16-year-old children who said that, if they were trying to decide what best to do after age of 16, they would ask their father/mother to help them decide	**10%** of children said their father	**33%** of children said their mother	DfES (2003c), using data from survey of 1,000 children, conducted by NOP over three waves from 2002-03	Children aged 11-16 in England in 2002-03

Research findings are complex on whether there are differences in father–child conversation by children's gender. In one large-scale survey, girls reported being less close to both their parents than boys did (Halle, 2001); but O'Brien and Jones (1995, 1996) report that boys were more likely to turn to their fathers than to their mothers, and vice versa for girls. Girls were less satisfied than boys with the amount of time that they had with their fathers, and they were much more likely than boys to feel that their father "did not understand them". This relative dissatisfaction of girls may reflect the aspirations that they have for chats with their parents; when asked about their favourite activity with their father, teenage girls were more likely than boys to choose "talking about things that matter" (O'Brien and Jones, 1995, 1996).

According to Lamb and Lewis (2004), fathers tend to be "more engaged with their sons, have less contact with daughters" and that daughters are relatively uninfluenced by their fathers. But there is conflicting evidence that teenage daughters in north-west England had more opportunity than sons to speak to their fathers, in particular because their fathers more frequently gave them lifts (Warin et al., 1999).

Evidence is also inconclusive on whether or not fathers are more involved in discussing educational and occupational choices with their children than everyday experiences of school. Catan (quoted in Lewis and Warin, 2001) in the UK writes that "fathers often offer careers advice, continuing their activity as a 'bridge to the outside world'"; and MORI's survey (Table 6) found that teenagers were equally likely to turn to mothers or fathers for advice on higher education. However, in one study, US adolescents[8] relied more on mothers than on fathers for advice on their life plans (including educational choices) (Tucker et al., 2001); and NOP's survey (Table 6) had similar findings in England.

We should note that none of this data reports on the quality or impact of father–child discussion, or on the frequency of fathers' involvement, only on the proportion of fathers engaging in this type of involvement.

Out-of-school educational activities with their children (Table 7)

Two research-based conclusions from the US are that "in practical terms, parental involvement tends to be aligned along traditional gender roles" (Brown et al., 2001); and "dads are not just substitute moms" (Halle, 1999). There is certainly much research showing that when children are infants and toddlers, fathers' involvement with their children is often different from mothers' involvement, with more "physically stimulating and unpredictable play" (Lamb and Lewis, 2004). This applies to most but not all cultures around the world (Lamb and Lewis, 2004). Does this gendered involvement for fathers persist when children are at school?

For UK children in primary school, mothers are more likely than fathers to be involved in many out-of-school activities including cooking, visiting the library, arts and crafts, learning about letters, numbers and shapes, writing letters, writing stories and music (Fitzgerald et al., 2003; West et al., 1998; Kids Club Network, 2003). In West et al.'s small-scale study in London,[9] only a very small minority of fathers got involved in these activities, although

---

8 Predominantly white adolescents, from middle-class and working-class districts in Michigan.

9 This source on fathers' involvement in primary schools in England was a small-scale study in 1994-5 in London of the parents of 107 children in the last year of primary school (West et al., 1998). The samples of schools and parents in this study were *not* selected randomly, but constitute quota/convenience samples. The sample of parents was selected from 19 state and independent schools in four LEAs in London. The researchers note that their ethnically and socially diverse sample (around one-third were from minority ethnic groups, 21 per cent were professionals, and 19 per cent were skilled manual workers) is likely to be biased towards parents more involved in their children's education. A relatively high proportion of parents interviewed were school governors. All data on fathers' involvement was obtained from the parent who was interviewed, who was generally the mother, but sometimes the father was interviewed as well as or instead of the mother. It is not clear from the published papers whether or not all the fathers were resident with their children and/or were biological fathers. Small sample sizes, ranging from 56 to 86, depending on the type of involvement.

percentages were much higher in the National Adult Learning Survey 2002 for children aged 3-7 (Fitzgerald et al., 2002). The only type of out-of-school activity in which fathers were more likely to be involved than mothers in West et al.'s study was educational computer games.[10] Fathers got involved with 15 per cent of children who engaged in this activity at home, whereas mothers got involved with 6 per cent of these children.

Computer use is one out-of-school activity for which children attending out-of-school clubs in England reported that their mothers and fathers spent about equal time with them (Kids Club Network, 2003). A BBC news item reports an NOP survey commissioned by British Telecom (300 parents of school-age children) showing that before a family bought a computer, only 9 per cent of fathers took the lead in their children's home learning (BBC News, 1998). But, after buying a computer, the figure rose to 16 per cent.

Likewise, in the 2002 National Adult Learning Survey, fathers of children aged 8-18 were more likely than mothers to have looked up information on the internet (43 per cent of fathers and 31 per cent of mothers) and learned about computing (20 per cent of fathers and 15 per cent of mothers) to help their children's learning (Fitzgerald et al., 2002). Mothers were more likely than fathers to have looked up information in books (55 per cent of fathers and 61 per cent of mothers), and to have got advice from a teacher (34 per cent of fathers and 50 per cent of mothers) or friend and relative (25 per cent of fathers and 33 per cent of mothers) or other professional (10 per cent of fathers and 14 per cent of mothers).

Building/repairing, other practical tasks and hobbies, and in particular outdoor activities and sport, are other areas of learning where fathers are more likely than mothers to get involved with their primary school children (Kids Club Network, 2003; Brown et al., 2001) and their teenage children (Warin et al., 1999). Shared activities such as car repairs had explicit learning goals for a group of teenagers in north-west England (Warin et al., 1999).

In fact, much of the literature accessed discusses fathers' contribution to their children's learning as recreational and activity-based, with a focus on play ("male preserve parenting" in Warin et al., 1999), along with sport, having fun, and family outings such as to the park (Lamb and Lewis, 2004; Lewis and Warin, 2001; Warin et al., 1999; O'Brien and Jones, 1996). Warin et al. write about the "public sites of fathering" – that fathers are very involved with their children outside the home in public spaces. In an analysis of the essays of over 3,000 predominantly white children in the US, the children were most likely to refer to "helping with homework" when talking about their mothers, and to playing, sports and other joint activities when writing about their fathers (Milkie et al., 1997). Fathers' greater involvement than mothers in recreational activities may reflect the fact that full-time working fathers are most likely to be around their children in recreation time on weekends and in evenings.

Resident fathers in one US study consistently reported more positive emotion during family leisure activities than did either resident mothers or their adolescent children (Larson et al., 1997). Fifty-five[11] white, middle-class and working-class fathers, mothers and teenagers (average age 12 years) in two-parent families in Chicago carried pagers for one week and reported on their experiences at random moments. The authors claim that:

---

10 Fifty-six children took part in educational computer games at home, high proportions of whom involved neither their mother nor their father, but did so alone or with someone else (West et al., 1998).

11 The response rate was 45 per cent (Larson et al., 1997).

> *"for fathers...family leisure is the primary context that counterbalances their strenuous work life...fathers may find this time pleasurable as their primary opportunity to experience affiliation and attachment to their families."*

In contrast, mothers feel much obligation of care and organisational responsibility during family leisure.

US non-resident fathers' contact time with their children is primarily recreational ("restaurants or movies" and "sharing good times together", Amato and Sobolewski, 2004). In turn, the more psychologically intimate 'parenting' role of fathers decreases after divorce, including their monitoring and supervision of their children. Amato and Sobolewski report the findings of a national US survey showing that, during visits, about 60 per cent of non-resident fathers got involved mainly in leisure activities with their children (Stewart, 1999). This emphasis must be seen in context, as many non-resident fathers see their children in day-time only (mainly at weekends) with no overnight stays. The remaining 40 per cent of the fathers in Stewart's survey also got involved in activities such as helping with school work and discussing the child's problems (also see Bradshaw et al., 1999 in Table 9). It seems likely that overnight contact facilitates this role.

Interestingly, there is a similar emphasis on leisure in non-resident mothers' time with their children, and Amato and Sobolewski (2004) argue that "the logistics of living in separate residences leads parents...and children to have relationships that are primarily recreational in nature". Amato and Sobolewski write that these recreational activities "contribute little to children's development" even if they are enjoyable. However, there appears to be an important opportunity here for schools and family learning providers to create recreational activities with a learning/educational emphasis for non-resident fathers and their children to enjoy together during their contact time.

But, in Britain, Bradshaw et al.'s (1999) qualitative research with non-resident fathers[12] found a wide range of at-home activities that the interviewed non-resident fathers engaged in with their children, such as playing, reading stories, using computers, and sports, as well as outings. Some of these fathers said that the costs of paying child support meant that they could not spend too much money on "expensive recreational activities outside the home". Bradshaw et al. write that:

> *"It was not all fun and games...the men were keen to point out that life carried on more or less 'normally' with arguments and household chores to be done...some [non-resident fathers] settled into a more mundane routine of parenting."*

---

12 The non-resident fathers who were interviewed in this qualitative research were all in contact with their children, and had been non-resident for at least two years (Bradshaw et al., 1999).

Table 7: Fathers' and mothers' out-of-school educational activities with their children

	Fathers	Mothers	Source	Population
Percentage of fathers who helped their children in 'extra-curricular activities' like music and sports	**19%** of fathers never, **22%** every day, **36%** once or twice a week, **13%** once or twice a month	No data	National Center for Fathering (1999), using data from survey of nearly 900 adults in US (nationally representative)	US fathers of primary and secondary school children in 1999
Percentage of fathers/mothers who said they had helped their 3-7-year-old child in the past 12 months with...	**...drawing, painting and crafts** 80% of fathers[13] **...letters, numbers, shapes** **82%** of fathers	**...drawing, painting and crafts** 90% of mothers **...letters, numbers, shapes** **89%** of mothers	Fitzgerald et al. (2003), using data from National Adult Learning Survey 2002 (large-scale and nationally representative)	Parents (aged 16 and over) of children aged 3-7 in England and Wales in 2002
Percentage of children who said they cooked with their father/mother	**27%** with father	**71%** with mother	Kids Club Network (2003), using data from survey of over 1,400 children between 4 and 13 years (average age of 8).	Children attending out-of-school clubs in England in 2003
Percentage of resident fathers/mothers who said they helped their children build or repair something at least once a week	**25%** of resident fathers	**13%** of resident mothers	Brown et al. (2001), using data from US Panel Study of Income Dynamics (large-scale and nationally representative)	US resident parents of children aged 3-12 in 1997
Percentage of children who said they played sports with their father/mother	**49%** with father	**22%** with mother	Kids Club Network (2003), using data from survey of over 1,400 children between 4 and 13 years (average age of 8).	Children attending out-of-school clubs in England in 2003
Percentage of resident fathers who said they played sport or did outdoor activities with their children at least once a week	**68%** of resident fathers	**54%** of resident mothers	Brown et al. (2001), using data from US Panel Study of Income Dynamics (large-scale and nationally representative)	US resident parents of children aged 3-12 in 1997

13 Both resident fathers, and non-resident fathers who saw their children at least every month (Fitzgerald et al., 2003).

	Fathers	Mothers	Source	Population
Percentage of fathers/ mothers who said they had helped their 3-7- year-old child in the past 12 months with...	**...teaching them about nature** (e.g. visits to zoo and farm) **76%** of fathers **...taken them to museum, gallery or historical building 47%** of fathers	**...teaching them about nature** (e.g. visits to zoo and farm) **74%** of mothers **...taken them to museum, gallery or historical building 44%** of mothers	Fitzgerald et al. (2003), using data from National Adult Learning Survey 2002 (large-scale and nationally representative)	Parents (aged 16 and over) of children aged 3-7 in England and Wales in 2002
Percentage of non-resident fathers who engaged in out-of-school activities with their children	**6%** of non-resident fathers played sports **12%** of non-resident fathers went on outings **14%** of non-resident fathers played **20%** of non-resident fathers watched TV/ video	No data	Bradshaw et al. (1999), using combined data from two surveys[14] of non-resident fathers in England in 1995/96 (large-scale and nationally representative)	Non-resident fathers with a school-age child in Britain in 1995/96
Percentage of 7- and 11-year-old children whose resident father/mother took them on outings most weeks	**73%** of 7-year-olds **53%** of 11-year-olds	**87%** of 7-year-olds **56%** of 11-year-olds	Flouri and Buchanan (2003b), using data from 1965 and 1969 waves of UK National Child Development Study[15] (large-scale and nationally representative)	UK children with resident father and mother, aged 7 in 1965, and 11 in 1969

14 The non-resident fathers were identified through screening of two large-scale, nationally representative Omnibus surveys (Bradshaw et al., 1999). Data on these fathers' involvement with their children (and a range of other issues) was collected directly from the fathers in follow-up interviews. The response rates in the follow-up interviews were 30 per cent and 56 per cent respectively for the two surveys. Analyses showed that there was under-representation of single, working-class, unskilled, unemployed non-resident fathers in the interviewed samples as compared with the non-resident fathers identified by the screening. The researchers re-weighted their data to correct for this bias.

15 The National Child Development Study (NCDS) is used in several key research papers to look at factors associated with fathers' involvement, and at the impact of parental involvement

Do fathers' shared activities with their teenagers differ according to the children's gender? Interestingly, despite fathers playing more sport and engaging in more hobbies and practical tasks with their sons than daughters, Warin et al. (1999) report that fathers in north-west England were more likely to have shared activities overall (including accompanying the teenager on shopping trips) with daughters than with sons. The researchers suggest that this may due to the greater freedom given to boys. Similarly, O'Brien and Jones (1995, 1996) found that, when asked about their favourite activity with their father, the teenage children in their research in London, but especially the boys, spoke most commonly about "going out and doing things related to leisure" (26 per cent of the children).

Reading with their children (Table 8)

Reading is a core skill for children's educational attainment as it "permeates the entire school curriculum" (Lynch, 2002); and poor literacy can contribute to and magnify boys' problems (Lloyd, 1999). More specifically, 80 per cent of boys excluded from school in Years 10 and 11 have problems that can be traced directly back to their poor literacy in Years 3 and 4 (Lloyd, 1999). Joint reading between fathers and their younger children can also model relaxed, quiet activities and conversational skills, and build quality attachments and relationships (Herb and Willoughby-Herb, 1998).

As with many other aspects of children's learning, resident fathers in England are less likely than mothers to read with their children (Kids Club Network, 2003), but it is encouraging that it is a substantial minority at least (50 per cent or even much greater in some studies) of resident fathers in the UK and US who engage in this at-home activity, often frequently (Brown et al. 2001; National Center for Fathering, 1999; Lugaila, 2003; Fitzgerald et al., 2002; The National Literacy Trust, 2003; West et al., 1998). Interestingly, seven-year-old boys interviewed for a qualitative research study[16] in London said that their father gave them encouragement to read, and fathers were more often mentioned than mothers in this respect (Lloyd, 1999). Similarly, most of the Bristol fathers interviewed in a needs analysis (Bryant et al., 1998) read with their primary school children; in fact, this was the most common way in which these fathers engaged in their children's learning. The National Child Development Study shows that regular reading with their children was a common activity for resident fathers, even in 1965 (Flouri and Buchanan, 2003b).

(and father involvement specifically) on children's outcomes (see Chapter 3). NCDS is an ongoing longitudinal study of about 17,000 children born between 3 and 9 March 1958 in England, Scotland and Wales with low drop-out. The children have been followed from birth through to adulthood. The sample is broadly nationally representative of the population in England, Scotland and Wales, although Flouri and Buchanan (2004) state that there have been "particularly high losses of participants in more disadvantaged groups". The sample is of course also out of date, as the children were 20 years old in 1978, and therefore entered secondary education in 1969. Parents or other primary caregivers were asked about the level or frequency of parental involvement, and teachers were asked about the level of parental interest in the child's education (Flouri and Buchanan, 2003b). Teachers' perceptions could have been biased by the child's characteristics, e.g. social class, ethnicity, school achievement, school behaviour. Over 90 per cent of the parents or caregivers interviewed were the mothers of the children in the study.

16 Focus groups were conducted with 20 boys aged four and five, 20 boys aged seven and eight, and 16 boys aged 13 and 14 (the latter group about their early reading experiences) in London and Bristol to investigate boys' and men's views on reading (Lloyd, 1999). The boys and fathers were from a variety of ethnic groups. Most of the fathers interviewed did not read regularly. However, we must note that these fathers were recruited from the researchers' existing networks in two family centres, a church and a nursery school, so it is probable that they are relatively involved fathers, and possibly less wary of 'women's spaces'.

What types of literature do fathers read with their children? Fletcher and Dally (2002) report from their review of research that fathers are less likely than mothers to take part in "conventional print-related literacy activities". Ortiz's research[17] in the US found fathers using "environmental print" and recreational materials with their young children such as road signs, maps, magazines, directories, manuals, comic strips in newspapers, instructions for board games, personal letters from relatives, religious materials, word-games, crossword puzzles, homework instructions, and notes sent home by teachers, as well as the more traditional materials of bedtime stories (Ortiz and McCarty, 1997). Similarly, in Lloyd's (1999) research in London, boys and fathers reported that, whereas mothers read women's magazines and novels, fathers were more likely to be reading male-oriented magazines and newspapers.

Table 8: Fathers' and mothers' involvement in their children's reading

	Fathers	Mothers	Source	Population
Percentage of resident fathers/mothers who reported that they read or looked at books with their children at least once a week	**39%** of resident fathers	**55%** of resident mothers	Brown et al. (2001), using data from US Panel Study of Income Dynamics (large-scale and nationally representative)	US resident parents of children aged 3-12 in 1997
Percentage of fathers who read to their children	**25%** every day, **23%** once or twice a week **40%** of fathers never,	No data	National Center for Fathering (1999), using data from survey of nearly 900 adults in US (nationally representative)	US fathers of primary and secondary school children in 1999
Percentage of children[18] whose resident mother reads to them between 1 and 6 times a week but who are never read to by resident father	**18%** of children	N/A	Lugaila (2003), using data[19] from US 1996 Survey of Income and Program Participation (SIPP) panel study (large-scale and nationally representative)	US children aged 6-11 years with two resident parents in 1999-2000
Percentage of children who were read to by both their resident mother and resident father between 1 and 6 times a week	**29%** of children	N/A	Lugaila (2003), using data from US 1996 Survey of Income and Program Participation (SIPP) panel study (large-scale and nationally representative)	US children aged 6-11 years with two resident parents in 1999-2000

17 Ortiz (2001) reports a small number of interviews with Californian urban fathers who volunteered to take part in his research project about fathers engaging at home in literacy activities with their young children. The sample included a range of educational levels and socio-economic status.

18 Thirty per cent of the children were not read to by any family member (Lugaila, 2003).

19 Data on resident fathers' involvement was obtained from a parent, who was the mother for 98 per cent of the children in the study sample (Lugaila, 2003). Resident fathers included both biological fathers and step-fathers.

	Fathers	Mothers	Source	Population
Percentage of fathers/ mothers who said they had looked at books or read stories together with their 3-7-year-old child in the past 12 months	**94%** of fathers (resident fathers, and non-resident fathers who saw their children at least every month)	**96%** of mothers	Fitzgerald, Taylor and La Valle (2003), using data from National Adult Learning Survey 2002 (large-scale and nationally representative)	Parents (aged 16 and over) of children aged 3-7 in England and Wales in 2002
Percentage of fathers/ mothers who said they helped with their 5-7-year-old/7-11-year-old child's reading at home	**50%** of fathers for 5-7-year-olds **25%** of fathers for 7-11-year-olds	**75%** of mothers for 5-7-year-olds **50%** of mothers for 7-11-year-olds	The National Literacy Trust (2003), reporting data from Primary Improvement Project at Exeter University (1994-97 research with 1,400 primary schools)	Children aged 5-11 years in UK in 1994-97
Percentage of children who had received help with their reading schoolwork from father/ mother	**52%** of children from father	**68%** of children from mother	West et al. (1998), using data from small-scale survey of parents in London (75 children had received help with reading schoolwork) (see footnote on previous page about this study)	Children in last year of primary school (aged 10-11) in London in 1994/95 (state and independent schools)
Percentage of 7-year-old children whose father/ mother reads to them most weeks	**37%** of children	**50%** of children	Flouri and Buchanan (2003b), using data from 1965 wave of UK National Child Development Study (large-scale and nationally representative)	UK children with resident father and mother, aged 7 in 1965

Helping with their children's homework (Table 9)

As with reading, helping with homework and other schoolwork is a common way in which fathers engage with their children's education, although fathers are generally less involved than mothers in this activity (Williams et al., 2002; National Center for Fathering, 1999; West et al., 1998).

Evidence from the US and UK suggests that fathers help out more with homework when their children are in secondary school than when they are in primary school. Shumow and Miller's (2001) analysis of nationally representative, large-scale cohort data[20] in the US showed an even balance between maternal and paternal help[21] with homework for adolescents with married resident fathers and mothers, but it is important to note that the data was collected between 1987 and 1994. In England, Warin et al. (1999) write about helping teenage children with homework as "a major site of fathering".

Research in the US and UK (Raymond and Benbow, 1986; West et al., 1999) suggests that when fathers get involved with their children's homework, they are more likely than mothers to help out with "stereotypically male" curricular subjects such as maths and science, although the differences can be small[22] (Raymond and Benbow, 1986). For teenagers in north-west England (Warin et al., 1999), maths homework was a niche left vacant by mothers for fathers' help.

This fits a general pattern in adult learning where "different areas of the curriculum have come to be strongly regarded as essentially masculine and feminine, reflecting the strongly sex-segregated labour market" (McGivney, 1999).

---

20 Shumow and Miller (2001) comment that, since refusals amongst sampled fathers were higher than amongst sampled mothers, fathers' involvement (in the population) may be lower than measured in this survey. The data on fathers' involvement was provided by the interviewed parent; either the mother or father was selected for interview at random.

21 Taking into account the time spent helping children with homework and special school projects, i.e. not simply a frequency measure (Shumow and Miller, 2001).

22 These small differences in fathers' and mothers' degree of involvement in curricular areas did not depend upon children's gender or area of talent (Raymond and Benbow, 1986).

Table 9: Fathers' and mothers' help with their children's homework

	Fathers	Mothers	Source	Population
Percentage of father/mothers who said they helped with their children's homework "every time"	**24%** of resident fathers	**37%** of resident mothers	Williams et al. (2002), using data from 2001 survey of parents in England (large-scale and nationally representative)	Resident parents of school-age children (aged 5-16) in England in 2001
Percentage of fathers/ mothers who had helped their 3-7-year-old child with "other schoolwork" in the past 12 months	**64%** of fathers	**67%** of mothers	Fitzgerald et al. (2003), using data from National Adult Learning Survey 2002 (large-scale and nationally representative)	Parents of children aged 3-7 in 2002
Percentage of non-resident fathers who helped their non-resident children with homework	**41%** of fathers	No data	Bradshaw et al. (1999), using combined data from two surveys of non-resident fathers in England in 1995/96 (large-scale and nationally representative)	Non-resident fathers with a school-age child in Britain in 1995/96
Percentage of resident fathers/ mothers who reported that they worked on homework with their children at least once a week	**52%** of resident fathers	Data not reported	Brown et al. (2001), using data from US Panel Study of Income Dynamics (large-scale and nationally representative)	US resident parents of children aged 3-12 in 1997
Percentage of fathers who help their children with homework	**Nearly 40%** every day **25%** once or twice a week **18%** of fathers never	No data	National Center for Fathering (1999), using data from survey of nearly 900 adults in US (nationally representative)	US fathers of primary and secondary school children in 1999
Percentage of fathers who had helped their children complete school project in past six months	**48%** of fathers	No data	National Center for Fathering (1999), using data from survey of nearly 900 adults in US (nationally representative)	US fathers of primary and secondary school children in 1999

Fathers' involvement in their children's schools

Table 10: Key statistics on fathers' involvement in their children's schools

In school	Fathers	Mothers	Source
Percentage of resident fathers/ mothers who said they had never heard of a home–school agreement	**47%** of resident fathers	**27%** of resident mothers	Williams et al. (2002), using data from 2001 survey of parents in England (large-scale and nationally representative)
Percentage of children in two-parent families[23] whose father/ mother was 'highly involved' in their school	**27%** of children	**56%** of children	Nord et al. (1997), using data from 1996 US National Household Education Survey (NHES:96) (large-scale and nationally representative)[24]
Percentage of children in contact with non-resident father[25] whose father had *not* participated in any school activity that school year	**69%** of children	N/A	Nord et al. (1997), using data from 1996 US National Household Education Survey (NHES:96) (large-scale and nationally representative)
Percentage of children whose father/mother attended at least one parent–teacher conference in current school year	**39%** of children in two-parent families	**68%** of children in two-parent families	Nord et al. (1998), using data from 1996 US National Household Education Survey (NHES:96) (large-scale and nationally representative)
Percentage of fathers/mothers who said they had helped as volunteer in the nursery, playgroup or school of their 3-7-year-old child in the past 12 months	**9%** of fathers	**37%** of mothers	Fitzgerald et al. (2003), using data from National Adult Learning Survey 2002 (large-scale and nationally representative)

23 Nord et al. (1997) write that the results on resident fathers and father-figures are "generalisable to all US children in kindergarten through 12th grade who have at least one biological, adoptive or stepparent in the home".

24 The 1996 NHES was a nationally representative (random) cross-sectional telephone survey of the parents/guardians of nearly 17,000 children (one parent or guardian per family was interviewed), including the resident parent or guardian of about 5,500 children who had a non-resident parent. Seventy-five per cent of survey respondents were mothers, and the survey response rate was 63 per cent.

25 Data on the involvement of a child's non-resident father was reported by the child's resident mother or guardian (Nord et al., 1997). The results on non-resident fathers are "generalisable to all children in kindergarten through 12th grade who have had contact with their non-resident father in the past year". Resident mothers may not accurately report the involvement of non-resident fathers especially. Nord et al. acknowledge this as a weakness of this survey.

Overall involvement in their children's schools (Tables 11 and 12)

There is consistent evidence from the UK and US that fathers are less involved than mothers in their children's schools (Williams et al, 2002; Nord et al., 1997; Clough et al., 2000; West et al., 1998; Shumow and Miller, 2001). This applies to all types of school activity (except possibly school governance[26]), and to both primary and secondary schools. This parental gender gap for in-school involvement is often greater than the gap for out-of-school involvement in children's learning and education. There is evidence from Williams et al. (2002) that resident fathers in England are less likely than resident mothers to feel very involved in their children's schools, and are less likely to know a variety of educational terms.

Despite this relative lack of knowledge of educational terms, and a US finding that only 57 per cent of fathers knew the name of their child's teacher (National Center for Fathering, 1999), it cannot be assumed that fathers tend not to be interested in their children's school experiences, nor that they tend not to influence the home–school interaction.

Ballard et al. (1997) report on the experiences of 15 fathers[27] of children with disabilities in the New Zealand education system. Although it was the mothers who usually had contact with school, the fathers were well informed about their children's school experiences and about their partner's school involvement. These fathers held strong views about their children's educational experiences, and the issues they discussed in interview were similar to those discussed in other research by mothers of children with disabilities.

Furthermore, in a nationally representative, large-scale US survey, 42 per cent of fathers said that they discussed their children's progress in school every day with their children's mother, 30 per cent did this once or twice a week, and 12 per cent once or twice a month (only 9 per cent never did so) (National Center for Fathering, 1999).

What about the in-school involvement of fathers in different family types? The most detailed source on this is an analysis of data from the 1996 nationally representative, large-scale, US National Household Education Survey of 17,000 US schoolchildren (full analysis in Nord et al., 1997, summarised in Nord, 1998 and in Nord et al., 1998).

- In two-parent families, children were twice as likely to have mothers who were highly involved[28] than to have fathers[29] who were highly involved.

---

26 No published statistical data was found on the gender of school governors. Ellis (2003) writes that "accurate records are not kept on governor demographic profiles".

27 The fathers in the sample volunteered to take part in this research, so they may not be typical of fathers of children with disabilities in New Zealand (Ballard et al., 1997).

28 High involvement in this survey comprised participation by the parent in three or four different types of school activity during the past school year. Moderate involvement comprised participation in at least two different types of school activity. Low involvement comprised participation in none or only one type of school activity. The four activities were: general school meetings; regularly scheduled parent–teacher conferences, school/ class events, and serving as a volunteer at the school. Seventy-five per cent of the respondents to this survey were mothers (Nord et al., 1997).

29 Including resident step-fathers and resident adoptive fathers, as well as resident biological fathers, in two-parent families (Nord et al., 1997).

- Fathers[30] who were 'single parents' were much more likely than fathers in two-parent families, and nearly as likely as single parent mothers, to be highly involved in their children's schools. These involvement levels were similar to those for mothers in two-parent families. Nord et al. comment that single-parent fathers may have higher involvement levels because there is no second parent to help them with their obligations.

- Non-resident fathers were much less involved[31] in their children's schools than were fathers in two-parent families, although about a third of children who had contact with their non-resident father did have a father taking part in at least one school activity. Nord et al. argue that the proportion of non-resident fathers participating in school activities is not at all trivial.

No equivalent large-scale quantitative data was found on UK non-resident fathers' involvement in their children's schools.

Schools may be a 'neutral' place where non-resident fathers and their children can have contact. However, they appear to be little used. In a nationally representative survey of about 310 non-resident parents[32] aged 16 or over in Great Britain, eight per cent of their children had contact with their non-resident parent at school (Blackwell and Dawe, 2004). This very small percentage compared with 39 per cent of children who had contact with their non-resident parent at a "place of leisure".

What about single-parent fathers and schools in the UK? Gingerbread, a national voluntary organisation for single parents in Britain, carried out a survey[33] amongst its members who were 'lone fathers' (Gingerbread, 2001). Thirty-five per cent of these Gingerbread members mentioned involvement in their child's education (including taking an interest, attending school activities, and taking and collecting children from school) as the main new skill needed on becoming a single-parent father. This was higher than the percentage of fathers who mentioned cooking or dealing with their children's health or any other skill. Only two per cent of fathers mentioned their children's school as a source of support when they became a lone father, although the school was mentioned more frequently than all other organisations except for Gingerbread. Just over 20 per cent of the lone fathers said that they didn't receive any support when they became a lone father.

---

30 Including step-fathers and adoptive fathers, as well as biological fathers, living with the child in a single-parent family (Nord et al., 1997).

31 According to resident mothers' reports. Non-resident fathers comprised non-resident biological fathers and non-resident adoptive fathers (Nord et al., 1997).

32 Parents in a nationally representative Omnibus Survey who had at least one child with a non-resident parent completed a questionnaire or were interviewed about child contact with non-resident parents (Blackwell and Dawe, 2004). The majority of respondents completed a questionnaire, which was used by the researchers to encourage honest answers and to avoid potential embarrassment on the part of respondents. The achieved sample of parents comprised 649 respondents who were resident parents and 312 respondents who were non-resident parents. The responses of the non-resident parents are reported here.

33 About 110 fathers responded, which was a response rate of just under 50 per cent (Gingerbread, 2001). Gingerbread's members may not be representative of all lone fathers in Britain.

Table 11: Resident fathers' and mothers' engagement with their children's schools in England

	Fathers	Mothers	Source	Population
Percentage of resident fathers/ mothers who said they felt "very involved" in their children's schools	**24%** of resident full-time working fathers **29%** of resident non-full-time working fathers	**26%** of resident non-full-time working mothers **35%** of resident non-full-time working mothers	Williams et al. (2002), using data from 2001 survey of parents in England (large-scale and nationally representative)	Resident parents of school-age children (aged 5-16) in England in 2001
Percentage of resident fathers/ mothers who said they had never heard of a home–school agreement	**47%** of resident fathers	**27%** of resident mothers	Williams et al. (2002), using data from 2001 survey of parents in England (large-scale and nationally representative)	Resident parents of school-age children (aged 5-16) in England in 2001
Percentage of resident fathers/ mothers who said they knew a lot about the terms National Curriculum Level or SATS	**32%** of resident fathers	**40%** of resident mothers	Williams et al. (2002), using data from 2001 survey of parents in England (large-scale and nationally representative)	Resident parents of school-age children (aged 5-16) in England in 2001
Percentage of resident fathers/ mothers who said they had never heard of the term Literacy Hour	**30%** of resident fathers	**13%** of resident mothers	Williams et al. (2002), using data from 2001 survey of parents in England (large-scale and nationally representative)	Resident parents of school-age children (aged 5-16) in England in 2001

Table 12: Fathers' and mothers' involvement in their children's schools in the US

	Fathers	Mothers	Source	Population
Percentage of fathers who knew the name of their child's teacher	**57%** of fathers	No data	National Center for Fathering (1999), using data from survey of nearly 900 adults in US (nationally representative)	US fathers of primary and secondary school children in 1999
Percentage of fathers who attended class events or school meetings	**23%** once or twice a month **37%** once every three months **just over 30%** of fathers never	No data	National Center for Fathering (1999), using data from survey of nearly 900 adults in US (nationally representative)	US fathers of primary and secondary school children in 1999
Resident fathers				
Percentage of children in two-parent families who had fathers/ mothers who had *not* participated in any school activity that school year	**25%** of children	**8%** of children	Nord et al. (1997), using data from 1996 US National Household Education Survey (NHES:96) (large-scale and nationally representative)	US school-age children in 1996
Percentage of children in two-parent families whose father/ mother was 'highly involved' in their school	**27%** of children	**56%** of children	Nord et al. (1997), using data from 1996 US National Household Education Survey (NHES:96) (large-scale and nationally representative)	US school-age children in 1996
Percentage of children in single-parent families whose resident father/ mother was 'highly involved' in their school	**46%** of children	**49%** of children	Nord et al. (1997), using data from 1996 US National Household Education Survey (NHES:96) (large-scale and nationally representative)	US school-age children in 1996

	Fathers	Mothers	Source	Population
Non-resident fathers				
Percentage of children in contact with non-resident father whose father had *not* participated in any school activity that school year	**69%** of children	N/A	Nord et al. (1997), using data from 1996 US National Household Education Survey (NHES:96) (large-scale and nationally representative)	US school-age children in 1996
Percentage of children in contact with non-resident father whose father participated in at least one school activity that school year	**31%** of children	N/A	Nord et al. (1997), using data from 1996 US National Household Education Survey (NHES:96) (large-scale and nationally representative)	US school-age children in 1996
Percentage of children in contact with non-resident father whose father participated in at least two school activities that school year	**18%** of children	N/A	Nord et al. (1997), using data from 1996 US National Household Education Survey (NHES:96) (large-scale and nationally representative)	US school-age children in 1996

Different types of in-school involvement (Tables 13 – 17)

As shown earlier, fathers are less involved than mothers in every type of in-school involvement, except possibly for school governance. But out of the different types of involvement in their children's schools, both resident and non-resident fathers are most likely to attend:

- parents' evenings in England (about 60 per cent of fathers, according to a small-scale study: Clough et al., 2000)

- general school meetings or class events[34] in the US (about 50 per cent of fathers in Nord et al., 1997).

In two-parent families in the US, fathers are almost as likely as mothers to attend school or class events (Nord, 1998). However, it is important not to be complacent as, in England, resident fathers (41 per cent of all parents in the survey) comprised 72 per cent of the parents who said that they never went to parents' evenings (Williams et al., 2002).

---

34 Such as plays and sports events (Nord et al., 1997).

These kinds of in-school involvement in support of their individual children's learning are much more common amongst both mothers and fathers (in both the UK and US) than their involvement in the 'life of the school' as a volunteer in the classroom (about 15 per cent of resident fathers in Williams et al., 2002, and about four per cent of children in contact with their non-resident fathers in Nord et al., 1997 – see Table 17

Nord et al. suggest that this relatively high attendance by both fathers and mothers at general school meetings or class events and at 'parent–teacher conferences' may be due to schools commonly scheduling these events outside the regular working day (i.e. evenings), as discussed further in Chapter 4. Additionally, activities such as classroom volunteering require more time commitment from parents (Williams et al., 2002). It is interesting that the percentages of full-time working fathers and full-time working mothers helping out in the classroom in England are very similar (Williams et al., 2002).

Another type of in-school involvement that resident fathers are relatively likely to share with mothers (between 40 per cent and 50 per cent of fathers in UK and US) is dropping their children off and picking them up from school, and talking informally to the teachers. Fathers' presence in the school playground or at the school gate (although still more limited than mothers' presence) may be increasing (Caddell, 1996) because of rises in working mothers, 'shift parenting', and flexible working hours (Joseph Rowntree Foundation, 2002). The case studies in Chapter 6 show that talking to fathers in the school playground is a method often used by teachers to recruit them to school-based family learning programmes. However, according to the Equal Opportunities Commission, schools usually telephone children's mothers rather than their fathers when children become unwell at school (EOC, 2003).

Many anecdotes were heard whilst conducting the research in this report about schools involving fathers only when children have serious behaviour problems, and only when the mother has already been involved but with no positive outcome. However, no clear evidence was found on this point, although fathers do tend to be involved in child health clinics and other family services only "when family distress is exceptionally high" (O'Brien, 2004).

Dudley-Marling (2001) in the US carried out in-depth research amongst a small, opportunistic but diverse, sample of 23 parents[35] whose children were struggling academically at school. She found that it was mothers rather than fathers who took on "the emotional burdens" and worry of their children's problems at school, although some of the fathers were involved in their children's school life and with their learning at home.

Making decisions about children's schooling can be considered to be a key part of a father's 'responsibility' (see Section 2.1). A small-scale research study in London[36] found that mothers were much more likely to take the lead in deciding on a primary school and secondary school for their children (David, 1998), although it can be seen that between 40 and 80 per cent of fathers were involved in some way in these decisions (David, 1998 in the UK; and Halle, 2001 in the US). David writes that mothers were also much more involved than fathers in conducting research on school choice, for example visiting schools. Mothers' informal social networks, through which they obtain information about local schools, are usually networks in which fathers do not participate. The fathers in David's study were most likely to be involved jointly in decision making (about school choice) in middle-class families, which was sometimes associated with the fathers paying for private education. It is encouraging that about half of the non-resident fathers participated in decisions about their children's secondary school.

---

35 There were more mothers interviewed than fathers due to some of the children living in single-mother families, and many fathers being unavailable for interview (Dudley-Marling, 2001).

36 This is the same research study as in West et al. (1998).

Table 13: Fathers' and mothers' attendance at general school or class events/meetings

	Fathers	Mothers	Source	Population
Percentage of children whose father/mother attended at least one class event in current school year	53% of children in two-parent families 65% of children in single-father families 22% of children who have contact with non-resident father	67% of children in two-parent families 60% of children in single-mother families	Nord et al. (1997), using data from 1996 US National Household Education Survey (NHES:96) (large-scale and nationally representative)	US school-age children in 1996
Percentage of fathers/mothers who attended[37] school induction meetings[38]	50% of fathers	Over 75% of mothers	Clough et al. (2000), using data from small-scale survey[39] of parents in north-east England (six schools in three urban LEAs)	Parents of children in reception classes in north east England in 1999-2000

37 It is not clear in the published report (Clough et al., 2000) whether this was attendance on at least one occasion.

38 Staff said that they had invited all mothers and all fathers to these events (Clough et al., 2000).

39 This source on fathers' involvement in primary schools in England was a very small-scale study of 36 mothers and 36 fathers of reception class children in six schools in three urban LEAs in north-east England (Clough et al., 2000). The samples of schools and parents in this study were *not* selected randomly, but constitute quota/convenience samples. The achieved sample had a higher percentage of single-parent households and a lower percentage of working parents than the average for this region. All of the staff at the schools were male except for one headteacher. All data on fathers' involvement was obtained directly from the fathers interviewed. It is not clear from the published report whether or not all the fathers were resident with their children and/or were biological fathers.

Table 14: Fathers' and mothers' attendance at parent–teacher conferences (US)/parents evenings (UK) about progress of children

	Fathers	Mothers	Source	Population
Percentage of children whose father/mother attended at least one parent–teacher conference in current school year	**39%** of children in two-parent families **64%** of children in single-father families **15%** of children who have contact with non-resident father	**68%** of children in two-parent families **71%** of children in single-mother families	Nord et al. (1997), using data from 1996 US National Household Education Survey (NHES:96) (large-scale and nationally representative)	US school-age children in 1996
Percentage of fathers who attended parent–teacher conferences	**45%** of fathers always **25%** sometimes almost **30%** almost never	No data	National Center for Fathering (1999), using data from survey of nearly 900 adults in US (nationally representative)	US fathers of primary and secondary school children in 1999
Percentage of children whose mother/father attended 'open evening'	**65%** of children had both mother and father[40] attend	**27%** of children had mother attend on her own, i.e. without the father	West et al. (1998), using data from small-scale survey of parents in London (105 children had parent/s or other adult who attended an 'open evening')	Children in last year of primary school (aged 10-11) in London in 1994/95 (state and independent schools)
Percentage of fathers/ mothers who attended[41] parent-teacher meetings[42]	**61%** of fathers	**97%** of mothers	Clough et al. (2000), using data from small-scale survey of parents in north-east England (six schools in three urban LEAs)	Parents of children in reception classes in north-east England in 1999-2000
Percentage of non-resident fathers who attended parents evenings for non-resident children	**41%** of fathers	No data	Bradshaw et al. (1999), using combined data from two surveys of non-resident fathers in England in 1995/96 (large-scale and nationally representative)	Non-resident fathers with a school-age child in Britain in 1995/96

40 The father only (i.e. without the mother) attended open evenings for a small percentage of children. The percentage is not recorded in West et al. (1998).

41 It is not clear in the report whether this was attendance on at least one occasion.

42 Staff said that they had invited all mothers and all fathers to these events.

Table 15: Fathers' and mothers' informal contact with teachers/ dropping children off and picking up children from school

	Fathers	Mothers	Source	Population
Percentage of fathers/mothers who dropped their child off at school in mornings	**42%** of fathers	**79%** of mothers	Clough et al. (2000), using data from small-scale survey of parents in north-east England (six schools in three urban LEAs)	Parents of children in reception classes in north-east England in 1999-2000
Percentage of children whose mother/father had informal discussions with teacher	**45%** of children had both mother and father having informal discussions	**49%** of children had mother only having informal discussions	West et al. (1998), using data from small-scale survey of parents in London (105 children had parent/s or other adult who had informal discussions with teacher)	Children in last year of primary school (aged 10-11) in London in 1994/95 (state and independent schools)
Percentage of non-resident fathers who picked up/ dropped off non-resident children at school	**27%** of fathers	-	Bradshaw et al. (1999), using combined data from two surveys of non-resident fathers in England in 1995/96 (large-scale and nationally representative)	Non-resident fathers with a school-age child in Britain in 1995/96
Percentage of fathers who walked or took their children to school	**20%** of fathers every day **11%** once or twice a week **15%** less regularly **52%** never	No data	National Center for Fathering (1999), using data from survey of nearly 900 adults in US (nationally representative)	US fathers of primary and secondary school children in 1999
Percentage of fathers who visited their children's classroom	**10%** at least once a week **20%** once or twice a month **31%** once every three months **37%** never	No data	National Center for Fathering (1999), using data from survey of nearly 900 adults in US (nationally representative)	US fathers of primary and secondary school children in 1999
Percentage of fathers who communicated with their child's teacher	**8%** every day **13%** once or twice a week **28%** once or twice a month **23%** once every three months **27%** of fathers never	No data	National Center for Fathering (1999), using data from survey of nearly 900 adults in US (nationally representative)	US fathers of primary and secondary school children in 1999

Table 16: Fathers' and mothers' responsibility for choosing their child's school

	Fathers	Mothers	Source	Population
Percentage of fathers/ mothers who were involved in/took main responsibility for decision on selection of primary school	**41%** of children had father who was involved **3%** of children had father who took main responsibility	**95%** of children had mother who was involved **70%** of children had mother who took main responsibility	David (1998), using data from small-scale survey of parents in London (111 families)	Children in reception class of primary school (aged 4-5) in London in 1994/95 (state and independent schools)
Percentage of fathers/ mothers who were involved in decision on selection of secondary school	**More than 78%** of children had father who was involved	**90%** of children had mother who was involved	David (1998), using data from small-scale survey of parents in London (120 families)	Children in last year of primary school (aged 10-11) in London in 1994/95 (state and independent schools)
Percentage of children with non-resident father whose father was involved in decision on selection of secondary school	**53%** of children had father involved	N/A	David (1998), using data from small-scale survey of parents in London (120 families)	Children in last year of primary school (aged 10-11) in London in 1994/95 (state and independent schools)
Percentage of fathers/ mothers reporting sole/shared responsibility for selecting childcare programme, pre-school or school for children	**60%** of fathers had shared responsibility **7%** of fathers had sole responsibility	**38%** of mothers had shared responsibility **60%** of mothers had sole responsibility	Halle (2001), using data from 1997 US Panel Study of Income Dynamics (large-scale and nationally representative)	US parents of children aged 3-12 in 1997

Table 17: Fathers' and mothers' volunteering in the classroom of their children's schools

	Fathers	Mothers	Source	Population
Percentage of resident fathers/ mothers who helped in their children's classroom	**15%** of non-full-time working resident fathers **14%** of full-time working resident fathers	**31%** of non-full-time working resident mothers **16%** of full-time working resident mothers	Williams et al. (2002), using data from 2001 survey of parents in England (large-scale and nationally representative)	Resident parents of school-age children (aged 5-16) in England in 2001
Percentage of fathers/mothers who said they had helped as volunteer in nursery, playgroup or school of their 3-7-year-old child in the past 12 months	**9%** of fathers	**37%** of mothers	Fitzgerald et al. (2003), using data from National Adult Learning Survey 2002 (large-scale and nationally representative)	Parents of children aged 3-7 in 2002
Percentage of fathers/mothers who had helped out in their child's classroom	**14%** of fathers	**25%** of mothers	Clough et al.(2000), using data from small-scale survey of parents in north-east England (six schools in three urban LEAs)	Parents of children in reception classes in north-east England in 1999-2000
Percentage of children whose father/mother acted as volunteers in their schools	**15%** of children in two-parent families **23%** of children in single-father families **4%** of children who have contact with non-resident father	**41%** of children in two-parent families **29%** of children in single-mother families	Nord et al. (1997), using data from 1996 US National Household Education Survey (NHES:96) (large-scale and nationally representative)	US school-age children in 1996
Percentage of fathers who had volunteered at their child's school	**60%** of fathers never, **13%** once or twice a month **18%** once every three months	No data	National Center for Fathering (1999), using data from survey of nearly 900 adults in US (nationally representative)	US fathers of primary and secondary school children in 1999

Fathers' participation in family learning programmes

As noted in Chapter 1, Ofsted (2000) wrote that "there is a disturbing absence of men involved in family learning". Research clearly and consistently shows that there is very low participation by fathers in family learning programmes which are not targeted especially at men.

- The 2002 National Adult Learning Survey reports that two per cent of fathers and six per cent of mothers with children aged 3-7 had attended a course with their children (e.g. literacy) in the past 12 months (Fitzgerald et al., 2003).

- An evaluation of LSC-funded family programmes estimated that about five per cent of learners participating in family language, literacy and numeracy (FLLN) programmes in 2002/03 were men (NIACE, 2003). The percentages were higher for wider family learning programmes (e.g. arts and crafts, design and technology, ICT) in which it was estimated that men comprised about 12 per cent of learners. Ofsted (2000) conclude in their review that wider family learning may have an important role in reaching parents, including fathers and other men, who do not have literacy and numeracy needs and/or who have fears about learning.

- The National Foundation for Educational Research (NFER) evaluation of the Basic Skills Agency (BSA) family literacy demonstration programmes, which worked with parents with poor basic skills and their children (aged 3-6), reports that 96 per cent of 360 parents in the research were mothers (NFER/BSA, 1996). These courses lasted 96 hours over 12 weeks, comprising six hours a week for parents and children separately, and two hours a week in joint parent–child sessions.

- In the evaluation of the BSA numeracy programme, 97 per cent of parents in the research were mothers (Brooks et al., 2002).

- Millard and Hunter (2001) report that men represent a minority of participants in the CEDC (now ContinYou) family learning programmes Share Key Stage 1 and Share Key Stage 2 for parents and their children.

- Macleod (2000) writes about an evaluation in 1994 of a large-scale family literacy initiative spread throughout England and Wales across 18 sites. The programme focused on disadvantaged children in the early years of school or pre-school in order to address an intergenerational under-achievement in literacy. The aims of the programme were to work with parents to improve their basic literacy skills; to work with children to support their language and literacy development; and to work with parents to help them support their children's learning. Fifteen of the 18 projects (10-week courses) were held at a primary school during school hours; 163 mothers, but only six fathers, participated. Furthermore, Macleod reports that "one programme, which stated the involvement of fathers as one of its main aims, recruited ten women and no men even though the project was sited in an area of high female employment and low male employment".

- Most family learning courses in Bristol were "almost exclusively attended by women", as shown by monitoring data (Bryant and Taylor, 1999).

These results mirror the lower involvement of men than women in non-vocational adult education, especially in adult and community education provided by LEAs and community organisations (McGivney, 1999). This is despite more men than women participating in adult learning overall (due to the greater involvement of men in employment-related learning), and women being more likely than men to have no qualifications.

Fathers are more likely to get involved when family learning programmes are shorter and run outside the working day. In the NFER/ University of Sheffield evaluation of the LSC-funded *Keeping Up with the Children* course (literacy and numeracy), which lasted 12 hours, nine per cent of the participants in the 31 observed sessions were fathers (Brooks et al., 2002).

A couple of research studies show that when fathers do join school-based family learning programmes held during daytime hours where mothers are in the great majority, they are likely to drop out significantly (Macleod, 2000; Lewis, 2000a). For example, the evaluation in Macleod (2000) found that five of the six men recruited dropped out of the course early on, which was a substantially higher rate of drop-out than for the mothers.

The reasons for this drop-out of fathers are not known. It could be due to a combination of factors: the high proportion of women in the programme (both teachers and participants); the school venue; the unemployed men who are enrolled finding work; the employed men who are enrolled changing their shifts; lower commitment of men (in general) to learning courses; other factors such as the nature of the curriculum and learning methods. Some of these barriers are discussed in Chapter 4. There is no evidence from the case studies that when fathers join family learning programmes oriented specifically towards fathers (even when these are held in schools), they drop out significantly, although their attendance at the sessions may be irregular.

No data was found during this research on the involvement of fathers in family learning programmes by their family status (resident, non-resident, single parent).

More encouraging is that our mapping for the research in this report uncovered many examples of family learning initiatives in Britain which are either targeted specifically at fathers, or which attract fathers in substantial numbers. Sometimes these were on stereotypically male themes such as sport, ICT and technology, but there were also examples in the curricular areas of the visual arts, music, reading and creative writing. The mapping also found that well-designed family learning programmes with exciting practical activities (e.g. robotics) can attract both fathers and mothers. Evidence on these initiatives (including the 13 selected for detailed case study) is presented in the remaining chapters of this report, but especially in Chapters 5 and 6.

Small-scale research suggests that even where fathers do not attend family learning sessions, they may increase their involvement with their children's learning as a result of the programme. Firstly, the mothers pass elements of their learning on to the fathers and, secondly, the children encourage their fathers to get involved in learning activities at home between sessions (Brassett-Grundy, 2002; Karther, 2002).

Is there a distinctive 'fathers' role' in children's learning and education?

Lamb and Tamis-Lemonda (2004) wrote that "fathers can and do engage with their children in many different ways, not only as playmates, and that they are more than role models". The evidence reviewed in this chapter shows that fathers' out-of-school involvement with their children's learning comprises:

- some specific roles, in particular supporting children's learning through building and repairing activities, other practical activities and hobbies, IT, maths, science, recreation and leisure, sports and physical play, outdoor activities, family outings, play and fun together

- some similar roles to mothers, in particular reading with their children, helping with homework, and giving praise and support to their children for their schoolwork, for substantial numbers of fathers

- particular kinds of literacy, for example newspapers, maps and 'environmental print'.

It appears to us that, in terms of Lamb et al.'s model of father involvement (Section 2.1), resident fathers' involvement in their children's learning and education consists primarily of:

- 'engagement', i.e. fathers' direct interaction with their children

- and, to a lesser degree, some 'indirect care' aspects of 'responsibility' (activities carried out for the child but not with the child), such as attending parents' evenings.

Resident fathers also support mothers' involvement in their children's learning and education.

The evidence supports the findings of Shumow and Miller in the US, and of Millard and Hunter in the UK, that fathers' overall involvement in their children's learning is less visible to schools than that of mothers (Shumow and Miller, 2001; Millard and Hunter, 2001). Shumow and Miller claim that this lower involvement of fathers in school than out-of-school leads some researchers and policymakers to "underestimate the interest of fathers and overlook them in designing parental involvement opportunities". Millard and Hunter similarly recommend that "schools should not confuse a lack of participation in school-run events/activities [by fathers] with a lack of interest". It is concluded that it is important for schools and family learning providers to learn about the roles of fathers in their children's learning so that they can effectively build on this.

2.4 Population groups of fathers who are more and less involved

The context

Before this chapter turns to look at factors statistically associated with the level of fathers' involvement in their children's learning and education, it is helpful to consider some of the factors which are associated with:

- men's participation in organised adult education and training after school
- 'parents'/mothers' participation in family learning programmes
- 'parents'/mothers' engagement with their children's learning and education/ schools

to give some context, as some of the same patterns apply to fathers' involvement in their children's learning and education.

Some specific groups of men in the UK tend to be under-represented ('missing') from organised education and training after school: long-term unemployed men, manual workers, men with poor literacy skills, men with few or no qualifications, men who left school at an early age, ex-offenders, and black and minority ethnic men (e.g. data from the National Adult Learning Surveys, as presented in McGivney, 1999). These same groups tend to be greatly disadvantaged in the job market.

The 2002 National Adult Learning Survey presents data specific to parents' involvement in family learning in the UK (Fitzgerald et al., 2003). Mirroring some of the findings on men's involvement in organised education, parents of older children, parents with low qualifications, parents with basic skills difficulties, and parents dependent on benefits were all least likely to have engaged in family learning programmes.

Parents are more involved in their children's education and in schools when:

- child is in primary school (Epstein, 2002; Nord et al., 1997; Williams et al., 2002)
- parent is more affluent/of higher social class, or lives in more affluent community, although there is often more communication between schools and families about children's problems and difficulties in more deprived communities (Epstein, 2002; Williams et al., 2002; Nord et al. 1997).
- parent has higher levels of education (Williams et al., 2002; Nord et al., 1997)
- parent believes they can help their child's learning (Nord et al., 1997)
- parent has high educational aspirations for their child (Nord et al., 1997)
- child's school has policies and teachers which promote parental involvement (Nord, Brimhall and West, 1997).

Parents are less involved when:

- parent is lone mother (Epstein, 2002; Nord et al., 1997)
- parent works full time compared with part time and not working (Nord et al., 1997)
- parent is doing paid work outside home (Epstein, 2002)
- parent lives far away from their children's schools (Epstein, 2002)

and, of course, as seen in this report, when they are male parents.

Which fathers are more and less involved in their children's learning and education?

Some descriptive data from large-scale, nationally representative surveys was found that shows levels of fathers' involvement in their children's learning and education for different population groups of fathers, mothers and children. This data was not systematically assessed for this report because of the limitations of descriptive ('bivariate') tables (see below), but a small selection is presented in Tables 18-20. Unfortunately, very little data was found from UK studies.

Table 18: Fathers' involvement in their children's learning and education, by characteristics of children

Group of fathers	Type of involvement	% of fathers in this group who are involved in this way (see column to left)	Source
By children's age			
Children aged 6-11 years (US resident fathers)	'High involvement'[43] in children's primary schools	33%	Brown et al. (2001) and Halle (2001) using data from 1999 US National Household Education Survey (large-scale and nationally representative)
Children aged 12-17 years (US resident fathers)	'High involvement' in children's secondary schools	25%	Brown et al. (2001) and Halle (2001), using data from 1999 US National Household Education Survey (large-scale and nationally representative)
Children in kindergarten to 5th grade (US resident fathers)	High involvement in children's primary schools	10%	Nord et al. (1997), using data from 1996 US National Household Education Survey (large-scale and nationally representative)
Children in 9th –12th grade (US resident fathers)	High involvement in children's secondary schools	7%	Nord et al. (1997), using data from 1996 US National Household Education Survey (large-scale and nationally representative)
By children's ethnicity			
White non-Hispanic (US)	Looked at books with their 3-12-year-old children	40%	Halle (2001), using data from 1997 Panel Study of Income Dynamics (large-scale and nationally representative)
Black non-Hispanic (US)	Looked at books with their 3-12-year-old children	45%	Halle (2001), using data from 1997 Panel Study of Income Dynamics (large-scale and nationally representative)
White non-Hispanic (US)	Played sports or engaged in outdoor activities with their children	70%	Halle (2001), using data from 1997 Panel Study of Income Dynamics (large-scale and nationally representative)

43 High involvement in this survey comprised participation by the parent in three or four different types of school activity during the past school year. The four activities were general school meetings, regularly scheduled parent–teacher conferences, school/class events, and serving as a volunteer at the school.

Group of fathers	Type of involvement	% of fathers in this group who are involved in this way (see column to left)	Source
Black non-Hispanic (US)	Played sports or engaged in outdoor activities with their children	67%	Halle (2001), using data from 1997 Panel Study of Income Dynamics (large-scale and nationally representative)
White non-Hispanic (resident fathers in two-parent families in US)	High involvement in children's schools	29%	Nord et al. (1997), using data from 1996 US National Household Education Survey for resident fathers (large-scale and nationally representative)
Black non-Hispanic (resident fathers in two-parent families in US)	High involvement in children's schools	20%	Nord et al. (1997), using data from 1996 US National Household Education Survey (large-scale and nationally representative)

Table 19: Fathers' involvement in their children's learning and education, by characteristics of fathers

Group of fathers	Type of involvement	% of fathers in this group who are involved in this way (see column to left)	Source
By resident fathers' work status			
Fathers working full time (UK)	Felt 'very involved' in children's schools	24%	Williams et al. (2002), using data from 2001 survey of parents in England (large-scale and nationally representative)
Fathers not working full time (UK)	Felt 'very involved' in children's schools	29%	Williams et al. (2002), using data from 2001 survey of parents in England (large-scale and nationally representative)
Fathers working full time (UK)	Helped out in classroom of children's schools	15%	Williams et al. (2002), using data from 2001 survey of parents in England (large-scale and nationally representative)
Fathers not working full time (UK)	Helped out in classroom of children's schools	14%	Williams et al. (2002), using data from 2001 survey of parents in England (large-scale and nationally representative)
Fathers working full time (US)	High involvement in children's schools	27%	Nord et al. (1997), using data from 1996 US National Household Education Survey for resident fathers (large-scale and nationally representative)
Fathers working part time (US)	High involvement in children's schools	30%	Nord et al. (1997), using data from 1996 US National Household Education Survey (large-scale and nationally representative)
Fathers not working and not looking for work (US)	High involvement in children's schools	18%	Nord et al. (1997), using data from 1996 US National Household Education Survey (large-scale and nationally representative)

Group of fathers	Type of involvement	% of fathers in this group who are involved in this way (see column to left)	Source
By resident fathers' educational level			
Fathers of 6- to 11-year-olds who were college graduates (US)	High involvement in children's schools	**45%**	Brown et al. (2001) and Halle (2001), using data from 1999 US National Household Education Survey (large-scale and nationally representative)
Fathers of 6- to 11-year-olds with some college or vocational/ technical training (US)	High involvement in children's schools	**36%**	Brown et al. (2001) and Halle (2001), using data from 1999 US National Household Education Survey (large-scale and nationally representative)
Fathers of 6- to 11-year-olds who had earned a high school diploma or GED (US)	High involvement in children's schools	**24%**	Brown et al. (2001) and Halle (2001), using data from 1999 US National Household Education Survey (large-scale and nationally representative)
Fathers of 6- to 11-year-olds who had not finished high school (US)	High involvement in children's schools	**10%**	Brown et al. (2001) and Halle (2001), using data from 1999 US National Household Education Survey (large-scale and nationally representative)
Fathers with educational level less than high school (US)	Looked at books with their 3-12-year-old children	**27%**	Halle (2001), using data from 1997 Panel Study of Income Dynamics (large-scale and nationally representative)
Fathers who were college graduates (US)	Looked at books with their 3-12-year-old children	**45%**	Halle (2001), using data from 1997 Panel Study of Income Dynamics (large-scale and nationally representative)
Fathers with educational level less than high school (US)	Played sports or engaged in outdoor activities with their children	**60%**	Halle (2001), using data from 1997 Panel Study of Income Dynamics (large-scale and nationally representative)
Fathers who were college graduates (US)	Played sports or engaged in outdoor activities with their children	**72%**	Halle (2001), using data from 1997 Panel Study of Income Dynamics (large-scale and nationally representative)

Group of fathers	Type of involvement	% of fathers in this group who are involved in this way (see column to left)	Source
By fathers' income			
Fathers classified as poor (US)	Looked at books with their 3-12-year-old children	26%	Halle (2001), using data from 1997 Panel Study of Income Dynamics (large-scale and nationally representative)
Fathers classified as *not* poor (US)	Looked at books with their 3-12-year-old children	72%	Halle (2001), using data from 1997 Panel Study of Income Dynamics (large-scale and nationally representative)
Fathers classified as poor (US)	Played sports or engaged in outdoor activities with their children	67%	Halle (2001), using data from 1997 Panel Study of Income Dynamics (large-scale and nationally representative)
Fathers classified as *not* poor (US)	Played sports or engaged in outdoor activities with their children	68%	Halle (2001), using data from 1997 Panel Study of Income Dynamics (large-scale and nationally representative)
Fathers in two-parent families classified as poor (US)	High involvement in children's schools	14%	Nord et al. (1997), using data from 1996 US National Household Education Survey (large-scale and nationally representative)
Fathers in two-parent families classified as *not* poor (US)	High involvement in children's schools	29%	Nord et al. (1997), using data from 1996 US National Household Education Survey (large-scale and nationally representative)
Non-resident fathers in contact with children and classified as poor (US)	High involvement in children's schools	6%	Nord et al. (1997), using data from 1996 US National Household Education Survey (large-scale and nationally representative)
Non-resident fathers in contact with children and classified as *not_* poor (US)	High involvement in children's schools	10%	Nord et al. (1997), using data from 1996 US National Household Education Survey (large-scale and nationally representative)

Table 20: Fathers' involvement in their children's learning and education, by characteristics of mothers

Group of fathers	Type of involvement	% of fathers in this group who are involved in this way (see column to left)	Source
By resident mothers' educational qualifications			
Child's mother had educational level less than high school (resident fathers in US)	Looked at books with their 3-12-year-old children	31%	Halle (2001), using data from 1997 Panel Study of Income Dynamics (large-scale and nationally representative)
Child's mother was college graduate (resident fathers in US)	Looked at books with their 3-12-year-old children	46%	Halle (2001), using data from 1997 Panel Study of Income Dynamics (large-scale and nationally representative)
Child's mother had educational level less than high school (resident fathers in US)	Played sports or engaged in outdoor activities with their children	60%	Halle (2001), using data from 1997 Panel Study of Income Dynamics (large-scale and nationally representative)
Child's mother was college graduate (resident fathers in US)	Played sports or engaged in outdoor activities with their children	70%	Halle (2001), using data from 1997 Panel Study of Income Dynamics (large-scale and nationally representative)
Mother of child had educational level less than high school (non-resident fathers in US in contact with children)	High involvement in children's schools	5%	Nord et al. (1997), using data from 1996 US National Household Education Survey (large-scale and nationally representative)
Mother of child was graduate (non-resident fathers in US in contact with children)	High involvement in children's schools	14%	Nord et al. (1997), using data from 1996 US National Household Education Survey (large-scale and nationally representative)

Group of fathers	Type of involvement	% of fathers in this group who are involved in this way (see column to left)	Source
By resident mothers' work status			
Child's mother not working (US resident fathers)	Looked at books with their 3-12-year-old children	46%	Halle (2001), using data from 1997 Panel Study of Income Dynamics (large-scale and nationally representative)
Child's mother was working (US resident fathers)	Looked at books with their 3-12-year-old children	36%	Halle (2001), using data from 1997 Panel Study of Income Dynamics (large-scale and nationally representative)
Child's mother not working (US resident fathers)	Played sports or engaged in outdoor activities with their children	72%	Halle (2001), using data from 1997 Panel Study of Income Dynamics (large-scale and nationally representative)
Child's mother was working (US resident fathers)	Played sports or engaged in outdoor activities with their children	68%	Halle (2001), using data from 1997 Panel Study of Income Dynamics (large-scale and nationally representative)
Mother worked full time (resident fathers in two-parent families in US)	High involvement in children's schools	28%	Nord et al. (1997), using data from 1996 US National Household Education Survey (large-scale and nationally representative)
Mother worked part time (resident fathers in two-parent families in US)	High involvement in children's schools	30%	Nord et al. (1997), using data from 1996 US National Household Education Survey (large-scale and nationally representative)
Mother did not work (resident fathers in two-parent families in US)	High involvement in children's schools	22%	Nord et al. (1997), using data from 1996 US National Household Education Survey (large-scale and nationally representative)

Descriptive data can be interesting and relatively simple to understand, but a much more robust way to show relationships between fathers' involvement and fathers', mothers' and children's characteristics is to use multivariate statistical analyses which control simultaneously for (i.e. hold constant) a wide range of factors that could influence the level of involvement.

For example, in the descriptive analysis in Table 20, it is seen that fathers were more involved in their children's schools when children's mothers had higher educational qualifications. But this relationship may occur not because there is any 'independent' association between these two variables, but because mothers' educational qualifications are correlated with, for example, fathers' educational qualifications, which in turn are associated with the level of fathers' involvement. In a multivariate analysis, fathers' educational level (and many other variables) can be held constant, and it can be seen whether or not there is still an 'independent' relationship between level of involvement and mothers' educational level.

Multivariate analyses show that fathers were more likely to be involved in their children's out-of-school learning and education in the UK in the 1960s (Flouri and Buchanan, 2003b[44]), and/or in their children's schools in the US in 1996 (Nord et al., 1997), when:

- **father was resident with the child** (Nord et al., 1997)

- **father was a single parent** (Nord et al., 1997)

- **child was younger/in primary school rather than older/in secondary school** (applies to both resident and non-resident fathers' involvement)[45] (Nord et al., 1997)

- **child was first-born** (applies to resident fathers' involvement with children in 'intact families') (Flouri and Buchanan, 2003b)

- **child had fewer siblings** (applies to resident fathers' involvement with children in 'intact families') (Flouri and Buchanan, 2003b)

- **child was doing well at secondary school** (applies to resident fathers' involvement with children in two-parent/'intact families')[46] (Flouri and Buchanan, 2003b; Nord et al., 1997)

- **father had higher educational qualifications** (applies to resident fathers' involvement with children in two-parent/'intact families' and to single-parent fathers' involvement) (Flouri and Buchanan, 2003b; Nord et al., 1997)

- **father was of higher social class** (applies to resident fathers' involvement with children aged seven in 'intact families') (Flouri and Buchanan, 2003b)

- **child's household had higher income**[47] (applies to non-resident fathers' involvement with secondary school children)[48] (Nord et al., 1997)

- **father paid child support** (applies to non-resident fathers' involvement with primary school children) (Nord et al., 1997)

- **father was younger** (applies to resident fathers' involvement with children in 'intact families' (Flouri and Buchanan, 2003b)

---

44 Flouri and Buchanan (2003b) looked at four indicators of father involvement as perceived by children's parents or primary caregivers (mainly mothers) and teachers in the National Child Development Study. Three of the four indicators (reads to child, takes outings with child, interested in child's education) relate strongly to involvement in children's learning and education, although Flouri and Buchanan call them 'middle-class indices'. Flouri and Buchanan's multivariate analysis looking at factors associated with father involvement included only 'intact families', i.e. those where the child had lived with both their parents.

45 Nord et al.'s multivariate analyses looking at non-resident fathers' involvement were restricted to non-resident fathers in contact with their children.

46 Causality could work in both directions or interact.

47 Both Flouri and Buchanan (2003b) and Nord et al. (1997) found no relationships between resident fathers' involvement and financial circumstances.

48 Flouri and Buchanan (2003b) found no associations in intact families between financial difficulties in the home and fathers' involvement in their child's learning and education.

- **father was unemployed, disabled or retired** (applies to resident fathers' involvement with children in 'intact families') (Flouri and Buchanan, 2003b)

- **good relationship between child's resident parents** (applies to resident fathers' involvement with children in 'intact families' (Flouri and Buchanan, 2003b)

- **father lived with child's step-mother (as opposed to biological/ adoptive mother) in two-parent families** (Nord et al., 1997)

- **child's mother was involved in child's learning and education** (applies to both resident and non-resident fathers' involvement) (Nord et al., 1997; Flouri and Buchanan, 2003b)

- **child's mother worked full time** (applies to resident fathers' involvement with primary school children in two-parent/'intact families') (Flouri and Buchanan, 2003b; Nord et al., 1997). This is likely to be related to more egalitarian roles within the household (Ortiz, 2001; Ortiz and McCarty, 1997)

- **child's mother had higher educational qualifications** (applies to non-resident fathers' involvement with primary school children; and to resident fathers' involvement with primary school children in 'intact families') (Nord et al., 1997)

- **child's mother had not remarried** (for non-resident fathers' involvement)

- **child's school had positive environment**[49] (applies to resident fathers' involvement with secondary school children in two-parent families, to single-parent fathers' involvement with primary school children; and to non-resident fathers' involvement with primary school children) (Nord et al., 1997)

- **father had earlier (post-natal/pre-school/primary school) involvement** (Flouri and Buchanan, 2003b) Flouri and Buchanan (2001) write that "generally once fathers are involved, they remain involved with that child throughout childhood", and this concurs with Pleck and Masciadrelli (2004) that there is moderate stability of fathers' overall involvement with their children over time.

Fathers were less likely to be involved in their children's out-of-school learning and education in the 1960s, and/or in their children's schools in the US in 1996, when:

- **father was manual worker** (Flouri and Buchanan, 2003b)

- **father worked evenings**[50] (applies to resident fathers' involvement in two-parent families, both poor and non-poor. There was an eight per cent decrease in the quality of the child's home environment when the father worked evenings, which was of the same order as the influence of the family being in poverty) (Heymann and Earle, 2001)

---

49 Welcoming, makes it easy for parents to get involved, has good classroom discipline, mutual respect between teachers and pupils (Nord et al., 1997).

50 Evening work hours were between 7.30pm and 9.30pm. Heymann and Earle (2001) used a measure of the quality of the child's home environment, which included cognitive stimulation, emotional support for the child, access to educational materials and ways in which parent and child spent time together. Therefore, it was not a direct measure of father involvement in his child's learning and education. Analysis found slightly stronger associations between this home environment measure and whether the mother worked evenings.

- **child had emotional and behavioural problems in primary school**[51] (applies to resident fathers' involvement with children in 'intact families') (Flouri and Buchanan, 2003b)

- **father was not biological or adoptive father, but a step-father, i.e. the child's mother has re-married** (applies to resident fathers' involvement with secondary school children in two-parent families) (Nord et al., 1997)

Ethnicity was a variable which was not included in Flouri and Buchanan's multivariate analysis, and which was not statistically significant in Nord et al.'s multivariate analyses.

With regard to **children's gender**, fathers in 'intact families'/two-parent families were more involved in the 1960s with taking their 7- and 11-year-old sons on outings than their 7- and 11-year-old daughters (Flouri and Buchanan, 2003b); and fathers were more involved in 1996 in their sons' secondary schools than in their daughters' secondary schools (Nord et al. 1997). This fits well with the UK research described in Section 2.3 showing that fathers are more likely to engage in hobbies, leisure and outdoor activities with their teenage sons than with their teenage daughters (Warin et al., 1999; O'Brien and Jones, 1995, 1996). It is important to remember that secondary school boys are more likely than girls of the same age group to have problems at school (Carter and Wojtkiewicz, 2000); and anecdotal evidence was cited earlier that fathers often get involved in their children's schools only in times of crisis.

However, for resident fathers' involvement more generally in their children's lives, the evidence is much more mixed for the relationship with children's gender. In more recent surveys, the amount of father involvement has not been related to the gender of the child (Pleck and Masciadrelli, 2004). Pleck and Masciadrelli speculate that "child gender exerts less influence on paternal involvement today than in previous decades". Lamb and Lewis (2004) report greater father involvement with sons for infants but that this association is "hard to detect...relatively small" for older children.

Chapter 3 reports similarly inconclusive evidence on whether or not fathers have different types of interactions with their sons than with their daughters during joint learning activities.

The level of mothers' involvement in children's learning and education was the variable which was most strongly related[52] to the level of fathers' involvement in their learning and education (Flouri and Buchanan, 2003b; Nord et al., 1997). In Flouri and Buchanan's analysis, in families where a mother was interested in her child's education, the father was more than 15 times as likely as fathers in families where the mother was not interested in her child's education to be interested in his child's education (Flouri and Buchanan, 2003b).

Nord et al. (1997) found that, for secondary school children, fathers were 175 per cent more likely to be highly involved in their children's schools for each additional type of mothers' involvement in the schools. This compared to fathers being 23 per cent more likely to be highly involved for each unit increase in fathers' educational level. These researchers speculate that mothers and fathers are likely to have similar educational aspirations for their children. Chapter 4 will discuss how mothers can be both facilitators and barriers to fathers' involvement.

Statistical analyses also show us that multiple forms of involvement by fathers coincide (Flouri and Buchanan, 2004; Nord et al., 1997). If a father is involved in his children's education in

---

51 Causality could work in both directions or interact.

52 Except in Nord et al.'s analyses for two-parent families for presence of step-mother in child's household.

one way, it is likely that he is also involved in other ways. Nord et al. found in their multi-variate analyses that fathers in two-parent families who were more highly involved in their children's schools were more likely to be involved at home or out-of-home in educational activities (for example, reading with their child or visits to a museum or historical site) and to help with their children's homework. Interestingly, this relationship did not apply to single-parent fathers, perhaps (Nord et al., 1997) because these fathers do not have time to be involved in both their children's schools and their children's learning at home.

Of course, all the multivariate data presented in this chapter were either for 40 years ago in the UK (Flouri and Buchanan, 2003b), or for a decade ago in the US (Nord et al., 1997). More up-to-date information is needed so that it can be seen whether these relationships with the level of fathers' involvement hold in today's societies in the UK and US.

Chapter 4 will return to some of these factors when discussing fathers' beliefs and attitudes, and barriers to fathers' involvement in their children's learning and education.

2.5 Black and minority ethnic fathers' involvement

The context

The relatively low educational attainment of some groups of black and minority ethnic teenage boys in Britain is of concern (National Statistics, 2002), as is the attainment of white working-class boys. McGivney (2004) and Bruneau (2002) report that there are high rates of school exclusion and truancy amongst African-Caribbean and Bangladeshi teenage boys. An analysis of 1991 census data shows that the ethnic groups with highest levels of educational qualifications were adults of African, Chinese and other Asian backgrounds, followed by white adults and adults of Indian backgrounds (McGivney, 1999). The ethnic groups with lowest levels of qualifications were adults of African-Caribbean, Pakistani and Bangladeshi backgrounds.

These differences between ethnic groups are likely to be due to a complex range of factors including pre-immigration educational and social background, as well as socio-economic factors and ethnic/racial/religious discrimination.

In 2001/02, men from Pakistani, Bangladeshi and Chinese communities were substantially less likely than men in other ethnic groups to take part in post-16 education and training, whereas men from African groups were substantially more likely to do so (McGivney, 2004). The relationship between social class and educational participation in minority ethnic groups is weaker than for the white population (McGivney, 1999).

Different black and minority ethnic groups vary greatly in their prevalent family structures, gender roles and religious and cultural orientations. South Asian communities tend to have relatively large families; traditionally differentiated roles for men and women (i.e. mothers as homemakers and fathers as economic providers); strong religious identities; high marriage rates; and relatively low levels of single parents, cohabiting couples and non-resident fathers[53] (Becher and Husain, 2003; Clarke and O'Brien, 2004; National Statistics, 2002; Bignall and Butt, 2001).

---

53 Traditional Hinduism does not accept divorce. In Islam, children legally belong to their father, but mothers are allowed custody until sons are aged seven, and until girls reach puberty. Mothers in both religious communities may of course use the British courts to gain custody of their children for a longer period (Becher and Husain, 2003).

Bruneau (2002) cites data from the 1991 Census which shows that 54 per cent of African-Caribbean households with children under age 16 were headed by a female single parent (also see National Statistics, 2002; and Bignall and Butt, 2001). Non-resident fathers are common in African-Caribbean communities, where extended families (e.g. grandmothers) often provide support to resident mothers.

In South Asian communities (Becher and Husain, 2003; National Statistics, 2002) and some African-Caribbean communities (Bruneau, 2002), children often have a range of 'father figures', for example older brothers, uncles and grandfathers, who are likely to live nearby or in the same household. These father figures act as sources of childcare, other practical and emotional support for children's parents, and additional male role models and playmates for children.

What many black and minority ethnic adults share is a relatively high likelihood of low income, unemployment, living in a deprived urban area, and being on the receiving end of crime and racism, compared with white adults (National Statistics, 2002). Immigrants may have grown up in a very different culture and education system outside Britain, and a minority will have also experienced the uncertainties and stress of refugee status along with traumatic times in their country of origin.

Involving fathers and 'father figures' may be an important way to improve black and minority ethnic boys' educational outcomes and subsequent employment opportunities. It was promising to find some small-scale research studies which investigated black and minority ethnic fathers' involvement in their children's learning and education, especially as Bignall and Butt (2001) and Clarke and O'Brien (2004) report limited information about fatherhood in black and minority ethnic communities, and Razwan (2002) reports very little research looking at South Asian parents' involvement in schools.

The research studies

All the research studies accessed on black and minority ethnic fathers' involvement with their children's learning and education were small-scale and localised, and they all interviewed volunteer or 'convenience' samples of fathers. Therefore, the findings may not be representative of entire black and minority ethnic populations in the UK, and the characteristics of the research samples are given in Table 21 as a guide for readers.

Table 21: Small-scale studies of black and minority ethnic fathers

Research study	Sample size and characteristics
Black Development Agency (2002)	Structured interviews with three small samples of fathers in a working-class area of Bristol: • About 30 Indian, Pakistani and Bangladeshi fathers, mainly Pakistani Muslims, but also small number of Hindu and Sikh fathers. Nearly all married. Most were aged 36-46+ years, with a small group aged 25-35. Were approached by development officer mainly through religious institutions, local media and shops, as well as community organisations. • About 20 African fathers, three-quarters of whom were Somali Muslims. Nearly all married. Most were aged 25-45 years. • About 20 African-Caribbean fathers. Mixture of Muslims, Rastafarians and Christians. Majority married but also fathers who were single or cohabiting. Mainly aged 36-45. Were approached by development officer mainly in leisure-oriented settings such as pubs and shops.
Razwan (2002)	Interviews with sample of about 20 South Asian Muslim fathers with primary school children in a working-class area of Bradford: • Almost all had Pakistani backgrounds; two were of Bangladeshi origin. • Most of the fathers had come from rural areas, and all but three were born in Pakistan or Bangladesh. Most of the fathers had lived in the UK for 10 years or more. • Most of the fathers were working in low paid jobs (about 40 per cent in catering industry and about a quarter as taxi drivers), and about a quarter were unemployed/had long-term illness. • Most of the employed fathers worked from early evening through the night and slept during the daytime. A minority of the fathers started work in the early afternoon and finished during the evening. Many had unpredictable and long working hours. • All the mothers were described by the fathers as housewives. The fathers tended to be the sole earners. • Most of the families lived in non-residential extended family networks, and there were no single-parent households. Nearly 80 per cent of the households included three or more children; and a third had five or more children.
Millard and Hunter (2001)	Focus group with sample of nine fathers and one grandfather in Bradford who were Gujerati Hindus (Indian backgrounds): • Their children were in a primary school with high commitment to home–school links and which had a Home School Liaison Officer. • Most of the fathers were skilled and unskilled manual workers.

87

Research study	Sample size and characteristics
Herrick and Ali (2003)	Interviews with sample of 10 British South Asian fathers/father figures in deprived area of Kirklees whose children attended the same primary school that they had as children: • Fathers were mainly of Indian (Gujerati) origin and nearly all had been born in UK (cf, Razwan where most had been born outside UK). • Included a few uncles who had regular contact with nephews and nieces. • Fathers of mainly pre-school and reception-aged children. • Fathers had been educated locally. Four of the fathers had HE qualifications, and the rest had been in further education. • All the fathers were working full time.
Bruneau (2002)	Semi-structured interviews with volunteer sample of about 20 older African-Caribbean fathers (mainly aged 35-45) in Wolverhampton. • Fathers were identified by community groups and local agencies; "the majority of interviewees were working, or had worked, with children in a paid or voluntary capacity". • About three-quarters were living with at least some of their children, either in their first family or in a subsequent family. • About three-quarters of the fathers were born in Britain. The great majority of the fathers born in the Caribbean left before they were 18 years old. • Just under half were A/B social grade, and about a third were social grade C1. • Nearly 60 per cent were practising Christians (many attended church regularly), and about a third had no religious faith. • The research team was unable to engage African-Caribbean fathers with limited or no involvement with their children, nor younger fathers.

Three research studies involved interviews with small groups of Muslim South Asian fathers (Razwan, 2002; Black Development Agency, 2002; Herrick and Ali, 2003). The findings suggest (bearing in mind the methodological limitations just discussed) that fathers in this group are similar in some respects to white fathers with regard to the level and types of their involvement in their children's learning and education:

• These fathers were much less involved overall than mothers in their children's care and education, and they were particularly less likely than mothers to be involved with their children's schools on a regular basis. In a Muslim South Asian community in Bradford primarily of Pakistani origin, fathers "appeared as shadowy background figures" to their children's teachers (Razwan, 2002). Parental involvement work had been developed in the children's primary school but the take-up was largely from mothers. Even when specific 'men-only' activities were arranged in the school, the take-up from fathers was very low.

• These fathers' participation in their children's learning and education tended to comprise going to parents evenings, taking their children to school, and engaging with their children in out-of-school learning activities (e.g. playing on the computer, helping with homework,[54] play and board games, sports, reading and singing together, outings to the park). Most of the fathers in Razwan's research mentioned parents' evenings as a useful method of contact with the teachers, although fewer than half of the interviewed fathers had attended one. A relatively high proportion of the fathers interviewed by Razwan had met the school's Home School Liaison Officer.

- Fathers' involvement with their children tended to occur in evenings and at weekends. However, this was constrained because employed and self-employed South Asian fathers in working-class areas tended to work long, irregular and atypical hours (Table 21), and have regular daily prayer times at the mosques, and their children often spent part of their weekday evenings at Muslim religion schools (madrasahs).

- Even when direct involvement in their children's schools was uncommon, some of these fathers were concerned about educational issues such as a lack of role models for boys and bullying in their children's schools. Some fathers were kept informed by their wives, who were involved in the schools.

There also seem to be some more distinctive[55] features of Muslim South Asian fathers' involvement with their children's learning and education (Razwan, 2002; Black Development Agency, 2002; Herrick and Ali, 2003):

- Cultural and religious activities and education were shared between fathers and children. Holy books such as the Koran may form the basis for regular reading in religious families.

- Some fathers took their children to school because they fear for their children's safety because of racism locally.

- Some fathers also took their children to and collected them from the Muslim religion schools (madrasahs) in weekday evenings after school.

- Children often lived in relatively large families with several siblings and sometimes also resident grandparents. Other male family members, such as grandfathers, uncles and older brothers, may help children with their homework and attend family learning activities in place of or in addition to children's fathers.

- Fathers were often more likely than mothers to speak English, and so they may then take on the family's responsibility for communication with their children's schools. In families where neither the father nor mother speaks much English, older brothers may take on this role and also help younger children with homework. Lloyd (1999) found in his interviews with boys in south London from a variety of black and minority ethnic groups that, in families where English was a second language, children often taught their fathers and mothers to read in English, rather than vice versa.

A focus group of 10 Hindu fathers with Indian backgrounds (Miller and Hunter, 2001) similarly found good relationships between the fathers and the school's Home School Liaison

---

54 Some fathers' limited knowledge of English may mean that they cannot help their children with homework. Barriers to minority ethnic fathers' involvement with their children's learning and education are discussed in Chapter 4.

55 Some of these issues may be relevant for other black and minority ethnic groups, and not just for South Asian fathers. More research is needed here.

Officer. These fathers talked about their roles as 'informal educators', for example discussing cultural issues and the importance of work with their children, and having a family decorating project at home.

A group of church-attending African-Caribbean resident and non-resident fathers (mainly aged 35 years+) interviewed in Wolverhampton were very involved in their children's lives, and most were substantially involved in their children's education specifically, even when they did not live with their children (Bruneau, 2002). However, it is important to remember that the majority of fathers in this research were working with children in a paid or voluntary capacity. These fathers mentioned several concrete activities such as helping with homework (most common), talking to the child's teacher (mainly at parents' evenings), giving their child extra tuition, reading with their children, play, sport, computers, language development, cultural activities, and shared practical activities such as art or cooking. These are the same types of activity that (as already seen) both white fathers and South Asian fathers engage in with their children. Most of the fathers were able to give their children's current teachers' names, and Bruneau writes that these fathers are "excellent role models for fatherhood".

In particular, as for South Asian fathers, many of these African-Caribbean fathers[56] were involved in their children's cultural and religious education, for example cooking Jamaican food and attending church together, especially when their children were resident with a non-Caribbean mother.

The Black Development Agency interviewed a small group of African-Caribbean fathers (also relatively older fathers) in Bristol who were recruited in pubs and other social venues. They report similar levels of involvement between the fathers and their children as in Bruneau (2002). A substantial minority of these fathers took their children to school.

No research could be located that was conducted specifically on younger African-Caribbean fathers' involvement with their children's learning and education.

With regard to African fathers, a small group (mainly Somali Muslims) interviewed by the Black Development Agency in Bristol had much lower levels of involvement in their children's care and education than those of the South Asian and African-Caribbean fathers that they interviewed in the same area of Bristol. About half of these African fathers reported only irregular involvement with their children. Small minorities of these fathers undertook shared sports, entertainment, cultural and religious activities, took their children to school, or helped with their children's homework.

In contrast, a voluntary organisation based in south London found that:

- African and African-Caribbean fathers were high users (70 per cent of total users) of services set up locally for men and fathers

- in two-parent households where both parents worked, often the mother worked during the day and the father in the evenings (i.e. 'shift-parenting'), so the fathers were relatively involved in childcare (Working with Men, 2004).

In this area of London, Christian African and African-Caribbean fathers were more likely to ask their church than their children's schools for advice about any school problems.

---

56 This focus on fathers engaging in their children's religious education was also found in Lloyd's (1999) interviews with seven fathers who attended a Seventh Day Adventist church in south London.

All this small-scale research is a very good start, but further research is needed to substantiate these findings for larger and more diverse samples of black and minority ethnic fathers in different areas of the UK.

Chapters 4 and 5 both include further evidence about black and minority ethnic fathers. Additionally, four of the case studies (Chapter 6) were of family learning programmes in schools targeted at or involving substantial numbers of black and minority ethnic fathers.

2.6 Summary

- Resident fathers are less likely than resident mothers to be involved in many aspects of their children's out-of-school learning and in their children's schools.

- Fathers contribute substantially to specific areas of their children's out-of-school learning: building and repairing, hobbies, IT, maths, science, sports, physical play, outdoor activities and family trips. There is a focus on play, leisure, practical activities and fun. Their involvement in these areas of learning is (in some research studies) at higher rates or more frequent than mothers' participation.

- Considerable proportions of fathers also read with their children, help with homework, and give praise and support to their children for their schoolwork, but at lower rates or less frequently than do mothers. When fathers read with their children, they often use non-fiction, environmental print and recreational materials.

- Additionally, considerable proportions of resident fathers attend parents evenings and general school meetings, and drop off and pick their children up at school, but at lower rates or less frequently than do mothers.

- Fathers are especially unlikely to be volunteers in the classroom, or participants in organised family learning programmes which take place during the daytime and are not targeted at men. A greater proportion of adult learners in wider family learning programmes are men than in family language, literacy and numeracy programmes.

- Much less data was found on the involvement of non-resident fathers and single-parent fathers than on the involvement of resident fathers in two-parent families.

- Non-resident fathers are especially unlikely to be involved in their children's schools. Involvement with their children's out-of-school learning often (but not always) takes place at weekends and has a recreational focus. Schools and family learning programmes have the potential to be a neutral place where non-resident fathers and their children can have positive time together.

- Single-parent fathers tend to get more involved in their children's schools than do resident fathers in two-parent families.

- Fathers are more likely to be involved if their child's mother is involved in the child's learning and education, they have good relations with their child's mother, they or their child's mother have relatively high educational qualifications, they are of relatively high socio-economic status, they got involved in their child's life early on, their child is in primary school rather than secondary school, their child is doing well in secondary school, and their child's school is welcoming to parents. The strongest association is with the level of mother's involvement.

- Fathers are less likely to be involved if they are a manual worker, they work evenings, or their child had emotional or behavioural problems in primary school.

- There are mixed findings on whether there are any differences between fathers' involvement in boys' learning and in girls' learning. There is some evidence that fathers spend more time with their sons than their daughters in sports, hobbies, practical tasks, outings and leisure, and that fathers are more involved in secondary schools when they have a male child.

- Different black and minority ethnic groups vary greatly in their prevalent family structures, gender roles and religious and cultural orientations. All the research studies accessed on black and minority ethnic fathers' involvement with their children's learning and education were small-scale and localised.

- There is a focus on religion and culture in some black and minority ethnic fathers' involvement in their children's learning. For some of these fathers, religious leaders and community workers are important sources of advice.

- In South Asian and African-Caribbean communities, children often have a range of 'father figures', for example older brothers, uncles and grandfathers, who are likely to live nearby or in the same household.

- Fathers in some families of South Asian origin are more likely than mothers to speak English, and so take on responsibility for communication with their children's schools.

- There are many examples of home–school and family learning programmes which specifically target and successfully engage fathers, including non-resident fathers, fathers in deprived areas, and black and minority ethnic fathers. Many of these are on stereotypically male themes such as sport, ICT and technology, but there are also programmes with learning in visual arts, music, reading and creative writing.

- Gaps in home–school and family learning programmes for fathers include work with teenagers, daughters, single-parent fathers and children with special needs.

3 | Why involve fathers?

"Until recently, fathers were the hidden parent in research on children's well-being...Their contribution...was often assumed to be secondary to that of mothers and was not usually examined."

Nord (1998)

"But research studies can only provide the rationale for recruiting fathers, the real passion for dads' involvement comes from the children. Their expressions of delight and approval (and sometimes cool acceptance) offer the most important rewards to dads and staff."

Bright et al. (2002)

A crucial question to ask when engaging in work with fathers is why do it when it can be challenging work? Many people need to be convinced – the funders, the policymakers, the managers in local education authorities (LEAs) and family learning providers, headteachers and teachers, family learning practitioners, the fathers themselves, and the mothers of the children. It is fortunate that there is now very good research evidence showing that fathers matter enormously for children's development.

This chapter focuses on the impact of fathers' involvement with their children on children's educational outcomes,[1] for school-aged children[2] (ages 4-16). Other outcomes, such as social and emotional development, are also crucial for children's happiness and future life chances, but a decision was made to focus only on one set of outcomes in this research.

In assessing the impact of fathers' involvement on children's educational outcomes, it is helpful to consider the impact on children's motivation, self-perceptions, expectations and attitudes connected with learning, as well as their performance. Several researchers cite

---

1 For the purposes of this research, 'educational outcomes' were defined to include educational performance on tests, public examinations and other forms of assessment; behaviour and conduct in school including school attendance and suspension/exclusion from schools; educational plans and choices; stay-on rates in school and in further education; and motivation, attitudes, enjoyment, aspirations, expectations, goals, behaviours and self-perceived competence related to learning and education (sometimes called 'learning dispositions').

2 Neither research looking at the impact of a father's involvement during the early years of a child's life (ages 0-3) nor research looking at the impact of fathers' involvement in Head Start programmes and other early years interventions, is reviewed in this report.

research studies showing the substantial impact of a child's 'learning dispositions' on their academic achievement and longer-term outcomes (Flouri and Buchanan, 2004; Nord et al., 1997; Trent et al., 1996; Lynch, 2002, Trusty and Pirtle, 1998). Many theories of how parents influence their children's educational outcomes have the children's educational beliefs and attitudes as a crucial mediating factor (e.g. see Trusty and Pirtle, 1998).

As important context, Section 3.1 first looks at what the research has to say about the impact of parental involvement in children's learning and education, and of other aspects of parenting on children's educational outcomes, mainly drawing upon key research reviews identified through contacts with experts in the field. Some of the research evidence on 'parents' is solely about mothers, but other research studies include both fathers and mothers in their samples. Section 3.2 presents evidence on the impact of fathers' overall involvement in their children's lives on children's educational outcomes, again drawing upon key research reviews; and then Section 3.3 looks at the central question of this chapter: what is the impact of fathers' involvement in their children's learning and education on children's educational outcomes, and what might be the mechanisms for this impact? This section draws its evidence from five quality research studies that were identified from comprehensive bibliographic searches. Finally, Section 3.4 assesses the impacts of fathers' involvement on fathers, mothers and schools.

3.1 Impacts of parental involvement in children's learning and education on children's educational outcomes

Spontaneous involvement in children's out-of-school learning

There is strong evidence from nationally representative longitudinal[3] large-scale research in the UK and US that parental interest in children's learning and education, and other aspects of 'at-home parenting', when children are in primary school and in secondary school are more powerful influences than socio-economic group, family size, or parents' educational level on children's educational attainment at age 16 or in adulthood (DfES, 2003d; Desforges and Abouchaar, 2003). This is after many other influencing factors[4] have been statistically controlled for (i.e. factored out of the model).

---

3   Longitudinal studies measure the development of a group of children at two or more time points, and sometimes over a period of many years. When they collect data on a wider range of variables, they are much better placed than cross-sectional studies (in which all the data is collected at one point in time) to show causal relationships rather than simply associations between variables. However, the long-term nature of some longitudinal studies means that analyses are investigating the impact of parental involvement several decades ago, when the social context would have been different from that of today.

4   High-quality non-experimental studies looking at the impact of parental involvement on children's outcomes control (factor out) simultaneously for a wide variety of variables which are also influences on children's outcomes, using advanced statistical techniques. These studies are therefore able to find out how much each factor (e.g. parental involvement or social class) independently contributes in explaining the outcome variable (e.g. exam grades). The variables often controlled for are the child's age, parental socio-economic status, income, employment status, working hours, education and age, ethnicity, family structure and family size. Some

Parents' interest in their children's education contributes to 10 per cent of variation in children's progress in English and maths at age 16 (Feinstein and Symons, 1999, using the UK National Child Development Study (NCDS)[5]). Feinstein and Symons write that:

> "...the combined advantage of coming from a high social class with parents who stayed on at school after 16 is only 5.98 percentage points in the All Exams index, compared to an effect of 24.4 from moving from no parental interest to the highest level of interest."

And not only does more parental interest lead to better educational progress, children's progress can be slowed down by lack of parental interest (Hobcraft 1998a, 1998b).

Positive 'at-home parenting' comprises positive interest, support, expectations/aspirations and encouragement for the child, warmth, nurturance, responsiveness, two-way communication, and setting appropriate firm limits, whilst giving the child sufficient autonomy.

The recent research review carried out for the DfES by Desforges and Abouchaar (2003) showed that direct parental involvement in children's out-of-school learning (e.g. reading and other learning activities together at home) is also substantially associated with children's achievement for *primary school* children. For primary school children, parental interest and involvement in their learning are much more important influences than factors associated with their school or their peer group at school. In one study that Desforges and Abouchaar cite, parental involvement had the same degree of impact on later achievement as the prior achievement of the child (Singh et al., 1995). The impact of direct parental involvement in children's learning on educational attainment decreases as a child gets older.

According to Desforges and Abouchaar, these strong relationships between parental involvement/parenting and children's educational outcomes apply to all social classes and ethnic groups[6] (also see Bryant and Zimmerman, 2003, citing research with African American youth).

The link between parental involvement in children's learning and children's educational achievement can be subject-specific. Desforges and Abouchaar write that "parental involvement has markedly different impacts on different areas of the curriculum". Research from Australia, the USA, Canada and the UK shows that parents' involvement in their children's literacy development can promote good literacy outcomes for children (Fletcher and Dally, 2002; DfES, 2003d). It is important for parents to give children books of their own, read to their children frequently, use the library with their children, and model their own literacy activities (Ortiz and McCarty, 1997). Research also shows positive relationships between (i) parents' positive attitudes to science/maths, and involvement in science/maths out-of-school activities and (ii) their children's science or maths achievement and attitudes towards science (Desforges and Abouchaar, 2003).

---

researchers also control for factors such as emotional and behaviour problems in the child, the child's general cognitive ability, the child's academic motivation, school 'peer group' characteristics, neighbourhood characteristics, school type, and other schooling inputs (e.g. Feinstein and Symons, 1999; Flouri and Buchanan, 2004).

5   The National Child Development Study is used in several key research papers to look at the impact of parental involvement, and father involvement specifically, on children's outcomes. It is an ongoing longitudinal study of about 17,000 children born between 3 and 9 March 1958 in England, Scotland and Wales with low drop-out. See footnote in Chapter 2 for more information.

6   The studies of various ethnic minority groups cited by Desforges and Abouchaar (2003) were all conducted in the US. The minority ethnic groups studied were African Americans, other Black Americans, Mexican Americans and Asian Americans.

Involvement in their children's schools

The quality of 'at home' parenting, and parental interest and direct involvement in children's out-of-school learning, have much stronger associations with children's educational outcomes than does parental involvement in children's schools (Desforges and Abouchaar, 2003). In a few studies that Desforges and Abouchaar cite, parents' involvement in their children's schools (e.g. volunteering in the classroom) had no or a very weak association with the educational achievement of those parents' children. However, Desforges and Abouchaar speculate that a minimal level of in-school involvement by a parent may be necessary, for example, to obtain information from the teacher about the curriculum, courses and assessments which supports the at-home involvement of the parent in their child's learning, i.e. it acts as "an essential lubricant".

Trusty and Pirtle (1998) report their research findings that the impacts of two types of parental involvement on children's educational expectations differed depending on the parents' socio-economic status (SES). When parents had higher SES, parental involvement in children's schools predicted expectations more strongly. When parents had lower SES, parental home-based involvement in their children's learning predicted expectations more strongly.

As seen later in this chapter (Section 3.3), *fathers'* involvement in their children's schools does have clear positive impacts on their children's educational outcomes.

Involvement in organised family learning programmes

In the UK, evaluations of the Basic Skills Agency's family literacy programmes (1994/5) for parents with limited literacy and numeracy skills (over 90 per cent were mothers) and their children aged 3-6 years demonstrated very substantial and "greater than expected" improvements (during the courses, and further improved or maintained[7] after 12 weeks, nine months or two years) in:

- children's language and literacy skills, and classroom behaviour

- parents' literacy skills

- parents' confidence and ability to help their children learn (Brooks et al., 1996, 1997; National Foundation for Educational Research/Basic Skills Agency, 1996).

Parents became more actively involved in their children's schools, including helping out in the classroom, and progressed to further study and into work. This evaluation did objectively measure parents' and children's skills before and after the course and at various time-points afterwards. Brooks et al. (1996, 1997) state that "comparison with a control group suggested that the improvements could be attributed to the courses".

Similarly, independent evaluations of the CEDC (formerly ContinYou) *Share* family learning programme demonstrated parents' progression to further education, and also benefits in children's attitudes to learning (Bastiani, 1999; Lewis, 2000a).

Most evaluations of the impacts of interventions such as home–school and family learning programmes on children's educational outcomes are "dramatically less well designed than research on parents' spontaneous behaviour" (Desforges and Abouchaar, 2003; also see Ofsted, 2000), for example with no reporting of sample characteristics, very small samples, no control or comparison groups, no systematic measures of children's outcomes, and no

---

7   Only some types of improvement were maintained for nine months or for two years.

statistical controls for children's characteristics in analyses. Many such interventions are not independently evaluated, even in the US, and the evaluations that do exist are small-scale local studies. It is therefore not possible to conclude on the basis of any substantial body of robust research evidence what impact family learning programmes have on children's educational outcomes; and there is, according to Desforges and Abouchaar, no strong evidence that the programmes are effective nor that they are ineffective.

However, more subjective evaluations of family learning programmes (based on parents' and practitioners' perceptions of benefits) do show "a coherent and consistent picture" (Desforges and Abouchaar, 2003), with a range of perceived benefits for children and parents (see Ofsted, 2000). Similar benefits were reported by practitioners and parents in small-scale evaluations of home–school and family learning programmes targeted at fathers (see Section 3.3).

How does this evidence on 'parents' relate to the involvement of fathers?

It has been discussed so far that "what parents do with their children at home is far more important to their achievement than their social class or level of education" (Desforges and Abouchaar, 2003), and that family learning programmes may have a variety of perceived benefits. But why is it important to involve fathers in their children's learning? Is mothers' involvement not sufficient?

Firstly, some writers on home–school relations (e.g. Nord et al., 1997) argue that fathers offer an opportunity for schools to make greater gains in overall parental involvement (in children's learning and in schools) than by maintaining their current focus on mothers only.

Secondly, some psychologists (e.g. Dunn et al., 2000) write about a "double dose" effect, in which children are influenced (positively or negatively) by the active involvement of two parents or carers and the interaction between them. Aldous and Mulligan (2002) argue that:

> "having two parents watching out for children and taking care of them would constitute a double dose of problem prevention."

It is better for children to have more than one active parent or carer (Lamb and Tamis-Lemonda, 2004) as this leads, not only to greater parental involvement in total, but also to a greater diversity of parental skills and interests, parenting styles, social capital and types of involvement. In this theory, the 'parents' or 'carers' need not both be biological parents; one of the pair could be a step-parent, a parent's partner, another 'father figure' or another 'mother figure'. This "double dose" effect does not require that one parent is male and the other female, just that there are two different parents or carers providing different inputs into a child's experience of life. This chapter returns later to the question of whether fathers can bring a specifically male input into children's learning (Section 3.3).

Third, parenting skills interventions with pre-school and older children which involve both the mother and the father are more effective than those which involve only the mother (O'Brien, 2004). O'Brien argues that:

> "mutual support, understanding and practice opportunities may be more likely in settings where both mothers and fathers have been exposed to the intervention at the same time."

This principle might also apply to family learning and home–school programmes which involve both mothers and fathers.

These arguments and theories certainly suggest that it is not sufficient just for mothers to be involved in their children's learning and education. However, to strengthen the case for involving *fathers* in their children's learning, it is key to look at research evidence not only on the impact of *parental* involvement, but on the impact of *fathers'* involvement specifically. Sections 3.2 and 3.3 review some of this vital research evidence.

Studies looking specifically at the impact of fathers' involvement on children's educational outcomes are much rarer than studies looking at the impact of aggregated parental involvement or of mothers' involvement (Flouri and Buchanan, 2004; Paulson and Sputa, 1996; Ortiz and McCarty, 1997; Fletcher and Dally, 2002). Some studies even seem to assume that the impact of parental involvement is the impact of mothers' involvement, although it is interesting to note Simpson's (2003) view that research looking at the impact of parents on the level or years of education that children receive has focused mainly on fathers' contributions (occupation, education and income) and that "the relative absence of mothers in the status attainment literature is striking", apart from mothers' level of education.

3.2 Impacts of fathers' overall involvement on children's educational outcomes

As seen in Section 3.1, the quality of 'at home' parenting has an important impact on children's educational outcomes. Is this true specifically of fathers? This section looks at the impact of fathers' active involvement in all aspects of their school-aged children's lives (not just in their learning and education) on children's educational outcomes.

There are mixed findings about whether or not the amount or frequency of fathers' involvement in their children's lives is associated with children's outcomes. Cross-sectional and longitudinal research evidence in the UK and US shows that the *level/frequency* of fathers' involvement[8] is associated with school-age boys' and girls' greater educational attainment, positive learning dispositions and school attitudes, and greater cognitive skills, as well as with their greater self-confidence, positive mental health, positive behaviours and positive relationships with others, both as children and as adults (see research reviewed in Le Menestrel, 1999; Updegraff et al., 1996; Flouri and Buchanan, 2004; Lewis and Warin, 2001; Yeung et al., 2000; Aldous and Mulligan, 2002; Pleck and Masciadrelli, 2004; Nord et al., 1997).

However, there are other research studies showing little impact of fathers' *level* of involvement (e.g. cited in Aldous and Mulligan, 2002, and Pleck and Masciadrelli, 2004). In relation to non-resident fathers, Amato and Sobolewski (2004) refer to a meta-analysis which "found that the frequency of father visitation following divorce was not generally associated with child outcomes" (Amato and Gilbreth, 1999). They also discuss research suggesting that conflict between the parents and also mothers' dissatisfaction due to the contact "may cancel out, or even reverse, any benefits".

There is much more consistent evidence from research reviews that the quality and content of fathers' involvement (e.g. types of activities) and of the father–child relationship (e.g. parenting style) matter much more for children's outcomes than the quantity of time for

---

8 Aldous and Mulligan (2002) describe this as: "go beyond their customary breadwinning activities and engage in daily, hands-on care of their offspring".

which a father and child are in contact or the frequency of contact and visits (O'Brien, 2004; Le Menestrel, 1999; Aldous and Mulligan, 2002; Amato and Sobolewski, 2004). This applies to both resident and non-resident fathers.

In particular, fathers' affection, support and 'authoritative' parenting styles are related to children's positive outcomes just as with mothers (O'Brien, 2004; Marsiglio et al., 2000, cited by O'Brien, 2004; Amato and Sobolewski, 2004). O'Brien (2004) writes that "the gender of the parent is less important…than broader parenting style". However, research with pre-school children shows that fathers are more likely than mothers to have an authoritarian parenting style, especially if the child is male (Lamb and Lewis, 2004). Additionally, the quality of a father–son relationship influences whether boys use their father as a role model; boys want to model "fathers whom they liked and respected and with whom their relationships were warm and positive" (Lamb and Tamis-Lemonda. 2004).

Positive father involvement can protect children from the negative impact of risk factors (e.g. financial hardship), but poor parenting by fathers (as well as by mothers) is associated with children's decreased educational attainment. Fathers' use of poor disciplinary style was associated with sons' difficult classroom behaviour, which in turn was associated with lower school achievement (Le Menestrel, 1999). Another research study shows that high levels of antisocial behaviour in fathers (e.g. not paying debts, criminal behaviour, aggressiveness) are associated with high levels of behavioural problems in five-year-old children, even when mothers' level of antisocial behaviour is controlled for in analysis (Jaffee et al., 2003).

In assessing this evidence, it is important to remember that:

> *"the body of research supporting positive child consequences…is still relatively small if attention is restricted to studies controlling for maternal involvement and using different source data."* (Pleck and Masciadrelli, 2004)

Implications for schools

It is concluded at this point that teachers need to find out about fathers' overall involvement in the lives of the children in their class (not just involvement in their curricular learning and education) so that they can understand the lives, successes and problems of these children much better, and then work with these children in a more appropriate way. This mirrors O'Brien's argument that "family service practitioners who only assess and work with mothers are excluding significant parts of children's family systems" (O'Brien, 2004). The case studies in this report show that some schools work with children's fathers (including non-resident fathers) to involve them, not just specifically in children's education, but in children's lives overall.

3.3 Impacts of fathers' involvement in their children's learning and education on children's educational outcomes

The key research studies to demonstrate the importance of fathers' involvement in their children's learning and education are those which measure the level, frequency and/or quality of this type of involvement, and show that it relates positively to children's outcomes, using high-quality research design and statistical analysis.

The research studies reviewed for this section of the report

Researchers have reported conflicting results about the relationship between parental involvement in children's learning and children's educational outcomes (Desforges and Abouchaar, 2003; Shumow and Miller, 2001; O'Brien, 2004). Some studies have reported positive impacts, others have reported negative impacts, and yet others have reported mixed impacts or no impact. These mixed findings are due to the different designs and methods of research studies, such as studies in different countries or localities; different definitions and ways of measuring parental involvement; some analyses not controlling for other key influences on outcomes; and different outcome measures. Desforges and Abouchaar (2003) very helpfully discuss at length the features of high-quality statistical studies investigating causal links between parental involvement and children's educational achievement.

Many research studies were identified that show statistical relationships between fathers' involvement in their children's learning and education, and children's educational outcomes. Following an assessment of their research design and methodology, three main types of study were distinguished.

Group 1: High-quality statistical studies using multivariate analyses of large-scale datasets (usually survey data), which isolate the *independent* impact of fathers' involvement in children's learning on educational outcomes by controlling simultaneously for a wide variety of other influencing factors, usually demographics and mothers' involvement (see footnote 4). Sample size is sufficiently large (sometimes thousands of children) to demonstrate relatively small statistically significant relationships in multivariate analysis, and to be broadly representative of a defined population, e.g. a country, a region, or an ethnic group. Includes cross-sectional and longitudinal studies. Samples usually selected from the population using random methods. Often high response rates and (in longitudinal studies) relatively low drop-out, meaning that the samples remain broadly representative of the population.

Group 2: Localised studies (e.g. one city, suburb or small rural area) using relatively small homogenous samples, for example parents who are all from the same socio-economic group, level of education, family type and/or minority ethnic group. These studies use the lack of variation in some of the sample's key characteristics as an alternative to the multivariate statistical controls used in Group 1 studies. A few of these studies go one step further than multivariate analysis, and they use matched control groups. Includes cross-sectional and longitudinal studies. Samples not often selected at random. One cannot generalise from these studies to the entire population, even for a single minority ethnic group or family type.

Group 3: Localised studies which use small and often purposively selected (not random) samples to try to represent the diversity in one local area, or even in an entire ethnic, regional or national population. Sample sizes usually relatively small, for example 350 parents. Can be cross-sectional or longitudinal studies. One cannot generalise from these studies to the entire population.

A meta-analysis of Group 1 and Group 2 studies would substantially enhance understanding of the research evidence in this area. According to Pleck and Masciadrelli (2004), the evidence supporting positive relationships between fathers' involvement and children's outcomes:

> *"has been accompanied by increased awareness of the methodological and conceptual complexity of the association between paternal involvement and children's development."*

For the purposes of this report, a decision was taken to focus on five high-quality Group 1 studies with large-scale, nationally representative samples of fathers and children in the UK and US.

One important factor to control for in multivariate analyses is the frequency, level or quality of mothers' involvement in their children's learning and education (Pleck and Masciadrelli, 2004; Nord et al., 1997). As seen in Section 2.4, when fathers have high levels of involvement, it is likely that mothers also have high levels of involvement. It could be that once mothers' involvement is taken into account in analysis, there is very little additional benefit of father involvement. It is key to find out whether fathers' involvement has an *independent* effect on children.

The findings of five high-quality research studies

Taken together, the findings from the selected five high-quality studies clearly show that:

- a greater level/frequency of *fathers' interest and direct involvement in their children's learning and education*[9] (Flouri and Buchanan, 2004;[10] Feinstein and Symons, 1999[11];

---

9   These three UK studies use data from the National Child Development Study (NCDS), where parental interest in children's education was assessed by teachers. The other measures of parental involvement were the reports of parents or primary caregivers, usually the child's mother. See footnote 15 in Chapter 2.

10 Fluori and Buchanan's analysis was based on a nationally representative sample from the NCDS of 3,300 children. The 'fathers' included resident fathers, non-resident fathers, and father figures such as step-fathers. The independent variable was an index combining scores on the frequency or level of "takes outings with the child", "father manages the child", "father reads to the child", and "father is interested in child's education" at age seven (in 1965). The dependent variable was child's highest school leaving qualification by age 20, with this data obtained from schools and education authorities in 1978. Hierarchical regression analysis was used, which controlled for other influences on educational attainment, including child's gender, parental socio-economic status at child's birth, child's birth weight, evidence of family financial difficulties, parents' ages at child's birth, parents' education levels, parents' employment statuses, family structure, number of siblings, level of domestic tension in the family when child aged seven, any mental illness in the family, emotional and behaviour problems in the child at age seven, general cognitive ability in the child at age seven, and level of mother's involvement in child's life and education. Together, these variables explained about 50 per cent of the child's later attainment. So, Flouri and Buchanan's analysis combined the frequency of 'at home' father involvement in the child's learning and education with the level of 'at home' parenting into one single measure. The published analysis does not show which element of 'father involvement' is most important for the child's educational attainment.

11 Feinstein and Symon's analysis and Hobcraft's analysis both used an independent variable of father's interest in his child's education (as assessed by the child's teacher in the NCDS). In Feinstein and Symon (1999), the dependent variables were the child's maths score at age 16 (as measured for the NCDS in tests), the child's highest grade in English in national exams at any age up to 21, and an index of the child's overall exam performance in all subjects at ages 16-18. These outcomes were technically equivalent to progress measures (progress between ages 11 and 16/21), as the analyses controlled for achievement in reading and maths tests at age 11. Controlled variables in the models were a range of demographic variables, peer group variables (e.g. proportion of children in the class with fathers in non-manual occupations when child was aged 16), school type, neighbourhood variables (e.g. unemployment rate in local area), and pupil-teacher ratios. R squared for the models ranged from 52 per cent to 66 per cent.

Hobcraft, 1998a and 1998b[12])

- a greater level/frequency of fathers' *involvement in their children's schools* (Nord et al., 1997[13])

- higher *expectations held by fathers about their children's educational level* (Trusty and Pirtle, 1998[14])

are associated strongly with better educational outcomes for children, including:

- better exam/test/class results

- higher level of educational qualification

- greater progress at school

- better attitudes towards school (e.g. enjoyment)

- higher educational expectations

- better behaviour at school (e.g. reduced risk of suspension or expulsion).

These associations were independent of associations between mothers' involvement/interest and the same outcomes, in all of the cited studies except for Trusty and Pirtle (1998).[15]

A more detailed examination of Hobcraft's analysis is illuminating. If the father had low interest at one or more of ages 7-16, this quadrupled[16] the child's risk of having no qualifica-

---

12 In Hobcraft (1998a and 1998b), the dependent variable was the child's qualifications by age 33 (in 1991). The analysis controlled for a very wide variety of childhood factors including experience of family disruption, poverty, contact with the police, social class, housing tenure, the child's personality attributes, and the child's educational test scores. The 'pseudo R-squared measure' for these models was about 30 per cent for no qualifications. This reduced to just over 20 per cent when educational test scores were removed from the model. Hobcraft regards these R-squared values as relatively low.

13 See footnotes 23, 24 and 25 in Chapter 2 for information on the methodology of the 1996 National Household Education Survey (NHES) which Nord et al.'s analysis used. The independent variable was the father's level of involvement in the child's school in 1996. The dependent variables were various measures of the child's educational outcomes, including their exam grades, their enjoyment of school, and whether or not they were suspended or expelled for bad behaviour, at the same time point in 1996. The multivariate analyses controlled for various factors including parents' educational levels, household income, child's gender, child's ethnicity, child's age, family type, mother's employment status, and the level of the mother's involvement in the child's school. The analyses for the impact of non-resident fathers' involvement also controlled for whether or not the father had paid child support in the past year.

14 Trusty and Pirtle (1998) used data from the 1988 US National Education Longitudinal Study. This was a national sample of over 7,000 adolescents which was representative of the US adolescent population. The independent variable was adolescents' perceptions (in 1992, when they were in high school) of their parents' educational expectations about what educational level (e.g. high school/college/masters) they would achieve in the future. The dependent variable was adolescents' own expectations at a later date (in 1994) of the educational level they would achieve. Trusty and Pirtle conducted a chi-square analysis in which they controlled for parents' and students' gender, parents' educational levels, family income and parents' socio-economic status

15 Trusty and Pirtle (1998) used chi-squared analysis, which cannot control for a wide variety of variables, for example the level of mothers' involvement.

16 The odds ratios were 4.4 for men, and 3.7 for women (Hobcraft, 1998a and 1998b).

tions in adult life (compared to when the father had a high level of interest). Furthermore, "fewer than two reports of the father being very interested in his child's schooling, but with no report of little interest, is still associated with an approximate doubling of the risk of the child failing to obtain qualifications". A father's interest had a stronger impact on a lack of qualifications than did contact with the police, poverty, family type, social class, housing tenure and the child's personality, for both men and women. If a mother had persistently low interest in her daughter's schooling, this added to the daughter's risk of being unqualified by two-and-a-half.

Hobcraft was investigating not only the impact of fathers' involvement, but the roles of childhood experience, education and qualifications in the onset of social exclusion outcomes in adulthood. He included 19 measures of adult disadvantage in his detailed analysis as indicators of social exclusion, covering demographic outcomes, psychological outcomes, welfare outcomes, economic outcomes and educational outcomes. Childhood poverty and contact with the police were linked to 15 of the 19 outcomes, educational test scores to 15, family type to 14, and the next most consistent influence was fathers' interest in schooling (linked to eight of the 19 outcomes[17]). Fathers' interest showed a strong association with the outcomes more frequently than did contact with the police or poverty. And, furthermore, the strength of the association between a father's interest and a lack of adult qualifications was stronger than for any other association (i.e. between any independent variable and any outcome) in the analysis for both men and women.

According to Hobcraft, "the associations found are probably more robust than is usual for such studies" because of the wide variety of variables incorporated into his analysis. Certainly, the results of his analysis are extremely convincing on the crucial importance of fathers' interest in their children's education. It is important, however, to note that "there is huge scope for many, if not most, individuals to escape from the patterns and tendencies observed", i.e. even where a father has low interest, a child can acquire good qualifications if other variables are positive.

Pleck and Masciadrelli (2004), drawing on the work of Lamb, write that "it may be that the positive effects of involvement do not occur across different contexts". In the selected five high-quality research studies, the positive associations between fathers' involvement in their children's learning/education and children's educational outcomes:

- were independent of *the level of* mothers' involvement (Flouri and Buchanan, 2001 and 2004)

- exist for children in two-parent families, children with single-parent fathers, and children with non-resident fathers (Flouri and Buchanan, 2001 and 2004; Nord et al., 1997), although the specific outcomes and the strength of effect can vary for different family types[18] (Nord et al., 1997)

---

17 These were having degree-level qualification, high and low income, social housing, receipt of benefits (particularly for men), extra-marital childbearing (only for women), psychological malaise (only for women) and teenage motherhood (only for women) (Hobcraft, 1998a and 1998b).

18 For example, Nord et al. (1997) found that mothers' involvement in their children's school, *but not fathers' involvement,* was associated with secondary school children's likelihood of suspension or expulsion from school *in two-parent families*. They speculate that this may be due to some fathers becoming involved in school because their children are having behavioural problems. But *single fathers'* involvement and *non-resident fathers'* involvement *were* associated with decreased likelihood of suspension and expulsion.

- exist for fathers' involvement both when the child is in primary school (Flouri and Buchanan, 2001 and 2004; Nord et al., 1997) and when the child is in secondary school (Nord et al., 1997; Trusty and Pirtle, 1998), although the specific outcomes and the strength of effect can vary for different age-groups of children[19] (Nord et al., 1997)

- exist regardless of the child's gender, i.e. for both sons and daughters (Flouri and Buchanan, 2001 and 2004; Hobcraft, 1998; Trusty and Pirtle, 1998).

Limitations of this research evidence

What are the limitations of this research evidence that fathers' involvement in their children's learning and education is associated with children's positive educational outcomes?

Firstly, since the NCDS collected data on fathers' involvement in the 1960s or 1970s in the UK, and much of the US data is from the 1996 NHES, it is not possible to tell whether fathers' involvement in current times will have the same impact on children's future outcomes. The context of fathers' involvement and its impact will have changed.

Secondly, one analysis using data from a cross-sectional study (Nord et al., 1997) and four analyses using data from longitudinal studies have been reported. It is not possible to determine the direction of causality in the cross-sectional study, as the variables assigned as causal and outcome variables in analysis are measured at the same point in time (see footnote 3). Parents' behaviour and characteristics can have impacts on their children, but children's behaviour and characteristics can also have impacts on their parents (Pleck and Masciadrelli, 2004). For example, fathers may be more likely to be highly involved because their children are doing well; or their children may be doing well because their fathers are highly involved. Jodl et al. (2001) suggest that:

> *"parents' perceptions of their own abilities may be influenced by the adolescents' self-perceptions and the value they place on various activities."*

Pleck and Masciadrelli (2004) note that:

> *"negative outcomes in the child may elicit increased paternal (and maternal) involvement, so that involvement is associated with negative rather than positive outcomes."*

Thirdly, the studies look at the level or frequency of fathers' involvement or interest, and not the quality of their involvement.

Fourthly, the involvement variables are measured by asking people for their perceptions of the involvement, rather than through observation by an independent observer. The perceptions tend to be those of mothers, children or teachers, not the fathers themselves.

Finally, even though the studies (with the exception of Trusty and Pirtle) controlled for many variables simultaneously, including demographics and the level of mothers' involvement, it is not possible to say for sure that such associations found are showing causal relationships between fathers' involvement in children's learning and children's educational outcomes.

---

19 For example, Nord et al. (1997) write that non-resident fathers' involvement in school is most important for secondary school children's educational outcomes.

Seemingly causal relationships, even in longitudinal studies, could be due to variables which were not controlled for in the analysis, and which are related both to the level or quality of the father's involvement (see Chapter 2) and to the child's outcomes, and sometimes also to the level or quality of the mother's involvement (see Lamb and Lewis, 2004 for a good discussion; also Pleck and Masciadrelli, 2004, and Hobcraft, 1998a and 1998b).

For example, it could be that there is no impact specifically of fathers' involvement *specifically in their children's learning and education* on children, but that fathers' positive interest or involvement *more generally in their children's lives* (e.g. authoritative parenting style, warmth, quality time, interest) is associated both with more specific involvement in learning by fathers and with children's educational outcomes (see section 3.2). Other examples of such variables (which were controlled for in some of the cited studies reported in this section) are the quality of the relationship between the father and mother (Lewis and Warin, 2001); fathers' mental health, well-being, personality and other psychological characteristics; children's sibling and peer relationships (Pleck and Masciadrelli, 2004); and children's achievement, behaviour or mental health.

Flouri and Buchanan (2004) write that lower father involvement is associated with a higher incidence of psychological problems in children, which, in turn, are associated with lower academic attainment. But they say that no evidence was found in their analysis that emotional and behavioural problems in adolescence mediate the relationship between fathers' involvement and educational attainment. Likewise, fathers' involvement at age seven was related positively to children's academic motivation at age 16. But (Flouri and Buchanan, 2004) say "there was no evidence that academic motivation mediated the relationship between father involvement and educational attainment".

Nord et al. (1997) show that associations between fathers' involvement in children's schools and educational outcomes remained for children in two-parent families, even when various measures of out-of-school parental involvement[20] were controlled for. This is good evidence for the "distinct and independent" impact of *fathers'* involvement in their children's schools (cf. Desforges and Abouchaar, 2003 for the impact of *parental* involvement in children's schools). It should be noted that, for single father families, the strong associations between fathers' involvement and children's grades disappeared once out-of-school parental involvement measures were added to the model, as did the associations between mothers' involvement and children's outcomes for children in two-parent families.

Large-scale, high-quality studies are needed which investigate:

- the relationships for specific groups, for example different ethnic groups, and more educated parents and less well educated parents

- the impact of specific types of direct involvement in children's out-of-school learning, e.g. involvement in homework, reading or outings, on children's outcomes.

Impact of fathers' involvement compared with impact of mothers' involvement

There are mixed findings on whether the impact of fathers' involvement is greater or less than the impact of mothers' involvement on children's educational outcomes. Nord et al.

---

20 For example, shared at-home and out-of-home learning activities, parental expectations about college graduation, help with homework, and discussions with children about educational plans.

(1997) speculate that mothers may be more important for children's social and emotional adjustment to school (especially young children), but that fathers are more important for children's academic achievement.

- In three of the studies reviewed, they were similar in strength (Feinstein and Symons, 1999; Trusty and Pirtle, 1998; Nord et al., 1997[21]).

- In two of the studies, the impact of fathers' involvement was greater in strength than the impact of mothers' involvement (Hobcraft, 1998a, 1998b; Nord et al., 1997[22]).

- In two studies, the impact of fathers' involvement was moderately weaker than the impact of mothers' involvement (Flouri and Buchanan, 2004; Nord et al., 1997[23]).

Obviously, the different studies relate to different types of involvement, different types of educational outcome, different age-groups and ethnicities of children, different time-periods, different countries, and so on. Kim and Rohner's small-scale study of Korean Americans, and the small-scale study of Chinese students that they cite (Chen et al., 2000), both show that, in these ethnic groups, fathers' involvement in their children's schooling had greater effects on the child's academic achievement than did mothers' involvement (Kim and Rohner, 2002). Kim and Rohner argue that this may be due to hierarchical family relations in these East Asian families, "with obedience and respect...due to...especially fathers".

Most importantly, some of the studies include non-resident fathers in their analysis and others do not.

Impact of fathers' involvement on boys compared with that on girls

There are mixed findings on whether the impact of fathers' involvement is greater for boys than for girls.

- In Flouri and Buchanan (2004), fathers' involvement and mothers' involvement both had similar strengths of association with girls' and boys' educational attainment.

- Trusty and Pirtle (1998) found that the associations between parents' educational expectations and their adolescent children's expectations were *not* stronger for same-gender pairs (i.e. fathers and sons; mothers and daughters) than for opposite-gender pairs (i.e. fathers and daughters; mothers and sons), nor vice versa, which was consistent with some earlier research they cite. In fact, fathers' and mothers' expectations were both more strongly associated with sons' later expectations than with daughters'.

- In contrast, however, Hobcraft (1998b) found that fathers' interest had a stronger impact on boys' later educational attainment than that of girls.

It is important to note that, although using the same source of data, Flouri and Buchanan used a composite measure of fathers' involvement, whereas Hobcraft used, more specifically, fathers' interest in children's education.

---

21 Specifically, for enjoyment of school and repetition of grades for children in two-parent families.

22 Specifically, for academic grades for children in two-parent families and for children with single parent father.

23 Specifically, for grade repetition and likelihood of suspension/expulsion for children in two-parent families and for children with a non-resident father.

Trusty and Pirtle (1998), in their review of the research literature, say that studies are inconsistent on both of these issues. The evidence presented in this section supports this conclusion.

The mechanisms of impact

Let it be assumed that the strong associations observed in high-quality quantitative studies between fathers' interest and involvement in children's learning and children's educational outcomes show a real impact of fathers' interest and involvement on these outcomes. What might be the processes and pathways ('mechanisms') for delivering that impact?

> *"...the research agenda has shifted from whether paternal involvement has positive consequences to questions about the context in which and the processes by which paternal effects occur."*
>
> Pleck and Masciadrelli, 2004
>
> *"...an important question concerns why parental involvement in school is important for children. There are several possible explanations that are not mutually exclusive."*
>
> Nord et al., 1997

There are theories in the educational research literature about *how* parental interest and involvement in children's learning might lead to better educational outcomes for children, and some of these processes could apply to fathers as well as to mothers. Jodl et al. (2001) cite Eccles' expectancy value model which "emphasises parents as role models, sources of reinforcement, and providers of information, resources, and opportunities for their children" in relation to children's occupational aspirations (Eccles, 1983).

In the fatherhood literature, there are theories from developmental psychology (including family systems theories, psychodynamic theories, social learning theories, attachment theory) on the father–child relationship and its impact on children (Clarke and O'Brien, 2004). Lamb and Lewis (2004) write that "there is impressive evidence that mothers and fathers may have different effects on child development", although they are not referring to educational outcomes specifically. Radin (1981) concluded that a father can have influence through his behaviour when interacting with his children, the attitudes he holds about himself and his children, the behaviour he models, his position in the family, the material resources he can give to his children, his ethnic heritage, and his aspirations for his children.

But most of the empirical evidence in the fatherhood literature relates to emotional aspects of the father–child relationship (e.g. attachments and affection) and children's emotional and social development, and/or to infants and pre-school children (Lamb and Lewis, 2004). According to Lamb and Lewis, the research literature on the relationships between fathers and teenage children is "relatively a-theoretical and descriptive", and researchers may have missed many paternal influences by focusing on emotional elements.

In Section 3.1, the 'double dose' theory was described, showing why a father's positive involvement is important. A positively involved father is a second parent/carer involved in his child's life, and therefore his input increases and also diversifies the total parental input into the child's life. But are there specific aspects to fathers' or other male carers' involvement with their children's learning which are likely to make their contribution different from that of a female parent or carer?

Chapter 1 noted the policy debate about the gender achievement gap at school, and the arguments that 'masculine' inputs[24] from fathers into children's learning are especially important for boys. Chapter 2 showed the distinctive typical role of fathers in certain areas of their children's out-of-school learning. As seen in the previous section, there are mixed research findings from large-scale statistical studies on whether fathers' involvement in children's learning and education is more important for boys' educational outcomes than for girls' educational outcomes. However, fathers' involvement could have impact on sons' and daughters' educational outcomes by different mechanisms, even if the overall strength of impact is similar. This possibility is considered throughout the following discussion.

There is very limited high-quality research evidence on mechanisms because of the limitations in many research studies of the data and sample size for complex analyses. It is rare to find statistical studies which convincingly demonstrate one specific mechanism by isolating it from others. Many studies show statistical correlations without specifying the mechanism at all (e.g. Yeung et al., 2000).

So, in this section a few ideas from the research literature are presented, along with evidence from a few selected high-quality quantitative research studies. The searches of bibliographic databases found many relevant smaller-scale studies based on localised samples with very specific populations of parents and children which shed light on all these proposed mechanisms. With so many small-scale studies, a systematic review or meta-analysis of all such studies could be beneficial as a further research project.

Of course, qualitative research can be very helpful in elucidating mechanisms of impact (see Boxes 3 and 4 later in this chapter).

Role modelling

The process of socialisation,[25] and in particular of role modelling,[26] is often used to explain the impact of parental interest and involvement in children's learning on children's interest and involvement in learning. Role modelling and other kinds of socialisation processes could also operate to transmit parents' education-related aspirations, expectations, values, attributions, behaviours (e.g. self-discipline), use of language, choice of activities and encouragement to the child (Tenenbaum and Leaper, 2003; Trusty and Pirtle, 1998; Lynch, 2002; Raymond and Benhow, 1986; Simpson, 2003). This role modelling mechanism also

---

24 The mix of 'masculine' and 'feminine' attributes and interests varies greatly across both men and women, and generalisations are being used.

25 For example, "*Children are viewed as learning most social behaviours from their parents, either through a process by which parents actively encourage or discourage children's behaviours or, as role model theory posits, by behaviours transmitted more passively as parents set examples with their behaviour.*" (Yeung et al., 2000).

26 In the role modelling of a parent, the child bases her/his own beliefs, attitudes and behaviour towards learning on those that the child assesses or observes that her/his parent holds. In more basic terms, the child imitates her/his parent's behaviour, and internalises her/his parent's beliefs and attitudes. Therefore, the greater, for example, the parent's interest in education, the greater the child's interest in education.

appears frequently in the fatherhood literature to explain fathers' influence on their children (Lamb and Tamis-Lemonda, 2004).

Bryant and Zimmerman (2003) write that "most adolescents look up to and view their parents as positive role models", and that parents are more influential role models than same-sex friends, siblings, extended family members, and teachers. They also acknowledge that "adolescents may adopt parent surrogates, such as older siblings and grandparents, especially when they have been unable to form these bonds with their own parents". However, it is important to remember that family and friends are not the total of a child's world (Lewis and Warin, 2001):

> "a child's ideas...are absorbed through the wider culture not just through the culture of their family."

Children will be more likely to model their parents "if they experience a warm, supportive parent–child relationship" (Jodl et al., 2001), and adolescents model individuals who they believe are "worthy of imitation", which links to the earlier discussion about the importance of a father's parenting style for his children's educational outcomes (Bryant and Zimmerman, 2003). Bryant and Zimmerman also write that adolescents' choice of their parents as role models is associated with whether their parents live with them and with overall parental involvement in their life, although they cite a finding that "44 per cent of male African American youth not living with their father reported that he was their role model" (Zimmerman et al., 1995). In their own research, 22 per cent of African American adolescents who did not live with their fathers "identified them as their male role models". They were more likely to select their brother or extended family, or to have no male role model, than youth living with their father.

For positive outcomes from the role modelling process, it is crucial that the parent has *positive* attitudes and behaviour around learning. Otherwise, role modelling of the parent will have *negative* outcomes for the child. Children's assessment of their parents' interest, attitudes and behaviours around learning and education may arise as a result of a number of sources of evidence, including:

- shared parent–child learning activities (Jodl et al., 2001)

- parent–child conversations about learning and education (Jodl et al., 2001)

- parents' discussions with others about learning and education, which are overheard by children

- parents' own involvement in learning/education,[27] for example in their children's schools or their own reading or participation in adult education

- parents' occupational status and type

- parents' level and type of educational qualifications (Dryler, 1998).

According to Nord et al. (1997), fathers' and mothers' involvement in children's schools matters "through its concrete demonstration to the children that education and school matters to their parents". So, parents do not need to be interacting with their children at all for role modelling to operate.

---

27 Which could include the parent's educational qualifications, involvement in the children's school, reading activities and adult learning activities.

According to Jodl et al. (2001), "parents' interpretation of reality...may be communicated in both subtle and overt ways". For example, parents may overtly demonstrate praise, support and encouragement for children's successes at school or particular kinds of activity (Simpson, 2003; Jodl et al., 2001), and/or disapproval for poor educational performance.

In role modelling of parents by children, the *gender* of the parent might be important. Rather than model a parent because they are a parent (of whatever gender), a child chooses to model a particular parent because they are a very significant adult of a specific gender, namely the same gender as the child (Dryler, 1998 discussing Kohlberg's 1960s theory). So girls would tend to imitate their mothers, whereas boys would tend to imitate their fathers. Much has been written about how gendered role modelling is responsible for the development of gendered attitudes and behaviour in boys and girls.

Many experts (see Chapter 1) propose the importance of fathers and 'father figures' acting as positive male role models for boys' learning and reading. Fathers and 'father figures' could alternatively be poor role models for boys. For example, if the parent reading at home (either on their own or with their children) is more often the mother than the father, this could lead to boys thinking that learning, and specifically reading, is a female activity (Fletcher and Dally, 2002).

Of course, positive role modelling of fathers could also operate for girls who model the father as a *parent* rather than as a very significant *male adult*. In fact, Dryler (1998) cites research showing that children choose to imitate "the most influential/dominant parent".

In particular, some researchers propose that both fathers and mothers can have a key *negative* influence on girls' lower involvement in maths, science and technical subjects, and on other gendered educational and occupational choices, by encouraging maths, science and technical activities in their sons but not in their daughters during conversation and joint activities. The research studies which focus on this issue for school-age children are nearly all small-scale, localised cross-sectional studies in the US, often with very specific populations of parents and children.

Some such studies (e.g. Tenenbaum and Leaper, 2003[28]) do indeed show differences in fathers' interactions with and encouragement for sons and daughters during joint learning activities; but others do not. Lewis and Warin (2001), reviewing the fatherhood literature, write that, when children are young, "fathers often respond differently to their sons and daughters. Researchers find that fathers engage in physical play more with sons than daughters, especially when there are other people around... However, large-scale reviews and meta-analyses do not support the assumption that men treat their sons and daughters differently".

---

28 Tenenbaum and Leaper found that fathers, but not mothers, used more cognitively challenging speech with their sons than with their daughters in a structured physics task carried out at home which was video-taped by the researchers. Additionally, both mothers and fathers who had daughters were more likely to believe that science was difficult for their child and less likely to believe that their child was interested in science (than were mothers or fathers who had sons), despite their sons and daughters showing no gender-differences in science ability nor in interest in science. The researchers conclude that "fathers may view physics as something to encourage in their sons but not their daughters". They speculate that this bias by fathers might contribute to differences in science achievement amongst adolescent boys and girls at older ages, and to the much greater percentage of men than of women in the science labour force which occurs both in the US and in Europe.

Fathers' involvement in daughters' learning could also convey ideas to girls about egalitarian gender roles. Lewis and Tamis-Lemonda (2004) cite research showing that:

> *"American fathers' involvement in routine child care was associated with... less stereotypical views about adult sex-roles on the part of daughters."*

Acquisition of information, skills and learning styles

Conversations between parents and children about learning and education, and direct involvement by parents in their children's out-of-school learning (e.g. reading, help with homework, outings) might:

- help children to think constructively about learning-related decisions and problems

- directly convey to children information and ideas leading to acquisition of specific skills, learning resources or knowledge, i.e. the parent acts in a 'teacher'/'direct instruction' role. Small-scale and observational studies show that children and teenagers "rely on their fathers to provide factual information" (Nord et al., 1997)

- if the learning is fun or related to everyday life, demonstrate to the child that learning can be fun and related to everyday life, perhaps more than for learning in school.

There could be a specifically 'masculine' aspect to fathers' direct involvement with their children's learning, which helps children to develop specific skills or areas of knowledge. As seen in Chapter 2, despite many similarities in the content of their involvement, fathers tend to play a greater role in some types of learning than do mothers (also see Flouri and Buchanan, 2004).

Fathers might also contribute specifically 'masculine' styles of learning and interaction during joint learning activities. Fletcher and Dally (2002) argue, in relation to children's literacy, that fathers often "act as a major resource" in developing children's skills in "other ways of knowing and relating", i.e. apart from talking, reading and writing. Fathers' interactions with children have a playful style, and fathers' activities with teenage children are goal-oriented (Lamb and Lewis, 2004). Fathers tend to spend less time overall with their children, and so they are less knowledgeable than mothers about their children's abilities, and therefore "more likely to speak in ways that challenge children's linguistic and pragmatic abilities" (Lamb and Tamis-Lemonda, 2004).

However, comparisons of mothers' and fathers' approaches to parenting are inconclusive, and research shows few differences between mothers' and fathers' interactional styles with adolescent children (Lamb and Lewis, 2004).

Are some aspects of fathers' direct involvement in their children's out-of-school learning more important for boys than for girls? There was some evidence in Chapter 2 that fathers do spend more time with their sons than their daughters in sport, hobbies, practical tasks and outings. It could be that boys are more likely to share interests (for example, types of reading material, sport, technology) with fathers than with mothers, which means that fathers' involvement would be more relevant and motivating for boys. Boys may also respond better to those learning styles used more often by fathers than by mothers. Certainly, many 'dads and lads' family learning programmes operate on this kind of basis (see Chapter 6 for case studies). A greater body of robust evidence is required to adequately answer this question.

Social capital

Another mechanism proposed in the literature for the impact of parental interest and involvement in children's learning and education is parents forming social contacts, relationships and networks ('social capital'[29]) outside the family with individuals and organisations which are directly useful for learning and education (e.g. increase the opportunities for children) or which benefit the quality of parenting (e.g. Yeung et al., 2000; Buchel and Duncan, 1998, based on Coleman, 1988; Bryant and Zimmerman, 2003; Nord et al., 1997).

More specifically, parents' involvement in schools and interactions with their children's teachers could have a positive impact on:

- the overall school environment and quality of teaching (Nord et al., 1997)

- teachers' behaviour towards their specific child (Flouri et al., 2000)

- teachers' likelihood of intervening early when a child displays difficulties in achievement or behaviour (Nord et al., 1997).

In a two-way process, the teacher could create learning opportunities in school which are better linked to children's out-of-school experiences and culture; and the teacher might recommend good educational resources and activities for parents and children to engage with at home (Fletcher and Dally, 2002).

Parents with one form of social capital are more likely to have other forms of social capital. In the US National Household Education Survey, fathers who were more highly involved in their children's schools were more likely to attend religious services, belong to community or professional organisations, or regularly volunteer in the community (Nord et al., 1997). However, parents' social and community activities outside the home can reduce the time they spend with their children (Buchel and Duncan, 1998).

It can be argued that the potential for fathers' to create social capital through their involvement in children's schools and family learning programmes would be greater if these settings were less feminised (Chapter 4). As seen in Chapter 2, fathers are less likely than mothers to participate in school life and to communicate with teachers about their children's progress. Despite this, it was seen in a previous section of this chapter that fathers' involvement in their children's schools has associations with children's educational outcomes which are independent of parents' out-of-school learning (Nord et al., 1997).

> Fathers "can connect children to other groups and institutions in the community such as schools, sports teams, and religious organisations".
>
> Amato and Sobolewski, 2004
>
> "...fathers may play a role that centers more around helping their children develop community ties than providing emotional support."
>
> Bryant and Zimmerman, 2003

---

29 Social capital as formulated by Coleman (1988).

"...fathers may play a special role as intermediaries between the family and the outside world"

Lamb and Lewis, 2004

Other possible mechanisms

Having quality discussions and joint learning activities, and parents' involvement in children's schools, could enhance the parent–child relationship more generally (e.g. 'my parent is taking an interest in me'), and so benefit children's emotional development and self-esteem, and consequently their learning. For example, parents' involvement in school "may be demonstrating to their children how much they care about them" as well as the importance they place on education.

Other possible mechanisms include parents' interest in and expectations for their children's learning and education leading to:

- concrete sanctions and rewards for poor and good school achievement respectively, which affect children's behaviour (Simpson, 2003)

- selection of a better school for the child

- provision of educational resources such as books, toys, computers, the internet, private tutoring, and money for other educational activities and experiences (this mechanism does not require parent–child interaction). This potential mechanism relates to fathers' typical 'provider' role, and it is called 'financial capital' by Coleman (1988).

Finally, fathers may influence children's positive educational outcomes by supporting and increasing mothers' involvement in their children's learning and education. Lamb and Tamis-Lemonda (2004) note the "extraordinary importance" of the indirect pathways through which fathers affect their children. They argue that children and their fathers "must be viewed as part of complex social systems... in which each person affects each other reciprocally, directly, and indirectly".

It is important to remember that different mechanisms may operate for different age-groups, for different population groups of children and parents, and in different contexts.

Four quality research studies relevant to the mechanisms of impact

In relation to the mechanisms of social capital acquisition, role modelling, father–child conversations, and father–child direct interaction, it is interesting to consider findings from a study by Yeung et al. (2000). They analysed data for two-parent families in the US Panel Study of Income Dynamics[30] to look at statistical associations between fathers' leisure-time activities (with no direct father–child interaction) when their children were growing up (as reported by the fathers) and their children's completed schooling (in years, as reported by

---

30 This is a longitudinal research study over 27 years since 1968. The sample for Yeung et al.'s analysis was nationally representative of the US, and comprised just over 1,000 families with children born in the years 1956-62. All the fathers were biological resident fathers.

the child in early adulthood). The analysis[31] found that the following variables did *not* relate to children's completed years of schooling:

- frequency of fathers' newspaper reading
- fathers' achievement motivation
- fathers' orientation towards the future
- how often the family ate main meals together
- fathers 'taking lessons'
- fathers watching TV
- fathers' frequency of going to bars or social clubs
- other 'spare-time activities' of fathers.

The beliefs and behaviours of fathers which did relate to children's completed years of schooling were:

- fathers' sense of personal control (only for sons)
- fathers' use of risk-avoidance behaviours (only for sons)
- fathers' church attendance (for both sons and daughters).

A similar analysis was carried out by Buchel and Duncan (1998), using the German Socio-economic Panel.[32] They found positive associations between fathers' involvement in active sports and in volunteer work in organisations (averaged over the period when their child was aged 9-14) and their children's educational attainment. They also found negative associations between fathers' socialising with friends, relatives and neighbours (and fathers' help to friends, relatives and neighbours) and their children's educational attainment, especially in low-income families and for boys. The researchers then controlled for the reported amount of time that the father spent in childcare of all the children in the household. They found that the negative association with time spent with friends, relatives and neighbours diminished but remained statistically significant. There were no statistically significant associations between mothers' corresponding involvements and children's attainment when the analysis controlled for demographics.

Buchel and Duncan's analyses did not control for variables such as parents' motivation and energy; and the involvement variable measured the frequency of involvement, rather than the quality of the social capital created by parents. They also note that (in comparison to the US) a relatively high proportion of German families are two-parent families with a male breadwinner; gender roles are relatively traditional in Germany; and informal social activity and support are relatively common in Germany, especially in rural areas.

---

31 The regression analyses in Yeung et al.'s paper controlled for a number of characteristics, activities of mothers, and conditions in the childhood home, for example mothers' and fathers' years of schooling, age at time of child's birth, work hours, housework hours, vacation time, family size, city size, ethnicity, earnings, occupation and disability status.

32 This is a large-scale, nationally representative, longitudinal study with a relatively high response rate. Buchel and Duncan looked at two-parent families in which children were living with both their biological parents, and restricted the sample to Western Germany. These analyses controlled for a range of demographic variables.

Another research study was carried out amongst about 700 African American adolescents with relatively low academic achievement in four Michigan high schools[33] (Bryant and Zimmerman, 2003). About 30 per cent of girls saw their father as their male role model,[34] compared with 43 per cent of males with their father as their male role model. Bryant and Zimmerman's analyses showed that, for girls, having their father as the male role model was associated with greater perceived likelihood of graduating than having a brother as a male role model or having no male role model. For boys, having their father as a male role model was associated with greater academic achievement than having extended family as their male role model or having no male role model. Having their father, brother or extended family as a male role model was associated with decreased truancy and better school-related attitudes than having no male role model. So, brothers seem to be role models for boys but not for girls.

Buchel and Duncan conclude that role modelling might be a vital mechanism for parents' influence on adolescents' outcomes above and beyond other aspects of good parenting, since they controlled in their analysis for parenting process and family structure. However, another mechanism could be that fathers are more likely than mothers to treat sons and daughters differently.

A large-scale, nationally representative, random-selection study[35] was conducted by Dryler (1998) in Sweden. The multivariate analysis looked at how children's choices about their academic programme at the 'upper secondary school' (age 16+) related to their mothers' and fathers' field of study and occupational sector, controlling for the children's school grades and for their parents' social class and levels of education.

Dryler found that fathers' field of study and occupational sector were important predictors of both girls' and boys' educational choices. For example, both girls and boys were more likely to choose an engineering or technical programme if their father worked or had studied in a technical sector. They were more likely to choose a humanities, social science or healthcare programme if their father worked or had studied in this field.

Another finding from this study was that parents' influence on their children's educational choices was stronger for father–son pairs than for mother–son pairs, i.e. boys were more likely to imitate their fathers than their mothers. Whereas, for girls, the gender of the parent *did not* change the strength of that parent's influence on her educational decisions, i.e. girls were *not* more likely to imitate their mothers than their fathers. Dryler discusses that alternative "rational choice" mechanisms could be responsible for their results, for example, children choose the same sector as their parents because they believe that they will get more help from their parents in this type of study.

---

33 Bryant and Zimmerman's study was of a localised, urban sample of African Americans with low academic achievement, and so is unlikely to be generalisable to all African Americans in the US. Additionally, all the variables except for academic achievement were based on adolescents' reports. The quality of the adolescents' relationships with their role models was not assessed. The researchers write that "our one-item measure of role modelling may not adequately distinguish role modelling from other socialisation processes", and that further research needs "more comprehensive measures of parenting and family process".

34 The adolescents were asked to name one male role model and one female role model whom they "looked up to".

35 Data was collected for 124,000 pupils born between 1972 and 1976 when the children were in their last year of secondary school (aged 15-16). The sample was limited to children living with both their parents. The data was taken from school administrative records and from the national Census.

Impact of home–school and family learning programmes targeted at fathers

Searches of bibliographic databases, and the review of recent and current practice and projects in England and Wales, did not find any high-quality, quasi-experimental evaluations which could show the impact of home–school and family learning programmes targeted at fathers on school-age children's outcomes. For example, no evaluations were found that used control or comparison groups, or measured children's or fathers' outcomes before and after the programme. This is unsurprising, as discussed in Section 3.1 for home–school and family learning programmes generally.

Additionally, a meta-analysis found only three experimental evaluations of the impact of involving fathers in early childhood interventions to improve parenting skills (Bakermans-Kranenburg et al., 2003). O'Brien (2004) reports that no systematic reviews have been conducted by the international Cochrane Collaboration on the effectiveness of father-based healthcare and social care interventions.

> "…few researchers have examined the effects of fatherhood programs on either the men's behaviour or the well-being of their children… [we] remain unable to pinpoint whether, how and why different types of program affect men, families, and children."
>
> Lamb and Tamis-Lemonda, 2004

Therefore, robust summative evaluations of family learning and home–school programmes which target fathers and school-age children are needed to fully demonstrate effectiveness in terms of children's outcomes. O'Brien (2004) gives a very helpful discussion of "father-sensitive evaluation" in her report on fathers and family support services.

The review of recent and current practice and projects in England and Wales did find several small-scale evaluations of family learning and home-school programmes specifically for fathers. However, the evidence in these evaluations that relates to outcomes for children is based on teachers', other practitioners' and parents' observations of a few specific children for whom there were behavioural or attitudinal changes following participation in a programme. Few evaluations were carried out independently of the programme implementers; and therefore the benefits reported may have a positive bias (see O'Brien, 2004).

Nonetheless, these evaluations and the case studies in this report show a wide and consistent range of reported outcomes for children, as shown in Box 3, and of reported outcomes for fathers which would support their children's out-of-school learning, as shown in Box 4.

Box 3: Observed or reported outcomes for children, as a result of home–school and family learning programmes targeting fathers

- enjoyment of and pride in their father's involvement
- learning new skills in curricular areas, including those which may more rarely involve mothers, such as IT, design and technology, and sport
- increased engagement with learning, reading, schoolwork
- stabilisation of school experience leading to better attendance and behaviour
- greater/higher quality father–child engagement and relationship, including more father–child conversation and joint learning (reading/outings/other activities at home) after the activity (including with the participating child's siblings)
- greater confidence

Box 4: Observed or reported outcomes for fathers which support children's learning and education, as a result of home–school and family learning programmes targeting fathers

- learning new skills which can benefit children in further learning activity at home once the family learning programme is over, e.g. IT or literacy or sports coaching
- aware of wider range of activities, resources and venues for learning (although can be difficult for fathers to generalise from specific activities to learning more generally)
- having a better understanding of child development and modern education
- learning from other fathers about positive parenting styles
- learning more about their specific child's learning styles, abilities and educational needs, and seeing their child in the context of other children in the school (*"you discover that your kid is like any other kid"*, Bright et al., 2002)
- being more comfortable with the school environment and other learning environments (e.g. libraries and museums), and starting to ask teachers about child's progress/ attend school meetings, etc
- increased library membership (where the programme specifically involved libraries)

Ofsted (2000) reported a very similar list of benefits resulting from family learning pro-grammes which were mainly with mothers. They reviewed family learning programmes (mainly literacy-based and targeted at deprived areas) in 28 LEAs based on inspections, i.e. observations, interviews and documentation, but not systematically measuring the outcomes for children.

3.4 Benefits of fathers' involvement for fathers, mothers and schools

This chapter has so far looked at the outcomes for children associated with fathers' involvement in their learning and education. Are there any associated outcomes for fathers, mothers and schools?

Fathers

When assessing the benefits for fathers as a result of involvement in their children's lives, there is of course the argument of gender equity/equal opportunities. Just as women are entitled to this in the work and public spheres, so men are entitled to this in the spheres of the home, the school and children's and family services.

There are also theories in the fatherhood literature that greater emotional intimacy with their children can bring emotional benefits for fathers. According to Herb and Willoughby-Herb (1998), there are three areas of men's development which are benefited by good fatherhood experiences: "emotional support and growth, maturing of direction/purpose in life, and increased feelings of generativity" (providing an input into the next generation). This could apply specifically to fathers' involvement in children's learning too. There are some very interesting studies showing that fathers' involvement overall is not significantly associated with 'generativity', but that there are relationships between generativity and involvement in specific parenting behaviours which include play, taking a child on routine jobs, consulting with teachers, and supervising homework (Pleck and Masciadrelli, 2004).

Certainly, in the case studies and in other small-scale evaluations of home–school and family learning programmes targeted at fathers, practitioners observed and fathers reported many emotional and social benefits for fathers (Box 5).

Box 5: Observed or reported emotional and social benefits for fathers, as a result of home–school and family learning programmes targeting fathers

- enjoyment, satisfaction, fun and pride in taking part in joint learning activities with their child

- increased confidence

- enhancement of their relationship with their children ('quality time' together and 'bonding')

- observing their children's enjoyment of and benefits from the activities (e.g. their child learning new skills and confidence)

- new friendships with other men

- discussions with other fathers about their children, and about parenting and education issues in a group with a male focus, including discussions about their relationship with their own father and a better understanding of themselves

---

However, several authors write that the juggle for involved fathers between work and family life can be a struggle (e.g. Burgess and Ruxton, 1996), and that this can lead to decreased life satisfaction and self-esteem, as compared to fathers who take on just the traditional provider role (Lewis, 2000b; Pleck and Masciadrelli, 2004). This has of course applied to working mothers for many years (Frieman and Berkeley, 2002). There are mixed research findings on this issue, and there is also some research showing that short-term costs for involved fathers (e.g. stress) are *not* associated with reduced satisfaction with being a parent (Pleck and Masciadrelli, 2004). Of course, the outcomes for fathers may depend on whether or not they want to be involved.

There can be a link between fathers' involvement in family learning programmes and their entry into other learning (including work-related training and improvement of basic skills), and ultimately a link with employment. Certainly, this pathway seems to exist for mothers (see Section 3.1). Millard and Hunter (2001) write that "the engagement of parents with education through an interest in their children's learning can be a powerful trigger for them to resume their education". Family learning may especially be a good route for fathers into adult learning, as the focus on helping their children can overcome men's typical reluctance to seek help for personal issues. However, it is important to note that most family learning programmes are free for fathers, but this is not the case for all adult learning, which could be a barrier to progression.

As well as helping to break a cycle of educational under-achievement, involving unemployed fathers in family learning may help them to find a job and reduce the social isolation of unemployment. According to McGivney (1999), many unemployed people obtain new contacts and then jobs through their informal networks of friends, former colleagues and acquaintances.

But little robust research evidence was found that demonstrated whether or not these potential benefits occur for fathers, especially any progression into further training or work, or the improvement of fathers' literacy and numeracy skills. Box 6 reports some evidence from the case studies (Chapter 6) and from small-scale evaluations of family learning programmes targeted at fathers and children. One programme initiated in a US maximum security prison for male prisoners with children involved prisoners writing stories or other text and making books (including computer design) to be sent to their children (Geraci, 2001). Geraci reports that the prisoners improved their skills in literacy, IT desktop publishing and creativity, and that some prisoners became tutors, teaching other prisoners the required skills.

Box 6: Observed or reported learning benefits for fathers, as a result of home–school and family learning programmes targeting fathers

- learned new skills for own benefit, as well as for children's benefit (e.g. IT, football coaching)
- taught skills to other fathers in the programme
- became mentors or volunteers, and occasionally paid workers, in family learning programmes or fatherhood initiatives
- some take-up of voluntary accreditation for adult learning
- pride in giving something back to the school and the community
- (for prisoners) decreased re-offending on release

Mothers

There are conflicting arguments in the literature about whether greater father involvement is good for mothers. Certainly, research suggests that some mothers are ambivalent or resistant to greater father involvement in their children's learning and education (see Chapter 4 on mothers' attitudes). One voluntary sector organisation set up several initiatives for fathers in a London borough. They were asked about whether their 'pro-father approach' would mean 'anti-mother' (Working with Men, 2004).

Pleck and Masciadrelli (2004) speculate that mothers' marital satisfaction may be lessened if fathers are more involved in their children's lives. If both the mother and father are actively involved with their children, arguments about child rearing may occur more frequently. But, conversely, greater father involvement could be related to better quality in their relationship with their partner because mothers will feel more supported and the partners will have more in common to bond them together as a couple. In fact, as seen in Chapter 2, greater father involvement in children's learning and education is related to a good relationship between children's parents in two-parent families.

Some argue that greater father involvement in their children's lives will decrease the burden on mothers who juggle both employment and family responsibilities (Macleod, 2000; O'Brien, 2004; Dudley-Marling, 2001). The primary focus of Scandinavian and other European countries on the role of fathers has been gender equity in families, and this focus also dominates British research on fathers due to the influence of feminism, for example the relative time contributions of men and women to housework and child care (Clarke and O'Brien, 2004; Pleck and Masciadrelli, 2004). Fathers' greater involvement in their children's lives is statistically associated to less stress in mothers' lives (Pleck and Masciadrelli, 2004).

> *"...mothers should not be expected 'to do it all'"*
>
> O'Brien, 2004
>
> *"...the co-ordination and supervision of children's educational activities often demands a significant portion of mothers' waking hours"*
>
> Dudley-Marling, 2001

But little high-quality research evidence was found on this important issue of whether increased fathers' involvement brings benefits for mothers. Pleck and Masciadrelli (2004) suggest that the effects of fathers' involvement on the couple relationship depend on whether mothers and fathers want fathers to be involved, and that research on this issue should control for fathers' and mothers' expectations.

Schools

> *"...fathers are a pool of supporters waiting to be tapped"*
>
> Bright et al., 2002

The involvement of parents in schools can lead to improvements in schools which can benefit all children in the local community (Desforges and Abouchaar, 2003). In fact, fathers can bring specific skills to schools, as shown in Section 6.5. Bright et al. (2002) argue that involving fathers as volunteers in schools is one way of increasing the adult–child ratio. This could apply, for example, to the involvement of fathers on school outings, although this type of in-school involvement is not that common amongst fathers (Chapter 2).

In the case study programmes (Chapter 6), some fathers did get fully involved in the life of their children's school, including school governance, classroom involvement as a volunteer (maths, IT and sports), and helping with school trips and after-school activities (sports). One teacher in 'It's a Man Thing!' said that she could use the family learning programme as an opportunity to identify a group of fathers with whom she could work further in future (Millard and Hunter, 2001).

3.5 Summary

- There is consistent evidence that the quality and content of fathers' involvement matter much more for children's outcomes than the quantity of time for which a father and child are in contact or the frequency of contact and visits. This applies to both resident and non-resident fathers.

- In particular, fathers' affection, support and 'authoritative' parenting style are related to children's positive educational outcomes. Poor parenting by fathers is associated with children's decreased educational attainment.

- It is important for teachers to find out about fathers' overall involvement in the lives of the children in their class so that they can understand the lives, successes and problems of these children much better, and then work with them in an appropriate way.

- Many research studies assessing the impact of fathers' involvement in their children's learning and education on children's educational outcomes are localised and small-scale. This report focused on five high-quality studies with large-scale, nationally representative samples of fathers and children.

- These high-quality studies show that fathers' greater interest and involvement in their children's learning and in schools are statistically associated with better educational outcomes for children, including better exam results, better school attendance and behaviour, and higher educational expectations. There are also associations with better social and emotional outcomes for children.

- In one high-quality study, a father's interest in his child's education had a stronger association with the likelihood of that child having qualifications in adult life than did contact with the police, poverty, family type or the child's personality.

- These statistical associations with fathers' involvement are independent of mothers' involvement. They exist for primary school children and secondary school children; for children in two-parent families, single-mother families with non-resident fathers, and single-father families; and irrespective of the gender of the child.

- Mothers' involvement is no substitute for fathers' involvement. Psychologists write about a 'double dose' effect in which children are influenced by the active involvement of two parents or carers. This leads, not only to greater total parental involvement, but to a greater diversity of parental skills and interests, parenting styles and types of involvement.

- There are mixed findings on any differences in the strength of impact of fathers' involvement and mothers' involvement.

- There are also mixed findings on whether or not the strength of impact of fathers' involvement is greater for boys than for girls.

- There is very limited, high-quality research evidence on the mechanisms of impact because of data and sample size limitations in research studies. It is rare for studies to isolate one specific mechanism from others.

- Proposed mechanisms include socialisation/role-modelling; direct acquisition of information, skills and learning styles; the formation of key social contacts such as a good relationship with the child's teacher; and enhancement of the father–child relationship. These mechanisms also apply to mothers.

- Small-scale evaluations of family learning programmes involving fathers consistently report many perceived benefits for children and fathers, including skill acquisition, greater confidence, a better father–child relationship, and increased engagement with learning. Children much enjoy it when fathers are involved. Fathers develop a better understanding of learning activities and resources for their children, and become more comfortable in schools.

- There is the potential for family learning to be a 'progression route' to adult learning for fathers, as it is for mothers. Small-scale evaluations of family learning programmes involving fathers reported some progression on to accreditation for adult learning; mentoring of other men in family learning programmes; and voluntary and paid work in schools, family learning programmes and the community.

- However, no evaluations of family learning programmes were found that systematically measured outcomes for children or adults, or had control or comparison groups.

- Some writers argue that increased fathers' involvement matters because of a need for gender equity. Just as women are entitled to equality with men in the work and public spheres, so men are entitled to this in the spheres of the home, the school and family services. Additionally, greater father involvement can relieve the burden on mothers who combine work and family commitments.

- There are theories in the fatherhood literature, and evidence from small-scale evaluations of family learning programmes, that greater father involvement can lead to emotional and social benefits for fathers. However, as for working mothers, the juggle for involved fathers between work and family life may be a struggle.

- There are conflicting arguments in the literature about whether or not greater fathers' involvement is beneficial for mothers, and little robust evidence.

4 | Beliefs, attitudes and barriers to involvement

"Fathers were also more likely than mothers to report a history of school failure in literacy, a dislike of reading aloud and the use of strategies to shorten the time spent on reading with their children."

Fletcher and Dally, 2002

"Programmes were largely initiated, planned, run and co-ordinated by women for women."

Cairney et al.,1995

"the terms, conditions and expectations of paid employment stand as the greatest barrier to men's involvement in childcare...the barriers to active fathering are more than a matter of attitudes."

Lewis, 2000b

Chapter 2 concluded that resident fathers are less likely than resident mothers to be involved in most aspects of their children's learning and in children's schools. Fathers are especially unlikely to be participants in organised family learning programmes which take place during the daytime and are not targeted at men. Non-resident fathers are especially unlikely to be involved in their children's schools. What are the barriers for the fathers who do not get involved?

Many writers and researchers have written about the barriers to fathers' active involvement in children's lives, and several have written more specifically on the barriers to fathers' involvement in children's learning and education. They differ (see Box 7) in whether they focus on:

- large-scale barriers (society, cultural belief systems, the economic system, the nature of work), or barriers at the level of individual fathers, mothers, practitioners, schools and family learning programmes

- beliefs and attitudes, or more practical issues (e.g. work hours, income, family-friendly employment, venues and timing of sessions)

- fathers' beliefs, attitudes, circumstances and behaviours, or the beliefs, attitudes, circumstances and behaviours of others. For example, is it fathers or schools that are hard-to-reach?

Many of the barriers presented in this chapter are interconnected and fuel one another. Pleck and Masciadrelli (2004) conclude that:

> *"variables associated with paternal involvement may act together additively, paralleling the concept of cumulative risk... Factors promoting father involvement may also operate interactively."*

Debates can take place about which came first ('the chicken or the egg'), but more productive is to try to understand all the barriers and then to try to address them at different levels. Schools can change the involvement opportunities they offer fathers, and their own practices, but they cannot on their own alter the gender pay gap or cultural belief systems, except perhaps in the long term through the education of the next generation.

Of course, the relative impact of each barrier differs for different groups of fathers. Throughout this chapter, findings are presented on barriers for particular groups of fathers: working-class fathers, unemployed fathers, black and minority ethnic fathers, non-resident fathers and single-parent fathers.

The final point in this introduction is that some of the barriers discussed in this chapter also commonly operate to restrict:

- fathers' relatively low active involvement in their children's lives (e.g. Lamb and Tamis-Lemonda, 2004; Amato and Sobolewski, 2004), and in family support and parenting education services (Henricson et al., 2001) compared with mothers – for example, cultural beliefs about gender roles; work and lack of time; fathers' beliefs; and mothers as gatekeepers

- mothers' involvement in their children's education and in family learning programmes (e.g. Brassett-Grundy, 2002; NIACE, 2003) – for example, fear of education; lack of transport and childcare; work and lack of time; and school practices

- men's relatively low involvement in all types of non-vocational adult learning and education compared with women (McGivney, 1999 and 2004; Fitzgerald et al., 2003[1]) – for example, fathers' beliefs; lack of transport and childcare; and work and lack of time.

What is done in this chapter is to bring all these barriers together as they relate to fathers' involvement in their children's learning and education. Sections 4.1 – 4.4 discuss large-scale barriers (at the levels of society, work and culture). Sections 4.5 - 4.8 discuss barriers at the level of individual fathers, mothers, practitioners, schools and family learning programmes. They incorporate research evidence on the relevant beliefs and attitudes of fathers, mothers, children and teachers. It will be seen that some of these beliefs and attitudes are potential barriers to fathers' involvement, but others are potential facilitators of fathers' involvement.

---

1   In the National Adult Learning Survey 2002 (England and Wales), 34 per cent of men and 25 per cent of women said that lack of time due to work was a barrier to adult learning. Fifteen per cent of men and 26 per cent of women said that lack of time due to family commitments was a barrier; and three per cent of men and six per cent of women said that caring for another adult was a barrier. Seven per cent of men and five per cent of women said that difficulties with reading and writing were barriers. Six per cent of men and 10 per cent of women mentioned problems with transport; and four per cent of both men and women mentioned health and disability as barriers (Fitzgerald et al. , 2003).

4.1 Cultural belief systems relating to gender roles in families

Traditional cultural belief systems[2] in the UK and elsewhere about fathers as economic providers and mothers as homemakers and childcarers continue to influence the beliefs and attitudes of fathers, mothers, teachers, other practitioners and children regarding fathers' involvement in their children's learning and education (see Lewis, 2000b).

Section 1.3 referred to fatherhood being in a time of change and negotiation, and "an extensive set of cultural images and icons of caring fathers" has been produced in recent decades (O'Brien, 2004). In a small-scale study in north-east England and in a consultation with fathers in London, although many of the fathers tended to see mothers as the primary carers for children, they were aware of increased father involvement in childcare, and of changing societal attitudes about fathers' and mothers' roles (Clough et al., 2000; Working with Men, 2004).

However, in the British Social Attitudes Survey, 53 per cent of men and 42 per cent of women agreed with a statement that the father's role is to 'provide' (cited in Gingerbread, 2001). In one research study in north-west England, only a minority of families challenged traditional gender role assumptions, including some single parents who had to take on both 'mothering' and 'fathering' roles (Warin et al., 1999).

Working-class parents tend to express less egalitarian attitudes than do middle-class parents (Lewis, 2000b). Teachers in north-east England expressed their perception of local attitudes in the following terms:

> *"The ethos of the area is that men do jobs and women deal with the kids." (Clough et al., 2000)*

Parents in some black and minority ethnic groups, for example South Asian families in the UK, may also have more traditional attitudes towards gender roles (Becher and Husain, 2003).

These cultural belief systems contribute to several other barriers discussed in this chapter, including the gender pay gap, fathers' long working hours, and schools and family learning programmes being 'feminised environments'.

4.2 Work, lack of time, and the gender pay gap

In the UK, fathers are more likely than men without children to work (O'Brien, 2004), and much more likely than mothers to work full time (Equal Opportunities Commission (EOC), 2003). When fathers work, they tend to work long hours (the longest working hours in Europe for fathers, and often atypical hours (i.e. outside the 9-5 working day) (see Section 1.3). In their out-of-work time, fathers may be tired from work stress (see the case study of Dads on Computers), or have other commitments. Frieman and Berkeley (2002) note that "men of the twenty-first century who want to place their child first and their work second are facing the reality that working women have had to deal with for decades".

Lack of time and long or atypical working hours are major barriers to fathers' involvement in their children' out-of-school learning, especially during the week. For example, one re-

---

2   Cultural beliefs and attitudes vary according to region, social class, age, ethnicity and so on.

search study included fathers who had no time to get involved in their sons' reading (Lloyd, 1999).

In nationally representative research in England and Wales by the National Centre for Social Research, fathers working shifts, weekends and evenings spent less time with their children and partners than fathers working more typical hours (Joseph Rowntree Foundation, 2003; La Valle et al., 2002). About a third of mothers and almost half of fathers who worked atypical hours said that their job "limited the time they could spend reading with, playing with and helping their children with their homework", compared with about a tenth of mothers and a fifth of fathers who worked between 9am and 5pm. In the US, Heymann and Earle (2001) also conclude that evening work limits the support that parents can give to their children's cognitive and social development.

The picture is similar for the impact of long working hours. In one UK research study, fathers in dual-earner families who worked more than 50 hours a week were less involved in childcare than other fathers (Clarke and O'Brien, 2004). Short-term stresses in fathers' lives caused by daily hassles are statistically related to lower levels of fathers' involvement in their children's lives (Pleck and Masciadrelli, 2004).

Long working hours and lack of time are also barriers more specifically to fathers' involvement in their children's schools (Nord et al., 1997; Clough et al., 2004; West et al., 1998) and in family learning programmes (Millard and Hunter, 2001; the case study of Hampshire Teenage 'Lads and Dads' Book Clubs). The impact of these barriers is exacerbated by the daytime and weekday timing of school hours and many family learning sessions (see Section 4.8).

Some argue that the gap in average earnings between men and women (the 'gender pay gap') (Equal Opportunities Commission, 2003; O'Brien, 2004), along with the high cost of childcare (Hatter et al., 2002), are key reasons why many families pragmatically adopt the traditional role of the father as full-time breadwinner (often working long hours), with the mother working part time.

Others point the finger at workplace cultures of 'presenteeism' and long hours, which are increasing despite an emphasis on organisations having family-friendly policies (Hatter et al., 2002). Much of the initial impetus for family-friendly policy was to meet the needs of working mothers, but this is changing (O'Brien and Shemilt, 2003; Hatter et al., 2002). Chapter 1 outlined the new focus in work-life balance policy and debate on fathers, and also the regulations introduced by the Department for Trade and Industry (DTI) in 2003 on rights for employees who are mothers, fathers, guardians or foster parents, or their partners, to apply to their employer for flexible, part-time and home working arrangements when their children are under six years old, or under 18 years old if their children have disabilities.

However, fathers' take-up of new rights and employers' increased flexibility may be low. The market research company MORI conducted over 60 in-depth interviews with employed fathers, their partners and personnel managers in six organisations in 2002 (Hatter et al., 2002). They found that fathers had low use of family-friendly policies and formal practices provided by their employer, with many fathers using only informal arrangements with their managers. Likewise, the voluntary organisation Working Families report for the DTI recommended that:

> "there is a need for more awareness-raising and training for both parents and employers. Fathers, in particular, need help and support in pursuing their rights under the legislation." (Camp, 2004)

The Government will carry out a review of the flexible working law in 2006, and is currently monitoring take-up. According to the DTI, on 5 April 2004:

> *"only 1 in 10 fathers are asking for flexible working – compared with nearly four times as many mothers." (Hewitt, 2004)*

This could be for a number of reasons. Many fathers may not know that family-friendly policies exist or apply to them. Our society accepts much less than for mothers that fathers will take time off work when their children are sick,[3] or pick their children up from school. Fathers may therefore feel uncomfortable discussing their family commitments in the workplace, and managers may not be understanding of fathers' family commitments (Hatter et al., 2002).

It is also important to remember that workplaces dominated by men, especially in traditional craft industries and occupations, are much less likely than other employers to offer flexible working arrangements to employees (EOC, 2003). It will be hardest to extend work–life balance to fathers in manual work and employed in small businesses, and to self-employed fathers.

Long and atypical working hours are common amongst fathers in all social classes, income groups and family types. In fact, the study by the National Centre for Social Research found that it was fathers in professional and managerial jobs who worked the longest hours (Joseph Rowntree Foundation, 2003; La Valle et al., 2002). However, Heymann and Earle (2001) in the US predict that:

> *"a significant number of the occupations with non-standard hours will be filled by low-skilled workers including cashiers, clerks, truck drivers, waiters and waitresses, orderlies and attendants."*

La Valle et al. (2002) found that parents in professional occupations were likely to say that they chose their working arrangements "to suit their career aspirations and family needs". In contrast, parents (especially fathers) in lower socio-economic groups were likely to say that they had no choice about working unusual hours, and "that there was no scope to negotiate more flexible arrangements".

It is widespread in some black and minority ethnic communities for fathers to be working long, unpredictable and atypical hours. South Asian, African-Caribbean and African fathers in small-scale research studies said that too much work, too much stress and pressure, being tired after work, temporary work, atypical working hours, unemployment and lack of time were major barriers to their attendance at parents' evenings and other activities at their children's school and helping with their children's homework (Razwan, 2002), or to their parenting role more generally (Black Development Agency, 2002). In Razwan's research with fathers of Pakistani origin in Bradford in 2001, most of the fathers were working in low-paid jobs (41 per cent in the catering industry and 24 per cent as taxi drivers), and 26 per cent were unemployed or had long-term illness (also see National Statistics, 2002). Most of the employed fathers worked from early evening through the night and slept during the daytime. A minority of the fathers started work in the early afternoon and finished during the evening. Some black and minority ethnic fathers who are immigrants or refugees additionally face complicated legal issues around immigration and asylum (Black Development Agency, 2002).

---

3   This is despite legal rights in the UK for adults (including both mothers and fathers) to take time off work (paid or unpaid) for family emergencies such as sickness, accidents, and unexpected disruptions in childcare arrangements. See www.dti.gov.uk/er/timeoff.htm

Single-parent fathers may be especially challenged to combine work and family commitments. About a tenth of single-parent fathers in a Gingerbread survey said that balancing work, childcare and home had been their main concern on becoming a single parent, and about a fifth mentioned it as an ongoing issue (Gingerbread, 2001). Almost 60 per cent of the fathers said that they had been only or mainly the breadwinner before lone fatherhood. About 40 per cent said that they had combined the breadwinner role with some responsibility for childcare and housework.

But long working hours is not a barrier which cannot be breached, and neither is it the only barrier. According to Lamb and Tamis-Lemonda (2004), "men do not trade work time for family time in a one-to-one fashion". Warin et al. (1999) asked fathers, mothers and teenagers in north-west England for their views on the interaction of work, time and father involvement. Some respondents spoke about fathers' long working hours leading to less involvement and time with their children. Others said that work did make a difference to fathers' parenting, but that the negative effects "could be overcome with 'effort'". There was also a view expressed that it was not work that made a difference, but other factors such as the father's personality, the particular relationship between father and child, assumptions about paternal roles, or the mother's reluctance to involve the father. According to Bright et al. (2002), "even men with full-time paid work can find the time to donate work and hours to a school" when they see a good reason for it and when the school makes an effort to involve them.

4.3 Schools and family learning programmes as feminised environments

Primary schools and family learning venues are often 'feminised environments'.

- Most teachers[4] and other staff in primary schools, and most home–school link practitioners and family learning practitioners, are women, although this is changing slowly.[5]

- Most participants in family learning, and most parents regularly involved in schools, are women (see Section 2.3).

- School reception and administrative staff, usually the first point of contact for fathers, are almost exclusively female.

The feminisation of schools and family learning venues contributes to several other barriers discussed in this chapter. These include fathers' beliefs about their own education and involvement in their children's learning, and predominantly female teachers and family learning practitioners sometimes acting as gatekeepers to fathers' involvement. The feminisation of learning venues can also deter men from training as teachers and family learning practitioners, so creating a cycle of feminisation in settings. Additionally, it can feminise the nature of the activities and publicity in home–school and family learning programmes, so again deterring fathers from participating (see Section 4.8).

---

4   DfES statistics on the school workforce in England show that in January 2003 there were 32,749 male qualified teachers and 183,786 female qualified teachers (including part-time staff) in maintained primary schools (National Statistics, 2003). In maintained secondary schools, there were 90,326 male teachers and 121,380 female teachers (including part-time staff).

5   A *Guardian* news item reported a nearly 30 per cent rise in applications by men for teacher training courses from 2002 to 2003 (Smithers, 2003). Government measures to attract more men into primary schools had included adverts in the sports pages of national newspapers.

4.4 Funding issues

Short-term funding offering little sustainability, and funding from multiple sources, have been significant challenges for family learning programmes in the UK (NIACE, 2003; Ofsted, 2000; the case study of the Fathers and Children in Education Project). Many of the case study family learning programmes were partly or fully funded by time-limited funding streams, for example by central government programmes. Funding sources often changed over time, especially after a pilot programme.

Running programmes for fathers and their children is resource-intensive, especially in terms of recruitment of fathers (Section 4.8). Of course, short-term funding is associated with staff being on short-term contracts, and subsequently high staff turn-over. Expertise in engaging fathers may be rapidly lost in an organisation when a fathers' worker leaves for a new job.

At the joint DfES/NFPI seminar, some practitioners working with fathers said that the amount of funding reaching individual projects was often very small, and that these projects are not often funded with sustainability in mind. This can mean that the projects become marginalized in the school or family learning provider, with staff feeling that they are 'victims of tokenism'.

Good progress has already been made towards greater sustainability, for example new three-year funding allocations to LEAs by local LSCs (NIACE, 2003, 2004).

4.5 Fathers' beliefs and attitudes

This section reviews evidence on the beliefs and attitudes of fathers that could be associated with their relatively low involvement in their children's learning and education. Of course, fathers are not a homogenous group, and their beliefs and attitudes vary according to region, social class, age, ethnicity and so on. It is also worth remembering in this context that people's behaviour correlates far better with their specific intentions to carry out that behaviour than with more general beliefs and attitudes (Fishbein and Ajzen, 1980).

Beliefs about fathers' family role as 'a breadwinner'

Section 4.1 discussed cultural belief systems about fathers as economic providers and mothers as childcarers which persist within many families in the UK. In Britain, fathers tend to see providing an income for the family (the 'breadwinner' role) as their central role, whether or not they are working (Warin et al., 1999; Hatter et al., 2002; Clough et al., 2000; Working with Men, 2004). In an exploratory study with working fathers across Britain, most fathers were satisfied with their current level of involvement with their children, although a substantial minority wanted to spend more time with their children (Hatter et al., 2002).

The provider role can have an important psychological function for men (McGivney, 1999). Warin et al. (1999) write that many of the fathers in their research "had a strong 'investment' in their role as provider, which helped them to identify themselves as 'masculine'". This role was strongly associated with feelings of emotional attachment to their family. Being the economic provider gave these fathers a clear rationale for their work, "which might otherwise seem quite meaningless", as fathers were much more likely than mothers to say that they did not enjoy their job. Their families expected fathers to maximise their earnings even if this greatly reduced their caring role in the family, but the fathers themselves were in any case very reluctant to let go of their traditional role. Likewise, some fathers in London were regretful about recent changes in fathering roles, and "would have preferred a return to the status they felt their fathers had" (Working with Men, 2004).

Consumer cultures, and the resultant demands of children for material goods, can be a key reason for the predominance of fathers' breadwinner role and their long working hours (Warin et al., 1999; Millard and Hunter, 2001). Fathers may give money to their children as an important way of expressing love and affection. Peer pressure amongst males can be another important factor in maintaining breadwinner attitudes.

However, in addition to providing money, many fathers were expected by their partners and children to be 'involved in the family' (Warin et al., 1999; Hatter et al., 2002). Fathers viewed their other fathering roles as additions to, rather than replacements for, their economic provider role. They found it difficult to define what 'father involvement' meant; they mentioned availability at home, shared activities, quality time together, discipline, being a role model, and practical involvement, as well as just 'being there' (psychological availability). Some of these fathers spoke about the tension between their different roles – a 'double burden', as discussed in Section 3.4 – as work often got in the way of other types of family involvement.

Reluctance to seek help

Fathers' reluctance to seek help, support and advice, and to disclose to others information about personal issues, are barriers to their involvement in family services and parenting programmes, even when there are serious problems in their families (Lewis, 2000b; O'Brien, 2004; Working with Men, 2004). The great majority of adult users of family support and parenting education services are mothers (Henricson et al., 2001; Ghate et al., 2000). Amongst fathers in London, there was enthusiasm for services for fathers "but not for themselves!" (Working with Men, 2004). This reluctance amongst men to seek help and support tends to co-exist with a related fear of showing failure or weakness, including any "educational limitations and deficiencies" (McGivney, 1999).

Beliefs that formal learning, education and schools are 'women's work'

Men tend to have lower involvement than women in non-vocational adult learning and education, and there is also the gender achievement gap in schools (McGivney, 1999: a "growing anti-education culture" amongst boys – see Chapter 1). McGivney (1999) writes about a wide gulf between academic success and masculinity that starts in school, although she also reports studies showing that:

> "in some learning environments, masculinity is associated with academic achievement...with careers, male status and power."

Men were more likely than women in the 1997 National Adult Learning Survey to say that:

- they prefer to spend their free time doing things other than learning (42 per cent of men and 35 per cent of women)

- they had not enjoyed learning at school (19 per cent of men and 15 per cent of women)

although it should be noted that these differences between men and women are relatively small. Dean (1999), Millard and Hunter (2001) and Clough et al. (2000) present similar findings about men being likely to have had poor school experiences.

Many writers and researchers discuss an intergenerational cycle of boys and the adult men that they grow into perceiving formal learning, education and schools as 'women's work', i.e. an activity for females. These beliefs and attitudes begin when boys are in primary school, and they are well established by the time they leave secondary education (McGivney, 1999). Boys tend to find school "more restrictive, less congenial and less relevant" than do girls (McGivney, 1999), as school learning and assessment methods may suit girls more than boys, and teachers (often female) may be more responsive to girls. This is reinforced when parents do not encourage or value education, and especially in working-class areas of high male unemployment where many young boys and their fathers do not believe that they will ever have a job and therefore feel sceptical about the relevance of education (Macleod, 2000). In these areas, finding a job is given greater priority for boys than achieving at school.

Reinforcing the 'women's work' beliefs still further, boys' fathers are much less likely to be involved in their education than are their mothers. A minority of children with a non-resident father have little or no daily contact with their father (Blackwell and Dawe, 2004). Many boys, therefore, have few (if any) positive male role models with regard to learning, especially as schools tend to be feminised environments with few male teachers in primary schools. McGivney (1999) writes that:

> "there are few cultural role models to persuade boys of the value of learning. Male pop stars and sport stars are admired for many other factors other than intellect and qualifications."

Peer pressure for adolescent boys emphasises "conforming to a set of attitudes and behaviours that are considered appropriately masculine" (McGivney, 1999).

In adulthood, the negative attitudes of men about learning and education may be reinforced by peer pressure from other men. Peer group influences tend to be important for men (McGivney, 1999). This peer pressure exerts its influence to a greater extent for some population groups, for example in working-class areas (Macleod, 2000; the case study of Super Dads at Pen Pych Community Primary School) and in prisons. According to McGivney (1999), white male manual workers are the most difficult group to engage in organised adult education programmes. This is partly due to education being seen as "the province of young people and women, while work is seen as the rightful province of men".

This proposed intergenerational cycle of negative attitudes towards education amongst some boys and men therefore involves the low achievement of boys at school; the low involvement of adult men in non-vocational adult education; and the low involvement of fathers in their children's learning and education (McGivney, 1999; Clough et al., 2000; Macleod, 2000; Fletcher and Dally, 2002). Disillusioned boys become fathers who play little role in their own children's education (see the next section), which influences the next generation of boys, and so on.

Beliefs about supporting their children's education

Beliefs which are potential barriers

Mothers (60 per cent) were more likely than fathers (54 per cent) to say that a child's education is equally, or more, the responsibility of parents as the responsibility of schools, in a large-scale, nationally representative survey of parents of school-age children in England (Williams et al., 2002). This fits with all the data reported in Chapter 2 showing lower rates amongst fathers than mothers of all types of involvement in their children's learning, and in particular in their children's schools. One researcher found that fathers are often "coerced" by mothers into involvement in literacy activities with their children, but that they do not value this involvement in the same way that the mothers do (Macleod, 2000).

Building on the evidence presented in previous sections of this chapter that men tend to see formal learning and schools as 'women's work', and that primary schools and family learning venues are usually feminised settings, some fathers see:

- schools, and adult and community education including family learning programmes, as 'women's spaces'[6] (Macleod, 2000; Razwan, 2002; McGivney, 1999)

- supporting their children's learning (particularly their literacy and in school) as 'women's work' (Fletcher and Dally, 2002; Clough et al., 2000; Macleod, 2000; the case study of Super Dads at Pen Pych Community Primary School)

- parental involvement in their children's schools as 'an extension of domesticity' (MacLeod, 2000).

It can be argued that differences in how women and men interact create problems in communication between fathers and teachers in female-dominated educational settings (Turbiville et al., 2000). Fathers in one small-scale study in north-east England said that they found it more difficult than their female partners to speak to female teachers, and that they found it easiest to speak to male teachers, such as the head teacher (Clough et al., 2000).

According to Turbiville et al., some fathers who try to become involved in educational settings find that they are not as welcome as mothers. Many of the single-parent fathers responding to a survey by the voluntary organisation Gingerbread felt that they were "ignored or invisible" in society as a whole (also see Working with Men, 2004). In relation to their children's schools, some of the fathers said that they felt like "outsiders", and that they were excluded from school-based networks of local mothers, for example being ignored in the school playground (also see Lewis and Warin, 2001).

Of course, gender is only one potential issue dividing fathers and teachers. The cultures of home and schools can also be far apart because of social class, ethnicity or age differences between teachers and parents. Fathers are more involved in their children's learning and education when they have higher educational qualifications, are of higher socio-economic status, and are not manual workers (Section 2.4).

One father in Lloyd's research said that some fathers are content with the feminised status quo in primary schools as they are concerned "about being replaced by a male teacher at school" in their children's affections (Lloyd, 1999). Similarly, some fathers not volunteering in their children's school may feel threatened by the relationships between their children and other fathers who are volunteers (Bright et al., 2002).

Some South Asian fathers said that groups of mothers in the playground inhibited their involvement in school (Razwan, 2002). These fathers saw the mosque as their social space, and they wanted to leave the school and its playground as mothers' social space. They described the school playground "as one of the few places which women could access easily, in confidence and feel safe". These fathers were also uncertain about whether the schools' family learning programmes were women-only activities, as there are cultural and religious traditions in Islam on social separation of men and women.

---

6   Other services for children and families, for example family centres and parenting support groups, are also seen by fathers as 'women's spaces'. See O'Brien, 2004, and Ghate et al., 2000.

The negative experiences in school of some fathers during their childhood are, of course, likely to be a substantial barrier to their involvement in schools when their children are there years later (Karther, 2002). In fact, fathers may have attended the same schools as their own children now do, and may even have been taught by the same teachers (Clough et al., 2000; Herrick and Ali, 2003). Teaching and discipline styles have changed over past decades but, for example, if teachers were more authoritarian in the past, this is the perception of teachers that fathers may still hold. This can, of course, be a barrier for mothers as well (Brassett-Grundy, 2002), although men are more likely than women not to have enjoyed school.

Fathers in the US are likely to be more involved in their children's lives when they believe that men are competent with children (Pleck and Masciadrelli, 2004). There is also evidence that parents who believe that they can influence their children's development are more proactive and successful in helping their children than parents who doubt that they have any impact (Lynch, 2002). In the Skills for Life 2002-03 survey[7] of literacy, numeracy and ICT skills in England, adults with lower literacy and numeracy levels were less likely to help their children with their learning than adults with a higher level of basic skills, and they were less confident about their help when they gave it (DfES, 2003b).

As do mothers (DfES, 2003d), some fathers with literacy problems report in qualitative research studies that they think they have inadequate skills to effectively help their children learn (Fletcher and Dally, 2002; Karther, 2002; Lloyd, 1999).

Do fathers tend to have weaker beliefs than mothers about their ability to help their child learn? Certainly, there is a tendency for fathers to talk about mothers having better overall 'parenting skills' than they do, especially in communication with children, for example being more patient and empathetic (Warin et al., 1999; Hatter et al., 2002; Lloyd, 1999). Quite a few of the fathers in Warin et al.'s research said that they felt guilty that they were not better at talking with and listening to their children. Other fathers suggested that they were making efforts to improve communication. But this view is not predominant; half the fathers in one study felt that mothers and fathers are equally able in caring for children (Hatter et al., 2002).

In one very small-scale quantitative study[8] in a rural area of Canada with middle-class parents, fathers' beliefs that they could help improve their sons' reading achievement were weaker than mothers' beliefs (Lynch, 2002). Yet, in a large-scale, nationally representative survey of parents of school-age children in England, fathers were substantially more likely than mothers to say that they were always confident about helping with their children's homework, despite giving help less often than did mothers (Williams et al., 2002).

So, the evidence on this issue is mixed and may depend on the area of learning. On a working-class estate in Bristol, a majority of the interviewed fathers[9] who had liked school as children had enjoyed sports, but only very small minorities of these fathers had enjoyed

---

7   This was a large-scale, nationally representative sample of men and women aged 16-65. Practical assessments of adults' basic skills (literacy, numeracy and ICT) were conducted.

8   The sample consisted of 92 middle-class parents of white children aged eight and nine. The children had been involved in a pre-school family literacy project for about one year.

9   Thirty-six fathers who had children at a local primary school were interviewed. This was a 60 per cent response rate, and nearly all these responding fathers said they were involved with their children's learning and education. The area was characterised by "high levels of unemployment, poverty and low take-up of further education and training".

English, art or music (Bryant and Taylor, 1999). In fact, in England in 2002-03, men and women had similar levels of literacy, but men had higher numeracy and ICT skill levels than women, after controlling for their education and employment (DfES, 2003b). Mothers were slightly more likely than fathers in the 2002 National Adult Learning Survey to say that they wanted to learn about maths so they could help their child's learning (Fitzgerald et al., 2003).

Similarly, on a housing estate in Bristol where men had rarely accessed adult learning, most of the interviewed fathers felt they had skills to contribute to their children's school or to family learning (Bryant and Taylor, 1999). The skill areas mentioned by at least four out of the 36 interviewed men were building, sport, computers, DIY and gardening. This is consistent with data reported on in Section 2.3 showing fathers being especially likely to help their children with sport, maths, computers, and building and repairing activities.

Fathers may of course not be aware of the importance of their involvement in their children's learning and education (Flouri and Buchanan, 2001; De Nicola, 1997; Lloyd, 1999; Working with Men, 2004), nor that schools want to involve them (Working with Men, 2004). Some fathers living in south London and Bristol were not sure whether, in relation to reading with their child, it was the relationship with their son that mattered most, or the reading itself (Lloyd, 1999). Some fathers thought that activities other than reading were just as important or could just as easily build the desired close relationship. But some fathers did speak about their special role as a father (cf. mother), for example being a male role model for reading, and "reading different types of story".

It might be expected that unemployed fathers will have more time to get involved in their children's learning, but when a family literacy course in Britain in 1994 targeted men in an area of high male unemployment and greater female employment, men did not attend (Macleod, 2000). Of course, this was some years ago when government funding for family literacy programmes was at a lower level. In another, more recent English study, unemployed men found it difficult to adjust to a childcare role even though they had the time to do so (Warin et al., 1999).

So is there anything distinctive about the beliefs and attitudes of unemployed fathers in relation to their involvement in their children's education? As seen in an earlier section of this chapter, attitudes of seeing education as 'women's work' and of cynicism about the value of education are especially strong in working-class areas which have much greater than average levels of long-term unemployment:

- Long-term unemployed fathers are especially likely to reject any 'feminisation of their identity' associated with taking on what they see as women's caring work (Macleod, 2000) because their masculinity is already seriously threatened by their unemployment (also see McGivney, 1999). Family learning programmes which these men perceive to be "a threat to their manhood" are unlikely to be successful.

- Fathers who are not working and not able to be good financial 'providers' for their families can develop "feelings of frustration, sadness and failure" and a lack of confidence about their ability to be a good father in any respect (Warin et al., 2000).

- Unemployed fathers may be depressed and especially "cynical about the value of education and training in helping them find a job" (Macleod, 2000; also see McGivney, 1999).

Yet, it is important to note that, despite these attitudinal barriers, some of the case study programmes successfully engaged unemployed fathers by using appropriate practices.

Working with non-resident fathers in prisons can also be challenging because of the very strong emphasis in prisons on values of masculinity and toughness (Geraci, 2001). Geraci writes about a programme that she initiated in a maximum security prison for male prisoners with children. The programme 'Reading Out the Write Way' involved prisoners writing stories or other text, and making books (including computer design) to be sent to their children. As the author states:

> "making children's books is not exactly an image inmates want to emit to the rest of the inmate population."

In relation to fathers' involvement in their children's schools when there are problems of bullying, it is interesting to note the findings of an English research study[10] looking at resident parents' and children's attitudes towards bullying in school. Fathers, like mothers, expressed largely sympathetic attitudes towards children who were bullied, but mothers were slightly[11] more sympathetic than fathers to victims and to school/teacher intervention. The specific items with which fathers were more likely to agree were "It can be funny to see people being teased", "A small amount of bullying can be a good thing", "I admire people who can usually get their own way" and "Kids shouldn't run to the teacher every time somebody teases them". In two-parent families, there was a significant correlation between mothers' and fathers' attitudes, but not between parents' attitudes and children's attitudes.

Beliefs which are potential facilitators

Despite the evidence just presented about some fathers' beliefs and attitudes acting as barriers to their involvement in children's education, there is also some more positive evidence. Some fathers do see it as their responsibility to get involved. For example, the majority of fathers in a small-scale study in north-east England disagreed that most fathers tend not to be interested in their children's education and do not see it as their role (Clough et al., 2000). Similarly, fathers living in south London and Bristol said that ensuring their sons could read was a responsibility that they shared with mothers and with schools (Lloyd, 1999). They wanted to have books in their home and to be seen reading by their children.

The case studies of schools and family learning programmes which successfully involve fathers, and their evaluation reports (in particular: Dads on Computers; Fathers and Children in Education Project; It's A Man Thing!), as well as several qualitative research studies, show that some fathers will get involved when they see very good reasons for it, even when there are many barriers facing them (Lloyd, 1999; Millard and Hunter, 2001; Bright et al., 2002; Ortiz, 2001; Karther, 2002; Stile and Ortiz, 1999; Bruneau, 2002).

The three most common reasons found in the research literature and the case studies (see Box 7) for fathers' initial involvement in their children's learning (and more specifically in schools and family learning programmes) are all 'child-centred reasons' as opposed to 'adult-centred reasons'. First children encourage their fathers to get involved. Second, fathers want to build better relationships with their children through shared activities. Third, fathers want to support their children's learning and school achievement. In Ortiz's qualitative

---

10 This survey asked 432 mothers and 227 fathers to complete a 'Parental Attitudes to Bullying Scale' which provides "an overall measure of 'sympathy' based on three subscales that also address specific attitudes towards victims, bullies and intervention"; 1,200 questionnaires were issued via children to the parents of children at four primary schools in Sheffield.

11 This difference was statistically significant.

study with fathers in California, children engaged their fathers in their reading through the children's curiosity about 'environmental print', for example when they were out together shopping, driving or in restaurants, and about newspapers and books that fathers read in their children's presence at home (Ortiz, 2001).

Of course, some of these reasons are also given by mothers for their involvement in family learning programmes (Brassett-Grundy, 2002). Yet it does appear from all the evidence reviewed that fathers are less likely than mothers to say that they get involved in family learning programmes because they wish to learn new skills for their own benefit, or to gain accreditation, or for social reasons (to meet other adults for friendship). This suggested gender difference in reasons for involvement would need to be substantiated using large-scale survey data.

Turning now to the educational expectations of fathers, there is some rather dated quantitative research evidence from the UK and US showing that fathers are similar to mothers with regard to their interest in and expectations for their children's education, which is presented below. Chapter 2 included the comment from one researcher in the UK that "schools should not confuse a lack of participation in school-run events/ activities with a lack of interest" (Millard and Hunter, 2001). Research was also reported showing that considerable proportions of resident fathers do frequently praise or reward their children for good schoolwork, talk with their children about school issues, and attend parents evenings at their children's schools.

Table 22 shows that, as reported by teachers[12] in the UK in the 1960s, fathers' were as likely as mothers to be "very interested" in, or even "over concerned" about, their children's education (Flouri and Buchanan, 2003b). Similarly, Trusty and Pirtle (1998) found that fathers'[13] and mothers' expectations for the level of education that their teenage children would achieve, as perceived by the adolescents, rarely differed (analysing data from the large-scale and nationally representative 1988 US National Education Longitudinal Study[14]). Over 93 per cent of adolescents perceived that their parents either had the same expectations or that their expectations differed by no more than one level. Where there was a discrepancy between fathers' and mothers' expectations, fathers were slightly more likely to have lower expectations than mothers.

In a much smaller-scale study of the parents of a diverse sample of 244 ninth grade (adolescent) children in the south-east and midwest of the US, mothers and fathers again held very similar values towards their children's achievement at school, although mothers were more interested in schoolwork and were more involved in school events (Paulson and Sputa, 1996).

In a survey in 1998 of about 1,350 teenage boys across Britain, 35 per cent of boys with low self-esteem and 79 per cent of boys with high self-esteem said that their father showed an interest in their schoolwork (Katz, 2003). Katz does not report figures for mothers' interest so we cannot make any comparison here.

---

12 Parents' level of interest in their children's education was assessed by teachers, so there may be some bias.

13 Of these adolescents, 82 per cent lived with their mothers and 62 per cent lived with their fathers.

14 This survey had a national sample of over 7,000 adolescents. Adolescents were asked in 1992 about their perceptions of their parents' expectations about what educational level (e.g. high school/ college/ masters degree) the adolescents would achieve.

Table 22: Percentage of fathers and mothers in 'intact families' perceived by teachers to be "very interested" or "over-concerned" in their children's education

	per cent of fathers	per cent of mothers
Children aged 7	44 per cent	44 per cent
Children aged 11	44 per cent	48 per cent
Children aged 16	47 per cent	48 per cent

Source: UK National Child Development Study as reported by Flouri and Buchanan (2003b). Large-scale, broadly[15] nationally representative sample of parents of 7-year-olds (in 1965), 11-year-olds (in 1969) and 16-year-olds (in 1974) in England, Scotland and Wales.

What about the relationship of fathers' educational expectations for their children with children's gender? Carter and Wojtkiewicz (2000) found that US parents in 1988 had higher educational expectations[16] for their daughters than for their sons, using the 1988 National Education Longitudinal Study (NELS). Trusty and Pirtle (1998) found, again using the 1988 NELS, that this was true specifically of fathers in the US in 1992, and also that fathers' expectations[17] for sons were generally lower than mothers' expectations for sons in families with low or middle socio-economic status (SES). These researchers suggest that "low SES fathers may tend to value work more than academics for their sons". Of course, this data may now be rather out of date.

In a large-scale, nationally representative research study[18] in Finland in 1997, parents were asked to estimate their child's school success (relative to other children in different subjects), abilities and attitudes towards school, using self-completion questionnaires (Raty et al., 1999). In their assessment of their child's problem-solving ability, both mothers and fathers attributed these skills more to girls than to boys; and fathers emphasised these skills less than mothers did. There were no differences between fathers and mothers in their assessment of their child's determination/ positive school orientation, nor in their assessment of their child's practical creativity.

Large-scale research is needed in the UK which collects data directly from fathers about their interest in and aspirations for their children's education.

---

15 Fluori and Buchanan (2003b) note that the long-term National Child Development Study may under-represent disadvantaged parents because of differential drop-out.

16 Adolescents' perceptions of their fathers' educational expectations and their mothers' educational expectations were combined into a composite 'parental expectations' variable (equal weight to each).

17 As perceived by their adolescent children.

18 Raty et al. (1999) carried out research in Finland with a nationwide sample of 938 parents with a child aged 9-10 or 12-13 years. The response rates were 51 per cent for the fathers, and 66 per cent for the mothers.

Box 7: Reasons[19] commonly given by fathers for their involvement in their children's learning, and in schools and family learning programmes

- As a response to their children's interest, curiosity and encouragement
  - children asking their fathers to get involved
  - invitations from children to their fathers inviting them into their school or family learning programmes (see Chapter 5 on good practice)

- To build stronger relationships ('bonding') with their children through shared activities

- To help their children's learning and educational achievement (even where their school experience was poor and/or they are not themselves involved in learning, reading, etc.)
  - because they have high expectations for their children's educational success
  - because they want their children to do better than they did
  - because they believe that helping their children to learn and do well in school is important for their children's lifetime outcomes, e.g. employment
  - (involvement in schools and family learning programmes) to learn new skills to help their children's learning
  - (involvement in schools and family learning programmes) to learn more about their children's schools and modern education
  - (involvement in schools and family learning programmes) to help their children's behaviour problems at school or poor educational progress

- To give more help to their children than their parents had given them/to be 'a better father' than their own father was

- Because of peer pressure/ encouragement
  - (involvement in schools and family learning programmes) other fathers in their community are involved and invite them along
  - (involvement in family learning programmes) the programme becomes well known in the community, and is perceived as 'the thing to do'

- Because their female partner encourages them to get involved

Single-parent fathers and non-resident fathers may have additional reasons for wanting to get involved in their children's schools. Gingerbread (2001), a national voluntary organisation for single parents in Britain, carried out a survey[20] amongst its members who were 'lone fathers'. Bereavement is a relatively common reason for a father being a single parent, and these fathers spoke about schools needing to give support to their children for emotional

---

19 These are the most common reasons for fathers' *initial* involvement in their children's learning and education. Once fathers get involved, they perceive a variety of benefits (see Section 3.4) which can sustain their involvement.

20 Gingerbread received responses from 111 fathers, which was a response rate of just under 50 per cent. Gingerbread's members may not be representative of all lone fathers in Britain.

and behavioural problems associated with their mother's death or absence from the home. Yet only a very small minority of the lone fathers said that their children's education was a worry on becoming a lone father. It is not known how representative these single-parent fathers (who were members of Gingerbread) are of single-parent fathers generally.

One research study was found that investigated the beliefs and attitudes of non-resident fathers concerning involvement in their children's schools. Baker and McMurray (1998) interviewed a small sample of Australian non-resident fathers who had replied to the researchers' advertisement in a regional newspaper for volunteer participants. The interviewed fathers were from "a range of socio-economic backgrounds", and they were not currently involved in family court proceedings. Most of the fathers interviewed were not currently involved in their children's schools, and most of them had poor relationships with their children's mothers.

All these non-resident fathers said that they strongly wanted to be involved in their children's schools, and that they believed they had a responsibility to be involved. These fathers reported that losing involvement in this and other aspects of their children's lives caused them much pain, anger and frustration, and a sense of much loss and hopelessness.

The fathers in Baker and McMurray's research may not be representative of non-resident fathers more widely because of the way in which the volunteer sample was selected. This small group of non-resident fathers may have had more negative experiences of their children's schools than non-resident fathers in general. Baker and McMurray recommend that further research at a national level is needed.

Furthermore (according to this research paper) at the time of the research, Australian Education Department practice "was for schools to contact the resident parent for instructions whenever they were uncertain of a contact issue"; and Baker and McMurray report that in most Australian schools at that time, non-resident parents were not included in school-based activities unless they had been invited by the children's resident parents, usually their mothers.

These non-resident fathers' perceptions of the barriers facing them in their involvement in their children's schools are reported in later sections of this chapter.

Amato and Sobolewski (2004), writing about non-resident fathers' overall involvement in their children's lives, discuss "divorce-activated fathers" and "divorce-deactivated fathers" (citing Hetherington and Kelly, 2002). The former group may get more involved following divorce because "they fear losing their children's affection". The latter group may get less involved because they find seeing their children infrequently too painful, or because they become preoccupied with their new lives, as well as because of mothers and schools acting as gatekeepers.

Findings are now reported from the small-scale research studies of black and minority ethnic fathers which were outlined in Section 2.5. Fathers[21] from South Asian and African-Caribbean minority ethnic groups who were involved in different ways in their children's learning and education expressed the following reasons for getting involved:

- they had high aspirations for their children's educational success (Bruneau, 2002; Razwan, 2002; Herrick and Ali, 2003)

- they wanted their children to do better than they had done educationally (Lloyd, 1999; Herrick and Ali, 2003; Razwan, 2002).

---

21 The British small-scale research studies that we refer to here are detailed in Section 2.6 of this report. The fathers interviewed may not be representative of all fathers in that minority ethnic group.

They believed that helping their children to learn and do well in school was important for their children's lifetime opportunities and outcomes, for example for employment and security (Bruneau, 2002; Razwan, 2002; Herrick and Ali, 2003). Adults from black and minority ethnic groups often face discrimination at work, and they often live in working-class areas with relatively high levels of unemployment. For example, Bruneau writes about involved African-Caribbean fathers feeling that black people need to be seen to achieve academically because of racism.

When they were the British-born children of immigrants, they wanted to give more educational help and quality time to their children than their fathers had been able to give them (Bruneau, 2002; Herrick and Ali, 2003; Working with Men, 2004). They wanted to be better role models than their fathers could be. Their fathers had had similarly high aspirations for their educational success, but they had not had the skills, English language, knowledge of the British educational system, or time necessary for engaging in their children's education or schools. Sometimes their elder siblings had taken on this parenting role. African-Caribbean fathers interviewed by Lloyd (1999) did speak about their own fathers helping their reading when they were children.

Racism was an issue commonly discussed by fathers of different black and minority ethnic groups in relation to their children's education. Involved African-Caribbean fathers said that they could not rely on schools to teach their children to read because of racism by some teachers, and therefore it had to be their responsibility as parents (Lloyd, 1999). Involved Muslim South Asian fathers born in Britain said that they had themselves experienced racism, bullying and other difficulties in English secondary schools, but not in the local primary school which their children now attended (Herrick and Ali, 2003).

Another commonly discussed issue in relation to their involvement was the importance of imparting religious and cultural values to their children. Involved African- Caribbean fathers said that they were concerned that, when they were not resident with their children, and the children were living with a non-African-Caribbean mother, these children needed to have contact with "and understand their Caribbean roots", and in particular the values of family, education, discipline, Christianity and morality. Similarly, involved Muslim South Asian fathers born in Britain said that they appreciated the modernised madrasah (Muslim religion school) and its important role in children's lives in providing a religious education, moral values and sense of discipline. In the Black Development Agency's research (Black Development Agency, 2002), Asian fathers said they wanted religious activities, social and cultural gatherings and family values seminars to engage in with their children.

Concerns amongst South Asian Muslim fathers regarding their children's education were about teachers not understanding South Asian Muslim values and traditions; a lack of positive male role models in schools; bullying and a lack of discipline in schools; frequent changes of teachers; and a lack of information for parents about school governance and other school issues (Razwan, 2002; Black Development Agency, 2002; Herrick and Ali, 2003). Some of the South Asian Muslim fathers also mentioned the 'generation gap' in values between themselves and their children. When asked about the preferred gender of their children's teachers, some fathers mentioned they wanted males who could influence their sons.

The research reported so far has focused on the beliefs and concerns of relatively involved black and minority ethnic fathers. African fathers, mainly Somali Muslims in Bristol who had much lower involvement in their children's lives, said that they felt uncomfortable about this (Black Development Agency, 2002). These fathers were also demoralised by the lack of appropriate support services for their children and wives.

4.6 Potential 'gatekeepers' to fathers' involvement: mothers, children and practitioners

Mothers, children, teachers, other school staff and family learning practitioners could potentially be barriers to or facilitators of fathers' involvement in their children's learning and education, depending on their beliefs, attitudes and motivations. For example, as reported in Section 2.4, fathers are more involved in their children's learning and education when:

- there is a good relationship between the children's resident parents

- children's mothers are involved in the children's learning and education

- children's mothers have higher educational qualifications.

Australian research by Bright et al. (2002) looked at the experiences of fathers and other men who acted as volunteers in primary schools. Fathers mentioned the following "special challenges that men face for being men":

- mixed responses from parents and from teachers; some were positive and welcomed their help, but others not so

- *"being a man and therefore having to be cautious where and how you interact with children...a suspicion, distrust and regulation of men's behaviour within educational institutions...all men carry the burden for a few... other parents worrying if their kids are safe with you... the mothers and teachers questioning your presence in the school"*

- people's stereotypes of male behaviour ("expectations about what men do").

Mothers

According to Macleod (2000), many women "unconsciously operate within the norm of male un-involvement". This means that mothers often see the limited involvement of fathers in their children's learning and education as unproblematic. It is something which they are so used to that they take it for granted as a "natural division of labour", and they do not question it.

However, a high proportion of mothers do believe that the involvement of fathers is important. For example, in a small-scale study in north-east England, 83 per cent of mothers interviewed disagreed that "mothers are more important than fathers in the care and upbringing of the child", compared with about two-thirds of fathers and of school staff (Clough et al., 2000). In another research study, mothers said that they saw sport as an important way to involve fathers in schools, for example integrating learning quizzes into half-time during school football matches (Millard and Hunter, 2001).

Mothers can, however, be 'ambivalent' to fathers' involvement in their children's lives (Pleck and Masciadrelli,[22] 2004), and to their school involvement specifically (Clough et al., 2000). This means that they have mixed feelings about this issue. Some mothers may believe, in principle, that substantial fathers' involvement is important for their children, but find it

---

22 It should be noted that Pleck and Masciadrelli, reviewing statistical literature, conclude that "although there is some evidence for maternal gatekeeping, it is not robust", since there are mixed findings on statistical associations between mothers' attitudes and the level of fathers' involvement.

a struggle to accept this emotionally or in practice. Some mothers, therefore, hold on to their traditional role in the home and in childcare (Warin et al., 1999; O'Brien, 2004), just as some fathers hold on to their provider role (see Section 4.5). These mothers may want fathers to be more involved in family life, but on "their own terms" (Warin et al., 1999), retaining control and overall "process responsibility" (Lamb et al.'s model of father involvement in Section 2.1).

For example, in Warin et al.'s research in north-west England, some mothers reported that they kept control over the relationship between their male partner and the children by referring the teenager to the father in specific circumstances. Mothers were reluctant to give up their role as the main listener in the family, and they did not like being excluded from father–teenager conversations. More specifically related to children's education, some fathers felt excluded by their partners from involvement in their children's life at school (Millard and Hunter, 2001). In the research in north-east England, one mother said that she would be very wary of some fathers if she was a teacher (Clough et al., 2000). NIACE (2003) report that mothers on family learning programmes saw the group "as a safe place for women to be".

Section 3.4 showed that there are conflicting arguments in the literature about whether greater father involvement is good for mothers, and little robust research evidence on this.

Mothers may be most likely to act as gatekeepers when they are not resident with their children's fathers and have a poor-quality relationship with him (Amato and Sobolewski, 2004), although poor-quality relationship between married parents is also associated with low levels of fathers' involvement. Baker and Murray (1998) found that, according to the small sample of Australian non-resident fathers they interviewed, mothers were the "single most important" barrier to school involvement. In family literacy programmes in prisons, some mothers return story tapes made by fathers to the prison or refuse permission for them to be sent to the child (see 'The Big Book Share', one of the case study programmes). It is important to remember, though, that many mothers want their former partners to be involved substantially in their children's lives (Amato and Sobolewski, 2004).

Children

It is important to consider children's perspective on fathers' involvement, and to look at whether children can be barriers and/or facilitators of fathers' involvement in their lives. Article 12 of the United Nations Convention on the Rights of the Child affirms that children's voices should be heard and taken into account in issues which concern them. There has certainly been a new emphasis in UK government initiatives and in research to consult children and young people, and to take their views into account when making decisions. The Government has recently made plans to appoint a Children's Commissioner.

One UK research study[23] shows that some children, especially as they get older, actively try to prevent their parents' involvement in their education, for example rejecting help offered with homework, not passing on school communications, and discouraging their parents from coming into their school (Allared and David, 2002). Children may want to be independent (especially middle-class children); want to keep home and school separate (especially boys and working-class children); accept that barriers such as long working hours, lack of English

---

23 This research comprised discussions and interviews with about 70 children from diverse social backgrounds, aged 9 and 14 at primary and secondary schools in inner-city London, a London suburb, and Brighton.

or lack of interest prevent their parents' involvement; or not want their school to judge their home life.

When it comes to shared out-of-school learning activities between fathers and children (e.g. family outings), teenagers are often unavailable and desire independence from their parents, wanting to be either alone in their bedroom or out with their friends (Larson et al., 1997; O'Brien and Jones, 1995, 1996).

In a qualitative research study in north-west England, one father spoke about the mother being the parent at home when their teenage child came home from school, so the teenager had already discussed school with the mother and didn't want to go through it again with the father when he returned home from work later in the evening.

There has been little research looking at children's and young people's views on fatherhood roles (see Milligan and Dowie, 1998 for a review). In some of the research that has been conducted, children tended to have relatively traditional views on their fathers' and mothers' roles. For example, just as their fathers and mothers did, some teenagers in north-west England saw providing a family income as the central role for fathers (Warin et al., 1999). Likewise, most teenagers in research in a working-class area of East London[24] thought that, for fathers, earning money was "the most important activity, followed by giving care and love and being involved in domestic duties", although 70 per cent of these young people agreed with the statement that "children need a father to be as closely involved in their upbringing as the mother" (O'Brien and Jones, 1996).

In the midwest of the US, Milkie et al. (1997) carried out a quantitative and qualitative content analysis of over 3,000 essays written by mainly white children aged 6-12 years. The analysis found clear differences in what children said about their mother or father when they were asked why their parent was "the best". Interestingly, although the children mentioned paid work more often in relation to fathers than to mothers, paid work was mentioned much less frequently for fathers than were cooking, play and sports activities.

These US primary school children were also more likely to value their fathers than their mothers in recreational terms (e.g. plays, ride bikes, movies/TV, sports), and in terms of time spent together in activities. They were more likely to value their mothers in instrumental terms (e.g. paid work, cleans, cooks, provides transport, helps) and emotional terms (e.g. listens, talks, understands). There was no significant difference between the frequency with which the children used educational terms (e.g. help with homework, reads, helps with computer) to describe mothers and to describe fathers, although children were more likely to refer specifically to "helping with homework" when writing about mothers than fathers.

Milkie et al. conclude that children do not see their fathers' paid work as especially salient. Perhaps they take it for granted in the same way that mothers "unconsciously operate within the norm of male un-involvement" (Macleod, 2000).

However, in contrast to these three studies, in Milligan and Dowie's research[25] (Milligan and Dowie, 1998; Milligan and Smith, 1999) with groups of 67 children (aged 4-17) in Edinburgh about their fathers and mothers, children rarely discussed their mother and father having different roles according to their gender, nor sons and daughters having different needs

---

24 Using data from a survey of about 600 children, aged on average 14 years, from six state schools in "a predominantly working-class urban East London locality".

25 Using drawings and photos of their fathers, and games about their fathers, as stimuli for discussion.

for support from their parents. What these children said they needed could be provided by either of their parents. The most frequent themes were fathers acting as a role model (e.g. active at home, leisure, having fun, employment, respect and trust, setting boundaries, appearance, money); children needing quality time with their fathers (activities, friendship and conversation); and children needing supportive behaviour from their fathers (taking an interest in their lives, protection and security, life essentials and treats). Children mentioned their fathers "paying attention to notes from school and giving help with schoolwork", their fathers asking about school and being picked up from school, as well as their fathers playing games, watching TV and joining in with sports and hobbies. Less frequently mentioned were children needing love from their fathers and children needing physical contact from their fathers. This research did not explicitly ask the children what was the most important role for their fathers.

So there is mixed research evidence on whether children's views on fatherhood are a potential barrier or facilitator to fathers' involvement.

Teachers, other school staff, and family learning practitioners

Teachers in schools are primarily trained to work with children rather than adults. The induction standards for newly qualified teachers in England do include "liaise effectively with parents or carers on pupils' progress and achievements", but references are not made specifically to either mothers or fathers (TTA, 2003c). Ofsted (2000) found "a lack of understanding on how to deal with adult students, particularly those with negative memories of their own schooling" amongst teachers involved in family learning programmes in schools.

As noted in Chapter 1, National Occupational Standards are now being developed for family learning practitioners and a national Family Learning, Language and Numeracy (FLLN) Professional Development Programme has been introduced for teachers of children and of adults. FLLN practitioners have to attain qualifications in a Skills for Life Teaching Qualifications Framework.

Teachers tend to be supportive of the key principles of parental involvement in children's education. The Association of Teachers and Lecturers and the Institute for Public Policy Research (IPPR) jointly carried out a postal survey[26] in 2000 of 2,000 teachers who were members of ATL (a teaching union). Nearly 90 per cent of these respondents agreed that "unless parental support for learning increases, the Government's ambitions to raise standards in education will not be met"; and nearly 75 per cent agreed that "the legal obligations of parents towards their child's education should extend beyond responsibility for attendance". However, when it came to specific types of involvement, teachers in this survey were much less likely to be positive. About a quarter agreed that "schools are required to give too much information to parents", with almost 45 per cent disagreeing and about a third being neutral. Nearly three-quarters of these teachers disagreed that "parents should have a greater say in the way schools are run".

Teachers and family learning practitioners' attitudes specifically towards men and fathers may affect their behaviour towards fathers and limit their efforts to involve them in children's learning and education. It has already been noted that teachers in primary schools and family learning practitioners tend to be women, and that fathers tend to perceive schools and family learning venues as 'women's spaces'. Only limited research evidence has been

---

26 The response rate was 47 per cent, with an even split between primary school and secondary school teachers.

found on teachers' and other school staff's beliefs and attitudes regarding fathers and their involvement; this is reported below. No literature was found on the attitudes of family learning practitioners towards fathers.

Although the majority of teachers and other school staff[27] (predominantly female) interviewed in north-east England disagreed that "most fathers tend not to be interested in the child's education and do not see it as their role", some expressed views that fathers in their area saw childcare and school involvement as the "the mum's job" (Clough et al., 2000). These teachers expected the fathers to have very little involvement in their school. They said that fathers "don't seem interested, or they have excuses", for example they don't come along because of their work commitments. About a quarter of these teachers also said that they interacted more with mothers at parents evenings, felt more comfortable talking to mothers, and had more in common with other women than with men.

These beliefs amongst teachers about the likelihood of fathers' involvement could, of course, become a self-fulfilling prophecy. And of course teachers' stereotypes are not confined to gender. Clough et al. (2000), citing Dean (1999), write that some teachers assume that working-class parents are not particularly interested in their children's education, especially if these parents do not come into the school very often.

What about teachers' beliefs about the importance of fathers' involvement? The majority of the mainly female school staff in Clough et al.'s research disagreed that "it is more important for teachers to engage and connect with the child's mother than the father". But there was a range of views. Some believed that mothers and fathers were of equal importance in children's care and education. Others saw the mother as more important but the father still of significance. Working with Men (2004) found that many workers in family and children's services are reluctant to engage fathers for fathers' own needs, being much more motivated by benefits for children.

Teachers, like other practitioners in services for children and families (Working with Men, 2004; O'Brien, 2004; Ghate et al., 2000), may have substantial ambivalence and fears about involving fathers in schools. Some teachers in feminised schools may be content to maintain a women-only environment (Clough et al., 2000). Macleod (2000) argues that teaching and motherhood are sometimes equated in professional writings: "Mothers and teachers are expected to be both nurturers and educators." She sees the school as an extension of family structure, with female teachers being 'mum', but a male as headteacher playing the role of 'dad' in the position of authority and power. In fact, Clough et al. (2000) speculate that involving fathers and other male role models in a school might be a threat to a male headteacher's authority.

Some teachers fear possible aggression and child abuse from fathers (Clough et al., 2000; Bright et al., 2002), or alienating and upsetting mothers, especially when involving non-resident fathers, when teachers' fears may extend to child abduction (Baker and McMurray, 1998). In the case study of Dads on Computers, schools' worries about men working with children were a barrier to these fathers' subsequent volunteering in the classroom.

In Baker and McMurray's small-scale research in Australia, a few of the interviewed fathers said that their involvement in their children's school was refused by the headteacher acting on the mother's wishes, even in cases where the father had a court order "stipulating that they were to have school involvement". School administrative staff could also be a barrier as non-resident fathers needed to negotiate with them to gain access to their child and to their child's teachers.

---

27 Six reception teachers, six headteachers, six classroom assistants and six school secretaries (one in each of six primary schools in three urban LEAs) were interviewed at their schools.

It must be remembered that some teachers, other school staff and mothers may have been the victims of domestic violence, child abuse or crime perpetrated by males, and also that "in some cases, of course, involving fathers may not be in the child's best interest" (Flouri and Buchanan, 2001). According to Turbiville et al. (2000), one of the reasons why fathers are "not welcome" in educational settings is an issue of power between men and women. Turbiville et al. argue that men have historically been seen as more powerful than women, and that:

> "some women, particularly those who are single parents or have
> experienced abusive relationships, feel anger over the physical
> presence of the fathers or resentment of the power that these men
> had in their lives."

Teachers can also be concerned about upsetting or embarrassing children who are not resident with or even in contact with their father (Lloyd, 1999; Working with Men, 2004), although the children themselves in Lloyd's work in south London "appeared to be very informed and matter-of-fact about each other's lives".

Gingerbread's survey of single-parent fathers did not report specifically on these fathers' perceptions of their relationship with their children's teachers. It is relevant though that 61 per cent of the responding fathers felt that society in general had a negative attitude towards them, compared with 14 per cent who felt they were viewed positively. Some of these fathers specifically mentioned that awareness of possible child abuse meant they were viewed with suspicion, especially when they had daughters, and that they were sometimes perceived as inadequate carers of children (also see Working with Men, 2004).

Box 8: Beliefs, attitudes and behaviours amongst potential gatekeepers to fathers' involvement

Mothers

- Some mothers see the limited involvement of fathers in children's education as expected and unproblematic. Other mothers value fathers' involvement and actively facilitate it.

- Mothers may want fathers to be more involved in family life, but on 'their own terms', so retaining control. Mothers may be most likely to act as a gatekeeper when they are not resident with their child's father.

Teachers

- Teachers may expect fathers to have very little involvement in their school and feel more comfortable talking to mothers.

- Some teachers fear possible aggression and child abuse from fathers, or alienating and upsetting mothers, especially when involving non-resident fathers.

Children

- Some children take active steps to prevent their parents' involvement in their education as they want to keep home and school separate.

- Teenagers may want minimal parental involvement.

- There are mixed views amongst children and teenagers on fatherhood roles.

4.7 Fathers' circumstances

Section 2.4 presented statistical findings showing the characteristics of fathers which correlate with higher and lower levels of involvement in their children's learning and education. These characteristics relate to some barriers as a result of fathers' individual circumstances, which are presented in Box 9. Of course, the practices of societal institutions, schools and family learning programmes, as well as cultural attitudes, can deepen or lessen the impact of some of these barriers.

> ### Box 9: Fathers' current circumstances as potential barriers
>
> - Non-resident fathers: Frequency of contact with child, and geographic distance from child
> - Many children in the family
> - Cost of involvement including travel
> - Low levels of education and literacy
> - Limited English language skills
> - Poor health or disability

Some of these barriers are especially common in particular population groups of fathers.

Working-class fathers and black and minority ethnic fathers often face unemployment, low income and poor living conditions which can be barriers to their parenting role (Black Development Agency, 2002; National Statistics, 2002). Some of these fathers may also have limited education and literacy. Amongst some black and minority ethnic fathers, limited English language skills and large families can also restrict their involvement in their children's learning and education (e.g. Razwan, 2002; Black Development Agency, 2002; the case study of Share for Dads).

Most of the South Asian fathers in Razwan's research (most of whom were born in Pakistan or Bangladesh) said they could read and write well in their first language, but some did not have literacy in their first language. About half of these fathers were able to speak, read and write fluently in English and had attended school in Britain. Some did not have time to learn English because of their long working hours. A large minority of the fathers mentioned their lack of English as an obstacle to helping their children with homework. Some wanted a homework club set up at their children's school where their children could be helped by someone who had good English.

Nevertheless, it is important to remember that language issues can also be a facilitator for black and minority ethnic fathers' involvement. In one research study, South Asian fathers (mainly born in the UK) were sometimes married to women from India who spoke little English and did not know much about education in England (Herrick and Ali, 2003). Therefore, some of these fathers took the lead in the family on communicating with their children's school.

Fathers in prisons are a population group much more likely than average to have literacy problems, which can be a barrier to their involvement in prison family learning programmes (Geraci, 2001; the case study of The Big Book Share). McGivney (1999) reports that 45 per cent of prisoners in 1991 had left school before the age of 16, and that half of the prison population had literacy problems. Over 40 per cent of young offenders had been excluded from school, and 20 per cent had a statement of special educational needs.

Unemployed fathers' lack of involvement in their children's lives may be due to the same reason that they are unemployed, for example ill-health; or, alternatively, for some fathers unemployment can cause depression (see the discussion on unemployed fathers' beliefs in Section 4.5). Some non-resident fathers and single-parent fathers may have mental ill-health associated with separation, divorce and bereavement. In the 1998 General Household Survey, 14 per cent of single-parent fathers became single parents as a result of their partner's death (Gingerbread, 2001).

Some non-resident fathers are substantially restricted in their involvement in their children's learning and education (and in their children's lives more generally) by infrequent contact. In a recent UK survey of non-resident parents, about 15 per cent of non-resident parents said that they never saw their children, but 28 per cent of resident parents said that the non-resident parent never saw their child (Office for National Statistics, 2003). About a quarter of non-resident parents said that they saw their children less than at least once a month. There may be large geographic distances between non-resident fathers and their children (Amato and Sobolewski, 2004), which have both financial and time implications for their involvement, and especially prevent participation in school and family learning events held on weekdays.

Non-residency with their children can be common for fathers in some black and minority ethnic groups (see Section 2.5). A small group of African-Caribbean non-resident fathers in Bristol mentioned not enough contact time with their children as a barrier to their overall parenting role (Black Development Agency, 2002). In the same research, a small group of Somali fathers said that refugee-related legal issues prevented their wives and children from joining them in the UK, and that unstable family systems were one barrier to their parenting role.

4.8 Policy and practice in individual schools and family learning programmes

Lamb and Tamis-Lemonda (2004) writes that:

> "institutions such as childcare and educational institutions have traditionally made little effort to involve fathers and have often acted in ways that exclude them or include them only in gender-type ways."

Similarly, in small-scale research amongst primary schools in north-east England, "there was no evidence of specific strategies to accommodate and invite men into the classroom", and there were no specific school policies to increase fathers' involvement (Clough et al., 2000). These researchers conclude that:

> "in spite of the preponderance of male heads, there was no great drive to challenge the perceived prevailing culture."

So, what are the potential barriers to fathers' involvement at the level of individual schools and family learning programmes? These are presented in Box 10, and good practice solutions are covered in Chapter 5.

Box 10: Potential barriers in individual schools and family learning programmes

SCHOOL INFRASTRUCTURE

- No school policy about parental involvement and/or involving fathers and non-resident parents

- Little parental involvement activity in the school

- Lack of information about children's fathers, particularly non-resident fathers

WEEKDAY/ DAYTIME TIMING of school hours and family learning programmes

INAPPROPRIATE DELIVERY and CONTENT of home-school and family learning programmes

- Using one model of practice 'to fit' all fathers

  - Not taking account of diversity amongst fathers

  - Culturally inappropriate for fathers from black and minority ethnic groups

  - Not taking account of fathers who have limited literacy or English language skills or communication or visual disabilities

- A female orientation to delivery and content of family learning programmes

  - Inappropriate learning materials, curricula and learning styles for men

  - Inappropriate physical environments and venues for men

- Too much monitoring or assessment, or insensitive assessment, of learners' skills

INAPPROPRIATE RECRUITMENT AND OUTREACH TO FATHERS by schools and family learning programmes

- Not going to where the fathers are

- Fathers less likely than mothers to be in school playground

- Mothers and children don't pass 'pupil post' to fathers

- Recruitment and outreach which does not reach some specific groups of fathers, for example non-resident fathers

- Recruitment message is based on help-giving model

PRACTICAL MATTERS AND ACCESS

- Not offering help with transport and childcare to participating fathers

- Lack of access for disabled fathers

No school policy and lack of information

In the small-scale study in north-east England, one-quarter of the staff interviewed did not know whether the school had a policy about parental involvement (Clough et al., 2000). Of the remainder, 46 per cent of the staff said that their school did have a policy, and 29 per cent said their school did not. None of these schools had a clear policy about communicating with non-resident parents. The schools had adopted a 'gender agnostic approach', i.e. they had not thought about whether engaging fathers required a particular approach.

It is interesting to note that, in a survey of all LEAs in England and Scotland in 1998 about their efforts to involve fathers in family learning programmes, fewer than 25 per cent of the authorities said that they were taking any special steps to engage fathers, although about 70 per cent agreed that "the real priority is to get more fathers involved. Family learning is seen as the mother's job" (McCormick, 1998). Authorities which were trying to engage fathers tended to do so through programmes for fathers and sons, but were not attempting to 'mainstream' fathers into family learning programmes overall.

Teachers may not know how involved fathers are in children's lives (Lloyd, 1999), and schools may lack details of non-resident fathers on their databases. However, in the small-scale study in north-east England, most of the interviewed school staff believed that they had contact details for both resident and non-resident parents (Clough et al., 2000). It is not known how representative this is for schools in England overall.

The DfES does give guidance to schools that:

> "Headteachers should ask parents or guardians the names and addresses of all parents when they register a pupil. These details, where known, must be included in the admission register. They should also be included in manuscript or computerised pupil records (which need to be kept up to date) and be available to the pupil's teachers. The information should be forwarded to any school to which the pupil moves." (DfEE, 2000)

Prisons running family learning programmes around literacy (see the case study of The Big Book Share) may find it difficult to identify fathers, as prisons don't routinely keep records of prisoners' family status.

Timing

Many school and family learning events take place in normal working hours, i.e. during the daytime in the week (NIACE, 2003). This is a major barrier to fathers' involvement (Millard and Hunter, 2001; Nord et al., 1997; West et al., 1998; Clough et al., 2000) because of the high proportion of fathers who work full time. Fathers are most likely to "put weekends aside for family life" (EOC, 2003), and many non-resident fathers tend to see their children only at weekends. Single-parent fathers in the Gingerbread survey said that "school activities do not always fall on the right days or at the right times", even if fathers' overall working hours are reduced (Gingerbread, 2001).

However, some research finds little increase in fathers' participation when family learning sessions are scheduled in evenings (Fletcher and Dally, 2002). And, of course, regular classroom involvement by fathers cannot be scheduled for evenings or weekends, although atypical working hours and shifts can give some fathers more flexibility. Fathers may have other commitments on weekends (see the case study of Basic Cookery for Dads).

Timing is not just about work for some fathers. Local sports fixtures, and national and international sports events on TV, can be substantial barriers to fathers' attendance at specific sessions and meetings if these are mistimed (see the case studies of Design and Technology whole-family workshops (Webster Associates), the Fathers and Children in Education Project, and Bradford YMCA Dads and Lads). Late evening timings will not be appropriate for family learning with younger children as they tend to be in bed by then, especially during the week. South Asian fathers' and children's shared time at home during the week was limited by prayer times at the mosque, children's time spent in religion school (madrasah) after school, and children's high level of homework (Razwan, 2002; Herrick and Ali, 2003; see the case study of Share for Dads). Likewise, family learning activities in schools sometimes coincided with daily prayer times, madrasah times and religious festivals.

It can therefore be almost impossible to find one timing that suits all fathers in a local area.

Inappropriate delivery, content and recruitment

Section 4.3 noted that schools and family learning programmes are feminised environments. According to Turbiville et al. (2000), their activities have a female orientation.[28] Macleod (2000) writes about the curriculum in many family literacy programmes being:

> *"devoid of masculine content or any other content that could be seen as relevant to the reality of people's, especially fathers', lived lives."*

Family learning practitioners and teachers need to pay attention to whether their programmes will appeal to men, in terms of learning materials, curricular content, learning styles, physical environments and venues.

Working-class fathers who were interviewed in Bryant and Taylor's research in Bristol said that the content of existing family learning activities had failed to appeal to them (Bryant and Taylor, 1999). Howzat!, and female librarians setting up Hampshire Teenage 'Lads and Dads' Book Clubs, two of the case study programmes, found it difficult at first to find high-quality, male-oriented reading which appealed to fathers and their sons.

In terms of learning styles, informal learning methods involving participants' personal experiences and disclosure may threaten or embarrass men because of a common fear of exposing weakness (McGivney, 1999). Men may find traditional instructive teaching more comfortable. The curriculum in many family literacy programmes is based on the feminine values of '"caring, sharing and helping"(Macleod, 2000). In Share for Dads, Hampshire Teenage 'Lads and Dads' Book Clubs, and Dads on Computers, three of the case study programmes, too much focus on talking during sessions had sometimes been challenging for the fathers and/or their sons.

Recruitment strategies used for in-school activities and family learning programmes may fail to reach fathers. Clough et al.'s (2000) study of fathers' and mothers' involvement in the reception class of primary schools found that, for almost every type of school involvement by parents, a much greater proportion[29] of mothers than of fathers felt that they had been

---

28 This female orientation can also apply to pre-school family learning activities offered in, for example, family centres. See Ghate et al., 2000.

29 For example, although all the interviewed school staff claimed that all mothers and fathers were invited to induction activities, one-third of fathers said that they had not been invited.

invited or encouraged to get involved by their children's school. This was despite the great majority of staff at these schools claiming that they had invited or tried to involve both mothers and fathers equally. Likewise, most of the Bristol fathers interviewed in a consultation said that they did not know about any family learning programmes in their local area, despite being involved with their children's out-of-school learning (Bryant et al., 1998).

What might be the reasons for these failures of communication?

In a survey of family learning provision, many LEAs relied for recruitment of learners on school newsletters, posters and leaflets, including sending information home from school with the children ('pupil post'), and conversations between school staff and parents (NIACE, 2003). Other strategies included visiting supermarkets, holding daytime events ('coffee mornings'), and working with early years and childcare practitioners. Most learners were referred informally by friends or relatives, i.e. the 'grapevine' effect.

However, men and women tend to get information from different sources. Whereas women use a wide variety of sources, including friends, families and professionals (McGivney, 1999), men tend to have smaller social networks which "provide them with less encouragement and fewer resources relevant to parenting" (Pleck and Masciadrelli, 2004). The most common source of information for men is their employer and, for unemployed men, their Jobcentre (McGivney, 1999).

As reported in Chapter 2, fathers are less likely than mothers to be in the school playground and to have regular contact with their children's teachers, and so there is less opportunity for face-to-face outreach to them there by teachers (Clough et al., 2000). Unemployed men in particular can become very isolated from information as they have lost their work-based friendship networks.

When letters specifically inviting fathers to events are sent home from school, mothers may not pass them to the fathers. Clough et al. (2000) report that:

> "women are the gatekeepers for information. They find the letter in the school bag and decide what to do with the invitation, sometimes sharing the information with fathers, but not always."

Family learning practitioners and teachers may therefore not make sufficient effort to invite fathers in person. In Bryant and Taylor's research, men lacking confidence had been reluctant to come forward because they had not been approached directly. Schools in London organising Fathers Breakfasts in primary schools were often very surprised to find that there were many fathers "that just needed to be invited" (Working with Men, 2004). Recruiting fathers to home–school and family learning programmes was commonly reported in the case studies to be challenging and resource-intensive (Basic Cookery for Dads, Hampshire Teenage 'Lads and Dads' Book Clubs, It's A Man Thing!).

Schools are especially likely to have poor or no communication with non-resident fathers. Frieman (1998) claims that schools often exacerbate "the schism created between the divorced father and his children…by leaving the father out of the educational process", which can lead to further withdrawal by the father from his children's lives. The following three small-scale research studies show little communication between fathers and schools.

In the small-scale study of primary schools in north-east England, despite most of the interviewed school staff reporting that they had contact details for both resident and non-resident parents,

- about 40 per cent of these staff said that their school did not send information such as school bulletins and newsletters to non-resident parents

- about a quarter of these staff said that their school did not send children's school reports to non-resident parents

- most staff said that non-resident fathers were sent reports if they provided the school with a stamped addressed envelope

- about a fifth of these staff reported that non-resident fathers were involved with home–school agreements (Clough et al., 2000).

Baker and McMurray (1998) paint a similar picture in their qualitative Australian research study on the school involvement of a small group of non-resident fathers. They write that, in most Australian schools, non-resident parents are excluded from school-based activities unless they are invited by the resident parent. At the time of the research, Australian Education Department practice was for schools to contact the child's resident parent for instructions whenever they were uncertain of an issue of father–child contact. The interviewed non-resident fathers in this study, most of whom were not currently involved in their children's schools and had poor relationships with their children's mothers, believed that the problem was that there was no communication between schools and the family courts. Baker and McMurray recommend that further research on non-resident fathers and school is needed at a national level.

Austin (1993), cited in Baker and McMurray (1998), conducted a random survey of 77 school districts in the US. These school districts were reluctant to include non-resident parents in their children's schools. Nearly half of the districts did not collect non-resident parents' names, addresses or phone numbers on school registration forms. Only 38 per cent forwarded school information to both resident and non-resident parents; 13 per cent reported that they would not pass information to non-resident parents in any circumstances.

No research was found that can show whether or not these practices also apply to the involvement of non-resident fathers in the UK.

Apart from the communication methods used in recruiting fathers, the nature of the message can also be a barrier to their participation. Macleod (2000) argues that the publicity message for family literacy events is often based on a "deficit model", i.e. that the father and his family have a problem that needs to be solved, which puts off men as they tend to be "reluctant help seekers" (see Section 4.5).

According to Turbiville et al. (2000), some family learning providers approach the participation of fathers with a 'one size fits all' approach, but this does not work. The huge diversity amongst fathers needs to be acknowledged. Similarly, in the evaluation of It's A Man Thing!, one of the case study programmes, "what suits one group may not please another" (Millard and Hunter, 2001).

Some families from black and minority ethnic communities may need services which target them in community languages and provide for their specific needs (Henricson et al., 2001). Somali fathers in the Black Development Agency's research said that "cultural differences" between them and local agencies were a barrier to their parenting role (Black Development Agency, 2002). A small group of South Asian Muslim fathers in a different research study wanted more Asian teachers in schools, although other fathers interviewed in this research were not concerned about the ethnicity of teachers (Razwan, 2002). Their children's school had recently appointed an Urdu-speaking parental involvement officer to work alongside the home–school liaison officer.

Moving on from this discussion of recruitment and outreach, the amount and/or style of delivery of monitoring and skills assessment in programmes may discourage fathers from participating. Family learning programmes funded by the LSC must create an Individualised Learner Record for each learner. NIACE (2003) report that many LSC-funded FLLN programmes are required to incorporate several assessments, including initial assessment, and that this can "frighten them away", referring to learners who were mostly women. This could be even more likely to deter fathers, given that men are generally more reluctant than women to show any lack of knowledge or skill. Of course, it can also be argued that quality teaching requires formal skills assessment, and it may be possible to conduct this assessment in a sensitive and appropriate way that is a positive or neutral experience for learners.

Some practitioners participating in a workshop at a conference in 2003 on engaging men in family learning expressed the view that there is too much form-filling for male learners. They also said that targets and inflexible frameworks do not take into account that it tends to be much more difficult, time-consuming, risky and expensive to recruit fathers than mothers.

Practical matters and access

There is a view amongst some practitioners that due to the relatively high prevalence of poor school experiences amongst men, family learning programmes working with fathers will not be successful if they take place in schools or other venues viewed as 'women's spaces' (e.g. Macleod, 2000). This can, of course, apply to mothers too. However, contrary to this view, there are successful family learning programmes for fathers running in schools (see the case studies in Chapter 6).

Family learning programmes may not offer parents any help with childcare or travel, sometimes because of restricted funding. A lack of transport was mentioned as a barrier to overall parenting by South Asian and Somali fathers in the Black Development Agency's research (Black Development Agency, 2002). A lack of childcare was a barrier to the participation of fathers in Basic Cookery for Dads and Dads on Computers, two of the case study programmes. Transport in rural areas is, of course, a particular difficulty. In the Fathers and Children in Education Project in rural Suffolk (one of the case study programmes) some of the fathers had an hour's travelling time from their homes to attend the family learning sessions.

Disabled fathers may be prevented from participating in schools and family learning programmes by inaccessible venues and communication. Similarly, fathers without literacy or English language skills may not be able to read publicity or use learning materials.

4.9 Summary

Large-scale barriers (cultural belief systems, the economic system, the nature of work, the education system)

- There are **traditional cultural belief systems** about fathers as economic providers, and mothers as childcarers. These beliefs contribute to several other barriers, including the attitudes of some fathers, mothers, children and teachers; the gender pay gap; fathers' long working hours; and 'feminised environments' in education.

- Fathers in the UK are much more likely than mothers to work full time. When fathers work, they tend to **work long hours** (the longest working hours in Europe for fathers). Some fathers also have **atypical working hours** (i.e. outside the 9-5 working day).

- The **gender pay gap** and **employment which is insufficiently family-friendly**, may both contribute to long working hours. Fathers may not know that family-friendly policies exist or apply to them. Fathers may feel uncomfortable discussing family commitments in the workplace, and managers may not be understanding.

- It is widespread in some black and minority ethnic communities for fathers to be working long, unpredictable and atypical hours.

- Single-parent fathers may be especially challenged to combine work and family commitments.

- Primary schools and family learning providers are often **feminised environments with few male teachers, practitioners or other adults**.

- **Funding offering little sustainability and from multiple sources** have been challenges for family learning programmes, although there has been recent progress.

Barriers at the level of individual fathers, mothers, practitioners, schools and family learning programmes

- Many **fathers** see their family role as predominantly 'a breadwinner'. This view is exacerbated by a consumer culture amongst children. Some fathers feel that they have to work long hours to meet all their families' material expectations.

- Some men see schools, their own education, and involvement in their children's education as 'women's work', and schools and family learning programmes as 'women's spaces'. This is exacerbated by a relatively high prevalence amongst fathers of bad experiences of school when they were children (higher prevalence than amongst mothers). There is an intergenerational cycle of these beliefs within some families, and a link with the gender achievement gap. These attitudes tend to be especially strong in areas with high long-term unemployment.

- Men tend to be much more reluctant than women to seek help from health and family services or to disclose information about personal issues.

- Peer pressure can be an important factor in maintaining these beliefs and attitudes.

- Differences in how women and men interact may create communication difficulties between fathers and teachers in female-dominated educational settings.

- Some single-parent fathers say that they are excluded from school-based networks of local mothers. Some Muslim South Asian fathers see the mosque as their social space, and prefer to leave the school and its playground as mothers' social space.

- Fathers are less likely than mothers to think that children's education is equally or more parents' responsibility than that of schools. But quantitative evidence from the UK and US suggests that fathers are similar to mothers in their levels of interest in and expectations for their children's education. Low-qualified fathers may have little confidence or interest in learning. Evidence is mixed on whether fathers' confidence in helping their children learn is lower than mothers' confidence.

- Some fathers do see it as their responsibility to help their children with their learning and education, and to join family learning programmes. Three common reasons for getting involved are because their children ask them to, to build a closer relationship with their children, and to support their children's educational achievements. Issues commonly discussed by involved black and minority ethnic fathers are wanting their children to do well in school, and the need to impart religious and cultural values. Evidence from small-scale research studies suggests that fathers are less likely to get involved in family learning programmes because they wish to learn new skills for their own benefit, or to gain accreditation, or to meet other adults for friendship.

- Some **mothers** see the limited involvement of fathers in their children's learning and education as unproblematic. They expect low involvement and do not question it. Other mothers value fathers' involvement and actively facilitate it.

- Mothers may want fathers to be more involved in family life, but on 'their own terms', so retaining control. Mothers may be most likely to act as a gatekeeper when they are not resident with their child's father.

- Some older **children** take active steps to prevent their parents' involvement in their education. In some research studies, children tend to have traditional views on fathering roles, seeing provision of a family income as central.

- Only limited research evidence has been found on **teachers'** attitudes towards father involvement. In one study, teachers expected the fathers to have very little involvement in their school and felt more comfortable talking to mothers.

- Some teachers fear possible aggression and child abuse from fathers, or alienating and upsetting mothers, especially when involving non-resident fathers.

- **Individual fathers' circumstances** (e.g. geographical distance from child, large family, poor health or disability) may be barriers. Some fathers have low literacy levels, and some minority ethnic fathers have limited English language skills.

- There is **inappropriate policy and practice in some schools and family learning programmes** for engaging fathers including:
  - lack of information about children's fathers, particularly non-resident fathers
  - weekday/daytime timing of events and meetings
  - a female orientation to delivery and content of family learning programmes, and recruitment of fathers.

Part Two

Effective practice and case studies

5 | Effective practice in engaging fathers in schools and family learning programmes

Over the past few years in the UK, there has been a growing collection of good practice guides and related research[1] about how services for children and parents can work successfully with fathers. But to our knowledge, there has not been any substantial research-based publication in the UK which has focused on how best to engage fathers in schools and family learning programmes. As mentioned in Chapter 1, the Department for Education and Skills (DfES) has recently published a good practice guide[2] for schools working with fathers *Engaging fathers - Involving parents, raising achievement* which has drawn extensively from our research in this report (DfES, 2004a).

In this chapter, two key questions are addressed:

- What is the range of models that has been used to involve fathers in their children's learning and education?

- Are there particular approaches to engaging fathers in schools and family learning programmes which are most successful? For example, what communication channels work for schools and family learning providers to engage fathers?

The many recommendations found in the literature are reviewed and synthesised. The searches of bibliographic databases found several short articles and papers written by practitioners, journalists and researchers in the UK, Australia and the US since 1996. The UK, Australia and the US obviously do have many important differences in the structural and cultural context for involving fathers, but some initiatives (for example, fathers breakfasts in schools) have worked successfully in all three countries.

In the literature accessed, recommendations are sometimes presented by experienced practitioners on the basis of their valuable experience (e.g. Berger, 1998; Reissman, 2001; Geraci, 2001). At other times, writers based their recommendations on conference and seminar discussions (e.g. Bryant and Henderson, 2002). The best evidence-based approach, from a researcher's perspective, is one in which recommendations are based on research (e.g. Clough et al., 2000; Lloyd, 1999; Ortiz, 2001; Ortiz and McCarty, 1997; Turbiville et al., 2000; Karther, 2002) and on reviews of research evidence (e.g. Fletcher and Dally, 2002).

---

1   Including Burgess and Bartlett, 2004; Lloyd, 2001; Burgess, 2002; Lloyd et al., 2003; Ghate et al., 2000.

2   This guide is published by the DfES on Teachernet, and is also available in print: http://www. teachernet.gov.uk/wholeschool/familyandcommunity/workingwithparents/engagingfathers/

Additionally, evidence is incorporated from:

- the case studies of successful home–school and family learning programmes engaging fathers (full case studies are presented in Chapter 6)

- other initiatives uncovered through the review of recent and current practice and projects in England and Wales that engage fathers in family learning and in schools

- discussions of the DfES Fathers Advisory Group 2003/04 (see Chapter 1). The information from these meetings, which is included in this and other chapters, does not necessarily reflect the views of the DfES – the group included a range of policymakers, voluntary organisations and practitioners

- discussions at a joint DfES/NFPI seminar, 'Father involvement in education and family services', in December 2003.

One point arising from this seminar was that 'father-friendly' services need to take diverse social, religious and cultural factors into account. Throughout this chapter, references are made (where appropriate) to single-parent fathers, non-resident fathers, black and minority ethnic fathers, working fathers, and unemployed fathers.

Some of the good practice recommendations in this chapter also apply to involving mothers in schools and family learning programmes, especially those mothers in hard-to-reach groups[3] (Brassett-Grundy, 2002). However, research suggests that they are even more crucial for fathers because of fathers' greater likelihood of full-time work, reluctance to seek help, lower involvement in parenting generally, greater likelihood to have had bad experiences at school, and so on (see Chapter 4).

Our final point in this introduction is that the guidelines and good practice in this chapter are just that. They are not "iron rules", and "involving fathers is not rocket-science" (DfES/ NFPI seminar). Every organisation and every practitioner needs to find out about the fathers they are working with, ideally in the planning stages, and adapt their practice as needed, using their own creativity. At the same time, it is crucial that schools and family learning practitioners seeking to engage fathers do not 're-invent the wheel', but learn from what has already been done, including some well-established family learning programmes for men.

5.1   General principles of good practice

Some overall principles of good practice for 'father-friendly' schools and family learning programmes emerged very strongly from the literature, the case studies, and the discussions of the DfES Fathers Advisory Group 2003/04 and the joint DfES/ NFPI seminar. These are presented in Box 11.

---

3   Mothers in a qualitative study in England wanted family literacy initiatives to have the following features: small numbers of people they already knew; an informal friendly learning environment ("not reminiscent of parents' early formal education"); free courses; clear, interesting, flexible, diverse and relevant content; free on-site childcare; simple language in publicity (not "wordy letters"); being asked along by someone they already knew; and staff who were supportive, non-intimidating, respectful, and tolerant of some degree of irregular attendance (Brassett-Grundy, 2002).

Box 11: General principles of good practice in working with fathers

- Put the children first

- Include children's fathers (resident and non-resident), but also other male carers, 'father figures' and the extended family (for example, grandfathers, uncles, older brothers, step-fathers, male mentors, family friends, foster fathers)

- Develop policies, programmes, strategies and recruitment specifically to engage fathers and male carers (as a starting point)

- Consult fathers, mothers and children in planning service design and content of programmes

- Recognise, respect and adapt to individual and cultural diversity

  - one model of practice is not sufficient

  - offer alternatives to fathers

- Work in partnership with other organisations, and share good practice

Develop programmes specifically to engage fathers and male carers

It is not clear-cut whether home–school and family learning programmes must be specifically for fathers and other male carers (and their children) if they are to successfully involve fathers. Many experts do recommend this very targeted approach, for example:

> "fathers (or father figures) need to be the focus of specific school outreach programs." (Reissman, 2001)

Almost all of the case study programmes do fit this model, although it is likely that there was much under-reporting (in response to our consultation) of initiatives which engage both mothers and fathers in roughly equal numbers. When asked for feedback on family learning programmes, some participating fathers said that they particularly liked the male camaraderie in the group, with the introduction of mothers on occasion leading to changed group dynamics (e.g. Hampshire Teenage 'Lads and Dads' Book Clubs, Super Dads at Pen Pych Community Primary School, Share for Dads, the Fathers and Children in Education Project).

The mapping did find a design and technology family learning project which successfully engaged whole family groups (mothers and fathers, other family members and their children), so it can be done with appropriate curricular content, learning methods and publicity (see the case study of Design and technology whole-family workshops – Webster Associates). Some family learning projects created specifically for fathers and children in Bristol and the US similarly found that the men-only feature was not that important a factor for fathers' participation (Bryant and Taylor, 1999; Turbiville et al., 2000). Some programmes have concluding sessions to which other family members are invited.

Overall, the evidence suggests that, for many schools and family learning providers, father-only programmes are a good starting point, with marketing and recruitment differentiated for fathers and male carers (see Section 5.9). Perhaps some father-only projects will become family clubs at a later stage with the involvement of both fathers/male carers and mothers/female carers.

Some of the case study programmes combined time with fathers and children together and time with the fathers on their own (Bradford YMCA Dads and Lads; Super Dads at Pen Pych Community Primary School; Share for Dads; Dads on Computers; The Big Book Share; It's A Man Thing!). This allowed fathers to discuss more personal issues amongst themselves, such as fatherhood and their relationships with their children, and to develop their own confidence in learning and their own skills.

Include a range of male carers

Children often have a range of male carers and other 'father figures', particularly if they grow up in single-parent or step-parent families. Some black and minority ethnic groups are especially likely to have traditional extended family networks. It is important for home–school and family learning programmes to be available to any male adult caring for a child (see the case study programmes in Chapter 6) to avoid excluding or alienating children not in contact with their father, or whose father cannot attend. As in the rest of this report, when the term 'father' is used in this chapter, all male carers and 'father figures' are included.

Consult fathers, mothers and children

Several of the case study programmes, and other projects found in the review, incorporated a distinct consultation with fathers into their planning or initial meetings (e.g. Working with Men, 2004; Herrick and Ali, 2003; Bryant and Henderson, 2002). For Pen Pych Community Primary School's Super Dads project with fathers, understanding the ethos, values and needs of the local community had been a key enabling factor. It is especially important to consult fathers when the teacher or practitioner is from a different socio-economic group, locality or ethnic group from the fathers.

Consultation before implementing programmes should include children and mothers (Fletcher, 2001; Berger, 1998), although it is consultation of fathers that is most commonly found in the good practice literature that was accessed. As seen in Chapter 4, both mothers and children can act as gatekeepers to fathers' involvement in their children's learning and education. It is important to persuade mothers that involvement by their children's father is really beneficial for their children (DfES Fathers Advisory Group 2003/04).

Recognise, respect and adapt to individual and cultural diversity

Schools and early childhood programmes working with fathers should "encourage cultural diversity" (Berger, 1998). Turbiville et al. (2000) remind us that "one size does not fit all", and that providers need to offer a range of alternatives for involving fathers in different population groups and with different interests.

Work in partnership with other organisations and share good practice

NIACE (2003) found that partnership working was crucial to the effectiveness of family learning programmes. The lead organisation in nearly all the case study programmes worked with a range of partner organisations, sometimes in joint ownership of the programme (Chapter

Box 12: Consult fathers

Why?

- Do not make assumptions about what fathers want or are interested in; "We must open a dialogue with fathers." (Turbiville et al., 2000)

- Need to "address the needs of learners, not those providing the funding" and avoid "an approach from the top down." (Bryant and Henderson, 2002)

- Understand why fathers are involved (Working with Men, 2004)

How?

- Collect information on fathers' family status, work status, occupation, attitudes, skills, interests, hobbies, reading preferences, involvement with homework, and languages (Tranter and Bright, 2004; DfES Fathers Advisory Group 2003/04; Karther, 2002)

- Ask fathers what they can contribute to their children's learning and to the school curriculum (Bryant and Taylor, 1999; Reissman, 2001)

- Hold a meeting or focus group (e.g. case study of Pen Pych Community Primary School; Herrick and Ali, 2003; Working with Men, 2004)

- Telephone or email survey of fathers (Reissman, 2001; Bryant and Taylor, 1999)

- Interviews with fathers (Bryant and Taylor, 1999)

6). Partnerships were often crucial to achieve sufficient staff capacity (including volunteers), suitable venues, and a mix of skills and gender amongst the programme facilitators. Some of the programme organisers saw enhancement of partnership working as a secondary benefit of their work.

Some of the case study programmes in which an LEA was not the main provider worked in partnership with LEAs and found this important to the success of their work (e.g. It's A Man Thing!, Dads on Computers). The DfES good practice guide *Engaging fathers – Involving parents, raising achievement* includes a list of questions for schools to ask their LEA to identify how the LEA can best support their work with fathers (DfES, 2004a).

5.2　A father-friendly organisation

In most cases, it is not sufficient just for individual teachers or family learning practitioners to think about the details of specific programmes when trying to engage fathers, although this is important. Headteachers and senior managers need to implement a 'whole school' or 'whole family learning programme' approach to involving fathers, which often involves 'changing cultures' (DfES Fathers Advisory Group 2003/04).

These organisational systems and structures do not all need to be in place before embarking on any work to engage fathers, and it is important to be realistic about what is possible, for example on recruiting a mixture of male and female practitioners.

Box 13: A father-friendly organisation

- High-level strategy and planning to engage fathers, with commitment of headteachers/senior managers

- Clear policies to engage fathers, including why involving fathers is important to your school/organisation (Millard and Hunter, 2001; Fletcher, 2001; Working with Men, 2004; Clough et al., 2000; DfES Fathers Advisory Group 2003/04)

- Funding for the work with fathers

- Availability of staff with appropriate skills and sufficient time to deliver home–school strategies/family learning programmes targeted at fathers

- Building positive attitudes amongst headteachers/managers, all teachers/practitioners (not just those working with fathers) and mothers towards fathers' involvement, using training and/or self-evaluation and reflective practice (Bright et al., 2002; Fletcher, 2001; McGivney, 1999; Berger, 1988):

  - purpose, commitment, creativity, perseverance, flexibility, sensitivity

  - understand and discuss views within the organisation towards men and fathers, and any concerns about working with them

  - make fathers welcome and appreciated

- Where possible, recruiting a balance of male and female teachers and practitioners

- Collecting information about fathers and their involvement in family learning programmes and school activities (Fletcher, 2002)

- Good research and evaluation to assess the benefits of and processes in involving fathers (Fletcher, 2001; DfES Fathers Advisory Group 2003/04)

High-level strategy, clear policies and commitment at a senior level

Schools and family learning providers should have a clear policy specifically about engaging fathers (including non-resident fathers). Where appropriate, they should also incorporate fathers into other organisational policies. The Big Book Share, one of the case study programmes, found that an important facilitator of their work was the inclusion of this project in the prison's and county council libraries' mainstream planning and targets.

> *"should place the agency's relationship with fathers clearly within the context of a whole-school policy on parental involvement which should be fully debated with staff and parents."*
>
> *"ask of every initiative in the...development plan... 'What are the implications for the involvement of fathers?'"*
>
> Millard and Hunter, 2001

Schools and family learning providers need to know why they need to involve fathers, and which groups of fathers, so that genuine commitment can be built. Fathers' involvement can be linked (see Chapter 2) to the central issues of:

- children's educational achievement, literacy, behaviour and emotional development, and child protection (Fletcher, 2001; Working with Men, 2004; DfES Fathers Advisory Group 2003/04)

- adults' lifelong learning and basic skills (DfES Fathers Advisory Group 2003/04).

> *"Schools should see fathers as potential allies both for the child and for the agency."*
>
> Millard and Hunter, 2001

With some of the case study programmes which ran in schools, headteachers (in addition to class teachers) were very committed and took much interest in the work with fathers. Sometimes headteachers had initiated the programme and/or co-facilitated sessions. Often, they were fully involved in planning, and they frequently 'popped into' sessions with the fathers and children. Similarly, The Big Book Share in HMP Nottingham secured the commitment of the prison governor and the senior library services manager in the local authority. In the LEA co-organising Share for Dads, there was a strong commitment to parental involvement in children's education.

Obtaining funding

As seen in Chapter 4, most (but not all) of the case study schools and family learning programmes obtained specific funding to run their father involvement work, often from multiple sources, and frequently from short-term, time-limited funding streams. The organiser of Howzat! said that obtaining sufficient funding for a high-quality programme (not having to "rely on goodwill") was a key facilitator of their work with fathers.

Box 14: *Sources of funding used by the case study programmes*[4]

Learning and Skills Council/Training and Enterprise Councils

School budgets

Local authority/LEA budgets (schools; family learning; other adult and community education; libraries)

Government education and children's/family programmes (Education Action Zones; Behaviour Improvement Programme; Children's Fund including On Track; Sure Start local programmes; Family Support Grant; Ethnic Minority Achievement; Adult and Community Learning Fund)

Government regeneration and social inclusion programmes (Single Regeneration Budget)

Voluntary organisation budgets

Grants from charitable trusts and other grant-making bodies (Arts Council; Paul Hamlyn Foundation)

Grants from research councils through universities for research and evaluation

Workers' Education Association

Companies (Boots PLC; News International; Marks and Spencer; children's publishers)

---

4   Some of these sources of funding are no longer in existence or have been replaced by new funding sources or structures (e.g. Training and Enterprise Councils and the Adult and Community Learning Fund).

Characteristics of staff working with fathers

Having quality staff with relevant skills is crucial to the success of engaging fathers, as it is for any educational programme. The case study programmes were run and facilitated by an enormous variety of practitioners, as shown in Box 15.

As mentioned in Section 5.1, many of the case study programmes used organisational partnerships to create a team of sufficient size and with a good mix of skills and gender. For example, the Hampshire Teenage 'Lads and Dads' Book Clubs are facilitated jointly by a children's librarian and librarians who work with adults. Howzat! is facilitated by a combination of teachers, classroom support staff, school librarians and professional sports coaches. Group work was commonly perceived as a core skill in the case study programmes.

Some case study programmes included sixth formers, students, fathers and other volunteers amongst the staff team (e.g. Design and technology whole-family workshops – Webster Associates). Others brought in guest facilitators when needed for specialist skills or 'celebrity appeal' (e.g. Fathers and Children in Education; Hampshire Teenage 'Lads and Dads' Book Clubs; Bradford YMCA Dads and Lads).

Box 15: Practitioner groups working with fathers in the case study programmes

- Project managers and other staff in local authorities/LEAs (including Parental Involvement Co-ordinators and Fathers Workers)
- Project managers and development workers in voluntary organisations
- Curriculum consultants
- Teachers of children (e.g. responsible for Ethnic Minority Achievement; pupil–parent liaison officer; teaching English and PE for sports/literacy programme)
- Teaching and learning support assistants (including special needs assistants and language support workers)
- Adult and community education practitioners/Teachers of adults
- Headteachers
- Sixth formers (as volunteer helpers)
- Students and trainees (e.g. IT courses, teacher training, social work)
- Professional sports coaches
- Community and early years workers including Sure Start practitioners, family centre project workers, and home–school liaison workers in schools
- Fathers who had participated in earlier programmes or were former pupils of the school
- Police officers (on secondment to government crime-prevention programme)
- Children's and adults' librarians in public libraries
- School and prison librarians
- Prison visits staff

Recruiting fathers and maintaining organisational partnerships is usually time consuming, and for this reason most of the case study programmes had some dedicated time from practitioners for this purpose. This could be from local authority fathers workers, practitioners and project managers (Basic Cookery for Dads, Hampshire Teenage 'Lads and Dads' Book Clubs, Share for Dads, Howzat!), designated teachers and school staff released part time from the classroom (The Fathers Inclusion Project at Kensal Rise Primary School, Share for Dads, Super Dads at Pen Pych Community Primary School), prison librarians and prison officers (The Big Book Share), an educational consultant (Design and technology whole-family workshops – Webster Associates), or voluntary organisation staff (Dads on Computers, Fathers and Children in Education Project). Similarly, work in Australia to involve fathers in primary schools in disadvantaged areas used designated home–school workers (Fletcher, 2001). In the Family Action Centre's Fathers and Schools Together (FAST) Literacy Program for fathers and children, schools release teachers from their classroom and extracurricular duties so they can attend project meetings (Tranter and Bright, 2004). This 'designated time' appears to be a key enabling factor for father involvement programmes to be successful, and this brings us back to the need for sufficient funding.

The ideal gender of teachers and other practitioners working with fathers in children's education settings is a disputed issue in the literature. Some writers and some practitioners on the DfES Fathers Advisory Group 2003/04 recommend having male staff (Fletcher, 2001; Berger, 1998; Bryant and Henderson, 2002). However, as seen in Chapter 4, most primary schools and family learning settings have few males on their staff, although this is changing slowly. The male input to some programmes working with fathers therefore comes from male volunteers and students (see the case study of Dads on Computers), fathers who are already involved (Stile and Ortiz, 1999; see the case study of the Fathers and Children in Education Project), male guest facilitators, or the few male members of staff who are asked to contribute (DfES Fathers Advisory Group 2003/04; see the case study of The Fathers Inclusion Project at Kensal Rise Primary School).

However, it is not always necessary to have male workers (Turbiville et al., 2000; case studies of Share for Dads and Basic Cookery for Dads; some practitioners on the DfES Fathers Advisory Group 2003/04). Bryant and Taylor (1999) interviewed working-class fathers in Bristol, and none of these men had any preference about the gender of course tutors or facilitators for adult learning.

It is more important that staff of either gender welcome and appreciate fathers and have relevant skills. After all, as seen in Chapter 4, some male teachers in schools may find involved fathers a threat to their authority. Additionally, male practitioners do not ensure male participation. In an evaluation of a *SHARE* family learning programme, even when the group was run by a male teacher, all participants were female (Bastiani, 1999). Female workers can sometimes take on 'honorary male' status within the group, they can encourage fathers to open up about more personal issues such as family life, and they can bring a 'female perspective' to the fathers (see the case study of Basic Cookery for Dads).

Table 23: Gender of practitioners in case study programmes

	Number of case study programmes
All female facilitators	3
All male facilitators	2
Mixed female/male	1

Gender is not the only relevant characteristic of facilitators. Bryant and Taylor (1999) found that it worked well to have a local man organising family learning activities on an estate in Bristol. When working with black and minority ethnic fathers, having facilitators from a similar ethnic and cultural background to the fathers may be important at helping to put these fathers at ease.

However, as with gender, this is not essential, and of course within every ethnic group are a number of subgroups which have different identities and traditions. Much more important is that whoever facilitates has a good understanding of the religions, cultures, family structures, gender norms and social customs of the fathers, is respectful of these, and asks questions when unsure about culturally appropriate behaviour. The case studies of Share for Dads, Bradford YMCA Dads and Lads, and The Fathers Inclusion Project at Kensal Rise Primary School found that female facilitators with these attributes were very well received by black and minority ethnic fathers from cultures with strongly gendered family roles. However, Muslim fathers in Razwan's research did request a male practitioner in their children's school (Razwan, 2002).

If some fathers do not speak English, it is vital to have someone present at the school meeting or family learning session who can interpret, who may be a member of staff (see the case study of The Fathers Inclusion Project at Kensal Rise Primary School) or another father or a child.

Building positive attitudes amongst managers and staff

Positive attitudes towards involving fathers are needed throughout the whole school or organisation – amongst senior managers, teachers, practitioners and mothers – so that fathers feel genuinely welcome and appreciated, and to overcome the barriers to fathers' involvement. In particular, any concerns about male power and influence, or about male abuse and violence in relation to child protection and family conflict, need to be discussed openly (DfES Fathers Advisory Group 2003/04; DfES/NFPI seminar). Some practitioners working with fathers who were at the joint DfES/NFPI seminar said that fathers workers can feel very isolated if they are not supported by their colleagues and managers. Similarly, male teachers and practitioners will leave any educational environment which does not welcome men.

> *"Front-line or contact staff [in primary schools] need to be convinced that father involvement is relevant to their needs, possible to achieve, and beneficial."*
>
> Fletcher, 2001

> *"Convince female staff it is safe and desirable."*
>
> DfES Fathers Advisory Group 2003/04

> *"develop a mind-set which will become embedded in the culture of the school."*
>
> Millard and Hunter, 2001

> *"Create an atmosphere where men as well as women are expected to be involved."*
>
> Berger, 1998
>
> *"Are staff comfortable talking to men of all backgrounds?"*
>
> Fletcher, 2002
>
> *"training programmes for people working with men could usefully incorporate an emphasis on understanding male conditioning and concepts of masculinity."*
>
> McGivney, 1999

In conversations with the organisers of the case study programmes, and in the meetings of the DfES Fathers Advisory Group 2003/04, references were commonly made to purpose, commitment, creativity, perseverance, flexibility and sensitivity as crucial enabling attitudes.

> *"Recognising that change takes time."*
>
> *"Difficult but can be done."*
>
> DfES Fathers Advisory Group 2003/04

Training and self-evaluation/reflective practice on working with fathers may be important tools to influence and discuss attitudes. One good example of an integrated training, quality improvement and self-evaluation system specifically for schools on working with fathers is the Australian Family Action Centre's[5] FAST Literacy Program (Tranter and Bright, 2004). This programme supports primary school teachers in their work to involve fathers in literacy activities with their children in the classroom and at home. The programme uses an action research approach. A small group of teachers in a school forms a FAST group which meets regularly, sets goals, tries methods of involving fathers, reviews and reflects on progress, adapts practice, and then disseminates effective practice to other schools. The teachers complete an Action Learning Journal each week on the projects they have tried out with the fathers, which includes ways of evaluating learning activities.

At least four UK voluntary organisations have accreditation and training frameworks on engaging fathers which can be delivered to schools and family learning programmes:

- Fathers Direct runs specialist training courses on fathers and schools (www.fathersdirect.com)

- Working with Men has delivered advice to schools on engaging fathers (Working with Men, 2004)

- ContinYou/Children North East jointly have a programme 'Developing Men-Friendly Organisations' accredited by the Open College Network. This comprises taught days and work-related field study that will make organisational cultures (e.g. in feminised sectors) more 'men-friendly' and increase the skills of workers to recruit and work with men.

---

5   The Family Action Centre is at the University of Newcastle in Australia. Its website is www.newcastle.edu.au/centre/fac/efathers (on 5/9/03).

Research, monitoring and evaluation

Research, monitoring and evaluation bring many benefits to schools and family learning programmes which seek to engage fathers. They may also be required by funders of home–school and family learning programmes. For example, the Learning and Skills Council (LSC) requires monitoring information from the programmes that it funds.

These processes can:

- facilitate intelligent planning and strategy

- allow quality improvement of strategies and programmes

- demonstrate the success and importance of the work with fathers to managers, funders and local policymakers

- encourage and help other schools and family learning programmes to work successfully with fathers.

Minimum good practice would be to collect information about the fathers and 'father figures' of children on enrolment forms and school records (Fletcher, 2002).

Ideally, schools and family learning programmes would also:

- document fathers' attendance and involvement (Fletcher, 2001)

- document the characteristics of involved fathers and non-involved fathers; the first realistic goal of many home–school and family learning programmes will be to recruit a small group of fathers, but a second-stage goal would be to recruit harder-to-reach fathers

- document the processes in successful models of father involvement in schools and family learning programmes (Fletcher, 2001)

- carry out research to assess the benefits of fathers' involvement in schools (Fletcher, 2001)

- share good practice and successful models internally, with their LEA, and with other schools or family learning programmes, for example submitting case studies to the Teachernet and National Family Learning Network websites.

The DfES good practice guide *Engaging fathers – Involving parents, raising achievement* includes a list of questions that schools should ask themselves in order to carry out an audit of the current involvement of fathers (DfES, 2004a).

Additionally, the Family Action Centre in Australia has developed:

- a *Checklist for Including Fathers and Father Figures in Schools* – for self-evaluation of schools' work with fathers (Fletcher, 2002)

- a *Father Involvement Inventory* – to document how many fathers are involved in schools and what types of activity they are involved in (Fletcher and Silberberg, 2002).

A research report has recently been published by the NFPI which looks at *Fathers and Family Support Services: Promoting involvement and evaluating impact* (O'Brien, 2004).

Fletcher (2001) argues that it is important for schools that involve fathers to provide "solid evidence" of benefits of this work, including measures of children's increased well-being. He recommends that schools link with academics, and he acknowledges that quality research needs time and commitment. Similar points were made at the joint DfES/NFPI seminar.

This degree of evaluation would be ideal, but it does not appear realistic for every school or family learning organisation involving fathers to carry out robust 'impact research'. Chapter 3 reported that this kind of systematic summative evaluation is very rare amongst any family learning and home–school programmes, and none of the case study programmes had one in place. Additionally, some fathers will be resistant to too much 'form filling', especially where there are legal sensitivities or social services involvement in their family.

In fact, only a very small minority of the case study programmes have been evaluated by independent researchers. Most of the programmes have used small-scale in-house evaluations, collecting feedback (perceived benefits and outcomes) from fathers, children and schools, and some have written evaluation reports. A few of the programmes have not yet had any evaluation activity but plan to do so in the future.

> ### Box 16: Methods in the case study programmes of collecting feedback from fathers, children and teachers
>
> - Informal discussion and comments during sessions (most common)
> - Thank-you letters from participants
> - Records and observations of sessions
> - Diaries completed by participants
> - Written questionnaires for fathers and teachers (need to take literacy into account)
> - Interviews with fathers and teachers
> - Video and photography by fathers and children
> - Drawings, poems and other written work by children

In addition to process evaluations by individual projects, there is a need for funding of independent high-quality, evaluations of different 'demonstration models' of involving fathers in schools and family learning programmes.

5.3 Welcoming to fathers

> *"Convince men it's not hostile territory."*
>
> DfES Fathers Advisory Group 2003/04
>
> *"Listen and learn from fathers."*
>
> *"Acknowledge the important roles of mothers."*
>
> Berger, 1998

Chapter 4 presented the many potential barriers to fathers' involvement in their children's learning and education. In particular, men are more likely than women to have had poor experiences at school during their childhood, men are less likely than women to seek help, even for serious family issues, and "men fear exposing educational limitations and deficiencies" (McGivney, 1999).

Therefore, it is vital for schools and family learning programmes to create an environment that welcomes and appreciates the fathers whom they want to involve (Millard and Hunter, 2001; Clough et al., 2000; Turbiville et al., 2000; Berger, 1998; Brookes, 2002; Bright et al., 2002; Karther, 2002). Fathers will then feel valued and important, and trust will develop between teachers and fathers (Fletcher, 2001). Some of the organisers and evaluations of the case study programmes mentioned provision of a "non-threatening environment" and "non-patronising" attitudes as key enabling factors. Pen Pych Community Primary School and Kensal Rise Primary School both mentioned there being an 'open door' to fathers.

Many writers and the DfES Fathers Advisory Group 2003/04 strongly recommend telling fathers why their contribution to their children's learning and education is so important (Lloyd, 1999; Stile and Ortiz, 1999; Millard and Hunter, 2001; Berger, 1998; Fletcher, 2003; Working with Men, 2004). Bryant and Henderson (2002) write in relation to involving fathers in family learning: "Sell the activity as 'something' you are doing for your children."

Box 17: Be welcoming and appreciative

- Be friendly!

- Build one-to-one relationships with fathers / Get to know their names

- Chat with fathers who drop off and pick up their children from school

- "take an interest in what they're doing...give them some recognition" (views of fathers who have volunteered in schools in research by Bright et al., 2002)

- "appoint a child to be a welcoming person" (Berger, 1998)

5.4 Curricular content, learning methods and information for fathers in family learning programmes

Curricular content

As seen in Chapter 2, when fathers get involved in children's out-of-school learning, it tends to be in building and repairing activities, other practical activities, hobbies, ICT, maths and science, recreation, sports, outdoor activities, family trips, play and fun together. Additionally, evidence was presented showing that fathers are more likely to participate in LSC-funded wider family learning programmes than in LSC-funded family language, literacy and numeracy programmes. In relation to adult education, McGivney (1999) writes that women tend to learn in a wide range of general and self-development programmes, whereas male learners are "more restricted in their subject choices". Men stereotypically prefer factual and practical subjects such as IT, foreign languages and sports, whereas women prefer "more caring subjects".

As for the gender of teachers and family learning practitioners working with fathers, there are mixed views in the literature on the curricular content which is recommended when working with fathers in family learning programmes.

"Realism about the hooks that engage male parents."

DfES Fathers Advisory Group 2003/04

"Give men strong and masculine things to do."

Macleod, 2000

but...

"Take 'appropriate risks'."

Bryant and Henderson, 2002

Many writers and practitioners recommend being realistic about typical male interests. Family learning programmes should use curricular content with 'a male focus' and meaningful relevance to everyday life when working both with fathers and boys (Macleod, 2000; Fletcher and Dally, 2002; McGivney, 1999; Bryant and Henderson, 2002). Fletcher and Dally (2002) argue that practitioners should value fathers' "alternate literacies" which are practical skills such as handling money, mechanical skills, technology and map-reading.

This may indeed be important for many fathers as an initial 'way in' to supporting their children's learning. The most popular choices amongst white and South Asian working-class fathers consulted in Bristol and Kirklees, and the fathers in some of the case study programmes, were physical games, sport, outdoor activities, gardening, computers, motor mechanics, carpentry, bricklaying, electronics and robotics (Bryant and Taylor, 1999; Herrick and Ali, 2003; Super Dads at Pen Pych Community Primary School, and Design and technology whole-family workshops – Webster Associates). Section 4.5 also presented evidence on fathers feeling most confident about the skills that they had to offer in these specific areas of learning.

The fathers at Pen Pych Community Primary School valued being able to engage in challenging, messy, outdoor activities with their children in the absence of the mothers. The YMCA has a large-scale parenting programme for fathers and their sons called 'Dads and Lads', which combines sports sessions with parenting discussions (see Lloyd, 2001 for a case study). One of the YMCA Dads and Lads programmes is included as a case study in this report (Bradford YMCA Dads and Lads).

However, although traditionally masculine activities were most popular, some of the fathers consulted in Bristol wanted learning events covering cookery, music, toy making, first aid, fishing, teaching, printing, art and childcare (Bryant and Taylor, 1999).

The case studies too show that a much broader variety of curricular content can successfully engage fathers, and indeed some fathers may not be at all interested in sport or car mechanics. Bradford YMCA Dads and Lads, the Fathers and Children in Education Project, and Share for Dads all report that fathers are very open about trying a wide range of new activities. In the Fathers and Children in Education Project, fathers preferred some of the curricular areas with more 'feminine appeal' (e.g. literacy and arts and crafts) to the more competitive sports activities. In another fathers project, although the fathers at first said they wanted sports, they moved on to less 'safe ground' at a later stage when they felt comfortable (Super Dads at Pen Pych Community Primary School). Literacy projects with fathers and children can be very successful if specifically oriented towards fathers, and these are covered in a later section of this chapter.

Of course, although many family learning programmes are targeted towards 'dads and lads', many fathers have daughters, and some do not have sons. Therefore, less stereotypically male activities may be needed to engage fathers with their daughters, for example see the case study of Basic Cookery for Dads.

There are very valid reasons for not perpetuating gender stereotypes (McGivney, 1999), and "taking appropriate risks" (Bryant and Henderson, 2002) once fathers are more comfortable or at their request. Family learning providers also need to cater for both majority interests and minority interests amongst fathers, taking account of some reduction in stereotyped gender roles in our society.

Some programmes use a combination of stereotypically male curricular content and taking more risks in a very varied family learning programme. Some programmes have a non-stereotypically male curricular area as their focus (e.g. literacy), but then engage fathers with games, ICT, internet, design and technology, audio and video being used as learning methods (see the next section on learning methods).

When working with fathers from black and minority ethnic communities in family learning programmes, it is important to check that activities are culturally and religiously appropriate, for example not planning high-energy physical games during Ramadan for Muslim fathers and their children (see the case study of Bradford YMCA Dads and Lads). Incorporating ethnic, religious and cultural traditions and stories into the curriculum can be very successful (see the case study of Share for Dads; also Mitchell, 1993). African-Caribbean fathers consulted in one small-scale research study wanted family learning that would create links between children and elders, especially grandparents, "to share their cultural heritage with their children and use the oral tradition" (Bruneau, 2002). Sports such as football and cricket can appeal to a wide variety of black and minority ethnic fathers as well as white fathers, for example in the literacy and sport programme Howzat!, one of the case studies.

The deciding factor on curricular content should always be the fathers and children themselves (see Section 5.1 on consulting fathers) or, as Fletcher and Dally (2002) and Bryant and Henderson (2002) respectively write, "valuing fathers' abilities and interests" and ""taking the lead from those receiving the service". Some of the case study programmes mentioned the need to be flexible about programming and open to new ideas, in response to fathers' requests. ContinYou run an 'Active Dads' programme, in which fathers and children re given a choice about which eight activities they do together.

Our final point in this section is that, as with the gender of practitioners, male-oriented curricular content is not sufficient good practice on its own. McGivney (1999) reports in relation to community-based adult education that:

> "attempts to attract men by mounting courses in subjects they are
> ostensibly interested in, such as IT, often founder. This has been
> attributed both to the feminine image of community education and
> to men's reluctance to admit learning needs."

It is the overall 'father friendliness' of children's education settings which is vital for engaging fathers.

Tables 23 and 24 show examples from the case studies and from the wider review of recent and current practice and projects in England and Wales, by curricular area.

Table 24: "Give men strong and masculine things to do" (Macleod, 2000)

Curricular area	Examples from the case study programmes	Some other examples from the review of projects and practice in England and Wales
Physical activities, outdoor activities, adventurous play, and sport	Howzat! Super Dads at Pen Pych Community Primary School Kensal Rise Primary School's Bring Dad to School Day [The Fathers' Inclusion Project] Bradford YMCA Dads and Lads Fathers and Children in Education Project	YMCA Dads and Lads (and Lassies) projects (Lloyd, 2001, and www.ymca.org.uk) Dads and Lads sports skills and coaching sessions at Playing for Success centres and other sports clubs (www.dfes.gov.uk/playingforsuccess) Family Learning Through Football, a project of Family Leaning in County Durham, Sunderland Association Football Club and Durham LEA (information accessed at www.givemefootball.com/community.html in October 2004); also see Chisholm et al., 2004) FASTLANE's Men and Family Learning Project (Herrick and Ali, 2003) Football and IT family learning courses Fishing family learning courses Allotments/gardening family learning projects
ICT, internet, digital photography, video, science, design and technology, tools, construction	Dads on Computers Design and technology whole-family workshops – Webster Associates Fathers and Children in Education Project Kensal Rise Primary School's Bring Dad to School Day [The Fathers' Inclusion Project] Super Dads at Pen Pych Community Primary School Howzat!, Hampshire Teenage 'Lads and Dads' Book Clubs, The Big Book Share, and It's A Man Thing! are family literacy programmes which all incorporate use of the internet and other ICT	Bristol Men's Family Learning Project including Woodwork Club and Exploring Computers Together (Bryant and Taylor, 1999; Bryant et al., 1998; Bryant, 2000) Football and IT family learning courses IT and practical media activities in Dads and Lads Family Learning at Playing for Success centres (www.dfes.gov.uk/playingforsuccess) Film making and multi-media family learning courses.
Popular culture, for example cinema, newspapers, and TV	It's A Man Thing! Howzat!	

Table 25: "Taking appropriate risks" (Bryant and Henderson, 2002) on curricular content[6]

Curricular area	Examples from the case study programmes	Some other examples from our mapping
Visual arts, design and crafts	Share for Dads Fathers and Children's Education Project Super Dads at Pen Pych Community Primary School It's A Man Thing! Bradford YMCA Dads and Lads Design and technology whole-family workshops –Webster Associates	Bristol Men's Family Learning Project including Arts and Crafts Day, Spray Art and Carnival Workshops (Bryant and Taylor, 1999; et al., 1998; Bryant, 2000) Other creative family learning workshops, for example fathers working with their children to produce pictures of themselves
Cookery	Basic Cookery for Dads Share for Dads	
Music	Kensal Rise Primary School's Bring Dad to School Day [The Fathers' Inclusion Project]	Father Figures, a project which included drama and drumming days for children (information accessed at www.eventus.org.uk/fewer/fathers in September 2003) Bridging the Generation Gap, a music project with fathers and sons, set up by Beyond the Will Smith Challenge (BTWSC)
Literacy	See Table 26	See Table 26
History	Howzat! (history of cricket)	Our History on the Net, a project for father/son and grandfather/grandson pairs, receiving award from Reading Families Millennium Award Scheme (information accessed at www.campaign-for-learning.org.uk/projects in August 2003)
Parent–child relationships	Bradford YMCA Dads and Lads Fathers and Children in Education Project Super Dads at Pen Pych Community Primary School The Fathers Inclusion Project at Kensal Rise Primary School The Big Book Share	Other YMCA Dads and Lads (and Lassies) projects (Lloyd, 2001, and www.ymca.org.uk) Family Learning Through Football (http://www.givemefootball.com/community.html in October 2004; also see Chisholm, Haggart and Horne, 2004)

---

6   Literacy programmes for fathers and children are covered in another section of this chapter.

Curricular area	Examples from the case study programmes	Some other examples from our mapping
Children's learning, development and education	Bradford YMCA Dads and Lads

It's A Man Thing!

Fathers and Children in Education Project

Super Dads at Pen Pych Community Primary School

Howzat!

The Big Book Share | Other YMCA Dads and Lads (and Lassies) projects (Lloyd, 2001, and www.ymca.org.uk)

Family Learning Through Football (http://www.givemefootball.com/community.html in October 2004; also see Chisholm et al., 2004) |

Learning and facilitation styles

As seen in Section 4.5, men do not want to suggest a lack of knowledge or skill, or divulge personal information, and this begins in childhood. According to McGivney (1999):

> "boys...prefer tasks that give quick results and they often do better in one-to-one teaching relationships as their peer culture discourages them from volunteering answers or engaging in open-ended, shared tasks."

The learning and facilitation styles that were recommended or used successfully in the literature, and the case study programmes for engaging fathers, are given in Boxes 18 and 19. The two most frequent messages to emerge from the case studies, the DfES Fathers Advisory Group 2003/04 and the literature are, firstly, to have fun, and, secondly, to base the programme around practical "hands on" activities, rather than having "too much sitting still or talking" (Fletcher, 2003). Using information and communications technology (ICT) was a learning method very commonly used by the case study programmes, as were games and quizzes (e.g. It's A Man Thing!, Bradford YMCA Dads and Lads, Share for Dads, Fathers and Children in Education Project, Hampshire Teenage 'Lads and Dads' Book Clubs, Super Dads at Pen Pych Community Primary School).

In several of the case study programmes, visits and outings were very popular learning experiences (e.g. Bradford YMCA Dads and Lads, It's A Man Thing!, Share for Dads, Howzat!, Super Dads at Pen Pych Community Primary School, Hampshire Teenage 'Lads and Dads' Book Clubs). In Bradford YMCA Dads and Lads, outings to museums and the coast dissipated some fathers' fears about whether they would fit into these unfamiliar environments, and some of the fathers made return visits with their families.

Macleod (2000) argues that "the language of the programme needs to be changed away from caring, sharing and helping", referring to family learning programmes which wish to engage men. However, fathers do need sensitive and supportive facilitators, as do mothers (NIACE, 2003).

Bryant and Henderson (2002), based on their experience as men's family learning development workers, suggest that facilitators should talk about "manly subjects". Two of the case study programmes recommended encouraging humour and banter during the sessions, especially when there are mistakes or problems. One of the case study programmes, the Fathers and Children in Education Project, sometimes paired families up with others ('buddying') to promote mutual support; and others also drew on this kind of peer-led learning (e.g. Design and technology whole-family workshops – Webster Associates; Basic Cookery for Dads).

As with curricular content, guidelines on learning styles can be broken if the fathers feel at ease, and with skilled facilitation. Several of the case study programmes successfully incorporated discussions with fathers and their children into the planned programme, although facilitators often needed to provide much encouragement at first (e.g. Bradford YMCA Dads and Lads; It's A Man Thing!; the Fathers and Children in Education Project; Hampshire Teenage 'Lads and Dads' Book Clubs). Others used father-only discussions at times in their programme, without the children (e.g. Super Dads at Pen Pych Community Primary School; Bradford YMCA Dads and Lads; The Big Book Share). Of course, even without explicit discussion in the schedule, valuable informal discussion accompanied practical activities in all the case study programmes (see the case studies of Design and technology whole-family workshops – Webster Associates, Share for Dads, and Basic Cookery for Dads).

Other case study programmes successfully used workbooks and written exercises, including some to be used by fathers and children at home (e.g. the Fathers and Children in Education Project, It's A Man Thing!, Howzat!, Hampshire Teenage 'Lads and Dads' Book Clubs, Bradford YMCA Dads and Lads, Design and technology whole-family workshops – Webster Associates). The key was making these written materials with bright, catchy visuals, and, of course, ensuring that the activities were fun and relevant. In the Fathers and Children in Education Project, the optional 'homework' activities were amongst the most popular elements of the family learning programme.

Of course, learning methods need to take account of fathers' language and literacy skills.

Box 18: Recommended learning styles for working with fathers

- **Have fun!**
- **Use male-oriented, active, fun, focused, 'hands on' learning styles**
  - "dynamic activities" (De Nicola, 1997enderson,Hender)
  - "physical games-based activities" (Fletcher, 2001)
  - "make things a game, not an exercise" (Bryant and Henderson, 2002; Herrick and Ali, 2003)
  - take fathers and children on outings and residential trips
- Use information and communications technology, such as computers, audio, video, photography and the internet
  - "working on a computer is safe and private with no risk of humiliation or losing face" (McGivney, 1999)
  - "...a means of encouraging participation by men in family learning, is joint ICT provision" (Ofsted, 2000)
  - many of the case study programmes used cameras to record learning

> ### Box 19: Recommended facilitation style for working with fathers
>
> - **Have fun and use humour!**
> - **Make it clear what the task is**
>   - "Have written instructions setting out the task and someone to explain what the informal rules are." (Fletcher, 2003)
>   - "Model activities with children so that fathers do not feel they are being taught, and the learning process is more subtle." (Bryant and Henderson, 2002)
> - **"Give fathers a sense of control and get a result."** (DfES Fathers Advisory Group 2003/04)
> - **"avoid setting men up to look stupid."** (Fletcher, 2003)

Information for fathers about learning with their children at home

Family learning programmes are a good start, but the sessions eventually come to an end. The goal should be encouraging fathers to incorporate learning with their children and involvement in their children's education into their everyday life. Therefore, it is important to give fathers information about learning with their children at home, and about their children's school-based education. In some of the case study programmes, an important element was modelling learning activities that fathers could carry out at home.

Fathers in three focus groups in the UK wanted more information and advice from their children's school on:

- the National Curriculum

- activities their children did at school

- the changes in schools and in education since their childhood

- "clearly-explained and manageable" activities they could do with their children at home to help their learning

- detailed comments on their child's homework (Millard and Hunter, 2001).

Similarly, some black and minority ethnic fathers would like information sessions about the school curriculum and the English education system, written in their community languages (Black Development Agency, 2002; Herrick and Ali, 2003; Razwan, 2002).

Mass media are one vehicle for delivering information to fathers, and these communication methods have the advantage of reaching a very large audience. In 2002, the Department for Education and Skills launched a national media campaign called 'Dads and Sons' to raise awareness of the importance of fathers' involvement in their teenage sons' (11-14-year-olds) learning, and to increase fathers' involvement. The campaign comprised two booklets and a website www.dfes.gov.uk/dadsandsons/ (DfES, 2002a). The booklets were available in cinemas, supermarkets, restaurants, sports venues and computer/electrical retailers.

The booklets and website, which were designed with colourful graphics and many photos, suggested different activities that fathers and sons could do together at home and when out and about. Some activities were based around curricular areas, and others were based around themes such as sports, shopping, TV, film, computers and work. There were incentives, offers and competitions focusing on travel, outings, DIY, cinema (male-oriented films), computers and football/other sports, which were made possible by commercial sponsorship of the campaign. The booklets also told fathers in a variety of ways that their input really matters. There were case studies of dads who learnt with their sons, and there were role models from sport and TV talking about their father–son relationships. Lists of resources were given, for example organisations, DfES literature, telephone helplines and websites. There was also advice for fathers about school issues, for example homework and bullying.

However, it may be more effective to deliver information to fathers when they are engaged in a family learning programme which offers them face-to-face support from other fathers and trained facilitators. As mentioned in the previous section, several of the case study programmes developed written resources for fathers which made suggestions for learning activities they could engage in with their children, at home or in their local community.

Involving fathers in family literacy

Literacy is not a typically male activity. In fact, as seen in Chapters 2 and 4, fathers are less likely than mothers to read with their children at home, and many fathers see reading as 'women's work'. Developing reading skills is a vital part of children's education, and a key area of LSC-funded family learning in England. It is important to find ways of engaging fathers in family literacy programmes.

There are several family literacy programmes specifically for fathers /'father figures' and their children (often their sons), or oriented towards typical male interests.

Table 26: Family literacy programmes oriented towards fathers

Examples from the case study programmes	Some other examples from our mapping of projects and practice in England and Wales
It's A Man Thing! Howzat! (and other Dads and Lads literacy and sport projects run by Lancashire County Council) Hampshire Teenage 'Lads and Dads' Book Clubs The Big Book Share	'DIY Dads', Fathers and Sons Reading Groups in Primary Schools (Working with Men, 2004)
	Reading event at Cranmer Middle School (Pendleton, 2003)
	Several family literacy programmes in prisons and young offenders institutions (The Reading Agency, 2003)
	Several family literacy projects for fathers and children which received awards from Reading Families Millennium Award Scheme (information accessed at www.campaign-for-learning.org.uk/projects in August 2003)
	Several family literacy projects for fathers and children on the Reading Initiatives: Men and Boys section of www.literacytrust.org.uk (information accessed in August 2003) including Kick Off!
	Reading Champions, an initiative of the National Literacy Trust, which celebrates the existing work of boys and men (including fathers and father figures) who are promoting reading to others. Information accessed from www.literacytrust.org.uk in August 2003.
	4Leeds4Reading2Together (Leeds United, Leeds Libraries and National Literacy Trust) (information accessed at www.literacytrust.org.uk/football in November 2003)

Some other case study programmes incorporated literacy elements (Fathers and Children in Education Project, Share for Dads, Kensal Rise Primary School's Bring Dad to School Day - The Fathers' Inclusion Project).

There are also literacy programmes for fathers in Australia and the US including:

- the FAST (Fathers and Schools Together) Literacy Program (Tranter and Bright, 2004). Activities include focus on play and activity, using computers for spelling and writing activities, and using environmental print, maps, dictionaries and bedtime stories

- the PROJECT DADS programme in the US (Stile and Ortiz, 1999).

So, how have schools, libraries (Herb and Willoughby-Herb, 1998) and other family learning providers successfully involved fathers in family literacy programmes and subsequently in informal literacy activity at home?

It is especially important when working with fathers and their sons to consider what reading materials they will enjoy, as it is not then just the fathers who may be resistant to reading and want male-oriented literature, but the boys too (Lloyd, 1999; see Chapter 4).

Some programmes combine literacy with stereotypically male interests, male-oriented learning methods, or fun activities (e.g. Howzat!, Hampshire Dads and Lads Book Clubs, and It's A Man Thing!).

Box 20: Effective ways to interest fathers in family literacy

- Quality programmes and learning materials
- Sports
- ICT, audio and internet research
- Play and practical activity
- Games and puzzles
- Visits to libraries, local archives, and other community venues which are sources of literacy materials
- Arts and crafts
- Visits from celebrity authors, poets, dramatists and storytellers

Some libraries and other organisations have produced reading lists for fathers and their sons which suggest suitable literature (Herb and Willoughby-Herb, 1998; Working with Men, 2004; Hampshire County Council Library Service, no date). Some of the case study programmes provide books to the fathers and their children, and/or use high-quality, visually attractive written resources (e.g. It's A Man Thing!; Howzat!; The Big Book Share; Hampshire Teenage 'Lads and Dads' Book Clubs).

Despite general advice not to include too much programmed discussion time in family learning programmes for fathers, it is possible for librarians to establish successful discussion-based reading groups for fathers and their sons in public libraries, schools and other venues, so long as the books appeal to the participants, and the facilitators are skilled (the case study of Hampshire Teenage 'Lads and Dads' Book Clubs; Brookes, 2002; Working with Men, 2004). Herb and Willoughby- Herb (1998) recommend that libraries should encourage "read-aloud programs that involve fathers and other male role models in the community".

For younger children, Reissman (2001) suggests "Dad's Book Choice or Dad Reading/Story-telling Time", where fathers can read to the class or talk about their favourite books. For geographically distant non-resident fathers, including those in prisons (see the case study of The Big Book Share), and for fathers who cannot come into the classroom for other reasons (Reissman, 2001), audio- or video-taped stories can be used. Several family literacy programmes have now been set up in male prisons, and these are summarised with good practice recommendations in The Reading Agency (2003): *The Big Book Share: Libraries and Family Reading in Prisons: A Handbook*.

The librarians in the Hampshire 'Dads and Lads' Book Clubs found that they could not assume what the fathers and their sons liked to read. Participants in the pilot reading group did not think of genres, but just "according to what sounded interesting" (Marley, 2000). Reading poetry and creative writing can work too if they are in the right context and presented as one of several options in the programme (see the case studies of Howzat!, the Fathers and Children in Education Project, Share for Dads, and It's A Man Thing!).

> ### Box 21: Think about fathers' and sons' likely reading and writing interests
>
> - Facts, knowledge, action, adventure, fantasy and sci-fi, sports, humour, travel, autobiographies, TV/popular culture, and practical relevance for men and boys
> - Non-fiction, newspapers, environmental print, maps, dictionaries, written instructions, comics and 'graphic novels'
> - Websites
> - Songs, book reviews and journalism
> - Fathers "often have different reading habits...men and boys are reading, but not necessarily novels: web pages, magazines and non-fiction" (Brookes, 2002)
> - Use "books with traditional male themes" (Karther, 2002)
> - Use "fathers' personal interests and hobbies" (Ortiz, 2001)
> - "Value home-based literacy" (Macleod, 2000)
> - Provide fathers with "reassurance that all reading should be encouraged" (Brookes, 2002)

As some fathers do not have literacy or English language skills (see Section 4.7), family learning programmes need to take this into account if incorporating family literacy activities or using written materials (see the case studies of Share for Dads, The Big Book Share, The Fathers Inclusion Project at Kensal Rise Primary School, and Super Dads at Pen Pych Community Primary School). There has been a bilingual reading scheme[7] for Turkish-speaking fathers in London involving storytelling, reading, writing and prop making. Of course, family literacy can be a good first step for fathers who want to improve their basic reading and writing skills (see the case studies of Howzat!, It's A Man Thing!, and The Big Book Share).

Apart from the ones already mentioned, other useful written resources for teachers, librarians and family learning practitioners wishing to support fathers' involvement in their children's reading are Fajerman (2000) and Orme (1999). The organisation Working with Men produce posters showing images of literacy between fathers and sons (www.workingwithmen.org).

---

7   *Okuma Kulubumuz* ('Our Reading Club') – Reading Families Millennium Award Scheme (information accessed at www.campaign-for-learning.org.uk/projects in August 2003).

5.5 Involving fathers in their children's schools

Schools can provide group-based family learning programmes for fathers and their children, but they can also involve fathers in many other ways, for example keeping them in touch with their children's progress, inviting them to school meetings and events, and working individually with fathers to help their children's educational progress and emotional development, all of which many schools already do with mothers. Examples of what schools can do are given in Box 22. A good source of case studies of involving fathers and other men in schools is Fletcher, 1997.

Box 22: Involve fathers in children's school lives and in the life of schools

Help fathers to support their own children in school

- Work individually with fathers to help them support their children's educational progress, attendance and behaviour
- Make sure fathers are regularly kept informed of their children's progress and achievements, using telephone and email if no face-to-face contact
- Invite fathers to school events and parents evenings (face to face, by telephone or email, as well as by pupil post), and send them their own copies of school newsletters and children's school reports

Introduce fathers to school life

- Hold a weekday 'Bring Your Dad to School Day' – see the case study of The Fathers' Inclusion Project Kensal Rise Primary School – also organised by other schools and LEAs, including Windsor and Maidenhead's 'Dads Into School Day'
- Organise a weekend 'Father Festival'/'Dads' Day Workshop' (Reissman, 2001)
- Arrange Dads Breakfasts before school (Working with Men, 2004; Fletcher, 1997; Bright et al., 2002)

Ask fathers to support the school curriculum

- To mentor or teach or read with the children (De Nicola, 1997; Reissman, 2001; Bryant, 2000; Fletcher, 1997; Bryant et al., 1998)
- To talk about their work, hobbies and personal experiences (Reissman, 2001; Fletcher, 1997)
- To write for or talk to the class about what it means to them to be a father (Reissman, 2001)
- To volunteer as an email or telephone resource for all the children in the class, e.g. giving help and advice with specific curricular subjects, training children in activities – this could help children in the class who do not have an adult male at home (Reissman, 2001)
- To take pupils (not just their own children) to their workplace on shadowing visits (Reissman, 2001)

Ask fathers to volunteer in other ways to support the school

- To help out with after-school sports, school sports teams, and outdoor activities (Fletcher, 1997)
- To help out with DIY, gardening and other practical help for the school (Fletcher, 1997; Bryant et al., 1998)
- To join the Parent Teacher Association, or become a school governor

'Fathers breakfasts' held in schools by the voluntary organisation Working with Men at the start of the school day "provided a brief, but effective method of bringing fathers into schools" (Working with Men, 2004), as did similar breakfasts organised by the Family Action Centre in Australia (Bright et al., 2002; Fletcher, 1997). Similarly in the US, Frieman and Berkeley (2002) recommend the specific strategy of providing coffee for fathers who drop their children off in the morning to encourage the father to stay to discuss his child with the teacher.

One of the case study schools in London, Kensal Rise Primary School, holds a Bring Dad to School Day, but this school also works individually with resident and non-resident fathers and 'father figures' to engage them in their children's education and lives more generally, as does Pen Pych Community Primary School.

Email and telephone are communication methods that can be used to keep non-resident fathers (and fathers with long working hours) in touch with their children's progress and with school news, events and meetings. One email system which has been developed in the UK is Parentmail (www.parentmail.co.uk), a service for schools. Their website stated (at the time of writing) that "by sending school letters directly to you electronically you can benefit from being up-to-date and informed on ALL school events and announcements".

When children have poor attendance or behaviour, it may be crucial to involve their fathers. This report includes a case study of one very interesting project, Family Group Conferences in Education. These are family meetings used as a way of making plans and decisions to help children with school attendance and behaviour, as well as to help resolve other family issues which are causing difficulties in school. Family Group Conferences are voluntary and involve the wider family network of that child as well as the immediate family and professionals. Fathers are successfully involved, including non-resident fathers.

Involving fathers in the classroom is one way of providing male role models for boys (Fletcher, 1997), especially where schools have mainly female teachers, and with the rise of single-mother families. It may also be a way for schools to make use of fathers' abilities, for example in sport, ICT and building (Bright et al., 2002; Bryant and Taylor, 1999). De Nicola (1997) writes that "whatever you do in work or as a hobby can be made into a learning experience for kids"; and Reissman (2001) reports on a car-building school project where fathers taught children technical skills. When working-class fathers were interviewed in Bristol, they were asked what skills they could offer to their child's school or nursery (Bryant and Taylor, 1999). Most commonly mentioned were building skills, sport, computers and gardening; but cookery, art, sign language, pottery, winemaking, outdoor activities, music, and history were also mentioned.

Fathers' classroom involvement is dependent on them having free time during the working day, and so it is unlikely to become a regular or majority activity amongst fathers. However, schools can more easily involve fathers in extracurricular activities in evenings or at weekends (for example, in sports teams), occasional school trips, and out-of-school-hours voluntary work in the school.

In Bristol, the men's family learning development worker encouraged a number of men to get involved in the local primary school, helping with gardening, reading and maths classes, decorating the school corridors with murals, and teaching computers and guitar to children and other fathers (Bryant et al., 1998).

Family learning programmes can, of course, be a very good initial step in involving fathers in their children's schools more generally. Nearly all of the case study programmes reported that one outcome was that fathers felt more comfortable in the school, talking to their children's teachers, and attending school meetings. A few of the participating fathers went on to become school governors and classroom volunteers.

There are child protection issues to consider when involving fathers in schools, as there are with any adults, but these should not prevent work with the great majority of fathers. The Australian Family Action Centre's 'Five Rules for Attracting Fathers and Father Figures' recommends confronting the child protection issue positively in the context of the fathers learning about and contributing to child protection issues in schools:

> *"Men, in our experience, are keen for their children to be protected and readily see the point of police checks and care around being alone with children." (Fletcher, 2003).*

One voluntary sector organisation set up several initiatives for fathers in a London borough. One of their underlying principles was:

> *"While we are pro-fathers, this is not to the detriment of children and women. We will not support individual fathers' actions when they have a harmful effect on children and mothers (e.g. domestic violence and sexual abuse)." (Working with Men, 2004).*

Involving non-resident fathers in schools

Chapter 2 noted that schools and family learning programmes can be neutral venues for non-resident fathers to spend quality time with their children. Some of the case study family learning programmes and schools also had this role (e.g. Design and technology whole-family workshops –Webster Associates and The Fathers Inclusion Project Kensal Rise Primary School). Some African-Caribbean fathers in a small-scale research study wanted venues where non-resident fathers could take their children for quality time together (Bruneau, 2002).

Frieman (1998) argues that it is the role of the school to "proactively reach out to divorced fathers and involve them in the educational process". Frieman and Berkeley (2002) that "teachers need to treat divorced fathers as if they were single parents".

Kensal Rise Primary School, one of the case study schools, reaches out proactively to non-resident fathers who have had no or little involvement in their children's lives. The school successfully obtains contact details for non-resident fathers from children's mothers; and follows this up with a letter or phone call to the father. Fathers may agree to a specific plan, such as regular visits to the school or involvement in a mentoring group. Fathers are given regular information about their children's progress, for example using the telephone, and there is an 'open door' to them. In one case, a previously uninvolved father became a governor at his child's school. This approach required teachers to have persistence and sensitivity, and to put the children's well-being firmly at the centre of their work.

In fact, a DfES guidance note for schools (*Schools, 'Parents' and 'Parental Responsibility REF: DfEE 0092/2000*) recommends that schools involve both parents wherever possible, including non-resident parents, unless this would be contrary to the child's needs (DfEE, 2000). Non-resident parents have rights under education law to be involved in their children's education.

In discussion at the joint DfES/NFPI seminar, points were made that involving non-resident fathers is very challenging where there is conflict between the child's separated parents, for example, if a resident mother does not want the school to involve a non-resident father, or if a non-resident father's decision about his child's education differs from a resident mother's.

> ## Box 23: Involve non-resident fathers
>
> - Have contact details for non-resident fathers on school database (where possible)
>
> - Have school policy on involving non-resident fathers
>
> - Refer to DfEE guidance note on schools working with all parents (DfEE, 2000)
>
> - Discuss any concerns of teachers and practitioners about engaging non-resident fathers
>
> - Send school newsletters and invitations to both non-resident fathers and any resident step-fathers or 'father figures'
>
> - Invite non-resident fathers to parents evenings and other school events. Have two separate meetings if necessary to discuss child's progress, one with the mother and another with the father
>
> - Use telephone or email to keep non-resident fathers in touch with their child's progress
>
> - Negotiate contact with non-resident father with child's mother where possible
>
> - Do not make children the 'go-between' between fathers and mothers who are in conflict
>
> - Know about any court orders restricting non-resident fathers' access or parental responsibility.
>
> - Be aware of the possibility of violence or abuse, but realise this will not generally be the case

Extended schools and fathers

Extended schools (see Section 1.3) can involve children's fathers in the range of services that they offer to parents and their local community, for example in sports, leisure and adult education. This could be a first step for 'school-phobic' fathers who wish to get more familiar with the school and then support their children's education. Two of the case study programmes organised adult learning in basic computer skills for fathers (sometimes combined with family learning) at their children's schools (Dads on Computers, Share for Dads).

In an area of Bristol, courses organised for fathers at the local primary school included basic computer skills, spray art, computer art and design, woodwork, and bricklaying (Bryant, 2000). The woodwork course led on to the formation of a workshop at the school, with the venue being hired out to Bristol Community Education and a women's group to cover overheads. Items were produced for community groups such as school playground furniture and puppet theatres.

Some black and minority ethnic fathers with limited English language skills would like language classes (Black Development Agency, 2002; Razwan, 2002), and their children's schools may be a convenient venue for these.

Schools should "meet fathers' needs as well as children's needs", on the basis that some fathers may need help before they can become effective role models for their children (DfES Fathers Advisory Group 2003/04). Some authors also argue that schools can support fathers in their overall parenting role. For example, Frieman and Berkeley (2002) and Frieman (1998) recommend that:

- school newsletters can include articles about fathering as well as about mothering

- teachers give non-resident fathers information and advice on parenting

- teachers can work with school counsellors to run groups for fathers to explore their feelings about fatherhood.

In Wales, at Pen Pych Community Primary School (one of the case studies), the headteacher works with groups of fathers about fatherhood and education issues, for example their relationship with their own fathers and their own experiences at school. These fathers are from a working-class 'macho' culture, but they feel able to be open in all-male groups, and they much value this time together.

Herb and Willoughby-Herb (1998) make similar recommendations for libraries to support fathering in a time of changing and fragile fathering roles: "supporting fathers as parents by acquiring and making visible resource material related to fathering", with the library as "an ideal community partner in supporting parenting". In The Big Book Share (Chapter 6), developing links with a local library was a resource and support for ex-offenders' reading, learning and community re-integration.

Single-parent fathers may especially appreciate support and advice from their children's school which goes beyond children's learning and education. In a survey of its lone father members by the UK voluntary organisation Gingerbread, 25 per cent of these fathers said their main worry on becoming a lone father was legal, 22 per cent financial, 14 per cent childcare and 10 per cent supporting their children; 22 per cent of the lone fathers said that they didn't receive any support when they became a lone father (Gingerbread, 2001). Nearly 80 per cent said they would have welcomed more support, with only 21 per cent saying that extra support would not have been necessary.

5.6 Physical environments

Section 4.8 suggested that schools and other feminised educational settings may not be the best venues for engaging fathers in family learning because many fathers had poor childhood experiences of school and are deterred by the predominance of women.

However, most of the case study programmes, including those for working-class and minority ethnic fathers (who tend to have traditional beliefs about gender roles – see Section 4.5), ran successfully in school and public library venues. In fact, as noted in the previous section, many of these programmes found that family learning sessions introduced fathers to the school environment and encouraged them to become more involved in their children's education more generally.

Table 27: Venues used in the case study programmes

Venue	Number of case studies
Infants and primary schools	7
Middle and secondary schools	4
Special school (children with special needs)	1
Outdoor venues (countryside, gardens, allotments, coast, outdoor activities centres, local parks)	4
Home	4
Local amateur and professional sports clubs	2
Arts and cultural venues, e.g. museums[8]	2
Community centres	2
Public library (as main venue[9])	1
Leisure centres	1
Prison[10]	1

Professional sports clubs have become popular venues for family learning programmes because they interest fathers and boys, and they are neutral venues (e.g. the case studies of Howzat! and It's A Man Thing!). In particular, the DfES, LEAs, professional sports clubs and business sponsors have set up Playing for Success study support centres at professional sports clubs with 'state-of-the art' equipment such as internet and video (www.dfes.gov.uk/playingforsuccess). These were first used for study support for teenage children in literacy, numeracy and ICT, but a number of Dads and Lads initiatives are now also in operation at these venues.

Some black and minority ethnic fathers may be especially comfortable in religious or community venues, for example black churches for African-Caribbean fathers (see Working with Men, 2004), and mosques or madrasahs (children's religion schools) for Muslim fathers. However, three of the case study programmes successfully engaged black and minority ethnic fathers in school venues (Share for Dads, Bradford YMCA Dads and Lads, and The Fathers Inclusion Project at Kensal Rise Primary School). Some black and minority ethnic fathers may want separate men-only venues to meet cultural and religious traditions on social separation of men and women. South Asian Muslim fathers in one research study wanted a men-only room in their children's primary school for fathers and children to use for family learning (Razwan, 2002).

Of course, it is not sufficient to base conclusions about optimal venues on participating fathers' reports of satisfaction with the chosen venue, as non-participating fathers may have been deterred by the venue, so a balance of school settings and other settings would be best to give fathers choices.

Even when home–school and family learning programmes for fathers run in schools, it may be best to recruit the fathers in other venues, as discussed in Section 5.9.

---

8   Other family learning programmes incorporate visits to museums (e.g. Bradford YMCA Dads and Lads and Share for Dads).

9   Other home-based family learning programmes for fathers and children incorporate visits to libraries (e.g. It's A Man Thing!, and Howzat!).

10 There are several family literacy programmes in male prisons and young offenders institutions (The Reading Agency (2003).

The type of venue is not the only consideration relating to the optimal physical environment for engaging fathers in their children's learning and education. The literature, the DfES/ NFPI seminar discussion and the case studies included recommendations for:

- pictures of fathers and children, as well as of mothers and children, on walls, in classrooms and in school newsletters, taking account of social and ethnic diversity (Berger, 1998; Fletcher, 2002; Millard and Hunter, 2001) – in some of the case study schools, pictures of fathers and children engaging in family learning were prominently displayed

- magazines in reception areas which appeal to men

- informal seating (not desks or a classroom format) – some school-based programmes used family learning rooms

- spaces large enough for physical activity, e.g. school halls

- furniture and spaces for tall men, as schools and some other family learning venues are spaces generally used for children, mothers and female teachers/practitioners.

There are good-quality posters with images of fathers and children available from the English voluntary organisations Fathers Direct and Working with Men.

5.7 Costs, incentives and accredited learning

Costs

Like mothers (NIACE, 2003; Fitzgerald et al., 2002), fathers participating in family learning programmes and in their children's schools can find any course fees and materials, and other costs of participation (e.g. childcare and transport), to be barriers (see Section 4.8). Nearly all of the case study family learning programmes were completely free to fathers and other participants. Bryant and Henderson (2002) recommend that family learning practitioners who want to involve fathers should "avoid...material costs for learners". All LSC-funded family learning programmes are expected to be delivered to the learners at no cost to them (LSC, 2004).

However, in some of the case study programmes, fathers were prepared to contribute small amounts towards the cost of the learning, even when they were low-paid workers. For example, in Pen Pych Community Primary School, fathers pay towards the cost of weekends away at an outdoor activities centre, and in It's A Man Thing!, fathers contribute towards the cost of some materials.

Berger (1998) recommends that early childhood centres and schools "provide or pay for transportation, and offer childcare" as one strategy to engage fathers, which of course also applies to mothers (NIACE, 2003). In research with working-class fathers in Bristol, only two out of the 36 men wanted transport to be provided, but about a third wanted childcare facilities (Bryant and Taylor, 1999). Two of the case study programmes mentioned that the lack of childcare provision had been a barrier to some fathers attending.

One of the case study programmes, Howzat!, provided transport from the school to the local cricket club for the programme's final session. The Big Book Share paid travel expenses for prisoners' families to enable them to attend the special family visits in the programme. The Fathers and Children in Education project offered childcare on site in a school where the

Sure Start local programme was a key partner. In other programmes, younger siblings could attend the family learning sessions, for example the Hampshire Teenage 'Lads and Dads' Book Clubs. Family literacy, language and numeracy programmes which are funded by the LSC provide free childcare or meet the costs of childcare, and sometimes arrange transport where required.

Incentives

What was relatively common in the case study programmes, and frequently recommended in the literature, is to offer fathers and their children some incentives for their participation (e.g. Millard and Hunter, 2001). The incentives referred to in the literature and the case studies are in Box 24.

What was especially common in the case study programmes was to give participating fathers and children a certificate at the end of the course, to display their work, and/or to hold an end-of-project celebration to which whole families were invited. Food and drink were also very prevalent incentives.

> ### Box 24: Incentives offered to fathers and children in family learning programmes
>
> - Certificates and prizes for participating fathers and children
> - Displaying fathers' and children's work
> - Taking away the learning, for example a cooked meal or a robotic toy
> - End of programme celebration
> - Outings
> - Food and drink
> - Sports match tickets
> - Cinema tickets
> - Loans of sports kit
> - Sports coaching
> - Books and educational resources
> - Free use of internet in libraries
> - Free loans of CDs and videos from libraries
> - Involvement of celebrities (local, sports)

Some programmes attract sponsorship from the commercial sector, including professional sports clubs, to offer incentives such as children's books, cinema tickets and sports match tickets (DfES, 2002a; the case studies of Dads on Computers, Hampshire 'Dads and Lads' Book Clubs, and The Big Book Share).

Incentives, for example food and drink, must of course meet the religious and cultural re-quirements of the target groups of fathers, for example taking into account local cultures, and the religious dietary and alcohol rules for Muslims, Hindus, Jews, some Christians, and other groups.

Although sometimes very helpful, these kinds of incentives are not crucial. Some projects find that the incentives of helping their children's learning and of quality time together with their children (see Section 4.5) are sufficient. One of the case study programmes, Dads on Computers, found that the prizes offered had little impact on recruitment, although another, It's A Man Thing!, found that incentives were an important factor.

Accreditation for learning

Accreditation for adult learning may be an incentive for some fathers to engage in family learning programmes, and also an important first qualification for some fathers which gives them confidence in their ability to learn. Two of the case study programmes, It's A Man Thing! and Share for Dads, offered Open College Network accreditation as an option, as does the programme Family Learning Through Football (Chisholm et al., 2004). Several prison family literacy programmes offer accreditation, although not The Big Book Share because there are no long-stay prisoners in HMP Nottingham (The Reading Agency, 2003).

However, Bryant and Henderson (2002) recommend that family learning programmes for men avoid "too much emphasis on accreditation". Similarly, the DfES Fathers Advisory Group 2003/04 warned against making accreditation a central concern because of local authorities' and Learning and Skills Council's targets, rather than because of fathers' wishes and needs. It is key to remember that fathers often get involved in family learning programmes to help their children rather than themselves.

Similarly, NIACE (2003) report mixed views amongst family learning practitioners to accreditation. Further research is needed on this complex issue.

5.8 Time and timing

Planning family learning programmes and school meetings requires three decisions about time. Firstly, the length of a learning programme, i.e. the number of sessions. Secondly, the length of a learning session or school meeting. Thirdly, when the event is to be held.

Family learning sessions – length and frequency

As seen in Chapter 2, fathers are more likely to participate in family learning programmes when courses are shorter, and in schools for one-off or infrequent events like induction meetings and parents evenings. Some family learning providers use one-day events, 'taster' sessions at first, or 'drop-in activities' (Berger, 1998; Bryant and Henderson, 2002; Working with Men, 2004; see the case studies of Basic Cookery for Dads and The Fathers Inclusion Project at Kensal Rise Primary School's 'Bring Dad to School Day').

But, as with so much good practice, this is not an iron rule. Some of the case study family learning programmes consisted of between six and ten sessions (generally one a week), and this was the programme length recommended by practitioners in the DfES Fathers Advisory Group 2003/04. In Howzat! and Hampshire Teenage 'Lads and Dads' Book Clubs, the fathers of teenagers were required to attend learning sessions just a couple of times in the school term. However, in the Fathers and Children in Education project, any break between sessions of longer than a week tended to lead "to a significant drop-off, both in attendance and interest" (Martin, 2003). Some projects reminded children or fathers between sessions, and many mentioned the need to be accepting of irregular attendance and lateness.

Most of the case study family learning programmes had individual sessions lasting between one and three hours, but with longer time commitments needed for outings.

Scheduling of school and family learning events

Section 4.8 showed that inappropriate scheduling of school and family learning events can be a barrier to fathers' involvement. When it comes to decisions on the timing of family learning and school events that seek to involve fathers, flexibility, taking account of local diversity, and consulting local fathers are all important. The recommendations on timing found in the literature or which emerged from the case studies are in Box 25.

There is no one good time even for working fathers (e.g. Bryant and Taylor, 1999; Frieman and Berkeley, 2002; Razwan, 2002); and, if possible, different times should be offered to meet the differing needs of fathers working full-time standard (daytime) hours, fathers working different shift patterns, fathers working on weekends and in evenings, and fathers in part-time work or who are not working at all. Non-resident fathers who do not live in the neighbourhood, or who see their children only on visits, may be able to come only on weekends with their children to family learning programmes, and to visit their children's schools. Extended schools offer an opportunity here with their extended opening hours.

Frieman and Berkeley (2002) suggest that teachers are available early mornings, late afternoons and early evenings to speak to fathers. They recommend that the fathers who do have flexibility over their work times could be invited into the school to "have lunch with their child or share some time reading to a child's class, or tutor children in their child's class". Section 5.5 referred to 'fathers breakfasts'.

Some of the case study programmes ran successfully in the daytime during the week, engaging unemployed fathers, those working part time or on shifts, and those sharing weekday childcare with their female partner (Dads on Computers, Share for Dads, Kensal Rise Primary School's Bring Dad to School Day – The Fathers Inclusion Project). Some of these fathers re-arranged their shifts, negotiated time off with their employer, or came straight from nightshifts to sessions, although this meant they could be very tired. Kensal Rise Primary School and Pen Pych Community Primary School maintained an 'open door' to fathers, which meant they could visit at any time during the school day.

More common in the case study programmes was to have sessions just after school (three programmes), in evenings (four programmes), or at weekends (six programmes). Webster Associates found that evening timings (in contrast to straight after school) can exclude younger children. Of course, home-based family learning like Howzat! and It's A Man Thing! allow fathers to decide what times are best for learning with their children, which is especially helpful for non-resident fathers.

The organisers of the case study programmes found that the timing of family learning events for fathers needs to take into account the scheduling of football matches and other sports events (also see Millard and Hunter, 2001) and a range of religious festivals, as well as religious obligations for some fathers in minority ethnic groups (e.g. Muslims) who pray at set times during the day.

> ### Box 25: "Have flexible schedules" (Berger, 1998)
>
> **Most fathers work full time, but not all**
>
> - Take account of local industries/working patterns
> - Remember about unemployed fathers, and shift and weekend workings – daytime may be fine for some fathers
> - Give fathers sufficient warning so can take time off work (Clough et al., 2000)
> - Remember that low-paid workers and self-employed fathers may have no flexibility over their work time and/or will lose earnings (Frieman and Berkeley, 2002; Black Development Agency, 2002)
>
> **And also consider:**
>
> - May need school caretaker to open and close premises
> - Being flexible; accept some irregular attendance and lateness
> - Dads breakfasts
> - Football, TV sport, local events
> - Taking account of religious festivals and daily prayer times (e.g. Muslim fathers)

5.9 Publicity and recruitment

One clear message coming from the case studies and the literature is that recruiting fathers into school involvement and family learning programmes is challenging and time-consuming. It requires persistence, creativity, patience, sensitivity, time and sufficient practitioner resource. The Family Action Centre write in their 'Five Rules for Attracting Fathers and Father Figures' that "for dads...just turning up at the school may be a big step" and recommend that schools should not be too ambitious (Fletcher, 2003).

However, it is possible to recruit fathers, and evidence from the literature and case studies is now presented on what can work successfully.

Reaching non-resident fathers and fathers with long working hours requires special determination. Successfully engaging black and minority ethnic fathers may require developing a knowledge of community languages and of where these fathers tend to be, for example socially and in places of worship. References to some of these specific groups of fathers are made in the following discussion.

Printed/written publicity and school information

In order to successfully engage fathers, family learning providers need to consider the language and message they use in their publicity, and make it clear and specific. Factual language usually works better than emotional language (Bryant and Henderson, 2002), and other authors make similar points, as shown in Box 26. Some of the case study programmes chose 'catchy titles' which would engage fathers and boys, with the emphasis on having fun rather than learning or education (e.g. Design and technology whole-family workshops – Webster Associates; Howzat!; Hampshire Teenage 'Lads and Dads' Book Clubs). Some of the case study programmes used publicity with bright visuals, for example posters, leaflets, stickers and flyers, rather than more formal letters.

Box 26: *Effective written publicity*

- Use post or email (e.g. Parentmail, www.parentmail.co.uk); do not rely on 'pupil post'
- Proactively send information and invitations to non-resident fathers (Berger, 1998) – try hard to obtain their contact details
- Place publicity imaginatively
- "Experience shows that fathers respond more favourably to any publicity or information which is factual" (Millard and Hunter, 2001)
- Invitations to Dads Breakfasts were "kept brief and to the point" and "then fathers came, sometimes in large numbers" (Working with Men, 2004)
- "avoid jargon and 'touchy feely' wording" (Bryant and Henderson, 2002)
- Make sure that fathers know how they or their children will benefit
- "Sell the activity as 'something' you are doing for your children" (Bryant and Henderson, 2002)
- Have the name 'Fathers/Male carers' in the title of letters, flyers and other written publicity to make clear to mothers and children that fathers specifically are required (Fletcher, 2003)
- Ask children to create invitations in class for their fathers
- Include pictures and articles about fathers in school newsletters (Berger, 1998; Fletcher, 2002)

'Pupil post' (where children take school letters and information home to their parents) and school newsletters are generally an unreliable way of getting written invitations and other information to fathers. Letters do not often reach fathers, as the children or mothers filter them out and sometimes even respond on behalf of the father (Brookes, 2002; Millard and Hunter, 2001). Pupil post will be especially unlikely to reach non-resident fathers, and the regular postal system or email would be better methods to use.

If using pupil post (and a few of the case study programmes did so successfully), it is usually important to be explicit that children' fathers and male carers are needed. However, it should be noted that one of the case study programmes managed to engage many fathers without targeting publicity to them, through a growing local reputation for technologically exciting workshops for all family members (Design and technology whole-family workshops – Webster Associates).

As seen in Section 4.5, fathers are more likely to participate in family learning for their children's benefit than for their own benefit, and so a good message is to explicitly tell fathers how their involvement will help their children (Bryant and Henderson, 2002). This worked for many of the case study programmes, and for Working with Men when advertising their fathers breakfasts and father–son literacy initiatives in schools (Working with Men, 2004). In some programmes, children make invitations themselves in class time.

It is important to be sensitive and inclusive of children who do not have a father or other resident male adult in their household. One good solution, especially if using 'pupil post' is to give all children in the class, including those with no resident father or other male, a copy of an invitation addressed to "Dear father or male carer" (Millard and Hunter, 2001).

When working with black and minority ethnic fathers, the use of printed publicity and written information from schools needs to take account of local languages, using translation wherever possible (see the case study of the Fathers Inclusion Project at Kensal Rise Primary School; also Razwan, 2002). It can be helpful for publicity to include visual images of black and minority ethnic fathers with their children (Working with Men, 2004).

Methods and locations of communication with fathers

According to McGivney (1999) in relation to adult learning, "women obtain information from a wide range of sources such as friends, family, education providers, TV and newspapers", whereas men commonly use their employer, and unemployed men use Benefit Offices or Job Clubs. As seen in Section 4.8, publicity methods commonly used to involve mothers in schools and family learning programmes will not be as successful in reaching fathers, for example by word of mouth, through local friendship networks, holding coffee mornings, or sending letters home from school with the children (NIACE, 2003; Brookes, 2002; Millard and Hunter, 2001).

Several researchers and practitioners and some of the case study programmes strongly recommend using direct personal approaches to individual fathers, face to face or by telephone, for example asking them to help on school trips or to come to school events (Clough et al., 2000; Bryant and Henderson, 2002; McGivney, 1999; Turbiville et al., 2000; Millard and Hunter, 2001; Bright et al., 2002). This kind of recruitment is essential for recruiting fathers with literacy difficulties or visual disabilities who cannot read written publicity. Several of the case study programmes combined written publicity with more personal approaches.

Achieving face-to-face contacts can sometimes be challenging, as fathers (and especially non-resident fathers) are less likely than mothers to drop off or pick up their children from school. In research in north-east England by Children North East, about 40 per cent of mothers but only about 15 per cent of fathers said they were personally invited by teachers to take part in classroom activities (Clough et al., 2000). Of the participating fathers, four of them (five in total) had been personally invited.

However, fathers' presence at the school gate is relatively common and increasing (see Chapter 2), and some of the case study programmes did successfully recruit their fathers this way (e.g. Share for Dads, and Dads on Computers), or they speak to fathers at school events such as parents' evenings and school sports matches. The Fathers and Children in Education Project felt that recruiting fathers through their children's schools is a good method, as parents tend to trust the school their children attend. It is likely that recruiting fathers solely through schools will miss some fathers out, in particular non-resident fathers and fathers with long or atypical working hours.

An alternative is to use "imaginative outreach strategies" (McGivney, 1999), either through home visits, by meeting fathers in locations like pubs and other social spaces, sports clubs, workplaces, places of worship and job centres, or by using local media like free newspapers and radio. This imaginative selection of recruitment venues applies both to face-to-face recruitment of fathers and to placing printed publicity (see the case study of Hampshire Teenage 'Lads and Dads' Book Clubs). One of the case study programmes, Super Dads at Pen Pych Community Primary School, held their initial meeting in the local rugby club where local fathers tended to feel comfortable. It is important to remember that pubs are an important social space for many fathers, but not for all, especially some black and minority ethnic fathers.

Community workers, for example fathers workers and home–school liaison practitioners, can be a great help in achieving personal contacts with fathers, which can be very time-consuming (Millard and Hunter, 2001; Razwan, 2002). This can be particularly important when working in ethnically diverse areas where recruitment should be conducted in the varied languages of the local communities (Razwan, 2002).

Other recruitment methods used by schools and family learning providers are to recruit fathers through people they already know, either:

- the children themselves (Fletcher, 2002) – some of the case study programmes relied mainly on this recruitment method, for example placing publicity in schools and youth clubs programmes (e.g. Hampshire Teenage 'Lads and Dads' Book Clubs)

- fathers who are already involved in the school or family learning programme and respected in their local community (McGivney, 1999; Reissman, 2001; Berger, 1998; see the case studies of Super Dads at Pen Pych Community Primary School, and Basic Cookery for Dads) or who were ex-pupils of the school (Herrick and Ali, 2003)

- through mothers of the children (McGivney, 1999; Karther, 2002; Clough et al., 2000; Lloyd, 1999; Bryant and Henderson, 2002) (see the case study of Super Dads at Pen Pych Community Primary School), although some mothers are resistant to or ambivalent about fathers' involvement (see Chapter 4).

Peer group norms are often more important to men than to women (McGivney, 1999) so the power of the peer group can be used successfully, especially in communities with strong group norms. McGivney (1999) suggests that it may be more helpful to recruit men into learning through workplaces and community organisations than by approaching individuals. In Pen Pych Community Primary School, three of the initial group of six fathers in Super Dads were miners who were revered by the local community and "viewed as the most masculine of men" (Todd Jones and Evans, undated). These fathers' participation gave the group instant local credibility and encouraged other local fathers to come forward. Similarly, in HMP Nottingham, the success of The Big Book Share family literacy programme was facilitated by this programme attaining 'street cred' within the prison.

Some of the case study programmes told us that their reputation built up locally, and then the main vehicle for recruitment was 'word of mouth', from school to school, father to father, and child to child (e.g. Howzat!, Super Dads at Pen Pych Community Primary School, It's A Man Thing!, Design and technology whole-family workshops – Webster Associates, Hampshire Teenage 'Lads and Dads' Book Clubs). Some programmes raise their local profile (or have plans to do so) through using local media (including black and minority ethnic media – see Working with Men, 2004), making videos of their work, displaying fathers' and children's work in school, and holding special events, sometimes with celebrities attending (e.g. Howzat!, Super Dads at Pen Pych Community Primary School, Bradford YMCA Dads and Lads, Share for Dads).

Box 27: "Relationships are better than posters" (Bryant and Henderson, 2002)

"Going to dads – not expecting dads to come to you" (DfES Fathers Advisory Group 2003/04)

- "Reaching non-participant men can be time-consuming...it requires one-to-one contact and dialogue in familiar local venues" (McGivney, 1999)

- "Imaginative outreach strategies are needed for those who are geographically and socially isolated" (McGivney, 1999)

- Use pubs, workplaces, job centres, sports centres, football and other sports clubs, weekend study support, free local newspapers

Fathers are not in school playground or at school gate as frequently as mothers, but still relatively common and increasing

- "During daily drop-off and pick-up, talk with fathers as well as mothers...Encourage fathers to come early and participate with the children" (Berger, 1998)

- Know the names of fathers, have specific events coming up to talk to fathers about, talk to fathers about their child's work (Fletcher, 2003)

Other methods

- Make home visits (Bryant and Henderson, 2002; Berger, 1998)

- Use telephone and email (e.g. Parentmail)

- Use community workers, for example home–school liaison workers

- "Children are the most effective recruiters" (Fletcher, 2003; DfES Fathers Advisory Group 2003/04)

- "Match up new dads with current participants and form peer support groups" (Berger, 1998)

- Appeal to mothers where there is a good relationship (and even where not if done sensitively and convincingly) (DfES Fathers Advisory Group 2003/04)

Targeted recruitment

Some of the case study programmes targeted the fathers of specific children, commonly those with problems in school, either for their entire recruitment to the programme, or occasionally along with much wider recruitment (e.g. Bradford YMCA Dads and Lads, The Fathers Inclusion Project at Kensal Rise Primary School, Super Dads at Pen Pych Community Primary School, Fathers and Children in Education Project).

5.10 Summary

- Some of the good practice recommendations in the report apply to working with mothers as well as fathers, but research suggests that they can be even more crucial for fathers because of traditional cultural belief systems about gender roles in families, fathers' greater likelihood of full-time work, fathers' greater likelihood to have had bad experiences at school, and so on.

- It appears easiest to engage fathers in home–school and family learning programmes developed especially for fathers, although practical family learning activities such as design and technology can engage both mothers and fathers when appropriately designed.

- There are some tried and tested ways of effectively involving fathers in schools and family learning programmes:
  - include non-resident fathers, and a range of male carers and 'father figures', not just resident fathers
  - consult fathers, mothers, children and practitioners
  - welcome and appreciate fathers
  - recognise, respect and adapt to individual and cultural diversity
  - work in partnership with other organisations, and share good practice.

- In most cases, it is not sufficient to think about the details of specific programmes when engaging fathers. Headteachers and senior managers need to implement a 'whole school' or 'whole family learning provider' approach involving:
  - high-level strategy, planning and commitment with clear policies
  - obtaining sufficient funding
  - staff with appropriate skills and sufficient designated time
  - building positive attitudes amongst all teachers and practitioners (not just those working directly with fathers) towards fathers' involvement, using training and/or reflective practice
  - collecting information about children's fathers and male carers, including non-resident fathers, on school records
  - research and evaluation on working with fathers.

- The two most frequent messages on engaging fathers in family learning programmes are: to have fun; and to use practical, dynamic, 'hands on' activities, rather than too much discussion. Outings, IT, audio, video, other technology and high-quality materials are popular with fathers. Discussions and workbooks can be used if fathers feel at ease and with skilled facilitation.

- The mapping found several examples of successful family literacy programmes specifically for fathers and children, oriented towards typical male interests, and using web pages and non-fiction.

- Incorporating religious and cultural traditions into family learning programmes can be very successful in engaging black and minority ethnic fathers.

- Professional sports clubs have become popular venues for family learning programmes.

- Ideally, family learning programmes for fathers should be free for the participants, and provide financial help with childcare and transport.

- Schools can involve fathers, including non-resident fathers, by regularly keeping in touch (by telephone and email where relevant), inviting them to school meetings and events, and working individually with fathers to help children's educational, emotional and social development, all of which many schools do with mothers.

- Schools can also ask fathers to support the school curriculum and to volunteer, for example with after-school sports and helping out with DIY. This can provide positive male role models for boys in schools which have few male teachers.

- Extended schools can involve children's fathers in the services that they offer the local community, for example sports, leisure and adult education. This can be a first step for 'school-phobic' fathers who wish to get more familiar with the school and then support their child's education.

- There are child protection issues to consider when involving fathers in schools and family learning programmes, as there are with any adults, but these should not prevent work with the great majority of fathers.

- Recruitment of fathers is often challenging and time-consuming. It requires persistence, creativity, patience, sensitivity and sufficient practitioner resource. A good recruitment message is to explicitly tell fathers how their involvement will help their children.

- 'Pupil post' (where children take school letters and information home to their parents) and school newsletters are generally unreliable methods to get invitations and other information to fathers, in particular non-resident fathers.

- Effective recruitment methods are through children, mothers and involved fathers, making use of peer-group power and imaginative outreach strategies. Offering fathers and their children incentives for their participation can also be very helpful.

- There is more inconclusive or complex evidence on the following issues:
  - gender mix amongst teachers and practitioners – male teachers and practitioners may be helpful but are not vital
  - number of sessions in family learning programmes – this may depend on the fathers and programme content
  - timing of sessions (daytime, evenings or weekends) – flexibility, taking account of local diversity, and consulting local fathers are all important – non-resident fathers who do not live locally or have limited access to their children may be able to come along with their child only on weekends
  - degree of 'traditionally masculine' curricular content – many writers recommend being realistic about typical male interests, and this is often a good first step, but a much broader curricular content can successfully engage fathers, and may be needed for programmes for fathers and daughters
  - venues – although school venues can be a barrier for some fathers, most of the case study programmes ran successfully in schools
  - accreditation for fathers – this may be a facilitator or inhibitor of fathers' involvement
- More research on these practice issues would be helpful.

6 | The case studies

This chapter presents 13 case studies of home–school and family learning programmes in England and Wales which successfully engage fathers in learning with their children and/or in schools. Each case study fits a descriptive "formative evaluation" model which aims "to describe, track and assess the implementation of the intervention" (O'Brien, 2004). O'Brien argues that "rich descriptive material" is especially important "at the early stages of new interventions where innovatory elements can be highlighted". She describes the kinds of issues that formative evaluation can address, including:

- clarifying goals and models of intervention

- description of the initiative by service planners, and evidence on how the initiative is conducted in practice

- methods of assessment of project outcomes

- the uptake of the initiative by fathers, and the characteristics of participating fathers.

The definition of 'success' used to select the case studies was that the initiative engages and retains fathers in significant numbers. Most of the programmes also have evidence of positive feedback and perceived benefits from fathers, children and practitioners. Due to the lack of rigorous independent evaluation of most of these initiatives (which is typical of home–school and family learning programmes – see Chapter 3), it is not often possible to define success in terms of robust evidence on learning achievements or long-term outcomes.

Methodological information on how the case study programmes were selected and on how the case study evidence was collected is in the Appendix.

It is the intention that these case studies will be a helpful resource for policymakers and practitioners working in this relatively new area of programmes to involve fathers in their children's learning and education.

6.1 Introduction to the case study programmes

Below are reported the main features of the case study programmes in terms of objectives, basic models, providers and target groups of fathers and children. Of course, it is not possible to make comparisons across the case studies since each project has different aims, target groups, processes, and levels of funding and other inputs.

Evidence from these case studies relating to perceived outcomes for children, fathers and schools has been reported in Chapter 3. Evidence relating to fathers' beliefs and attitudes, and barriers and challenges in working with fathers, has been reported in Chapter 4. Evidence relating to successful practice in working with fathers has been reported in Chapter 5.

	Name of programme	Main provider/s	Brief description	Special features
1	**Bradford YMCA Dads and Lads**	City of Bradford YMCA	A family learning programme (many different activities, not solely physical/sport) for fathers and sons taking place in a primary school	Fathers and sons Deprived area Asian Muslim fathers
2	**Basic Cookery for Dads**	Suffolk County Council Families Project (Family Learning)	A cookery session for fathers and children taking place at a school	Rural area Fathers and daughters, although not specifically targeted at daughters Non-stereotypically masculine activity
3	**Dads on Computers**	Children North East Fathers Plus project, two first schools, and the Workers Education Association (WEA)	A computer course for fathers and their children taking place in a school	Deprived area Learning with the fathers on their own (adult learning) and joint learning with their children (family learning) Fathers making use of a service for adults in an 'extended school'
4	**Family Group Conferences in Education**	Hampshire LEA	Voluntary family meetings used as a way of making plans and decisions to help children with school attendance and behaviour, as well as to help resolve other family issues which are causing difficulties in school	Behaviour and attendance Involves whole families, including fathers County-wide
5	**Hampshire Teenage 'Lads and Dads' Book Clubs**	Hampshire County Council Recreation and Heritage Department (includes County Library Service)	Five Lads and Dads reading groups set up in Hampshire public libraries for fathers and teenage boys	Teenage boys Literacy Public libraries County-wide

	Name of programme	Main provider/s	Brief description	Special features
6	Howzat!	Lancashire County Council (LEA)	A county-wide programme for fathers and teenage boys in Lancashire secondary schools to link sporting activities with literacy activities	Teenage boys Literacy and sport Partnership with local sports clubs Includes a special school, and black and minority ethnic fathers County-wide
7	It's A Man Thing : A Fathers and Reading Project	ContinYou (formerly CEDC)	A nationwide project providing opportunities for fathers and other significant males to help primary school children with reading activities at home, supported by the child's school	Literacy for primary school children Nationwide
8	The Fathers Inclusion Project at Kensal Rise Primary School	Kensal Rise Primary School	Works to involve fathers and male carers in their children's education and school, increasing communication and support. Most is individual work between fathers, children and teachers. The Project has also organised a Bring Dad to School Day	Deprived area Individual work with fathers Black and minority ethnic and non-resident fathers
9	Fathers and Children in Education Project	The Fathers and Families in Suffolk project of the Ormiston Children and Families Trust	A two-year programme ran activity-based family learning projects for fathers and children in five primary/middle schools in Suffolk and Essex	Rural area Several curricular areas including sport and play, arts and crafts, and literacy Included a special school
10	Super Dads at Pen Pych Community Primary School	Pen Pych Community Primary School	Fathers and children get involved together weekly in a variety of activities. There are occasional father-only groups to discuss fatherhood and education issues; and some weekends away	Deprived area Several curricular areas including design and technology, crafts and outdoor/sporting activities Weekends away

	Name of programme	Main provider/s	Brief description	Special features
11	**Share for Dads**	South Haringey Infants School and Haringey Adult Learning Service (LEA)	The group meets weekly in an infants school to carry out joint activities, sometimes with their children, sometimes without their children	Deprived area Black and minority ethnic fathers Several curricular areas including arts and crafts Fathers making use of a service (IT learning) for adults in an 'extended school'
12	**The Big Book Share: Libraries and Family Reading in Prisons**	The Reading Agency, Nottingham City Libraries and HMP Nottingham	Family literacy project for male prisoners at Nottingham Prison and their primary age children. Combines prison sessions for fathers and family visits	Prison project Literacy for primary school children
13	**Design and technology whole-family workshops (Webster Associates)**	Webster Associates, a primary science and technology educational consultancy. Boots PLC for the pilot project.	Whole families are involved in design and technology family learning workshops. The project has run in several sites in the Midlands and north of England	Design and technology Involves whole families, including many fathers and other male carers Both primary and secondary children

Initiatives targeted specifically on fathers and daughters, or on single-parent fathers and their school-age children, were not found in the review of projects and practice in England and Wales. Only a couple of programmes focusing on children with special needs or taking place in special schools were found in this review.

Case study 1: Bradford YMCA Dads and Lads

Basic description and objectives

The national YMCA England Dads and Lads programme aims to promote, encourage and enhance relationships between fathers and their sons (and recently also daughters) through joint activities, often with a sporting theme. This Dads and Lads project (many different activities, not solely physical/sport) was piloted by Bradford YMCA in summer 2002 in a primary school in a deprived area of Bradford for a group of Asian Muslim fathers and their sons who attended the school. The project was run for the second time at the same school for a (mainly) different group of fathers and sons in autumn/winter 2003.

Background

The project arose out of discussions between the school, On Track and the City of Bradford YMCA. This deprived area of Bradford has a higher than average crime rate. The project was devised with the fathers' help and input.

Main provider

City of Bradford YMCA

Partnerships

The school, the police, On Track and YMCA England.

Funders

The pilot was funded by the On Track initiative. The second project is being funded by the Children's Fund. YMCA England have also provided training and a grant.

Children

Boys aged 7-11 who (mainly) had difficulties at school (ranging from behavioural issues to lack of confidence).

Participants

There were 14 participants (seven dads and seven lads) in the first project. The dads were all Asian Muslims, mainly the children of immigrants to the UK. They had a mixed employment profile and mixed ages.

Venue/Physical environment

A large hall in a primary school in Bradford.

Timing

Saturday mornings – The school caretaker opened and shut the school each week.

Processes and implementation

The project consisted of eight sessions covering topics such as communication, the role of the police, stranger danger, promoting self confidence, drugs, friendship, bullying, male health and looking after yourself. Each session started with a short preview for both the fathers and boys. Then the fathers and boys had separate sessions (often on a common theme), followed by time together for a joint physical activity, evaluation and discussion. Most of the activities did not require literacy or writing skills.

The project included one session for the fathers on encouraging children's education. The activity planned for this session was looking through educational workbooks, a reading activity with the children, word puzzles, and talking about counting in everyday activities such as shopping. The session that took place was centred around discussion with the fathers and boys about school: the importance of regular homework, the place of team-working, listening skills, mistakes, encouragement, praise and discipline, and relating these themes to England's success in the rugby world cup.

Some materials were developed in-house, including workbooks with discussion points for the boys on communication and on looking after themselves; and a handbook for the dads about communication for use at home.

There were two visits: one to the National Museum of Film, Photography and Television in Bradford (for a session led by an artist), and another to the coast and a Sea Life Centre.

Publicity/Recruitment

For the first project, the school made the initial contact with the fathers of 10 boys who had been identified by learning mentors as having difficulties at school. Seven of the fathers were interested and participated. The YMCA then met with the dads to explain more about the project. For future projects, there are plans to make a video and to hold an information session at the end of the day in the school hall.

Accreditation

None

Costs for fathers

Free

Practitioners

For the first project, there were three facilitators – two women from the Bradford YMCA and one male police officer on secondment to On Track (who was known by the boys from school). The non-Asian non-Muslim female facilitators and the police officer were very well received by the fathers, and a lot of stereotypes were dispelled. The facilitators were aware of cultural and religious issues such as eye contact and appropriate clothing. The two female facilitators had experience in groupwork and family work. The police officer was given training.

For the second project, one of the facilitators was an Asian Muslim woman. This worked well.

Evaluation

There was an internal evaluation involving discussions with participants and facilitators throughout the project and especially in the final session.

Feedback from fathers and sons

The programme worked well. The boys reported enjoying spending time with their father and having fun, and feeling more confident about talking to their fathers. The fathers said they benefited from spending quality time with their sons, spending time with other fathers, discussing generational changes within Asian culture, and reviewing and being more confident about their fathering behaviour and (in some cases) also their relationship with their own father.

Both fathers and sons learnt more about one another (e.g. issues, life, abilities and interests), developed new skills, and practised listening to and supporting one another.

The fathers wanted more off-site activities, for example bowling and local museums.

Perceived and observed outcomes

(reported by the school, the fathers and the children)

- The fathers had started to go into school and get more involved, for example offering to help and asking the teacher about their child's progress. For many, the project had been their first positive experience of a school environment. Some of the fathers had bad memories of school from their childhood and came into the school as a father only in connection with their son's problematic behaviour. The fathers wanted future projects to be delivered in the school.

- The fathers were spending more time with their children (both during the project and once it had finished), for example re-visiting the museum with other children in the family, or having another trip to the coast. The project had modelled learning activities that were free or at low cost, and dissipated the fathers' fears about whether they would fit into environments such as museums and coastal towns.

- One father would like to train as a Dads and Lads facilitator for future projects in Bradford.

- Other reported benefits were greater community cohesion, and partnership working in running the project.

What was important in engaging fathers

- Creating a 'non-threatening' environment.

- Having a variety of activities on offer and not making assumptions about what the fathers would enjoy. The fathers were very open to trying new activities.

- Adapting the activities and programme where needed during the session to fit the group's needs.

- Making the environment 'male friendly', for example having images of males on the walls, and using appropriate language.

- The partnership working was beneficial and all involved were clear about their roles and responsibilities.

Working with Asian fathers

- A two-way dialogue about religion and culture between the Asian Muslim fathers and non-Asian non-Muslim facilitators was important, with neither making assumptions. Being respectful of cultural differences. Being aware of issues of minimal eye contact, not shaking hands and wearing suitable clothes when a female facilitator is working with fathers.

- Being aware of Ramadan when the project was run for the second time and adapting some activities to be less physically based. And being aware of the need to get back in the afternoon from visits/trips for prayer at the mosque.

Reference

Waugh, G. and Redding, J. (2003) *Dads and Lads Programme Report 14th June – 2nd August 2003*. Bradford: City of Bradford YMCA.

Contact

Geraldine Waugh

City of Bradford YMCA

McMillan Centre

Dorset Street

Bradford BD5 0LT

Geraldine.waugh@bradford.ymca.org.uk

Case study 2: Basic Cookery for Dads

Basic description and objectives

Suffolk Family Learning ran a cookery session for fathers and their children, and for fathers on their own, as a pilot for a longer course. The objectives were to:

- create learning opportunities and experiences for children and parents to share

- provide an activity which could result in the whole family benefiting

- promote speaking and listening skills between child and parent and use them in a shared activity.

Background

Suffolk County Council has a Families Project which holds various learning courses and workshops for fathers and their children (including pond dipping, fishing, IT and football, arts and crafts, video and film making); and also runs fathers' groups and parenting/health education for fathers. There are five locally based fathers workers in the county to work with fathers and their children. The cookery session originated in a request from one of the fathers involved in other activities.

Bungay is a small town with a surrounding rural area. The 1998 Ofsted report for the high school states that "Some students live in very isolated situations. The percentage of students entitled to free school meals is low compared to national averages. There are very few students from ethnic minority groups."

Main provider

Suffolk County Council Families Project (Family Learning)

Partnerships

Bungay High School, a Specialist Science College

Main funder

Local Learning and Skills Council

Children

Children aged 7-13

Participants

There were four family groups and a father on his own (he has a pre-school child who was too young for the cookery) at the session. There were seven children – one boy and six girls.

Venue/Physical environment

The home technology room (kitchen) of a local secondary school.

Timing

Sunday morning

Processes and implementation

Fathers and their children cooked a Sunday lunch in a three-hour session. Care was taken to avoid hazards for younger children, e.g. the oven was used rather than the stove. One of the fathers was a butcher so he was able to provide meat at a reasonable price. Each family group made roast beef, Yorkshire pudding, vegetables, a pudding and fairy cakes. Foil dishes were provided so that each family could take the food home to eat for lunch.

The session began with an short introduction. Each family group had a recipe for the sponge mixture and they selected the necessary ingredients. The facilitators gave help during the session. Families learnt from one another. Some fathers already had cooking experience, others had very little.

Publicity/Recruitment

Publicity (fliers and posters) was distributed through local primary and middle schools and local fathers' groups. Fathers already involved in other fathers' activities in the county were personally approached. The flier/poster asked children to "make sure your dad comes along and brings you with him!".

If a course is run, fathers attending the pilot session will be asked whether they can bring along a friend.

Accreditation

None

Costs for fathers, travel, childcare and incentives

Free. No childcare provided. Incentive of a free Sunday lunch!

Practitioners

The session was organised by one of the county council's fathers workers – who is female. There were two additional facilitators, who were female students on an IT course, who enjoyed cooking and could teach cooking skills to the fathers and their children.

Evaluation

Evaluation forms were given out at the end of the session. The session was documented with photos.

Feedback from fathers and children

Feedback from participants was generally very positive. The fathers and children had enjoyed the pilot session and wanted more sessions.

Perceived and observed outcomes

(based on the organiser's observations, and on some feedback from fathers at the end of the session and during the following weeks)

- The organiser observed that there was much conversation during the activity, and very strong engagement between fathers and their children. Fathers were observed to be praising their children. The organiser reported that one father had commented on how much he valued the quality time with his children.

- Cookery may serve a particular purpose in bringing fathers and their daughters together. Many other family learning activities for fathers and children organised by the council tend to have a stereotypically male focus, e.g. fishing, IT, and football, and so these attract mainly fathers and sons.

- The fathers and children learnt new skills, i.e. cookery. One dad had cooked the Sunday meal three times since at home. His daughter had helped him on one occasion.

- The organiser plans to run a four-session cookery course for fathers and children in the following school term in early evenings. All four fathers who brought along their children want to take part.

What was important in engaging fathers

- Having a practical and task-oriented activity. As a result of gender roles in flux, it is now much more common than it used to be for fathers to cook at home. So cookery is no longer seen as a 'feminine' activity by all fathers, although some fathers do still view it as very female-oriented.

- Keeping everything light-hearted. Having a sense of humour when there are mistakes or problems. Many men like banter, and men can get embarrassed if they expose lack of skill or knowledge, especially to female workers.

- Recruiting fathers by appealing to their children.

- Starting with a one-off session to get the fathers interested without the commitment of a longer course.

- Female facilitators are sometimes given 'honorary male status' by the fathers so they are not seen as invading male space. Female facilitators may encourage fathers to open up and talk about their children in a way that they would not with a male facilitator. They can also bring the female perspective to the fathers in conversations about relationships, parenting and the balance of work and childcare.

Challenges in engaging fathers

- Fathers have many competing commitments on weekends. Weekday evenings may be easier for them. Attendance may have been lower than expected because no childcare was provided and because the session ran closer to Christmas than originally planned.

- Recruiting the fathers.

Lessons learned

- Future cookery sessions may begin with a short demonstration.

Reference

1998 Ofsted Inspection Report for Bungay High School on www.ofsted. gov.uk/reports

Contact

Lindsay Wolton

Fathers Worker
Suffolk County Council
Bungay Youth Centre
Old Grammar Lane
Bungay, NR35 2QW

Tel: 01986 892609

Case study 3: Dads on Computers

Basic description and objectives

A computer course (basic skills) for fathers and their children ran in a primary (first) school in the north-east of England. The course incorporated both learning with the fathers on their own (adult learning) and joint learning with their children (family learning). The aims were to:

- enable fathers to feel more comfortable about school and about engaging with the teachers, and more welcome in school

- allow fathers to learn IT skills, and build self-esteem and confidence

- allow fathers to learn about their children's schoolwork and the school environment

- allow fathers to work with their children – building a better relationship and also helping fathers to support their children's education

- give children male role models at school

- assess any other learning and support needs for fathers.

Background

The headteacher of one of the first schools was interested in involving more fathers in the school, especially as all the teachers were female. It was hoped that this would provide encouragement to the children (especially boys) by providing male role models, and so increase boys' achievement.

Main providers

Children North East Fathers Plus project, two first schools, and the Workers Education Association (WEA).

Partnerships

Community Education Department of the LEA.

Funders

Children North East; WEA (provided the tutor); and Northumberland Training and Enterprise Council

Children

Children aged 5-9, both girls and boys

Fathers

Five fathers (resident with their children) and three grandfathers attended regularly. The schools draw most of their intake from working-class industrial areas which have very few residents from black and minority ethnic groups. Most of the men worked shifts; just one was unemployed. They had a variety of skill levels with IT. Some had a PC at home, others did not. Several men knew a lot about computers and could share knowledge with the others.

All the men were already very committed to supporting the children's learning (e.g. activities after school, in the evenings and on weekends; helping with homework; day trips; baking bread). Some of the fathers had a 'shift parenting' arrangement with their partner where they swapped work and childcare roles, with the men working evenings and taking care of the children in the daytime when their partner was working. It was likely that they were a self-selecting group of men (they were recruited from the school playground).

Only two fathers had previously taken an active role in school (except for parent evenings and school shows, which they all attended when they could). Most thought that school involvement was 'women's work' and that they could be very involved in their child's education without attending school or helping in the classroom.

Venue/Physical environment

Computer suite in one of the first schools.

Timing

Monday mornings. The children were released from their classes.

Processes and implementation

The course consisted of 10 learning sessions at the computer with the children working jointly with their fathers in weeks 7-10. The sessions covered basic ICT skills, such as keyboard skills and use of the internet. The tutor worked at each participant's individual pace. Two teachers came to the final session to speak to the fathers of children in their class to encourage them to help in the classroom.

It took about five weeks before the men grew comfortable enough with one another to chat informally over coffee. Before that, they had mostly interacted with the tutor and the development worker individually.

Accreditation

No accreditation

Publicity/Recruitment

There was an initial standard school letter sent to all parents via the children, but this was unsuccessful in recruiting fathers. The second (much more successful) method used was to hand flyers out in the school playground to fathers collecting their children. Two follow-up letters were sent out during the summer holidays to maintain the fathers' interest before the course started.

Costs for fathers, travel, childcare and incentives

Free. No crèche provided. ASDA supermarket and NTEC donated prizes, and these were advertised on the flyers to encourage attendance.

Practitioners

One female WEA tutor, one female Children North East development worker, and one male social work student. Some involvement by headteachers and class teachers.

Evaluation

There was an internal evaluation. Questionnaires were given to adult participants at the end of the course. These asked about reasons for attendance, previous involvement in school, previous familiarity with computers, enjoyment of course, what they had learnt, any disappointments regarding the course; any changes they would recommend, perceived benefits for their child; and other activities for parents in the school that they would like to see.

Feedback from fathers and children

(based on questionnaires and informal feedback)

The fathers said that they:

- valued a regular slot to spend time with their child

- had enjoyed the course and especially valued their children's enjoyment

- had learnt new IT skills, which increased their confidence and expertise, and made their skills better matched to their child's skills

- had benefited from the access to the internet during the course

- had gained confidence to go into the school and approach teachers

- had gained confidence to talk to other fathers

- now understood their child's abilities better

- now understood educational aims for different ages, and knew about the software in school

- were therefore better able to support their children's learning at home.

The evaluation did not investigate whether any of the fathers had gone into other learning/courses later on, nor whether they had volunteered at the schools as a result.

The children particularly stressed their pride and pleasure at their father coming into school and at spending time with their father. They also said that:

- they now recognised their father's ability

- their communication with their dad had improved

- their father had obtained more appropriate software for them at home

- they valued the opportunity to do research for use in class

- they had learnt new IT skills.

The headteacher of one of the schools went on to gain funding from BT for a successor project combining literacy and computer skills. This was described in *The Guardian*, Tuesday October 15 2002, 'Dads help their lads on the road to literacy'.

Perceived and observed outcomes

(reported by the schools)

- A foundation for future work with fathers. Some fathers have overcome their fear about school and feel more comfortable interacting with school personnel.

- Fathers understand their children's education better.

- Joint working with the other school involved.

What was important in engaging fathers

- The facilitators' commitment to making the group work. This kind of project really needs 'champions' to succeed.

- Having one male facilitator (the student) as a 'counterbalance' to the two female facilitators.

- The daytime slot allowed shift workers to attend. They preferred this to evenings, which were often interrupted by shifts. Some of the fathers re-arranged some shifts.

- Friendly atmosphere and approachable tutor.

What was not important in engaging fathers

- Free – the fathers were nearly all working (although mainly low-paid) and said they would be prepared to contribute to the cost of any follow-up course.

- It appeared that the prizes had little impact on recruitment as none of the fathers remembered that these had been offered. Most of the men joined the course because they wanted to help their children rather than to gain a prize or even learning for themselves.

Challenges in engaging fathers

- There was no crèche provided due to no suitable venue at the school (funding was available) and this inhibited some participation, especially as some of the fathers were in sole care of the children whilst their wife was working during the daytime. In one case, the wife took time off work so that her husband could attend the course.

- Engaging fathers who are hard to reach/not already involved in their child's learning/not in the school playground/less motivated.

- Having one time that suited everyone, e.g. fitting different employment and shift patterns.

- Some fathers arrived very tired following a night shift.

- Stigma about men working with children and slow police checks inhibited classroom involvement by the men following the course.

References

Arnold, H. and Higginson, J. (2001) *Dads on Computers*. Unpublished: Children North-East.

Wallace, W. (2000) Pa for the course. *Times Educational Supplement 17/11/2000*. Online at www.tes.co.uk.

Contact

Children North-East
9 Denhill Park
Newcastle upon Tyne
NE15 6QE

Tel: 0191-256-2444

Fax: 0191-256-2446

enquiries@children-ne.org

Case study 4: Family Group Conferences in Education

Basic description and objectives

Family Group Conferences (FGCs) are family meetings used in education in Hampshire as a way of making plans and decisions to help children with school attendance and behaviour, as well as to help resolve other family issues which are causing difficulties in school. FGCs are voluntary and involve the wider family network of that child as well as the immediate family and professionals. Fathers are successfully involved in FGCs, including non-resident fathers. To date, over 300 families have been involved in FGCs in Hampshire.

Background

FGCs have taken place since the early 1990s in England in the social work and child welfare sectors. Five years ago, Hampshire set up FGCs in the education sector as an embedded service. FGCs in education have since spread to other counties. The idea of a FGC is rooted in Maori community traditions of resolving family problems in New Zealand. It is a family-oriented way of making decisions for and about children.

Provider

Hampshire Education Department (the LEA)

Funders

Initially the project was funded by the Standards Fund, but costs are now met by the LEA.

Children

Mostly age 5-13 (Years 1-8). The key age-group is 10 and 11 years. FGCs are also helpful with older children where they are willing to participate.

Participants including fathers

Family members (seven on average) include the child, parents, step-parents, other significant family and household members and siblings.

The evaluation reports that in about 75 per cent of families, the parents of the child were not living together. In 50 per cent of the FGCs, both parents were present. Fathers were present in 72 per cent of FGCs. This compares with mothers being present at 94 per cent of FGCs. There were also nearly as many uncles present as aunts.

The family decides which professionals would be helpful in reaching a decision for their child. Family members usually outnumber professionals.

Venue/Physical environment

Informal, accessible community venues where the family feels comfortable. Examples are church halls, community centres and leisure centres. Refreshments are provided to create an informal 'family' atmosphere.

Processes and implementation

The presenting issues are usually around school attendance and behaviour. But FGCs often end up dealing more widely with child welfare issues, for example young carers, and contact with non-resident parents.

The FGC is a meeting of the child, family members, significant others (e.g. close family friends) and professionals (usually three or four) arranged by an independent co-ordinator in consultation with the family. The immediate and extended family members attempt to reach a shared understanding of the situation with the professionals involved. The family is always given private decision-making time. Professionals provide consultation and advice, but do not make decisions. A plan is agreed involving action points and resources to be put in by family members and school staff jointly. The family's action plan is respected by the professionals unless it is unlawful or leaves a child at significant risk of harm. Plans often involve consideration of home–school communication. The majority of FGCs meet again after about a month for a follow-up meeting, where the family can review the plans they make, check on progress and discuss the next steps needed.

The FGC and the resultant action plan are voluntary, and the family has ownership of the action plan. The child is always given voice at the meeting unless they do not want this or choose not to attend. Often the co-ordinator invites, e.g. a family friend, to work with the child as an advocate during the conference.

All FGCs happen in the first language of the family. FGCs work well in different cultural contexts.

There is flexibility over the timing of FGCs so it is convenient for the family. The evaluation reports that most of the FGCs were held just after school hours. A third were held on evenings, and a few at weekends.

Referrals

Most families using FGCs are referred by schools, education welfare officers, youth workers and other professionals.

Practitioners

The FGC is convened by a co-ordinator who is an independent person skilled in dealing with conflict and family dynamics. They may be social workers, teachers, health visitors, counsellors or other family workers. They are trained as FGC co-ordinators. Gender and ethnicity is taken into account in selecting the co-ordinator.

Evaluation

A detailed evaluation has been carried out by Sheffield University of the FGCs for the first 64 families.

What was important in engaging fathers

- Flexible timing of the meeting
- Can pay loss of earnings if necessary, e.g. for working fathers
- Pay for transport, e.g. for non-resident father if the family wants this
- Effort and creativity in approaching fathers.

Challenges in engaging fathers

There are challenges in involving non-resident fathers. Some mothers feel too vulnerable to reveal details about the father, especially where there are issues of domestic violence or mental illness. The co-ordinator tries to encourage this, but it doesn't always work. Sometimes, other family members are asked how best to engage the father. Sometimes the co-ordinator makes a personal visit to the father. In some cases, two separate FGCs are held, one involving the mother, and the other involving the father.

Website

www.hants.gov.uk/TC/edews/fgchome.html

Contact

Liz Holton

Family group conference and schools counselling service manager

County education office

The Castle, Winchester, Hants SO23 8UG

tel: 01962 846365 fax: 01962 846469

email liz.holton@hants.gov.uk

Case study 5: Hampshire Teenage 'Lads and Dads' Book Clubs

Basic description and objectives

Five Lads and Dads reading groups have been set up since September 2001 in Hampshire public libraries for fathers/male carers and teenage boys. The project objectives are:

- to encourage teenage boys and young males to use the library service more

- to encourage reading development (choices, variety, regularity) amongst these groups

- to increase confidence in choosing, reviewing, requesting and talking about books, and reading with peers and others.

Background

The pilot reading group in Test Valley School arose from a concern that "boys stopped reading once they had become teenagers" (Marley, 2000). This was thought to be due to other activities taking precedence (e.g. friends, computers, homework, sports) – "anything rather than reading, which is decidedly uncool and smacks of schoolwork". Another possible factor was that teenage boys "find it difficult to find material they want to read", and that parents and librarians find it difficult to advise them.

The school librarians therefore created a focus group of fathers and sons to inform a booklist for men and boys. This became an ongoing reading group. As a result, Hampshire Library Service produced a 'Dads N' Lads' reading list (Hampshire County Council Library Service, undated) covering fantasy/sci fi, travel, sport, teenage fiction, survival, thrillers, humour and autobiography. Reviews were provided by the school group and by a celebrity author and son.

Main provider

Hampshire County Council Recreation and Heritage Department (includes County Library Service).

Partnerships

Local public libraries in Hampshire, National Literacy Trust, (previously) Southern Arts, and local artists, writers and football clubs.

Funders

Currently, Hampshire County Council Literature budget. Previously also Arts Council England Regional Arts Lottery Programme.

Children

Teenage boys aged 11-15 and a few younger siblings (both boys and girls) there for childcare reasons. The librarians say it is likely that the groups attract more 'bookish' boys, although it can work both ways with bookish boys encouraging not so bookish dads to come, and vice versa. Many of the boys have stayed in the groups as they have moved up years, so the age-group is now generally wider than at first. The original age-group was 11- and 12-year-olds.

Participants including fathers

There are between eight and 16 father/step-father and son pairs in each reading group (not all attend each time) from a range of social backgrounds. Other family members are welcome, but the groups have not evolved into family groups. Librarians report that mothers, although initially reluctant to attend because of the male focus, are welcomed, and a few now attend regularly.

Venue/Physical environment

In a 'comfortable' section of the public library which is not too near to the children's section and which is sometimes near to the 14-19 section. Often with a poster display backdrop and with displays of books.

Timing

Each group meets twice a term in the evening when the library is closed. This gives members time to read their chosen books between sessions. Reminders of sessions are sent to participants.

Processes and implementation

Each session tends to last one-and-a-half hours. In the first meeting of each reading group, there is discussion about what the fathers and sons would like to get out of the group. Quizzes/games are very helpful as 'ice-breakers' (the lads and dads getting to know one another). In most groups, participants are initially given a 'menu' with reading ideas.

At subsequent meetings, libraries display relevant books and create specific book lists. Librarians/participants may read small sections of books as tasters, perhaps on a theme (e.g. 'favourite beginnings and endings'). Members give feedback in discussion, in a circle, on what they have read since the last meeting, and recommend books. Staff join in to delve deeper and to seek comments from others. Reading can quite often include graphic novels, magazines and non-fiction, but most participants read fiction. Refreshments are provided in a mid-session break to allow both selection of books and informal conversation with one another and the librarians.

The fathers and sons write reviews of books, discussing positive and negative points, their favourite characters, what was learned, how a story made them feel, and what they would ask the author. Book review sheets are provided – some are unstructured, and others (often seen as more fun) ask specific multiple choice questions. Male guests are invited to some meetings, such as Reading Champion footballers, storytellers, writers, dramatists, journalists and explorers. There are occasional outings, for example to author events and local institutions. Participants are introduced to 'behind the scenes' of the library, and are invited to a Hampshire Teenage Book Festival (230 participants) each year with authors.

Publicity/Recruitment

Recruitment is resource intensive, multi-method and mainly recruits fathers through their children. Word of mouth works best, such as in libraries to current teenage users, and from school to school. Time permitting, the organisers have gone to schools, youth clubs and sports clubs, taking publicity and sometimes talking to pupils directly or playing interactive book games. Publicity has also been placed in bookshops, GP surgeries, sports shops, church halls and pubs. There are eye-catching posters and fliers with tear-off reply strips, which may include a competition or prize draw. Schools may place adverts in their newsletters or send letters directly home via children. There are plans to liaise more with Hampshire Schools Library Service in the promotion of the groups.

Accreditation

None, although reviews written by members are displayed in libraries and on the reading groups' website. The project is looking into the potential for members' reviews on local radio.

Costs for fathers, travel, childcare and incentives

Local businesses have been asked for sponsorship of competition prizes, such as books and book tokens.

Refreshments are provided at each session. The library gives free loans of CDs and videos at some sessions.

Practitioners

For the first two years, each session was facilitated by the project manager and local librarians, in total between two and four people. Now, the local librarians run the sessions themselves most of the time. Involvement of the children's librarians is key. All the librarians and the project manager are female.

Feedback from fathers and sons

The fathers and boys report that they like the recommendations for reading from others in the group. Some of the fathers don't read very much themselves, but they attend for their children's development, and they enjoy hearing about other participants' reading. Librarians report that the fathers like to have their usual reading choices validated, for example the internet and newspapers.

Fathers and sons like the male camaraderie in the group, and the quality time together in a 'male space'. Too many females in the group can inhibit this and change the dynamic.

Evaluation

An evaluation is planned.

Perceived and observed outcomes

Despite initial reluctance of the men and boys to participate in the pilot group (Marley, 2000), they gradually started to interact. Participants tried new kinds of reading, increased their reading, and wrote book reviews. Some of the participants were already keen readers, but others were persuaded to join in by existing group members.

Librarians in the current groups observe that boys and fathers develop discussion/ communication skills and increased confidence. Fathers and sons gain skills in using the library's IT and display systems. The librarians observe that there is probably more impact on sons' reading than on fathers' reading. Interestingly, the participants prefer to handwrite their book reviews and give them in person to the facilitators, rather than emailing them to the website. Competitions have not always taken off.

Relationships are built between the fathers/sons and the local library. The library consults the participants on library issues. Librarians have learnt about male preferences for reading.

What is important in engaging fathers and sons in reading groups

- Effective and intensive recruitment, mainly through the boys encouraging fathers to attend.

- Recommendations of literature which is likely to appeal to fathers and sons. Marley (2000) writes that participants did not think in terms of genres, "just according to what sounded interesting when someone talked about it". Librarians in the current groups have realised that teenage boys enjoy adult titles as much as or more than teenage fiction, and not to assume anything about individuals' preferences. Father and son do not often like to read the same books as one another, but it can be very rewarding when they do.

- Being flexible and responsive. Making the participants feel important. Using humour and banter. Displaying completed reviews in the library and on the website. Applying lessons learned in one reading group to the other groups.

Challenges in engaging fathers and sons in reading groups

- Setting up the reading groups is 'high maintenance'. Marley (2000) writes about the challenges in setting up the pilot school focus group (although this pilot group was different in approach to the current five groups). Three out of the four schools approached could not get a group together despite teachers' and librarians' enthusiasm. Fathers were busy, and some boys did not have fathers at home. Only four fathers and sons turned up initially and were not that enthusiastic.

- Initial lack of familiarity and confidence of librarians with male-oriented literature, as they tend to be female and therefore don't read it themselves.

- Conversation in the pilot group can sometimes be static, especially in the first few sessions (see Marley, 2000), although this has not been such an issue in the subsequent five groups. Fathers and sons are not always keen to write book reviews, and need persuasion.

- Fathers' long working hours, although many of the fathers are very committed to the groups and come straight from work.

- Making the groups valuable for both keen readers and more reluctant readers.

References

Marley, A. (2000) The Lads and Dads Experiment. *Youth Library Review*, **Issue 28**, Spring 2000.

Hampshire County Council (2002) Lads and Dads are getting hooked on books! *Hampshire Now*, **Issue 7**, Summer 2002. Online at http://www.hants.gov.uk/hampshirenow/issue7/ladndad.html in April 2004.

Hampshire County Council Library Service (undated) *Dads 'n' Lads reading list*. Hampshire: Hampshire County Council Library Service.

Department for Education and Skills (2002b) *Parents and Schools*, Issue 5, Spring 2002. London: DfES.

Website

www.hants.gov.uk/library/ladsndads

Contact

Emma Dolman

Literature Development Officer, Hampshire County Council Recreation and Heritage

emma.dolman@hants.gov.uk

01962 845468

Case study 6: Howzat!

Basic description and objectives

Howzat! is a county-wide programme (since 2001) in Lancashire secondary schools (20 new schools per year), including a special needs school, which aims to involve fathers and male carers in their sons' education "by linking sporting activities with complementary reading tasks". Father and son pairs are provided, over seven weeks, with cricket kit, cricket and reading activity cards, and cricket-related literature of male interest. The schools keep the resources to run subsequent Howzat! projects for other children in school.

The aims of the programme are to:

- develop physical, intellectual and social skills whilst having fun

- develop teenage boys as "confident readers" and with more positive attitudes towards reading

- develop basic cricket skills and knowledge of the game of cricket by both parents and children

- enable fathers/male carers "to contribute more knowledgeably towards the physical, intellectual and social development of their children", and specifically to act as role models in their education

- promote health and physical workouts

- encourage access to local cricket clubs and local libraries.

Background

Howzat! is one of four family literacy and physical activity/sport programmes (the Lancashire Dads and Lads Scheme) run by the county council for different age-groups of boys and their parents:- nursery/ reception (Dads and Lads); Key Stage 1 and 2 (Dads and Bigger Lads); and Years 5-7 (Dads and Lads Rugby). These programmes have been implemented as a result of a concern about boys' literacy levels and school achievement (now a key issue in the county council's development plan). Fewer fathers than mothers read with their children. Parents and teachers want recommended reading for boys.

Main provider

Lancashire County Council (the LEA)

Partnerships

Schools, the England and Wales Cricket Board, Lancashire County Cricket Club, local cricket clubs and Lancashire County Libraries. The Howzat! organisers write initially to each school's headteacher, and the schools are fully involved in the planning of the project.

Funders

Adult education budgets, Single Regeneration Budget, the Children's Fund, and other sources.

Children

By the end of summer 2004, about 550 boys and their fathers/carers will have participated in Howzat! across the county. The boys are mainly aged 11-13 (Years 7 and 8), although the resources have been used with children aged 15 and 16 who have special educational needs. The activity cards include suggestions for activities of different grading for different ages and abilities.

Fathers

The programme involves fathers, uncles, grandfathers (especially in more deprived areas), older brothers (18 years and above) and foster fathers. Non-resident fathers are often involved, as activities can be carried out on weekends when father and son are together. Howzat! has included many fathers of Asian heritage. The fathers are very diverse in terms of income and employment. Howzat! runs both in deprived areas and more affluent areas (where fathers may not spend much quality time with their children).

Venue/Physical environment

Weekly sessions for boys in school libraries. Joint activities for fathers and sons at home and elsewhere, for example in libraries and outdoor spaces. Initial session for fathers and sons at the school. Final session for fathers and sons at the local cricket club.

Timing

The initial Howzat! projects, facilitated for each school by Lancashire County Council, run in the summer term of each year. Some schools then run follow-up Howzat! projects in summer holidays and the autumn term for other children. Weekly sessions for the boys are held during the school day. The final session in the cricket club is usually held on a weekday evening from 6pm-9pm.

Processes and implementation

Each school is given, for each father and son pair, a bag of high-quality cricket kit, a Howzat! Reading File of cricket and reading activity cards, and a collection of cricket-related fiction. Each week, the son takes home cricket equipment, activity cards, and a book or other written resource to share. Each week, the father and son practice a different cricket skill (using a cricket test card) and complete a different reading activity (using a reading activity card and seven reading tests). Each card gives tips on resources to use.

The reading skills developed include researching information (printed and electronic), using the local library, newspapers, magazines and internet; reading fiction, factual books (e.g. history of cricket) and autobiographies; interpreting other sources of information, including cricket journalism and maps; following instructions; writing reviews of articles and books, poems and explanations of cricket; and talking about books. The cricket skills cover catching, bowling, batting, rules and strategy.

The project starts with a meeting for fathers and sons. Sons then attend a weekly session when the activities are explained. Individual schools provide ongoing feedback to the boys and/or display their work. At the project's end, an event is held in the local cricket club with professionals giving coaching to fathers and sons. Advice is given on how fathers and sons can get involved in the cricket club and on local learning opportunities (e.g. adult basic skills; recreational learning). Partners, other family members, teachers, librarians, other facilitators, and sometimes adult education providers, are invited. The literacy work is displayed, refreshments are provided, and certificates and prizes are awarded.

Accreditation

Each father and son pair receives a certificate and two tickets for a Lancashire Cricket Club match.

Publicity/Recruitment

Each school selects 10-12 children for each project' and implements their own publicity and recruitment. Howzat! produces resources, e.g. posters and postcards addressed to fathers/male carers which the boys can take home. Some schools mention the project at parents evenings. The initial profile of the programme was raised by holding sportsman dinners for fathers and sons in a local

teacher training college and in a local football club; but this was too costly to maintain.

Costs for fathers, travel, childcare and incentives

The sessions are free for the families. Father–son pairs are given free internet access in the local library. Important incentives are the loaned sports kit and the coaching at the end of the project. Transport is often provided in the school minibus from the school to the cricket club for the final session.

Practitioners

The weekly sessions for the boys are facilitated by teachers (PE and English), teaching assistants, school librarians and special needs staff. Professional coaches facilitate the cricket club event.

Evaluation

Photographs are taken in schools and during the cricket club event, and teachers, fathers and sons are asked for written feedback using evaluation forms. Fathers and sons are asked to use a diary to comment weekly about the work they have been undertaking. Each father and son pair is given a disposable camera for one week of the project so that they can photograph their home and out-of-school activities.

Feedback from fathers and sons

Fathers and their sons report much enjoyment. In one project, all fathers and sons shared a practical cricket session or literacy activity at least once a week, with 50 per cent twice a week, and over 35 per cent on every day of the week. The most popular literacy activity was reading the cricket fiction supplied.

Perceived and observed outcomes

Schools have seen increased parental involvement in school that they say can be directly attributed to Howzat!. Teachers and librarians have reported:

- more positive attitudes towards reading amongst boys

- physical skill improvement, including better performance at inter-school events

- increases in some boys' reading ages

- fathers' commitment and enthusiasm, and their requests for books to share with their children

- fathers' depth of knowledge about the Howzat! literacy materials.

The project is seen as 'habit forming' for fathers and sons, as it changes education-related values and aspirations, and therefore it is likely that it will lead, in time, to substantial achievement improvements.

Benefits for schools have included:

- very useful high-quality resources for further use

- opportunities for staff to meet fathers and male carers, i.e. has promoted home–school links

- many more men in school, for example attending parents evenings and helping out with the school cricket team

- improved working partnerships between a range of working professionals.

In one Howzat! programme with pre-project low membership of the local cricket club, 68 per cent of fathers or sons got involved in the club following Howzat.

Some fathers have progressed on to other family learning, e.g. the Better Reading Scheme, a family literacy programme for both mothers and fathers provided by Lancashire County Council.

The Howzat! programme has been adapted for use in Staffordshire.

What has been important in engaging fathers

- Enjoyment and interest in cricket (sport as 'a hook') by a wide range of men, including those from black and minority ethnic communities. Fun activities which do not seem too much like schoolwork.

- Link with the 'neutral' venue of the local cricket club.

- Not requiring regular participation by fathers at sessions – this has enabled non-resident fathers, for example, to take part, as activities can be carried out at home or in other settings at weekends. It is also important for secondary schools, as parents rarely come to these schools on a regular basis.

- Non-threatening and visually attractive publicity and resources. Howzat! postcards carry the message 'Do you want to spend time with your child?'. This works better than more formal letters.

- Strong partnerships with a variety of professional skills.

- Enthusiastic introduction of the projects to all participants.

- Receiving sufficient funding for a high-quality programme, and not having to 'rely on goodwill'.

- The programme gaining reputation; people now want to be involved, and some fathers and sons have previously been involved in the family literacy/sports programmes run by the council for younger children in the feeder primary schools.

Challenges in engaging fathers

- Getting fathers involved and boys interested in reading before the programme had gained a good reputation.

- Finding high-quality reading materials to interest fathers and sons.

Reference

Lancashire County Council.
Lancashire's Dads read with their Lads - and they make a great team!
Preston: Lancashire County Council.

Website

www.lancsngfl.ac.uk/projects/dadsnlads

Contact

Bernard Poole/Nick Riley

Parental Involvement and Teaching Support Team

Lancashire County Council

Portakabin 4, P.O. Box 61, County Hall, Preston PR1 8RJ

Tel. 01772 532809

Nick.riley@ed.lancscc.gov.uk

Case study 7: It's A Man Thing: A Fathers and Reading Project

Basic description and objectives

This nationwide project, running since 1999, provides opportunities for fathers and other significant males in families to help their primary school child with reading activities at home, supported by the child's school/other local provider. Each family is given a pack of activity books and other materials. Schools and/or local community providers put on weekly sessions for fathers on their own or with their children.

The objectives include:

- to offer opportunities to fathers to learn about ways of supporting their children's reading at home

- to develop the skills, knowledge and values which teachers need for working with fathers

- to raise awareness about the need for positive male role models for children

- to provide a referral point for fathers who have basic skills needs.

Background

It's A Man Thing started with a 1999 pilot 'Fathers and Reading' project in 15 schools in five LEAs in Great Britain. The pilot was inspired by ContinYou's family learning project 'Share' (in which very few fathers attend sessions although they do often get involved with activities at home).

Main providers

ContinYou (formerly CEDC) with primary schools/other local providers (e.g. libraries, adult and community education providers and community workers, local football clubs).

Partnerships

The pilot was designed by a national partnership including CEDC, LEAs, Education Action Zones and the Basic Skills Agency. Ongoing partnerships with LEAs, basic skills /adult education services, and libraries.

Funders

Family Support Grant and the Adult and Community Learning Fund (central government). The pilot was funded by the Basic Skills Agency, News International and Marks and Spencer.

Children

Ages 5-11

Fathers

In the pilot project (Millard and Hunter, 2001), about a third of the fathers had higher technician or manager status, a third were at lower technician or clerical status, and a third were working in unskilled work. Only four out of the 52 participants were unemployed. Only a small number of the fathers had a degree.

Only a small minority of the fathers in the pilot said that they wanted to improve their own reading. The great majority said that they were confident about their own reading. A high proportion of fathers said that they had not enjoyed their time at school, had not been interested or had poor achievement there.

Venue/Physical environment

Home, school/other venues, and library. One project run by a football club ran the sessions after football activities, and with an incentive of free match tickets.

Timing

Flexible at home, and session timing to suit the specific group of fathers.

Processes and implementation

Each It's A Man Thing pack contains three adult and child activity books (at different levels), a reading diary, a library record, a favourite books record sheet, a pen and an audio tape (of poems, stories and rhymes). Each activity book explains the project,

how children learn to read and how fathers can support learning.

Activities outlined in the pack have been chosen to be fun and to reflect typically male interests. They include challenges for library visits, making a book using ICT, making finger puppets inspired by a story, and exploring the role of cinema, TV and video. It is stressed that 'reading isn't just about story books', but also about newspapers, comics, ICT and factual books.

Schools and other local providers put on sessions to explain activities, usually weekly for about one hour. Some sessions are for fathers and children together, others for fathers on their own. There is informal group activity to support fathers in understanding the 'building bricks' of learning, such as imaginative play, dialogue and manual dexterity. Fathers (with the help of the teacher) select the level of workbook that suits their child, and then (with their child) select activities to do at home over a period of 10 weeks.

Publicity/Recruitment

Schools are given advice about different ways of recruiting fathers, and about the design of leaflets and posters. The best publicity is 'word of mouth' and meeting fathers 1:1 'on their home territory'. Bright flyers inviting fathers to help their children, or invites designed by the children, are also useful. Where possible, outreach workers (e.g. community workers and school governors) recruit the fathers. This is particularly helpful when recruiting fathers from black and minority ethnic communities.

Accreditation

The library stamps the It's A Man Thing library card each time the father and child visits. The father records the child's achievements using the pack diary. Each father and child receive an 'It's A Man Thing – reading together' certificate. Fathers can use Share Open College Network accredited units if they wish.

Costs for fathers, travel, childcare and incentives

Some small costs for fathers for materials such as paper, pencils and glue; some schools offer these free.

Many of the schools offer incentives to fathers and children such as football coaching and use of the school's computers. ICT training may be used as an incentive, and this may include accreditation.

Practitioners

Each session has a group facilitator (teachers, adult and community education tutors, classroom assistants and home–school liaison workers). Schools/local providers are given a one-day training programme, and a day's follow-up when their projects are running. This covers developing home-based activities, recruiting fathers, and using groupwork skills and participatory learning styles.

Evaluation

The pilot project was externally evaluated by Sheffield University (Millard and Hunter, 2001). Pre-project and post-project questionnaires were given to fathers and children in collaboration with the class teacher. Some interviews with teachers were carried out. The report "draws mainly on the data collected from six schools, chosen from three different LEAs" as there were problems in gaining evaluation data from all the schools. This sample comprised 33 children, 52 fathers pre-project and 15 fathers post-project.

Outcomes (Millard and Hunter, 2001)

- *Outcomes – engagement with children*: Teachers and fathers reported that fathers got more involved in their child's reading at home. They showed more awareness of reading issues (e.g. that reading "can involve material other than books") and of their children's interests and abilities. Fathers enjoyed spending quality time with their children. They became more aware of the importance of encouraging their children and giving them positive support.

- *Outcomes – engagement with school and library*: Teachers reported that home–school links had improved. One teacher reported that the project enabled him "to identify a group of fathers he could contact and rely upon for future projects or school functions". Teachers learned how best to work with fathers. Library membership increased.

- *Outcomes – further courses for the fathers*: Most of the fathers did not have basic skills needs, although some welcomed further courses. But "More external support will be required to enable schools to link to local adult education programmes and other agencies, including the library, to identify and build on fathers' own interests in learning."

What was important in engaging fathers (Millard and Hunter, 2001)

- Sessions just for fathers/male carers and children.

- *Content:* Using practical and fun activities that appeal to male interests and relate to everyday life. Use of non-fiction/factual reading. Use of brightly coloured activity books and pack.

- *Reasons for joining the course:* Many of the fathers said that they joined the course because they wanted to help their child with reading and/or they wanted to learn something. Smaller numbers said that they wanted to develop their parenting, help their child do better than they had done, and/or to learn more about the modern school environment.

- *Recruitment:* Teachers thought that personal contact was the best method (e.g. telephone calls from the teacher in the evening rather than directly after school), and

that incentives (e.g. football and computer training) were important. The fathers said that their first contact had been through a school letter or by their children encouraging them to take part.

- *Timing of school-based sessions* needed to be flexible. It is important where possible to recruit a group of fathers who have some common time slots available for sessions.

- *Venue:* Schools said they needed to use "adult spaces, large furniture and non-desk seating arrangements...a more comfortable setting than a classroom" to help fathers reduce their anxiety about being involved with a school.

- *Liaison with other agencies,* especially library services. Clear objectives and goals for all partners were key. Active LEA involvement was very helpful in successful and timely implementation – one LEA got together a group of schools implementing the project so they could share practice.

What was challenging in engaging fathers (from evaluation report)

- *Recruiting and retaining fathers* required a lot of effort, and some of the schools delayed implementation due to problems in recruitment.

- *Location and time of course:* There were problems gaining access to school premises at the times most convenient for fathers. Projects need to make allowance for the school caretaker's time.

- *Content:* This needs to be varied for different groups and negotiated with parents. The evaluation report states that "what suits one group may not please another".

- *Other factors:* The project "made large demands on teachers' goodwill and personal time", and teachers said "they would have appreciated further training sessions".

Website

www.continyou.org.uk

References

ContinYou. *Fathers and Reading Project.* Coventry: Continyou

Millard, E. and Hunter, R. (2001) *It's a man thing!: Evaluation report of CEDC's Fathers and Reading Project.* Coventry: CEDC

Contact

Barbara Crosbie

Unit C1 Grovelands Court

Grovelands Estate

Longford Close

Exhall

Coventry CV7 9NE

024 7658 8440

Barbara@cedc.org.uk

Case study 8: The Fathers Inclusion Project at Kensal Rise Primary School

Basic description and objectives

The Fathers Inclusion Project works to involve fathers and male carers in their children's education and school, and to increase communication and support. Most of the work is individual work between fathers, children and teachers. The Project has also organised a 'Bring Dad to School Day'.

The aims of the project are to:

- enhance the educational opportunities of children in the school, especially the boys
- fulfil the requirements of the school's social inclusion policy in line with their equal opportunities policy
- provide support for children and their parents
- provide opportunity for parents to participate and benefit from school support.

Background

The project arose out of an awareness of some fathers' lack of involvement in their children's school lives, and that a few specific pupils who were not receiving support from either their father or a father figure were struggling at school/ had challenging behaviour. Single-parent mothers needed support. In addition, although many men are now playing a more active role in their children's lives (nurturing, passing on values and becoming a physical presence), their presence is not always felt at school.

Main provider

Kensal Rise Primary School

Partnerships

None to date. There is liaison with outside agencies, such as for children in care.

Funders

There is no specific funding for the fathers project. Brief therapy and other therapeutic interventions are funded through the Behaviour Improvement Project.

Children

Ages 4-11

The school serves pupils from a wide variety of ethnic backgrounds and social backgrounds. The proportions of pupils eligible for free school meals and with special educational needs are both higher than the national average. About a third speak English as an additional language. Pupils speak about 30 different languages, the main languages apart from English being Gujarati, Arabic and Portuguese (information from 2001 Ofsted inspection report).

Fathers

There are 20 fathers working directly with the school's Behaviour Improvement Project. Many non-resident fathers are involved, as well as resident fathers, step-fathers and 'father figures' (e.g. grandfathers, uncles and older brothers). The fathers have different levels of education and literacy.

The Bring Dad to School Day involved over 100 adult men (two-thirds of the school population) and 430 children.

Venue/Physical environment

At the school.

Timing

No set times – the school has an 'open door' to fathers. Most meetings are held within the school day with occasional after-school appointments. Teachers liaise with fathers to establish the most convenient times for them to come into the school and support their children.

For the Bring Dad to School Day, some fathers negotiated time off work with their employer as paid leave.

Processes and implementation

Most of the project is 1:1 work with fathers who have had no or little contact with their children and whose children are of concern – 'trying to build bridges'. Individual work is used, as it was felt that group sessions/workshops would not be as effective due to children's and fathers' very individual circumstances.

Fathers are invited to come into the school, when they can to talk to teachers about how they can support their child's learning and development, and whether/ how they can get involved in the school. For non-resident fathers, the school is 'neutral ground' for building their relationship with their child. The father may agree to a specific plan, such as regular visits or involvement in a mentoring group supporting children's transition to secondary school.

Fathers are given regular information about their child's progress if they want this, e.g. using telephone; in one case, this is as often as every other day. The school has an 'open door' policy so that fathers can come into the classroom or have time with their child outside the class. Support is offered where needed, e.g. brief therapy working with the parents and children together.

A fathers' forum is organised to give fathers an opportunity to discuss issues amongst themselves.

The Bring Dad to School Day was organised in the summer term in

2003 around Fathers Day. It ran all day with sessions comprising: 'Dads at Work', reading and story-telling, science workshop set in school's wildlife habitat, maths games with prizes, outdoor physical games, music, a fathers' seminar, lunch with the children, computers, and a Fathers Day celebration. Teachers were released from class to support the different activities. In sessions where learning activities were modelled, materials were used that the fathers could use themselves at home.

Publicity/Recruitment

Fathers whose children have educational and/or emotional difficulties are targeted (the school's Behaviour Improvement Project). The main carer (e.g. mother) is invited in and asked about other family members. Details of non-resident fathers are obtained where possible. The school then telephones the fathers and follows up with a letter.

For the Bring Dad to School Day, posters were put up around the school in different languages. A programme of events was developed.

Accreditation

For the Bring Dad to School Day, each participating father received a certificate (this was mentioned in the publicity), which they could show to their employer if they took the day off work. There were prizes as part of sessions and at the end of the day.

Costs for fathers

Free

Practitioners

The project is run by the school's female pupil–parent liaison officer/ inclusion manager. Most teachers at the school are female – but there are three male teachers, one male nursery nurse, one male learning support assistant and one male language support worker. The male learning support assistant is used to help translate into Arabic for Muslim fathers and if there are gender issues, especially in initial meetings.

However, gender has not been that great an issue because the focus is on the child.

Evaluation

There was an internal evaluation of the Bring Dad to School Day which involved written feedback forms. The feedback and outcomes reported below are based on the feedback forms and on the project organiser's knowledge of outcomes for specific children at the school.

For the individual work, outcomes are much easier to see than with group work.

Feedback from fathers and children

Bring Dad to School Day: The fathers really liked the day and wanted another one the following year. The children's feedback was about their pride and joy in seeing their father in school, and the importance of time spent with their dad. It was a novelty for many children to have their father/male relative involved.

Perceived and observed outcomes

The school has been able to engage all fathers that they have contacted.

Fathers have become aware of their importance in their children's lives, and have been "thrilled to be involved". The fathers learnt the importance of reading and taking part in the child's education. They learnt about the atmosphere and challenges of schools and of teachers' work in class.

Mothers have been happy to have this support from the fathers.

The project has revealed "how much sadness children conceal" and how passionate children are about their dads.

The project has benefited children's SATS results. One teacher reports that a pupil who had been excluded from another school had settled down well after the school had involved the father in the school "on neutral ground". Another pupil had made substantial changes in effort, study skills and concentration. The child had visited their dad's workplace and observed (and then modelled) their dad's productive behaviour.

The project has led to involvement of fathers in school trips. Fathers and other male carers have offered help at the school with IT, maths and sports.

In one case, the dad is now a governor at his child's secondary school.

The school entered and won a national competition organised by Fathers Direct and DfES to 'Write a message to Dad'. Some children read out their poems in a radio broadcast. BBC News ran a feature about fathers, and the Bring Dad to School Day was staged for filming.

What was important in engaging fathers

- Working in a way that does not make fathers defensive
- A non-patronising approach
- Persistence in contacting fathers
- Being committed and dedicated
- Putting the child at the centre
- Having firm beliefs about goals
- Developing good relationships with fathers
- Language support and use of interpreters where needed
- Accepting a lack of planning and routine when working with parents-flexibility
- Looking at teachers' perceptions and judgements of men.

Challenges in engaging fathers

Involving fathers in family literacy and adult literacy.

References

Pendleton, R. (2003) Involving Dads. *Teachers,* May 2003.

Fathers Direct website for poems written by children at the school (www.fathersdirect.com/news/)

Contact

Jennifer Coleman

Kensal Rise Primary School
Harvist Road, Kensal Rise
London N6 6HJ

020 8969 3846

Case study 9: Fathers and Children in Education Project

Basic description and objectives

This two-year programme, from 2002-2004, ran activity-based family learning projects (weekly workshops over six weeks) for fathers and children in five primary/ middle schools in Suffolk (including one special needs school) and one Essex school. Curricular areas included sport and play, arts and crafts, and literacy.

The programme objectives included:

- to strengthen family ties to "enable men to recognise...their ongoing role as a father", including communicating with their children and learning about their children's needs and development

- to develop relationships between fathers and their children's schools, and to encourage fathers to be "more informed and involved in issues related to their children's education"

- to improve children's educational, social and emotional development and attainment.

Background

The programme was inspired by research showing the importance of a father's involvement in their children's education and the direct links to educational attainment for children between the ages of 7 and 11. A pilot project was launched in a primary school, and this was then delivered in other schools.

Main provider

The Fathers and Families in Suffolk project of the Ormiston Children and Families Trust.

Partnerships

Suffolk LEA (family learning), the Robert Milne Family Centre (an Ormiston project), schools and The Children's Society. Some schools were involved only in recruitment of fathers and children; others had teachers around during session breaks to chat to participants; other schools co-facilitated sessions. Additional partners in Essex were Colchester Sure Start and Goodstart Greenstead.

Funders

Suffolk Children's Fund for the Suffolk schools, and Colchester Sure Start for the Essex school.

Children

There were 82 boys and 36 girls participating between the ages of pre-school and 14+ (the youngest and oldest children tended to be in the school nursery, older siblings of participants with special needs to give them support, or where the parent could not find childcare). Most children were aged 5-12 years, with 27 secondary school children. About 40 children had special needs (mostly moderate learning difficulties). The pilot project was for fathers and sons, but later projects included daughters too.

Participants including fathers

There were 56 fathers and 12 mothers participating in the programme, from a variety of social backgrounds and income groups, and mainly employed in different sectors. Most of the mothers/female carers attended the occasional session when the father was unable to come along, although one school ran FACE for the whole family. There were few black and minority ethnic participants. The 'fathers' included two step-fathers, two non-resident fathers, two single-parent fathers and a few other male carers (e.g. uncles or older brothers).

Venue/Physical environment

Usually the school hall; classrooms for some sessions, and also school playground/fields in good weather.

Timing

Usually Tuesday evenings between 6pm and 8pm in the Suffolk schools. The Essex project ran on Saturday mornings between 10 and 12 noon.

Each session in Essex was preceded by breakfast (very popular).

Processes and implementation

Each six-week project comprised six workshops linked to the national curriculum and to ways of supporting children.

- Session 1: 'Introduction and Project Launch' to discuss expectations, ground rules and the programme. It also included 'Problem Solving Activities' (physical, mental and logical) looking at how children solve problems.

- Session 2: 'Sport, Play and Learning' based on physical activities, and looking at sets of rules, health, and children's confidence.

- Session 3: 'Heroes and Villains' looking at men, masculinity and positive male role models through discussion about children's and fathers' heroes, using arts and crafts and a game.

- Session 4: 'Storybook, Picture Book, Poetry and Prose', a literacy activity where children chose the topic, and the fathers and children produced work using IT, arts, crafts and other learning tools.

- Session 5: 'Do-It-Yourself', an arts and crafts activity exploring everyday learning opportunities and how these can link to the curriculum.

- Session 6: a celebratory session where female partners and other family members were invited; or the participants made presentations to the group using poetry, song and pictures; or (in one project) a video diary was created.

Suggestions were made for optional home-based activities ('homework') at five of the sessions, for example using ICT and libraries. In each school, this framework was adapted and so individual projects were unique. The workshops were adjusted in different ways, for example having sessions outdoors when the weather allowed, and according to the needs of the group. A 'standby' set of sessions and activities supplemented the programme.

Publicity/Recruitment

Schools sent an invitation to each child's parents/carers. Posters and flyers were used, often with a covering letter designed by the school. Schools identified families who may benefit most from the project, and followed up the flyers with phone calls to these families. The evaluation sheets (mid-project report) asked fathers what attracted them to the project. The most common reasons (from 18 sheets returned) were doing things together, the child was keen on the idea, and there is little provision around for children with special needs. These were child-centred reasons.

Accreditation

None

Costs for fathers, travel, childcare and incentives

All sessions were free for the families. In the Essex school, the Sure Start local programme provided two crèche/play workers, which enabled fathers with very young children and a school aged child to attend.

Practitioners

There were generally two or three facilitators for each project, but with six facilitators in the special needs school. Facilitators included the FACE development manager, LEA fathers workers, teachers from the schools, two volunteers (a father who participated in an earlier FACE project, and a former pupil of one of the schools), a Sure Start worker, the FACE project assistant (from the Family Centre), a Children's Society social work trainee, and guest facilitators. There was a mixture of male and female facilitators.

Evaluation

FACE collected comments that families produced to record the project. Children drew pictures and wrote poetry about favourite sessions. One poem was written by an autistic girl and her father. Evaluation sheets were given to fathers in penultimate sessions, and 18 sheets were returned (out of 38). Older children were encouraged to help complete the sheets, which included questions about whether the father's relationship with their child had changed.

Feedback from fathers

The fathers were generally very positive, mentioning a good balance between activity and learning; activities appealing to both them and the children; and their liking of a project specifically for fathers. Schools reported that the children had fun and had talked about sessions at school the next day.

Interestingly, most fathers enjoyed the wide range of activities, including those with more 'feminine appeal' which had been adapted to interest men (e.g. literacy, and arts/crafts). The mid-project report states: "Most surprisingly, the physical games/sports...came very low in the rankings", as these activities could be overly competitive. Many fathers also welcomed home-based activities. There was only six per cent drop-out, with 72 per cent of all families attending at least half of the sessions. The fathers and schools suggested "more advice on play-related learning activities with older children", "more activities where families are grouped together", and a choice of activities within each session.

Perceived and observed outcomes

The FACE manager observed that at first, "individual families kept themselves very much to themselves, or grouped with families known to them" (mid-project report), but close bonding occurred later on between participants who had not known one another previously. Some friendships formed were maintained.

Benefits as reported by the fathers and older children on evaluation sheets and in informal discussion included:

- closer relationships between father and children; the fathers learnt about their children's needs

- the children gained confidence

- an opportunity for fathers to discuss children's education with and to learn from other fathers.

Benefits as reported by two schools returning evaluation sheets were similar and also included:

- bringing families together from different socio-economic groups

- allowed the school to engage with fathers in the playground and at school social events.

Feedback from these schools was that, although very valuable for father–child relationships, one short project such as this cannot in itself significantly change attendance or educational performance.

FACE has been adapted for use by a family centre, Sure Starts and regional providers (north-east of England). FACE has been followed up by summer holiday activities and fathers groups to maintain continuity. One of the fathers in an early project has become a volunteer for subsequent projects.

What was important in engaging fathers

- Working in strong partnerships with schools and other organisations, especially to provide facilitators with different skills, which improved the programme's quality. This skill mixture was more important than the gender of the facilitators.

- Recruiting fathers through schools as "parents generally trust the school their children will attend" (mid-project report). The flyers were aimed specifically at the father and presented child-centred reasons for participation ("to find out how they could support their children's education).

- Having weekly sessions: "any break of longer than a week tends to lead to a significant drop-off, both in attendance and interest" (mid-project report). Being flexible about occasional non-attendance and lateness. Some fathers made arrangements with employers and childcare providers and, being a rural area, some had an hour travelling time from home.

- Designing "manly enough" activities to attract fathers, with not too much discussion (especially in early sessions). Being flexible about the sessions. Giving everyone clear roles in each activity. Pairing families up with others ('buddying') to promote mutual support.

- Having groups specifically for fathers/male carers. In the school where FACE ran as a family project, mothers changed group dynamics to some extent. Most fathers welcomed mothers attending on occasion; but one or two fathers commented that, although they were happy for this to happen, the aim of the project was to engage fathers specifically. One single-parent father said that he would prefer it if mothers were excluded, but this did not affect his attendance.

Challenges in engaging fathers

- Engaging daughters as well as sons, single-parent fathers, and black and minority ethnic fathers.

- Having physical activities which do not become overly competitive.

- Sustaining the activities for fathers and children in schools once the FACE project has ended, and attracting sufficient funding for this. These projects are expensive in terms of staff time.

- Maintaining regular communication with the participating schools during the project.

- Competition from sporting events! One of the projects ran over England's success in the Rugby World Cup. This factor affected attendance, so arrangements were made to bring in a TV for the day of the final and have the match on in the background. Seven dads and 15 children attended!

Reference

Martin, P. (2003) *Mid-project Report on the findings of the Fathers and Children in Education Project: August 2002 to August 2003.* Ipswich: Ormiston Children & Families Trust (Fathers & Families in Suffolk).

Contact

Paul Martin, Development Manager

Fathers & Families in Suffolk,
Ormiston Children & Families Trust

333 Felixstowe Road, Ipswich, Suffolk
IP3 9BU

Tel. 01206 578978

Paul.martin@ormiston.org

Case study 10: Super Dads at Pen Pych Community Primary School

Basic description and objectives

The Super Dads project gives fathers and other male carers of the children in Pen Pych Community Primary School the opportunity to spend quality time on a weekly basis with their children in a "well controlled supervised environment" (Todd Jones and Evans, undated). Fathers and children get involved together in a variety of activities, including design and technology, crafts and sporting activities. There are occasional father-only groups to discuss fatherhood and education issues; and some weekends away at an outdoor activities centre. This project "enables recognition and assessment of the ongoing roles of the fathers" in supporting their children's development, and identifies positive ways to enhance father–child relationships.

Background

Pen Pych was a new community school founded in June 1999 around the principle of local regeneration. Super Dads began in December 2001.

The headteacher observed that there was no specific activity in school to encourage fathers to spend time with their children, although family learning was run for mothers and children. An initial meeting was held in the local rugby club, and six fathers attended.

Main provider

Pen Pych Community Primary School

Partnerships

The project was, for some time, without substantial partnerships. But, more recently, Sure Start local programmes and the LEA's family learning section have become involved. It will become increasingly important to develop partnerships as the group expands.

Funders

Pen Pych Community Primary School primarily. Additionally, the fathers have themselves applied for and obtained funding for specific activities, for example, grants from the LEA's family learning budget for outdoor pursuits and model car kits. The University of Glamorgan has funded a robotics project.

Children

3-11 years, both girls and boys.

Fathers

The group originally had eight fathers, but this has grown to 20. There is a full spread of different male carers, including resident fathers, non-resident fathers, grandfathers, uncles and step-fathers/partners of the child's mother. There is a mixture of employment status, with the majority doing small amounts of work.

The school is in the Welsh Valleys, a former coal mining area where industry went into decline during the 1960s and later. The Valleys have become deprived areas with relatively high unemployment, low wages, high long-term sickness rates, and poor housing. Todd Jones and Evans note in their paper that the coal industry's decline has resulted in the dissolution of the respected 'breadwinner' role for fathers. At the height of the mining industry, fathers were rarely involved in their younger children's lives because they had little non-work time and worked shifts. Todd Jones and Evans write that "what leisure time there was, was spent, as a man, socialising, drinking and taking part in sport-boxing to begin with and rugby later...The family was seen as women's work with the all pervading view of a man being 'looked after'...males, and fathers particularly, feel personally alienated from their youngest children". The view of the family as women's work continues in this area, which still has a very traditional 'manly' culture.

Venue/Physical environment

Weekly activities for the fathers and children take place in the school's family learning room, which is also used for mother–child sessions.

Outdoor pursuit weekends take place at a specialist outdoor centre.

Timing

Every Tuesday 3.30pm to 5.30pm; and occasional weekends away

Processes and implementation

The group is focused around father–child activities such as sport, design and technology, and outdoor pursuits in the summer. There have been robotics and kit car workshops, and other crafts activities such as making Christmas cards. Summer activities have included gardening in the school grounds, visits to an adventure playground, nature walks in the countryside, and games in the park. There have also been weekends away with orienteering and outdoor problem-solving events. Over time, the initial focus on sport (at the request of the fathers) has declined. Fathers and children have tried other activities and found less need to keep to the 'safe ground' of sport.

The group's facilitators have also worked occasionally with groups of fathers on their own on fatherhood and education issues, for example their relationships with their own fathers and their own experiences at school.

Publicity/Recruitment

Initial recruitment of the fathers took place in the local rugby club. Invitations to this meeting were sent out from the school to fathers via their children. Mothers were also asked to encourage their partners to attend, and were told how important fathers' involvement is to their children.

Super Dads now has a very good reputation in the local area, and it therefore expands naturally by word of mouth. The school may still proactively reach out to particular families in distress where the father's involvement would help the child. Fathers already in the group often act as mentors to involve others.

Accreditation

None currently.

Costs for fathers, travel, childcare and incentives

Weekly sessions are free for the fathers. The fathers pay a small amount towards the cost of outdoor pursuit weekends.

Practitioners

The sessions are supported and facilitated by senior members of the schools staff including the headteacher and the leader of the Sure Start local programme.

Feedback from families and children

The fathers:

- primarily appreciate the regular quality 'special' time with their children that the group enables on a weekly basis in a very supportive environment

- feel able to engage in more challenging and messy outdoor activities with their children than when in the 'moderating' company of the mothers

- like the opportunity to be with other men and to discuss fathers' relationships with children.

The children express much delight when their father is at school, and they see the weekly sessions as a 'special time'.

The mothers like the project as it equalises responsibilities in the family. They do not feel threatened by the group as they know school staff and appreciate that fathers' involvement is good for their children.

Evaluation

There has been no specific evaluation, but fathers in the group now plan to make a professional video of the fathers relating their experiences of the group. A video has been chosen rather than a booklet because of the limited literacy skills of some of the fathers. The intention is for this video to be made available for other groups and organisations to use in promoting fathers' involvement.

Perceived and observed outcomes

The headteacher, school staff and parents have observed that children's social skills and self-discipline have positively developed. There has been an improvement in classroom attainment across the whole school, especially for the youngest children, for example in baseline assessments.

The school reports that a few fathers who had previously had negative communications with the school have completely changed their attitude towards school and towards their children's problems as a result of being in Super Dads. Their children have shown very substantial improvements in confidence and behaviour, and the fathers have developed very good communications with school. The mechanism for these substantial benefits has been the intervention and support of other fathers in the group, which has had much more impact than the prior intervention of the school.

The fathers have learnt about what activities are appropriate for different ages of children, and they have started to proactively suggest activities to suit different age groups.

The fathers have taken the initiative to promote and develop the project, and a committee has formed. Some of the fathers have acted as facilitators in courses run by the LEA, Sure Start and Fathers Direct.

Super Dads has developed the school's relationships with the local community, and it has helped to regenerate the locality as, in this community, male input to regeneration is crucial. The local community has developed more positive views about the future, for example about the roles of children's education and of life-long learning. They have been motivated to improve the locality for the sake of their children.

Challenges in engaging fathers

- The local community regarding involvement with children as 'women's work'. Very strong peer group norms inhibiting men's involvement with children.

- Very negative experiences of school amongst many adults in the local community.

- Planning activities to suit the wide age range of children in the group.

- Being sensitive to and inclusive of the wide range of family forms and 'father figures' locally so as not to alienate anyone.

- Capacity is becoming an issue because of the high demand of fathers and children to participate! The group has expanded from one room into three rooms.

What has been important in engaging fathers

- Understanding the ethos, values and needs of the local community.

- Holding the initial meeting in the local rugby club: "on their territory, not ours" (Todd Jones and Evans, undated). Being patient in initial recruitment, as the area is one where new initiatives are treated with suspicion. Developing trust.

- Three of the initial group of six fathers were miners working at the only remaining deep mine in South Wales. These men are revered by the local community and "viewed as the most masculine of men" (Todd Jones and Evans). These men's participation gave the group instant credibility locally, and encouraged other fathers to come forward. Todd Jones and Evans argue that these men were the first to get involved because "they had nothing to prove to anyone...no one was going to question these particular men's motives or actions".

- Persuading mothers that the work with fathers is important.

- Practical activities and a sports/ outdoor focus which appeal to the local men.

- The fathers are very candid about how the want the group to be. They are proactive and constructive in running the group, and they regularly have new ideas for activities, which they discuss regularly with the headteacher. They are much more self-organised than the mothers of children in the school. It has been important for there to be an 'open door' to the fathers in the school, and in particular to have the active involvement of the headteacher.

- The fathers feel able to be very open in discussions about fatherhood and other personal issues when there are no women present.

References

Todd Jones, G. and Evans, M. (undated) *Developing Services for Fathers in a School Setting: Pen Pych Super dads Group.* Unpublished: Pen Pych Community Primary School.

BBC News (2003) *'Super dads' improve pupils' skills.* 9 June 2003. Online at www.bbc.co.uk in June 2004.

Contacts

Gareth Todd Jones
Headteacher

Maralyn Evans
Head of Community Development

Pen Pych Community Primary School
Blaenrhondda Road
Tynewydd
Treorchy
Rhondda CF42 5SD

Tel. 01443 771434

Fax 01443 776911

email: penpych_com@rhondda-cynon-taff.gov.uk

Case study 11: Share for Dads

Basic description and objectives

The aims of the group are to provide children with good role models, and to give fathers an insight into school life. The group meets weekly in an infants school on a Friday morning to carry out joint activities, sometimes with their children, sometimes without their children.

Background

The project has been in existence for about one year prior to this research being conducted, and it arose out of the ContinYou (formerly CEDC) SHARE family learning project. SHARE aims to: involve parents actively in their children's learning; increase parents' understanding of the important role they play and of the learning process; improve the educational attainments of children; enable parents to further their own education; and develop effective management and organisation of parental involvement in schools. Parents are invited into the school (90 per cent of SHARE providers are schools) for SHARE sessions with a teacher who has received training from ContinYou. SHARE provides activity books with activities which are flexible and adaptable and relate to the school curriculum.

Haringey LEA runs the SHARE programme in several schools, but it is unusual to have fathers involved. Therefore the Dads Only group was formed. There are plans to start a Dads Only group in another school.

Main providers

South Haringey Infants School and Haringey Adult Learning Service (in the LEA) working very closely together

Partnerships

ContinYou (formerly CEDC)

Funders

No specific funding for this group. Uses school's resources and LEA budget for family learning.

Children

Age 3-7 (infant school)

Fathers

The group consists of about 10 fathers. Not all the fathers attend each week, and there is a core of about five fathers. The fathers of children in the school are a mobile population, so the membership changes frequently.

They are a very international group of fathers – from Zambia, Somalia, Turkey, Armenia, Bangladesh, Italy and the Caribbean. The activities take into account the different languages and literacy levels of participants;

literacy and language are not barriers to participation. Many of the fathers have very basic education, and were at school outside the UK. This SHARE group is the first experience of school for some of the fathers.

Interestingly, many of the wives of the fathers are *not* involved in the school.

Venue/Physical environment

Infants school, in a family learning room.

Timing

The group meets weekly on a Friday morning during term-time. This daytime timing has not been a problem, as the group has recruited fathers who work part time or in the evenings/on shifts and non-working fathers. The fathers have *not* requested evening sessions.

Processes and implementation

The sessions are practical, informative and curriculum based. Some sessions take place with the children (they are released from class) and some without the children. The SHARE activity booklets are not used that often; many sessions arise from the school's curriculum for the children and how the fathers can support this at home. The facilitators have asked the fathers what they want to do, but the fathers are often happy for the facilitators to suggest the programme.

Activities with the children have included mosaics, playing board games, doing puzzles, writing poetry, photography and cooking. There are also visits, e.g. to art galleries and local museums. Three of the fathers put on a performance for the school at assembly displaying skills such as juggling and magic tricks. The activities often draw on the various ethnic cultures and traditions of the participants. One of the facilitators has commented that it is not necessary to have stereotypically masculine activities.

Activities without the children include an IT course to teach keyboard and word-processing skills. This has been specifically requested by the fathers. The course links with how the children are using computers to learn, e.g. get the fathers to type in children's poems and songs to show their children after school.

Photographs are frequently taken to document the group's activities, and displayed prominently in the school.

Referrals/Publicity

Many fathers were recruited individually by personal contact, approaching fathers who came into school and inviting them to participate. When the group started, the facilitators spent time at the school at the beginning and end of the school day so that they could consult fathers and then recruit them.

Promotion of the group by the fathers already involved to other fathers is important, as is publicity in school assembly on a regular basis. Children are asked to tell their father about the group, for example children created invitations to the group in class. There have also been coffee mornings. The class teachers remind the children about the group's sessions.

Accreditation

The fathers can gain SHARE accreditation with the Open College Network, for example 'Computers Don't Byte!' for the IT course. One member of the group has received the SHARE Best Adult Learner Award.

Costs for fathers, travel, childcare and incentives

Free

Refreshments are provided.

Practitioners

There are two female facilitators. One is a teacher in the school (responsible for leading on Ethnic Minority Achievement), the other is the LEA Parental Involvement co-ordinator who co-ordinates SHARE throughout the LEA. All the school's class teachers are aware of the Dads group and work in partnership with the group's two facilitators. An external trainer may be recruited to help lead the fathers-only IT course. The head teacher of the school takes a keen interest and often pops into the group's sessions.

All SHARE facilitators in Haringey attend two-day training delivered by the LEA.

Feedback from fathers and children

The group is a place of support and understanding and new friendships. Fathers exchange ideas and information about their lives and their children; they learn from one another and from shared experiences. Fathers may reflect on their relationships with their own father, as well as on their relationships with their children; the two are obviously linked. Male relationships are important.

Stronger father–child relationships and conversations.

Father and child learning about one another.

Fathers are learning new skills, e.g. IT, cookery, public speaking in class assembly.

Children feel special and really like it when their father visits the school.

Perceived and observed outcomes

(reported by practitioners)

Raises the profile of fathers in the school. Gives children positive role models of men; shows them that fathers can be an important part of their school lives and that fathers are connected to the school.

Fathers can talk to teachers more confidently. The fathers take much pride in local publicity about the group, e.g. photos in the LEA newsletter. The sessions validate the fathers' role and existing skills.

Some activities and visits are repeated by the fathers with their family outside of the group. The fathers learn about local learning resources and become more confident, for example about visiting local museums.

One father has gone on to a borough-run parenting course at a local community centre.

Children are learning new skills, and also all the activities are designed to promote their language and numeracy development. However, one of the facilitators has observed that it is difficult to assess improvement in reading and writing specifically as an outcome of the group.

Observed impact (by class teacher) on children's behaviour in classroom, for example one child much happier in school and with calmer behaviour since her fathers has been attending this group. Children have much pride when their father visits the school, and this leads to greater confidence.

Observed impact (by class teacher) on child's motivation to learn in classroom.

Evaluation

No formal evaluation.

What has been important in engaging fathers

- Staff who are flexible and open to ideas. Important characteristics of the facilitators are experience, sensitivity, much planning, groupwork skills and effort/

persistence. Skills are more important than gender. Having female facilitators working with observant Muslim fathers has not been an issue.

- Having an ongoing dialogue with the fathers. Awareness of fathers' issues and of cultural issues in parenting. Being respectful of others' traditions and values (e.g. gendered norms).

- Both the school/headteacher/class teachers and the LEA view parental involvement in children's education as a priority.

- Giving the fathers status and recognition for attending.

- Giving the fathers an opportunity to learn new skills, e.g. IT.

- Building 1:1 relationships with the fathers and knowing about their individual circumstances. Recruiting through subtle persuasion.

- Taking religious festivals into account when planning sessions and activities.

- The most successful activities have been visits and practical activities – having fun!

References

Haringey Council. Parental Involvement Celebration Day. *Haringey Ethnic Minority Achievement Bulletin*, **Issue 12.**

Sharma, V. and Nairn, L. Dads only!: Ground Breaking SHARE Group at South Haringay Infants. *Haringey LEA*

Ethnic Minority Achievement Team Bulletin, Issue 11.

Contact

Veena Sharma

Borough Parental Involvement Co-ordinator

Haringey Adult Learning Service

020 8489 8880

Case study 12: The Big Book Share: Libraries and Family Reading in Prisons

Basic description and objectives

The Big Book Share is a family literacy project for male prisoners at Nottingham Prison and their primary age children. In prison sessions, fathers choose books for the children, read stories on to tape, and talk about children's reading. Tapes and postcards are sent to families. There are special family visits for reading together. The project has now been extended to six other prisons, including women's prisons and young offenders institutions.

Its objectives are:

- to enable fathers in prison to contribute to their children's reading, including having a better understanding about children's books, reading and libraries
- to enable fathers in prison to play a key part in family life outside prison, supporting their relationships with their children and with their children's mother/ carer[1]
- to build closer links between the fathers/their families and public libraries, supporting shared family activity and the father's resettlement after release
- to build fathers' own reading and writing skills
- to reduce the risk of fathers re-offending on release (through the prior objectives).

Background

'Parenting' (general parenting/family relationships) courses are part of the prison core curriculum, and The Big Book Share includes a number of men doing this course. There are very high levels of poor education/illiteracy amongst prisoners, so family literacy in particular can be very helpful for prisoners' skills development. This project began in November 2000 at HMP Nottingham.

Main providers

The Reading Agency, Nottingham City Libraries and HMP Nottingham. The project is now run by the prison library in partnership with the prison education section as part of the prison's learning and skills activity. The prison library is a branch of Nottingham City Libraries.

---

1 The term 'mother' is used to refer to the child's mother or any other carer.

Partnerships

HM Prison Service, the Offenders' Learning and Skills Unit (DfES), the National Literacy Trust (linking with the National Reading Campaign and Reading is Fundamental), and other prisons and public library services.

Funders

Initially Marks and Spencer, East Midland Arts and 20 leading children's publishers, which provided free books. Now funded by the Paul Hamlyn Foundation to develop family literacy models in different prisons.

Children

Children are under 12 years (most under five years). About 600 children have participated over three years.

Fathers

There is an average of eight fathers/ father figures attending each session; about 490 over three years. Most of the prisoners are from the local area, as HMP Nottingham is a local prison and now takes only short-stay prisoners. There is a mixture of age, type of offence (including drug-related offences), ethnicity and literacy skills. High-risk prisoners are excluded, as well as those who have committed offences against children. Participants include some uncles (and one godparent) as well as fathers and grandfathers.

Venue/Physical environment

Two education rooms in the prison are used for prisoner-only sessions (one for the group session, and one to allow privacy for taping). The family visits venue changes (because of other room needs at the prison) but the chapel has made a good venue. Informal seating is used so that families can sit close together.

Timing

Prisoner-only sessions take place in the afternoon every two weeks. Family visits take place each month.

Processes and implementation

There are fortnightly three-hour sessions for prisoners, with a mid-session break (refreshments provided). Children's books (provided by the prison library and public library) are displayed. With the help of librarians, fathers choose books for their children (e.g. in conjunction with the children's mother via phone); practise reading aloud with other prisoners; read stories on to tape for the children to listen to; and write postcards for the children. Tapes and books can be sent to children or used on family visits. Fathers and children can write to one another on The Big Book Share postcards (space for a message from the father and for the child's reply). If language/illiteracy is a barrier, fathers ask library staff or another prisoner to read a story on to tape; the father adds a recorded introduction and message to their children.

The sessions also cover issues for prisoners around family visits, reading, storytelling, children's books and libraries, relating to their experience as parents and as children. The Big Book Share makes referrals for literacy support to the education section at prisoners' request.

There are special family visits (lasting two hours) in which parents and children can share books, listen to reading (including the stories they have taped), and tell stories together face to face. Sometimes, the librarians facilitate specific activities such as a summer reading challenge and colouring. Children may bring their school reading. A computer is provided with interactive story-based software, as well as drawing materials and a large collection of library books to use at the session and borrow from.

Publicity/Recruitment

Prison librarians recruited the fathers through posters, leafleting (prison workshops, in the education department and under prison cell doors), stickers (originally for the children but also stuck around the prison), visiting cells and induction talks. Word of mouth and 1:1 recruitment by the prison library staff have been most effective. The recruitment message was based around helping the children, not the fathers.

Accreditation

None in The Big Book Share because there are no long-stay prisoners. In some other prison family literacy programmes, the fathers may gain accreditation for the Open College Network 'Reading Together' units.

Costs for fathers, travel, childcare and incentives

Fathers are paid for attendance at the prisoner-only sessions as for other prison activities. The extra family visits are also a great incentive.

Babies are included in family visits. Travel expenses are paid to family members to enable them to visit.

Practitioners

Librarians from the prison library and the local public library (including children's librarians). Prison officers do not attend the sessions but they are on duty to be available if needed. The prison visits staff act as security personnel on family visits.

Nottingham Libraries provided ICT training for Marks and Spencer, who in return gave Customer Care training. Prison staff have been given awareness sessions about children's books and reading.

Evaluation

The evaluation has been an integral part of the project. Methods include session records, and feedback from prisoners, children, mothers, prison and library staff and teachers using questionnaires/more informal methods. To look at the impact on resettlement and repeat offending, feedback was gained through contacts maintained with ex-prisoners and their families. More in-depth longitudinal research is proposed.

Feedback from families

Prisoners have been keen to take part. Fathers and their families have often thanked the prison librarian.

Fathers report that the project:

- helps keep them in touch with their children

- the children really appreciate and benefit from the contact with the father, and the books, tapes and other gifts and communications.

Mothers have shown appreciation that the father is playing his part in helping with his children's reading.

Perceived and observed outcomes

The Big Book Share has enabled meaningful, quality, regular interaction between fathers and their children. It gives the fathers an opportunity to show affection and commitment, and a clear role in family life which they can build on when released. The Reading Agency (2003) writes that "sessions have often been extremely moving, especially where they have enabled contact...which has not been possible before".

Children's reading outcomes and relationship with their libraries have been enhanced.

Some prisoners have been motivated to take part in prison education courses to improve their own literacy and their employment prospects on release (and employment also reduces the risk of re-offending). Developing links with a local library (which is open and free to everyone) creates a resource and support for the prisoner's reading, learning and community re-integration when he leaves prison. Some of the men have used the library on release, bringing family members along.

Links have been built between the prison and the outside community. Library and prison staff have gained skills and awareness to enhance their work. Some initially sceptical staff now recognise the project's value.

What has been important in engaging fathers

- Shared understandings, mutual respect and joined-up delivery processes between project partners. The prison library being a valued branch of Nottingham City Libraries. Commitment of senior managers (prison governor and senior library services manager) to steering group. Inclusion of project in mainstream planning and targets, e.g. librarians' and prison officers' time. Training for staff (in both prison and public library), and their ownership of and high support for the project.

- Encouraging prisoners to take part (the prison library), and mentoring them where needed. Sensitivity to literacy difficulties and security considerations, with unobtrusive security staff. Keeping sessions informal. Responding to prisoners' feedback. Good resources. Giving prisoners private spaces to record stories if they want it. Persistence and flexibility.

- The Big Book Share having 'street cred' within the prison.

- Families often live nearby, so possible to keep in touch with them after release.

- The library service manager communicates with the child's school if required, e.g. when a family is seeking permission for the child's absence to attend a family visit. This means that schools are aware of this positive involvement by the fathers in the child's family and in the child's reading.

Challenges in engaging fathers

- Security issues: Staff not employed by the prison service need security clearance which can take several weeks. Family visits may be cancelled with little notice due to security alerts. All prisoners are checked by security before they are allowed to take part. A member of the prison library staff attends each session to support visiting staff and to deal with any arising security issues.

- Literacy difficulties of prisoners.

- Prisoners are in HMP Nottingham for a short time (e.g. one week). Every session must be meaningful.

- Children may have to miss school to attend a family visit, and this may be embarrassing for the child or lead to unauthorised absence.

- Staffing pressures on prison and library staff.

- A poor relationship between the father and mother of the child may deter men from applying to join the project – or they may create tapes and then the mother will return them/refuse permission for them to be sent to the child. There have been some instances where men have been allowed access to their children only through the structure of this project.

References

The Reading Agency *(2003)* The Big Book Share: Libraries and Family Reading in Prisons: A Handbook. *St Albans: The Reading Agency*.

Kings, T. (2004) Inside out: the Big Book Share. *Library and Information Update January 2004*, **Vol 3 (1)**, 24-26.

Contact

Tricia Kings
The Reading Agency
PO Box 96
St Albans
Herts AL1 3WP
Tel: 01736 332228
Mobile: 07974 365696

Case study 13:
Design and technology whole-family workshops (Webster Associates)

Basic description and objectives

Whole families are involved in design and technology family learning workshops. The project has run in several sites in the Midlands and north of England. Boots PLC ran a pilot project from 1997. Many fathers, grandfathers and other male carers have attended, along with mothers and children of all ages. Father participation has been especially high for workshops on robots, mechanical toys and outer space.

The aims of the pilot three-year Boots Family Learning project (see Webster, 1999) included:

- to support parents as children's first and natural teachers and to encourage parental involvement in education

- to support the school curriculum and raise the profile of design and technology

- to foster the participation of business and industry.

Background

The work was piloted in the Boots Family Learning Project over three years on an estate with predominantly white working-class residents in Nottingham with pockets of great poverty.

Main providers

Webster Associates, a primary science and technology educational consultancy, and Boots PLC for the pilot project.

Partnerships

Various schools (primary, secondary and technology colleges), LEAs, colleges, universities, industrial museums and the Neighbourhood Learning Net. Partners for the pilot Boots Family Learning project were Education Extra, Nottingham Trent University and Nottingham LEA.

Funders

Boots PLC funded the original project. Since then, workshops funded from a variety of sources: LEAs, LSC, regeneration strategies (e.g. Education Action Zones, Single Regeneration Budget), and an Engineering and Physical Sciences Research Council grant.

Children

Originally ages 3-13. Recently extended to ages 12-16 through the secondary 'robot' workshops.

Participants including fathers

Attending are mothers, fathers (many), grandparents, other adult carers, older children and younger children. Attendance commonly between 15 and 55 families; commonly between 80 and 100 individuals. Over 50 per cent of adult participants were fathers at the Sheffield family learning Sunday events and robot club.

Venue/Physical environment

Schools (both primary and secondary), industrial museums, community halls.

Timing

After school (e.g. 3.30-5pm) and weekends. Some holiday activities.

Processes and implementation

Some workshops are one-off events, but a set of three workshops is more common, with progression opportunity from one to another. Parallel challenges appropriate for adults and for children of different ages and abilities are an integral part of each workshop. The workshops are on themes such as robot-making, motorised model-making, puppet-making (with moving parts), designing puzzles and games (mazes, marble runs), circuit work, and designing fairground attractions. Each workshop lasts 90 minutes, and begins with a brief fun presentation on the activity and safety issues/tools. Each table has several families around it so that they can work together. Parents support their children's learning.

Very high-quality materials are used that would not normally be provided by schools. Families are given a booklet to suggest simple activities that they can do at home using everyday materials. Instruction sheets are used in the complex robot activities for secondary school children.

Publicity/recruitment

- For each workshop, pupils of nearby schools and their families are invited with letters. This can involve a partnership between one secondary school and its feeder primaries.

- Big colourful posters and displays in schools – advertised as 'family fun events' for the whole family. These don't mention fathers or mothers specifically.

- Schools place details about the workshops in their newsletters for parents.

- Reputation grows. Discussion is generated in the school and the community about the workshops.

- Children ask their parents to attend. One school tells other schools in the area.

- Names for the current workshops include 'Ugly Bug Ball', 'Moving Monsters', 'All the fun of the fair', 'Outer Space', 'Rowdy Robots', 'Tinkering with Toys' and 'Family Fun Engineering Day'.

- Some schools have targeted some children with behavioural problems.

Accreditation

A 'Special Award' certificate is given to each family. Each family that attends is also given a 'Passport', a small booklet with details of future events. When they attend an event, it is stamped in the booklet.

Costs for participants, travel, childcare and incentives

Free. Families take their creations home! Refreshments provided at the start of the workshop to allow social time. No childcare provided.

Practitioners

The workshops are designed and led by a former design and technology curriculum advisor (Webster Associates). She is helped by teachers, sixth formers, students and other workers depending on the venue. Where the workshop is held in a school, the headteacher is fully involved in planning.

Webster Associates runs training for teachers, sixth formers, students, community workers and LEA staff so that they can run future workshops themselves/use the ideas in classroom activities.

Evaluation

Feedback has been regularly obtained from both adults and children, for example using 'post it' notes left on tables, and there have been many thank you letters. The University of Sheffield with NIACE carried out an external evaluation of the Boots project. They observed workshops (and the impact on pupil and adult learning), issued questionnaires to parents, and spoke to participants and schools.

Feedback from participants

Much positive feedback from both parents (including many fathers) and children that the activities are great fun/enjoyable/exciting. They want to come again and look forward to the workshops.

- Challenging, thought-provoking, creatively inspiring.

- Friendly, a community event, social benefits for children.

- Quality time for families. Families worked well together without conflicts. Provides a neutral venue for non-resident fathers to spend time with their children.

- High standard of materials and resources.

Would have liked instructions/drawings – but the project manager thinks that this could inhibit creativity, problem-solving and family discussion with the younger children.

Older pupils are given instruction sheets for building the more complex robot models.

Perceived and observed outcomes

(based on external evaluation of the Boots project and on participant/teacher feedback from more recent workshops)

- Attendance is excellent and has far exceeded expectations. Many fathers attend.

- Children: gain self-esteem and acquire skills which they take back into the classroom; have great pride in their achievements/what they have made; value quality time with family and friends.

- In addition to design and technology skills, the children develop language, number, decision-making, communication, teamwork, support, concentration, creativity and problem-solving skills through discussion within and between families.

- Teenagers have an attractive after-school option, and gain from male role models in their families.

- Parents: gain self-esteem and acquire new skills; are introduced to creative learning; learn about the school curriculum; acquire ideas and confidence for activities and everyday resources to use with their children at home; experience quality time with/learn about their children's abilities.

- Some families model good behaviour and communication from other families, and this can help families where children have behavioural problems.

- Stronger home-community-school links are built; teachers get to know the parents.

- Teachers and sixth formers have run workshops themselves/started after-school technology club.

- The high-quality design and technology work has enriched the school curriculum.

- Provides opportunities for school staff and students to work with parents and with very mixed age-groups of children and to see whole families learning together. Students comment that it helps them see the value of working with parents when they start teaching.

- Governors have been recruited for the schools.

What was important in engaging fathers

- Practical events focused on activity and clear practical outcomes, with technology and tools.

- Themes with more 'masculine focus' attracted more fathers, especially robots and outer space.

- Flexibility about timings, lateness and lack of notice about participation. Knowledge of TV sport times; 3.30pm is fine for non-working fathers; some working fathers can arrange to leave work early/re-organise their shifts.

Later evening timings would exclude younger children. Saturday and Sunday workshops may suit working fathers better, and have been very popular.

- Publicity: not 'learning' but 'family fun', and 'user-friendly' workshop titles.

- Teaching in subtle ways and through children's learning in a non-threatening friendly environment.

- Flexibility about process: some fathers like to build the models themselves at the first workshop so they learn how to do it; then they feel comfortable about working with their children.

Challenges in engaging fathers

- Fathers less frequently at workshops on masks, puppets and fabrics. But many fathers have been to these workshops and enjoyed the new skills. Some of the fathers progress from robots to fabrics.

- Some fathers aren't used to working with their children in a collaborative way; they are used to making decisions without consulting their children.

Selected references

Department for Education and Employment (1998) Learning Together: family learning case studies. In *Study Support: A Code of Practice for the Primary Sector*. London: DfEE.

Webster, P. (1999) Raising the status of design and technology through a family learning focus. In C. Benson and W. Till (eds.) *Second international primary design and technology conference.* Birmingham: CRIPT at University of Central England

Contact

Pat Webster
Webster Associates
91a Furniss Avenue
Sheffield S17 3QN

0114 236 1648

p.websocc@gemsoft.co.uk

Part Three

Conclusions and policy implications

7 | Conclusions and policy implications

7.1 Conclusions about fathers' involvement in their children's learning and education

From this research review and the case studies of successful programmes emerge a number of clear messages about fathers' involvement in their children's learning and education.

Fathers' involvement in their children's learning and education is important for children

It matters for fathers and other 'father figures' to be involved in their children's learning and education. Fathers' interest and involvement in their children's learning and education are associated with better educational, social and emotional outcomes for children, including better exam results, better school attendance and behaviour, and higher educational expectations. These associations with fathers' involvement are independent of mothers' involvement. They exist for primary school children and secondary school children, for children in two-parent families, single-mother families with non-resident fathers, and single-father families, and irrespective of the gender of the child.

Mothers' involvement is no substitute for fathers' involvement, and many experts propose the importance of male role models for boys' learning and reading. There is the potential for family learning to be a 'progression route' to adult learning for fathers, as it is for mothers, but there is little robust research evidence on whether or not this occurs. Small-scale evaluations of family learning programmes involving fathers reported some progression on to accreditation for adult learning, mentoring of other men in family learning programmes, and voluntary and paid work in schools, family learning programmes and the community.

Fathers' non-economic contributions to family life can also relieve the burden on mothers who combine work and family commitments.

Fathers are less likely than mothers to be involved in many aspects of their children's learning and education

Despite the research evidence demonstrating how important it is for fathers to get involved, resident fathers are less likely than resident mothers to be involved in many aspects of their children's out-of-school learning and in their children's schools. Fathers are especially unlikely to be participants in organised family learning programmes which take place during the daytime and are not targeted at men.

Fathers are more likely to be involved if their child's mother is involved, they have good relations with their child's mother, they or their child's mother have relatively high educational qualifications, they are of relatively high socio-economic status, they got involved in their children's lives early on (post-natally and when the children were in pre-school), and their child is in primary school rather than secondary school. Non-resident fathers are especially unlikely to be involved in their children's schools, and single-parent fathers tend to get more involved than do resident fathers in two-parent families.

When fathers do get involved, it tends to be in certain areas of learning

There are some specific areas of children's out-of-school learning to which fathers tend to contribute substantially: building and repairing, hobbies, IT, maths, science, recreation, sports, physical play, outdoor activities and family trips. Considerable proportions of fathers also read with their children, help with homework, and give praise and support to their children for their schoolwork. Two common reasons for fathers getting involved in their children's learning and education are because their children ask them to be involved, and to build a closer relationship with their children.

7.2 Barriers to fathers' involvement and policy implications

In considering the policy implications of the research findings in this report, it is important to look at the barriers to fathers' involvement in their children's learning and education. What gets in the way of fathers' involvement, and what can policymakers in central government and educational organisations do to break down these barriers?

The wider context: Gender roles, work, childcare, and early fatherhood behaviours

> "even limited flexibility [work] can allow many fathers to play a more active role with children such as attending sports days."
>
> Hatter et al., 2002

> "Such change requires support through a raft of interconnected policies relating to the support of both working and parenting roles for mothers and fathers...policy needs to support men as parents in tandem with support for women in the labour force. Initiatives within either of these policy areas should not be seen to undermine the other."
>
> Warin et al., 1999

The research reviewed in this report demonstrates that there is only so much that schools and family learning providers can do to engage fathers, as fathers' involvement takes place in a much wider societal context.

Chapter 4 discussed two substantial large-scale barriers. Firstly, there are traditional gender roles within many two-parent families, with fathers, mothers and children tending to perceive fathers' family role as predominantly that of an economic provider. Secondly, many fathers have long, inflexible, atypical working hours, which leads to a lack of time and to unavailability during school hours. Traditional perceptions of gender roles can be exacerbated by a consumer culture amongst children and teenagers which means that some fathers feel that they have to work long hours to meet all their families' material expectations. Two other factors associated with the long working hours of many fathers are the gender pay gap and employment which is insufficiently family-friendly.

These large-scale barriers suggest that fathers' non-economic involvement in their children's lives, and in their learning and education more specifically, will be greatly facilitated by the development of:

- more flexible societal attitudes to masculinity and fatherhood, in which a greater number of fathers feel able to play non-economic roles in their children's lives, including their learning and education

- pay equality between men and women in employment

- more widespread family-friendly employment, including flexible working hours (shift swapping, compressed working hours, flexitime, and time-off-in-lieu schemes) and shorter working hours, for both mothers and fathers

- a greater supply of quality, affordable childcare.

The Government has implemented a number of policies and provided financial support to move closer to these goals, as described in Chapter 1[1]. Much has been written elsewhere about childcare, pay equality and family-friendly employment, and recommendations have been made for enhancements to policy and legislative changes, for example extension of the new flexible working and parental leave rights for parents (Camp, 2004; Fathers Direct, 2004a).

In particular, more flexible working hours (for example, flexitime arrangements) and greater understanding from employers would help fathers get more involved in their children's education (Hatter et al., 2002; Clough et al., 2000). The voluntary organisations Fathers Direct and Working Families have cited examples of good practice. One father started to work flexibly at home with his employer's support, and subsequently he was able to attend school events and help out at his children's schools at least once a term (Fathers Direct, 2004b). Another father worked 7.30am to 3.30pm in order to be with his children after school (Working Families, 2003).

Frieman and Berkeley (2002) in the US report how one teacher in an area where many fathers worked for the same employer asked the employer to donate one hour of each employee's time so that those employees who were fathers could attend a school event. A similar scheme in the UK, the DfES 'Give An Hour' campaign, was run by Comet (a large electrical retailer with nearly 70 per cent men amongst its workforce) in 2002 to give its employees who were fathers one hour to get involved in their teenage sons' learning and education (BBC News, 2002).

---

1   In addition to the policy developments described in Chapter 1 (for example, the Work-Life Balance Campaign, and new flexible working and parental leave rights for parents of young children), others include the implementation of an Equal Pay Questionnaire in the 2002 Employment Act (which enables employees to ask their employer for key information when they are deciding whether to take their case to a tribunal – see Women and Equality Unit, 2004), and a considerable expansion of childcare (DfES, 2004b, 2004c).

One possibility, building on 'Give An Hour', would be for large employers to set up pilots of paid parental leave schemes, supported by central government, which give fathers and mothers with school-age children (up to the age of 16) some time off work each year to attend school meetings and events, and to help out on school trips and other occasional voluntary work in schools. Employees who are not parents could be given similar time off to carry out other forms of caring or voluntary work in their communities.

Research evidence shows that father involvement in children's early years predicts later father involvement when children are in school (Chapter 2), and some fathers lack confidence in their parenting roles (Chapter 4). This suggests the need for a greater emphasis on parenthood education in schools (incorporating discussion of fatherhood and motherhood roles); and continued funding of parenting education targeting fathers, and also couples together, ante-natally, post-natally and in the early years.

Father-friendly schools and family learning programmes: policy implications for educational policymakers and funders

This section of the report discusses the policy implications for central government, national educational bodies, local policymakers and other organisations with a strategic role in influencing and funding schools and family learning programmes.

Evidence was presented in Chapter 4 that policy and practice in some schools and family learning programmes can be inappropriate for engaging fathers. Additionally, the beliefs of some teachers about fathers and their involvement may limit schools' efforts to involve fathers in children's learning and education. For example, like other practitioners in services for children and families, they may be ambivalent about involving fathers, considering greater father involvement as unlikely and even as a 'risk'.

Chapter 5 discussed the good practice and 'father-friendly cultures' which individual schools and family learning providers can develop to engage fathers successfully, and this report includes a number of case studies of effective programmes (Chapter 6). As mentioned in Chapter 1, the DfES has recently published a good practice guide for schools working with fathers *Engaging fathers – Involving parents, raising achievement*, which has drawn extensively from the research review and case studies in this report (DfES, 2004a). Fathers Direct, in their response to the Green Paper *Every Child Matters,* mention the "pioneering work" of the DfES in looking at engaging fathers in schools, arguing that "this is the most precisely and well-defined gender specific measure in the whole Green Paper" (Fathers Direct, 2003).

The new DfES guide is an important step towards promoting increased fathers' involvement in schools by disseminating effective practice on engaging and communicating with fathers (and the importance of this work) to local education authorities (LEAs), Learning and Skills Councils (LSCs), Ofsted inspectors, schools, teachers and family learning practitioners. Its impact would be strengthened by additional dissemination of the main messages using communication vehicles such as *Teachers* magazine, seminars for national and local educational policymakers, and training for teachers and family learning practitioners.

More specifically, it would be helpful if training modules for teachers, other school staff and family learning practitioners on working with fathers were developed for initial practitioner training and continuous professional development,[2] drawing on successful training provided

---

2 For example, for Initial Teacher Training and for the Family Literacy, Language and Numeracy Professional Development Programme.

by organisations like Fathers Direct, Working with Men, Children North East, and ContinYou. The new Continuous Professional Development agenda for teachers offers an opportunity here (DfES, 2004b), as does the development of National Occupational Standards for family learning practitioners (New Directions Consulting Ltd, 2004b). The case studies show the importance of headteachers taking an enthusiastic lead in work with fathers in their school. Therefore, one possibility would be for seminars for headteachers on 'whole school' approaches to working with fathers to be developed at the National College for School Leadership.

Most official guidance for schools on working with parents, and most government communications with parents, use the gender-neutral term 'parents and carers'. However, as shown in this report, in our society at present, fathers and mothers tend to have different family roles, and some different strategies are needed when recruiting and engaging men and women in learning. This suggests the need for a return to some gendered language ('mothers/female carers' and 'fathers/male carers') in the medium term.

It is therefore proposed that organisations such as DfES, Ofsted, the Adult Learning Inspectorate, the national LSC, local LSCs, the Basic Skills Agency, the Teacher Training Agency (TTA), providers of practitioner training and continuous professional development and LEAs use the terms 'mothers/female carers' and 'fathers/male carers' where appropriate in their strategies, targets, policies, guidance, inspection frameworks, training modules, and communications with parents. This would also apply to relevant National Occupational Standards.[3] Perhaps, in the long term, 'mother' and 'father' could once more be aggregated into the term 'parents'.

Some guidance[4] could be revised to explicitly recommend that schools engage both fathers and mothers, to suggest examples of the *different* strategies and good practice often needed to engage fathers and mothers, and to refer readers to the new DfES good practice guide for schools on engaging fathers. One possibility would be to incorporate gender dimensions[5] into all guidance as is currently often done for social class, ethnicity, culture, religion and disability. It would also be helpful if schools, local authorities, Ofsted and educational policymakers were encouraged to take reasonable steps to involve both mothers and fathers in consultations preceding inspections, home–school agreements and new policies.

The emphasis in the research literature (Chapter 5) and the case studies (Chapter 6) is on attracting fathers into schools and family learning programmes through recruitment and activities designed specifically for fathers and other male carers. The case studies describe programmes which successfully engage fathers in their children's learning and education, including non-resident fathers, fathers in deprived areas, and black and minority ethnic fathers. Sometimes these are on stereotypically male themes such as sport, ICT and technology, but there are also examples with learning in literacy, the visual arts, music and creative writing. However, home–school and family learning programmes for fathers and children

---

3   Good practice is demonstrated by the Draft National Occupational Standards for Work With Parents (New Directions Consulting Ltd, 2004a): "...opportunities and supportive activities to enable mothers and fathers, prospective parents and those in a parenting role".

4   The following guidance relating to parents and schools was reviewed in spring 2004: (i) DfES Teachernet 'Working With Parents' and The Standards Site (DfES) 'Partnership with Parents' guidance to schools on good practice in working with parents; (ii) Ofsted inspection criteria (Ofsted, 2003a and b); (iii) the TTA's standards for new teachers (TTA, 2003b, c and 2004).

5   Again, see the Draft National Occupational Standards for Work With Parents (New Directions Consulting Ltd, 2004a): "Provide environments that are sensitive to the culture, religion, gender or disability of the parents" (para. B1.3). Similar language is used in the Draft National Occupational Standards for Family Learning (New Directions Consulting Ltd, 2004b).

which work with teenagers, daughters, single-parent fathers, and children with special needs are less common. Additionally, a greater proportion of adult learners in LSC-funded wider family learning programmes are men than in LSC-funded family language, literacy and numeracy (FLLN) programmes.

Drawing on the evidence in this report, policy and funding options at national and local levels which would facilitate fathers' involvement in their children's learning and education include:

- inclusion of strategy on the engagement of fathers in LEAs' and Local LSCs' strategic plans such as LEAs' three-year development plans, LEA/local LSC family learning plans, and family literacy, language and numeracy action plans[6]

- developing and piloting approved FLLN programmes targeted at fathers and male carers for national roll-out, building on evidence to be gained in Phase Two of the Skills for Families initiative[7]

- increasing the status of[8] and funding for LSC-funded wider family learning programmes (without reducing the status or funding of FLLN programmes), which can be an effective first step in engaging fathers in their children's learning and possibly also in adult basic skills programmes

- funding the development and piloting of home–school and family learning programmes specifically for or inclusive of fathers and daughters, fathers and teenagers, non-resident fathers, single-parent fathers, black and minority ethnic fathers, and children and fathers with special needs and disabilities.

Evidence was presented in Chapter 5 that recruiting fathers to home–school and family learning programmes is often more challenging and time-consuming than recruiting equivalent groups of mothers. Consequently, one important facilitator in working with fathers is having practitioners with designated time. Two funding developments would facilitate this and contribute significantly to enabling effective work with fathers. One is specific funding for recruitment and outreach by schools and family learning providers to engage hard-to-reach learners such as fathers (also recommended by NIACE, 2003). The LSC has already specified in its 2004-05 guidance that funding for wider family learning programmes can include a contribution towards "outreach work in a new area or with a particular group of learners" (LSC, 2004). The second is specific funding for LEAs and schools to recruit home–school liaison practitioners, fathers workers and other community workers, and to give some teachers some non-classroom time. This would fit well with the Government's funding to support non-teaching co-ordinators and practitioners in extended schools.

6 These plans are referred to in DfES/LSC (2004b).

7 As noted in Chapter 1, the second phase of the Skills for Families initiative requires new partnerships to develop new approaches to family literacy, language and numeracy from a list that includes "promotion and content that brings in fathers, including non-resident fathers" and "programmes that use sport as a focus" (DfES/LSC, 2004a).

8 As noted in Chapter 1, this was also recommended by NIACE (2003), who reported that nearly 70 per cent of LEAs "have a higher demand for wider family learning programmes than they are able to supply". Some work on increasing the status of wider family learning is already underway, for example the DfES is encouraging the funding of family learning programmes in a sporting context (NIACE, 2004; LSC, 2004).

Putting resources into recruiting fathers, when it can be easier to recruit mothers, would also be encouraged if LEAs were required to monitor the number of fathers and male carers participating in family learning programmes and were set targets[9] where appropriate.

The policy implications discussed in the final part of this section relate to the research evidence that a major barrier to fathers' involvement is that many schools and family learning settings are feminised environments, with few male teachers, practitioners or other adults. This feminisation can deter fathers' participation, as fathers tend to see these settings as 'women's spaces', and learning and education as 'women's work'. This is exacerbated by fathers being more likely than mothers to have not enjoyed school when they were children. Additionally, fathers may find it more difficult than mothers to speak to the mainly female teachers in primary schools.

These barriers would be lessened by continued work by the DfES, the Teacher Training Agency, LEAs and schools to:

- increase the number of male teachers[10] and other staff in schools, and the number of male family learning practitioners, so that children's education settings and family learning settings are less feminised

- pilot initiatives[11] and subsequently make longer-term changes to make schools more attractive to current and future generations of boys (without disadvantaging girls) so that the men and fathers they grow into do not tend to see learning and education as 'women's work'. This may in time also lead to more men choosing teaching and family learning as careers.

7.3 Research gaps

This report has extensively searched for and reviewed research and other evidence published over a five-year period in the UK and some other English-speaking countries. As a result, the following research gaps in particular have been identified:

- a national large-scale survey in the UK to measure the extent of fathers' involvement in their children's out-of-school learning, and in primary and secondary schools, including non-resident fathers, step-fathers and other sub-groups

- questions in nationally representative large-scale surveys, and complementary qualitative studies, investigating the attitudes of fathers (including step-fathers and non-resident fathers), mothers, teachers, family learning practitioners, education welfare officers, and other local authority staff (e.g. parental involvement and family learning co-ordinators) towards fathers' involvement in their children's learning and education

---

9 LLSCs and LEAs now agree their own planned learner numbers ('targets') for participation and achievement in family literacy, language and numeracy. Local areas can define local priority groups, such as unemployed fathers. Male family members are a priority group for LSC wider family learning programmes. See LSC, 2004.

10 The Teacher Training Agency (TTA) aims to increase the number of male graduates who take up primary teacher training by a fifth for 2004-5 (TTA, 2003a).

11 As noted in Chapter 1, there are several initiatives taking place to reduce the gender gap in school achievement, for example, the Raising Boys' Achievement toolkit. See McGivney (1999) and www.standards.dfes.gov.uk/genderandachievement

- research on complex practice issues where there is inconsistent literature and advice, in particular:

  - research to investigate the role of male teachers and practitioners in facilitating fathers' involvement in schools and family learning programmes

  - research to investigate the roles of skills assessment and accreditation in facilitating or inhibiting fathers as learners in family learning programmes

- a meta-analysis of the large number of published statistical studies showing relationships between fathers' involvement in their children's learning and education, and children's educational outcomes

- robust summative evaluations of home–school and family learning programmes that involve fathers to measure the impacts on children and on fathers, with controls/comparison groups and systematically measured outcomes.

The beginning of Chapter 2 made the point that, although some research studies on parents' involvement in children's learning collect information from both mothers and fathers, these two distinct groups are often aggregated into one group of 'parents' for analysis and reporting. In other research, the samples of 'parents' are exclusively or mainly mothers, often because the 'parents' involved in home–school/family learning programmes are exclusively or mainly mothers.

The following research and analytic strategies would contribute substantially to our knowledge about fathers' involvement in children's learning and education:

- disaggregating 'parents' into 'mothers' and 'fathers' when reporting research on involvement of parents in education and family learning programmes

- making clear (including in abstracts) whether 'parents' are mothers and fathers, or just mothers, how many of each were in the sample, who reported data on resident and non-resident fathers' involvement, and whether step-fathers and other male carers were included

- where possible, obtaining data directly from non-resident fathers, not just from mothers or from practitioners

- disaggregating fathers' involvement overall from fathers' involvement specifically in children's learning and education.

7.4 Summary

The wider context: gender roles, work, childcare, and early fatherhood behaviours

- Fathers' non-economic involvement in their children's lives, and in their learning and education more specifically, would be greatly facilitated by the development of:

  - more flexible societal attitudes to masculinity and fatherhood, in which a greater number of fathers feel able to play non-economic roles in their children's lives, including their learning and education

- pay equality between men and women in employment

- more widespread family-friendly employment, including flexible working hours (shift swapping, compressed working hours, flexitime, and time-off-in-lieu schemes) and shorter working hours, for both mothers and fathers

- a greater supply of quality, affordable childcare.

- The Government has implemented a number of policies and provided financial support to move closer to these goals. One possibility would be for larger employers to set up pilots of paid parental leave schemes, supported by central government, which give fathers and mothers with school-age children (up to the age of 16) some time off work each year to attend school meetings and events, and to help out on school trips and other occasional voluntary work in schools. Employees who are not parents could be given similar time off to carry out other forms of caring or voluntary work in their communities.

- There is the need for a greater emphasis on parenthood education in schools (with discussion of fatherhood and motherhood roles); and continued funding of parenting education targeting fathers, and also couples together, ante-natally, post-natally and in the early years.

Father-friendly schools and family learning programmes: Implications for educational policymakers and funders

- The new DfES good practice guide for schools *Engaging fathers – Involving parents, raising achievement*, which has drawn extensively from the research review and case studies in this report, is an important step in disseminating effective practice to LEAs, local LSCs, Ofsted inspectors, schools and family learning providers.

- It would be helpful if training modules for the benefit of headteachers, teachers, other school staff and family learning practitioners on working with fathers were developed for initial practitioner training and continuous professional development.

- Most official guidance for schools on working with parents, and most government communications with parents, use the gender-neutral term 'parents and carers'. However, as shown in this report, in our society at present, fathers and mothers tend to have different family roles, and some different strategies are needed when recruiting and engaging men and women in learning. This suggests the need for a return to some gendered language ('mothers/female carers' and 'fathers/ male carers') in the medium term in the strategies, targets, policies, guidance, inspection frameworks, training modules, and communications with parents of key national and local educational organisations.

- Furthermore, some guidance could be revised to suggest examples of the different strategies and good practice often needed to engage fathers and mothers.

- Other policy options to facilitate fathers' involvement in their children's learning and education include:

  - developing and piloting approved FLLN programmes targeted at fathers and male carers for national roll-out, building on evidence to be gained in Phase Two of the Skills for Families initiative

  - increasing the status of and funding for wider family learning programmes (without reducing the status or funding of family literacy, language and numeracy programmes)

- funding the development and piloting of home–school and family learning programmes specifically for or inclusive of fathers and daughters, fathers and teenagers, non-resident fathers, single-parent fathers, black and minority ethnic fathers, and children and fathers with special needs and disabilities

- specific funding for recruitment and outreach by schools and family learning providers to engage hard-to-reach learners such as fathers

- specific funding for LEAs and schools to recruit home–school liaison practitioners, fathers workers and other community workers, and to give some teachers some non-classroom time to work with fathers and mothers.

• Increased fathers' involvement in schools would also be facilitated by continued work by the DfES, the Teacher Training Agency, LEAs and schools to:

- increase the number of male teachers and other staff in schools

- pilot initiatives and subsequently make longer-term changes to make schools more attractive to current and future generations of boys, without disadvantaging girls.

References

Aldous, J. and Mulligan, G. (2002) Fathers' Child Care and Children's Behavior Problems: A Longitudinal Study. *Journal of Family Issues*, **23(5)**, 624-647.

Allared, P. and David, M. (2002) Minding the gap: children and young people negotiating relations between home and school. In R. Edwards (Ed.), *Children, Home and School: Resistance, Autonomy or Connection?* London: Routledge Falmer.

Amato, P. and Gilbreth, J. (1999) Non-resident fathers and children's well-being: A meta-analysis. *Journal of Marriage and the Family*, **61**, 557-573.

Amato, P. and Sobolewski, J. (2004) The Effects of Divorce on Fathers and Children: Nonresidential Fathers and Stepfathers. In M. Lamb (Ed.), *The Role of the Father in Child Development*, 4th Edition. New Jersey: John Wiley & Sons.

Arnold, H. and Higginson, J. (2001) *Dads on Computers*. Unpublished: Children North-East.

Austin, J. (1993) The impact of school policies on noncustodial parents. *Journal of Divorce and Remarriage*, **20 (3/4)**, 153-170.

Baker, R. and McMurray, A. (1998) Contact Fathers' Loss of School Involvement. *Journal of Family Studies,* **4(2)**, 201-214.

Bakermans-Kranenburg, M., Van Ijzendoorn, M. and Juffer, F. (2003) Less is more: Meta-analyses of sensitivity and attachment interventions in early childhood. *Psychological Bulletin*, **129**, 195-215.

Ballard, K., Bray, A., Shelton, E. and Clarkson, J. (1997) Children with Disabilities and the Education System: The Experiences of Fifteen Fathers. *International Journal of Disability, Development and Education*, **44(3)**, 229-241.

Barber, B. (1994) Support and advice from married and divorced fathers: Linkages to adolescent adjustment. *Family Relations*, **43**, 433-438.

Bastiani, J. (1999) *SHARE: An evaluation of the first two years*. Coventry: CEDC.

BBC News (1998) *'Cyberdads' on the button*. 14 January 1998. Online at www.bbc.co.uk in June 2004.

BBC News (2002) *Time off call for fathers*. 7 August 2002. Online at www.bbc.co.uk in June 2004.

BBC News (2003) *'Super dads' improve pupils' skills*. 9 June 2003. Online at www.bbc.co.uk in June 2004.

Becher, H. and Husain, F. (2003) *Supporting Ethnic Minority Families: South Asian Hindus and Muslims in Britain: developments in family support*. London: National Family and Parenting Institute.

Beinhart, S. and Smith, P. (1997) National Adult Learning Survey 1997. *DfEE Research Report 49*. London: DfES.

Berger, E. (1998) Don't Shut Fathers Out. *Early Childhood Education Journal*. **26(1)**, 57-61.

Bignall, T. and Butt, J. (2001) Supporting fathers as parents. *Black and Minority Ethnic Families Policy Forum Discussion Paper 3*. London: REU.

Black Development Agency (2002) *Black Fathers Empowerment Project: Report for Black Development Agency. October 2002*. Unpublished: Black Development Agency.

Blackwell, F. and Dawe, F. (2004) *Non-resident parental contact with children*. London: National Statistics. Online at www.dfes.gov.uk/childcontactsurvey/ on 29/4/04.

Bradshaw, J., Skinner, C., Stimson, C. and Williams, J. (1999) *Absent fathers?* London: Routledge.

Brassett-Grundy, A. (2002) Parental Perspectives of Family Learning. *Wider Benefits of Learning Research Report No. 2*. London: Institute of Education.

Bright, K., Silberberg, S. and Fletcher, R. (2002) Men's Views of Volunteering in Schools. *Engaging Fathers Project Research Report*. Newcastle, Australia: The Family Action Centre at The University of Newcastle. Downloaded from www.newcastle.edu.au/centre/fac/efathers on 5/9/03.

Brookes, S. (2002) Reaching Fathers. *Literacy Today,* September 2002.

Brooks, G., Cole, P., Davies, P., Davis, B., Frater, G., Harman, J. and Hutchison, D. (2002) *Keeping Up with the Children: Evaluation for the Basic Skills Agency by the University of Sheffield and the National Foundation for Educational Research*. London: Basic Skills Agency.

Brooks, G., Gorman, T., Harman, J., Hutchison, D., Kinder, K., Moor, H. and Wikin, A. (1997) *Family Literacy Lasts: The NFER Follow-up Study of the Basic Skills Agency's Demonstration Programmes*. London: Basic Skills Agency.

Brooks, G., Gorman, T., Harman, J., Hutchison, D. and Wilkin, A. (1996) *Family Literacy Works*. London: The Basic Skills Agency.

Brown, B., Michelsen, E., Halle, T. and Moore, K. (2001) Fathers' Activities with Their Kids. *Child Trends Research Brief*. Washington DC: Child Trends, Inc.

Bruneau, S. (2002) *Research Report into the Levels of Involvement of African Caribbean Fathers in their Children's Lives and Education*. Unpublished: The Harmony Project, West Midlands Caribbean Parents and Friends Association.

Bryant, A. and Zimmerman, M. (2003) Role Models and Psychosocial Outcomes Among African American Adolescents. *Journal of Adolescent Research,* **18(1),** 36-67.

Bryant, D. (2000) *Hartcliffe and Withywood Fathers for Family Learning Report: November 2000*. Bristol: Bristol Community Education.

Bryant, D. and Henderson, A. (2002) *Men's Family Learning Conference Report: Royal Marriott Hotel, Bristol, Friday 11th October 2002*. Bristol: Bristol Community Education Service.

Bryant, D., Robinson, G. and Taylor, J. (1998) *Men's Family Learning Project, Hartcliffe, Bristol: April 1998.* Bristol: Bristol Community Education.

Bryant, D. and Taylor, J. (1999) What about men? *Adults Learning*, January 1999, pages 9-11.

Buchel, F. and Duncan, G. (1998) Do parents' social activities promote children's school attainments? Evidence from the German Socioeconomic Panel. *Journal of Marriage and the Family,* **60(1),** 95-108.

Burgess, A. (2002) Fathers and families. *Parenting Education & Support Forum In Practice Paper.* London: Parenting Education & Support Forum.

Burgess, A. and Bartlett, D. (2004) *Working with Fathers: a guide for everyone working with families.* London: Fathers Direct.

Burgess, A. and Ruxton, S. (1996) *Men and their children: Proposals for public policy.* London: Institute for Public Policy Research.

Caddell, D. (1996) *Roles, Responsibilities and Relationships: Engendering Parental Involvement.* Paper presented at SERA conference, September 1996.

Cairney, T., Ruge, J., Buchanan, J., Lowe, K. and Mumsie, L. (1995) *Developing partnerships: The home school and community interface, Vols 1 & 2.* University of Western Sydney: DEET.

Camp, C. (2004) *Right to Request Flexible Working: Review of Impact in First Year of Legislation. Report for the DTI.* London: Working Families.

Campaign for Learning (2000) *A Manifesto for Family Learning.* London: Campaign for Learning (NIACE, Scottish Council Foundation, CEDC, Education Extra).

Carter, R. and Wojtkiewicz, R. (2000) Parental involvement with adolescents' education: Do daughters or sons get more help? *Adolescence,* **35(137),** 29-44.

Chen, X., Liu, M. and Li, N. (2000) Parental warmth, control and indulgence, and their relations to adjustment in Chinese children: A longitudinal study. *Journal of Family Psychology,* **14**, 401-419.

Chisholm, C., Haggart, J. and Horne, J. (2004) *Starting points in developing wider family learning.* Leicester: NIACE.

Clarke, C. and O'Brien, M. (2004) Father Involvement in Britain: the Research and Policy Evidence. In R. Day and M. Lamb (Eds.) *Reconceptualising and Measuring Fatherhood.* New Jersey: Lawrence Erlbaum.

Clough, J., Johnson, R., Fundudis, T. and Le Couteur, A. (2000) Engaging parents in a primary school setting Children. *Children North East Research Report.* Newcastle upon Tyne: Children North East.

Coleman, J. (1988) Social capital in the creation of human capital. *American Journal of Sociology,* **94**, S94-S120.

ContinYou. *Fathers and Reading Project.* Coventry: Continyou

David, M. (1998) Involvements and Investment in Education: Mothers and Schools. *Journal for a Just and Caring Education*, **4(1)**, 30-46.

Dean, J. (1999) *Improving the primary school*. London: Routledge.

De Nicola, A. (1997) Dads in School. *New Moon Network*, **Vol. 4,** Issue 6.

Department for Constitutional Affairs, Department for Education and Skills and Department for Trade and Industry (2004) *Parental Separation: Children's Needs and Parents' Responsibilities*. Norwich: The Stationery Office.

Department for Education and Employment (DfEE) (1998) *Excellence in schools*. London: The Stationery Office.

DfEE (1998) Learning Together: family learning case studies. In *Study Support: A Code of Practice for the Primary Sector*. London: DfEE.

DfEE (2000) *Schools, 'Parents' and 'Parental Responsibility' REF: DfEE 0092/2000*. Online at www.standards.dfes.gov.uk in October 2004.

DfEE (2001) *Skills for Life: the national strategy for improving adult literacy and numeracy skills*. London: DfEE.

Department for Education and Skills (DfES) (2002a) *Dads & Sons: a winning team*. London: DfES. Online at www.dfes.gov.uk/dadsandsons/ in July 2004.

DfES (2002b) *Parents and Schools*, Issue 5, Spring 2002. London: DfES.

DfES (2003a) Family Learning: Dad's The Word. *Parents + Schools,* **Issue 8**, Summer 2003. Sheffield: DfES.

DfES (2003b) The Skills for Life survey: A national needs and impact survey of literacy, numeracy and ICT skills. *DfES Research Brief RB490*. London: DfES.

DfES (2003c) *Children and Young People Survey: Summary of Results: July 2003*. London: DfES. Downloaded from http://www.dfes.gov.uk/research in July 2004.

DfES (2003d) *The Impact of Parental Involvement on Children's Education*. London: DfES.

DfES (2003e) *David Beckham congratulates Reading Champions 2003*. Press notice, 10 December 2003. Online at www.dfes.gov.uk/pns in July 2004.

DfES (2004a) *Engaging fathers – Involving parents, raising achievement*. London: DfES.

DfES (2004b) *Five Year Strategy for Children and Learners*. Norwich: The Stationery Office.

DfES (2004c) *Biggest reform of children's services for 30 years set out in Children Bill.* Press notice, 04 March 2004. Online at www.dfes.gov.uk/pns in July 2004.

DfES and the Learning and Skills Council (LSC) (2004a) *August 2004 – July 2005: Skills for Families Phase Two Prospectus*. London: DfES/LSC. Downloaded from http://www. skillsforfamilies.org in October 2004.

DfES and the LSC (2004b) *Skills for Families: Information and Guidance for Local Education Authorities, Learning and Skills Councils and Partners. March 2003 – March 2004*. London: DfES/LSC. Downloaded from http://www.skillsforfamilies.org in October 2004.

Department for Trade and Industry (DTI) (2003a) *Flexible working – the right to request: A basic summary (PL516 Rev 1)*. London: DTI.

DTI (2003b) *Parental leave summary guidance*. London: DTI. Online at www.dti.gov.uk/er/ parental_leave.htm in October 2004.

Desforges, C. and Abouchaar, A. (2003) The Impact of Parental Involvement, Parental Support and Family Education on Pupil Achievement and Adjustment: A Literature Review. *DfES Research Report 433*. London: DfES.

Dex, S. and Smith, C. (2002) The nature and pattern of family-friendly employment policies in Britain. *Joseph Rowntree Foundation Family and Work Series.* Bristol: Policy Press.

Dryler, H. (1998) Parental Role Models, Gender and Educational Choice. *British Journal of Sociology*, **49(3)**, 375-398.

Dudley-Marling, C. (2001) School Trouble: a mother's burden. *Gender and Education*, **13**(2), 183-198.

Dunn, J., Davies, L. and O'Connor, T. (2000) Parents' and Partners' Life Course and Family Experiences: Links with Parent-Child Relationships in Different Family Settings. *Journal of Child Psychology and Psychiatry*. 41, 955-968.

Eccles, J. (1983) Expectanices, values and academic behaviours. In J. Spence (Ed.) *The Development of Achievement Motivation*. Greenwich, CA: JAI.

Ellis, A. (2003) Barriers to Participation for Under-represented Groups in School Governance. *DfES Research Report RB500*. London: DfES.

Epstein, J. (2002) School, Family, and Community Partnerships: Caring for the Children We Share. In J. Epstein, M. Sanders, B. Simon, K. Salinas, N. Jansorn and F. Van Voorhis, *School, Family, and Community Partnerships: Your Handbook for Action, Second Edition*. Thousand Oaks, CA: Corwin Press.

Equal Opportunities Commission (EOC) (2003) Fathers: balancing work and family. *EOC Research findings*. Manchester: EOC.

EOC (2004) *Facts About Dads Today*. Manchester: EOC. Online at www.eoc.org.uk in October 2004.

Eslea, M. and Smith, P. (2000) Pupil and parent attitudes towards bullying in primary schools. *European Journal of Psychology of Education,* **XV(2)**, 207-219.

Fajerman, L. (2000) *Involving fathers in their sons' reading*. London: Save The Children.

Fathers Direct (2003) *Fatherwork news: Fathers Direct response to the Green Paper, Every Child Matters*. On www.fathersdirect.com/fatherwork/news on 29/6/04.

Fathers Direct (2004a) *Strengthen parental rights to flexible working, demand fathers on first anniversary of reforms*. Press release, 4 April 2004. Online at www.fathersdirect. com/media on 29/6/04.

Fathers Direct (2004b) *Hewitt urged to back 'Charter for Father Friendly Britain' at Europe's largest Fatherhood conference*. Press release, 4 April 2004. Online at www.fathersdirect. com/media on 29/6/04.

Feinstein, L. and Symons, J. (1999) Attainment in secondary school. *Oxford Economic Papers*, **51**, 300-321.

Fishbein, I. and Ajzen, M. (1980) *Understanding attitudes and predicting social behavior.* Englewood Cliffs, NJ: Prentice Hall.

Fisher, D. (2004) *21st century Dad. Speech by Duncan Fisher, Director of Fathers Direct. at National Conference on Working with Fathers, 5 April, 2004, London*. Online at www. fathersdirect.com/news on 29/6/04.

Fitzgerald, R., Taylor, R. and La Valle, I. (2003) National Adult Learning Survey (NALS) 2002. *DfES Research Report 415.* London: DfES.

Fletcher, R. (1997) *Getting dads involved in schools: Recruiting Fathers to be Partners with Schools.* New South Wales: University of Newcastle Family Action Centre.

Fletcher, R. (2001) Engaging Fathers Project: Lessons from the first year. *Engaging Fathers Project Research Paper presented to the Parenting Australia Conference, 2001.* Downloaded from www.newcastle.edu.au/centre/fac/efathers on 5/9/03

Fletcher, R. (2002) *Checklist for Including Fathers and Father Figures in Schools.* Newcastle, Australia: The Family Action Centre at the University of Newcastle. Downloaded from www.newcastle.edu.au/centre/fac/efathers on 5/9/03.

Fletcher, R. (2003) *Five Rules for Attracting Fathers and Father Figures*. Newcastle, Australia: The Family Action Centre at the University of Newcastle. Downloaded from www. newcastle.edu.au/centre/fac/efathers on 5/9/03

Fletcher, R. and Dally, K. (2002) *Fathers' Involvement in Their Children's Literacy Development.* Newcastle, Australia: The Family Action Centre at the University of Newcastle. Downloaded from www.newcastle.edu.au/centre/fac/efathers on 5/9/03.

Fletcher, R. and Silberberg, S. (2002) *Father Involvement Inventory*. Newcastle, Australia: The Family Action Centre at the University of Newcastle. Downloaded from www. newcastle.edu.au/centre/fac/efathers on 5/9/03.

Flouri, E. and Buchanan, A. (2001) 'Father time'. *Community Care*, **4-10 October**.

Flouri, E. and Buchanan, A. (2003a) *Report for the ESRC R000223309: Father involvement and outcomes in adolescence and adulthood. End of Award Report. 24 October 2001*. Online at www.literacytrust.org.uk on 16/6/03.

Flouri, E. and Buchanan, A. (2003b) What predicts fathers' involvement with their children? A prospective study of intact families. *British Journal of Developmental Psychology*, **21,** 81-98.

Flouri, E. and Buchanan, A. (2004) Early father's and mother's involvement and child's later educational outcomes. *British Journal of Educational Psychology*, **74**, 141-153.

Flouri, E., Buchanan, A. and Bream, V. (2000) Adolescents' perceptions of their fathers' involvement: Significance to school attitudes. *Psychology in the Schools*. 39, 575-582.

Frieman, B. (1998) What Early Childhood Educators Need to Know About Divorced Fathers. *Early Childhood Education Journal*, **25(4),** 239-241.

Frieman, B. and Berkeley, T. (2002) Encouraging Fathers To Participate in the School Experiences of Young Children: The Teacher's Role. *Early Childhood Education Journal*, **29(3)**, 209-213.

Geraci, P. (2001) Fathering Program Implementation: A Teacher's Experience. *Journal of Correctional Education*, **52**(1), 2-3.

Gershuny, J. (2000) *Changing Times – Work and Leisure in Post-Industrial Society*. Oxford: Oxford University Press.

Ghate, D., Shaw, C. and Hazel, N. (2000) *Fathers and Family Centres: Engaging fathers in preventative services*. York: Joseph Rowntree Foundation.

Gingerbread (2001) *Becoming visible: focus on lone fathers*. London: Gingerbread.

Halle, T. (1999) The Meaning of Father Involvement for Children. *Child Trends Research Brief*. Washington DC: Child Trends Inc.

Halle, T. (2001) *Changing Parenthood: A Statistical Portrait of Fathers and Mothers in America*. Washington DC: Child Trends Inc. Downloaded from http://fatherhood.hhs.gov/charting02/Parenting.htm on 13/5/2004.

Hampshire County Council (2002) Lads and Dads are getting hooked on books! *Hampshire Now*, **Issue 7**, Summer 2002**.** Online at http://www.hants.gov.uk/hampshirenow/issue7/ladndad.html in April 2004.

Hampshire County Council Library Service (undated) *Dads 'n' Lads reading list*. Hampshire: Hampshire County Council Library Service.

Haringey Council. Parental Involvement Celebration Day. *Haringey Ethnic Minority Achievement Bulletin*, **Issue 12.**

Hatter, W., Vinter, L. and Williams, R. (2002) Dads on Dads: Needs and expectations at home and at work. *EOC Research Discussion Series*. Manchester: EOC.

Henricson, C., Katz, I., Mesie, J., Sandison, M. and Tunstill, J. (2001) *National Mapping of Family Services in England and Wales – a consultation document: Executive Summary & Consultation Questions*. London: National Family and Parenting Institute.

Herb, S. and Willoughby-Herb, S. (1998) A Focus on Fathers: The Role of Males in Children's Literacy Development. *Knowledge Quest*, **26(4)**, 44-49.

Herrick, C. and Ali, A. (2003) *Fastlane: Men and Family Learning: Report on an action-research project within an ethnic minority community*. Huddersfield: University of Huddersfield.

Hetherington, E. and Kelly, J. (2002) *For better or for worse: Divorce reconsidered*. New York: Norton.

Hewitt, P. (2004) *Keynote speech, Father's Direct, 'Working With Fathers' conference: London, Monday 5 April 2004*. Online at http://www.dti.gov.uk/ministers/speeches/hewitt050404.html in August 2004.

Heymann, S. and Earle, A. (2001) The Impact of Parental Working Conditions on School-Age Children: The Case of Evening Work. *Community, Work and Family*, **4(3)**, 305-325.

HM Treasury and DfES (2003) *Every Child Matters*. Norwich: The Stationery Office.

HM Treasury and Department for Trade and Industry (2003) *Balancing work and family life: enhancing choice and support for parents. January 2003.* Norwich: The Stationery Office.

Hobcraft, J. (1998a) Childhood experience and the risks of social exclusion in adulthood. *CASE brief 8, November 1998.* London: Centre for Analysis of Social Exclusion, London School of Economics. Downloaded from http://sticerd.lse.ac.uk/case.htm in April 2004.

Hobcraft, J. (1998b) Intergenerational and Life-Course Transmission of Social Exclusion: Influences of Childhood Poverty, Family Disruption, and Contact with the Police. *CASE paper 15, November 1998.* London: Centre for Analysis of Social Exclusion, London School of Economics. Downloaded from ttp://sticerd.lse.ac.uk/case.htm in April 2004.

Home Office (1998a) *Boys, young men and fathers: a ministerial seminar 16 November 1998: Seminar report.* London: Home Office. Downloaded from www.homeoffice.gov.uk/cpd/fmpu/boys.htm on 16/1/03.

Home Office (1998b) *Supporting Families: a consultation document.* London: The Stationery Office.

Jaffee, S., Moffitt, T., Caspi, A. and Taylor, A. (2003) Life with (or without) father: The benefits of living with two biological parents depend on the father's antisocial behaviour. *Child Development, **74**,* 109-126.

Jodl, K., Michael, A., Malanchuk, O., Eccles, J. and Sameroff, A. (2001) Parents' Roles in Shaping Early Adolescents' Occupational Aspirations. *Child Development,* **72(4)**, 1247-1265.

Joseph Rowntree Foundation (2002) The influence of atypical working hours on family life. *Joseph Rowntree Foundation Findings,* Ref. 982. York: Joseph Rowntree Foundation.

Joseph Rowntree Foundation (2003) Family Time. *JRF Search 3B,* **Winter 2003.**

Karther, D. (2002) Fathers with low literacy and their young children. *The Reading Teacher,* **56(2)**, 184-193.

Katz, A. (2003) *Leading Lads.* London: Young Voice.

Kids Club Network (2003) *2003 Buzz Survey.* London: Kids Club Network.

Kim, K. and Rohner, R. (2002) Parental Warmth, Control, and Involvement in Schooling: Predicting Academic Achievement Among Korean American Adolescents. *Journal of Cross-Cultural Psychology,* **33(2)**, 127-140.

Kings, T. (2004) Inside out: the Big Book Share. *Library and Information Update January 2004,* **Vol 3 (1)**, 24-26.

La Valle, I., Arthur, S., Millward, C., Scott, J. and Clayden, M. (2002) *The influence of atypical working hours on family life.* Bristol: Policy Press.

Lamb, M. and Tamis-Lemonda, C. (2004) The Role of the Father: An Introduction. In M. Lamb (Ed.) *The Role of the Father in Child Development,* 4th Edition. New Jersey: John Wiley & Sons.

Lamb, M. and Lewis, C. (2004) The Development and Significance of Father-Child relationships in Two-Parent Families. In M. Lamb (Ed.) *The Role of the Father in Child Development*, 4th Edition. New Jersey: John Wiley & Sons.

Lancashire County Council. *Lancashire's Dads read with their Lads - and they make a great team!* Preston: Lancashire County Council.

Larson, R., Gillman, S. and Richards, M. (1997) Divergent Experiences of Family Leisure: Fathers, Mothers and Young Adolescents. *Journal of Leisure Research*, **29(1)**, 78-97.

Learning and Skills Council (LSC) (2004) *Family Programmes: Guidance for Local Learning and Skills Councils and Local Education Authorities 2004/05, February 2004*. Coventry: LSC. Downloaded from http://www.skillsforfamilies.org in October 2004.

Le Menestrel, S. (1999) What do Fathers Contribute to Children's Well-Being? *Child Trends Research Brief*. Washington DC: Child Trends Inc.

Levine, J., Murphy, D. and Wilson, S. (1993) *Getting Men Involved: Strategies for Early Childhood Programmes*. New York: Families and Work Institute.

Lewis, A. (2000a) *SHARE at Key Stage 2: Pilot Project 1999, Evaluation Report*. Coventry: CEDC.

Lewis, C. (2000b) A man's place in the home: Fathers and families in the UK. *Joseph Rowntree Foundation Findings*, Ref 440. York: Joseph Rowntree Foundation.

Lewis, C. and Warin, J. (2001)[1] What Good Are Dads? *Father Facts*, Volume 1, Issue 1. Fathers Direct/NEWPIN Fathers Support Centre/ NFPI/ Working with Men.

Lloyd, T. (1999) *Reading for the future: boys' and fathers' views on reading.* London: Save the Children.

Lloyd, T. (2001) *What works with fathers?* London: Working with Men.

Lloyd, N., O'Brien, M. and Lewis, C. (2003) Fathers in Sure Start. *NESS Evaluation Report*, No. 02. London: DfES.

Lugaila, T. (2003) A Child's Day: 2000 (Selected Indicators of Child Well-Being). *Current Population Reports*, P70-89. Washington, DC: US Census Bureau.

Lynch, J. (2002) Parents' self-efficacy beliefs, parents' gender, children's reader self-perceptions, reading achievement and gender. *Journal of Research in Reading*, **25(1)**, 54-67.

Macleod, F. (2000) Low Attendance by Fathers at Family Literacy Events: Some Tentative Explanations. *Early Child Development and Care*, **161**, 107-119.

Marley, A. (2000) The Lads and Dads Experiment. *Youth Library Review*, **Issue 28**, Spring 2000.

Marsiglio, W., Amato, P., Day, R. and Lamb, M. (2000) Scholarship on Fatherhood in the 1990s and Beyond. *Journal of Marriage and the Family*, **62**, 1173-1191.

---

1 This date is not on the publication.

Martin, P. (2003) *Mid-project Report on the findings of the Fathers and Children in Education Project: August* 2002 to August 2003. Ipswich: Ormiston Children & Families Trust (Fathers & Families in Suffolk).

McCormick, J. (1998) *Family Learning: Parents as co-educators*. Edinburgh: Scottish Council Foundation and Institute for Public Policy Research.

McGivney, V. (1999) *Excluded Men: Men who are missing from education and training*. Leicester: NIACE.

McGivney, V. (2004) *Men earn, Women learn: Bridging the gender divide in education and training*. Leicester: NIACE.

Milkie, M., Simon, R. and Powell, B. (1997) Through the Eyes of Children: Youths' Perceptions and Evaluations of Maternal and Paternal Roles. *Social Psychology Quarterly*, **60(3)**, 218-237.

Millard, E. and Hunter, R. (2001) *It's A man thing!: Evaluation report of CEDC's Fathers and Reading Project*. Coventry: CEDC.

Milligan, C. and Dowie, A. (1998) What do children need from their fathers? *Occasional Paper No. 42*, Centre for Theology and Public Issues. Edinburgh: University of Edinburgh.

Milligan, C. and Smith, E. (1999) *Cool Dads: what do children need?* Edinburgh: University of Edinburgh.

Mitchell, M. (1993) School Dads. *Essence*, **24**(7), p132.

Morgan, A, and Hall, R. (1999) Learning Together: family learning case studies. In *Study Support: A Code of Practice for the Primary Sector*. London: DfEE

MORI Social Research Institute (2003) Higher Education An Aspiration for Most Young People. *MORI Education Research Unit Newsletter*, Issue 1, March 2003.

National Center for Fathering (1999) *1999 National Random Sample Poll Results: Father Involvement in Education*. Downloaded from www.fathers.com in August 2004.

National Foundation for Educational Research and the Basic Skills Agency (1996) *Family Literacy Works: Key findings from the NFER Evaluation of the Basic Skills Agency's Demonstration Programmes*. London: Basic Skills Agency.

National Statistics (2002) *Social Focus in Brief: Ethnicity*. London: Office for National Statistics.

National Statistics (2003) *Statistics of Education: Schools in England. 2003 Edition*. London: DfES.

New Directions Consulting Ltd (2004a) *Development of National Occupational Standards for Work With Parents: Draft Unit and element titles following consultation. May 2004. Version 5 – Post Consultation.* Downloaded from www.parenting-forum.org.uk in September 2004.

New Directions Consulting Ltd (2004b) *Development of National Occupational Standards for Family Learning: Draft Unit and element titles following consultation. May 2004. Version 3 – Post Consultation.* Downloaded from www.niace.org.uk in September 2004.

NIACE (2003) *Evaluation of LSC Funded Family Programmes*. Leicester: NIACE. Downloaded from www.niace.org.uk/Research/Family/ in August 2004.

NIACE (2004) *Evaluation of LSC Funded Family Programmes - Taking Forward the Recommendations: Updated Action Plan – March 2004*. Leicester: NIACE. Downloaded from www.niace.org.uk/Research/Family/ in August 2004.

Nord, C. (1998) Father Involvement in Schools. *ERIC Digest*, **ED419632**. Washington DC: US Department of Education, National Center for Education Statistics.

Nord, C., Brimhall, D. and West, J. (1997) Fathers' Involvement in Their Children's Schools. *Statistical Analysis Report: National Household Education Survey*. NCES 98-091. Washington DC: US Department of Education, National Center for Education Statistics.

Nord, C., Brimhall, D. and West, J. (1998) Dads' Involvement in their kids' schools. *The Education Digest*, **63**(7), 29-35.

O'Brien, M. (2004) *Fathers and Family Support Services: Promoting involvement and evaluating impact*. London: National Family and Parenting Institute.

O'Brien, M. and Jones, D. (1995) Young People's Attitudes to Fatherhood. In P. Moss (Ed.) *Father Figures*. Scotland: HMSO.

O'Brien, M. and Jones, D. (1996) The Absence and Presence of Fathers: Accounts from Children's Diaries. In U. Bjornberg and A. K. Kollind (Eds.) *Men's Family Relations*. Sweden: University of Goteborg.

O'Brien, M. and Shemilt, I. (2003) Working Fathers: Earning and Caring. *EOC Research Discussion Series*. Manchester: EOC.

Office for National Statistics (2003) *Census 2001: Children: 11.7 million dependent children in England and Wales*. Online at www.statistics.gov.uk/CCI in October 2004.

Ofsted (2000) *Family Learning – A survey of current practice*. London: Ofsted.

Ofsted (2003a) *Inspecting Schools: Framework for Inspecting Schools: Effective from September 2003*. London: Ofsted.

Ofsted (2003b) *Inspecting schools: A guide for parents (for inspections from September 2003)*. London: Ofsted.

Orme, D. (1999) *Read me another, Dad!* London: Save The Children.

Ortiz, R. (2001) Pivotal Parents: Emergent Themes and Implications on Father Involvement in Children's Early Literacy Experiences. *Reading Improvement*, **38(3)**, 132-144.

Ortiz, R. and McCarty, L. (1997) 'Daddy, Read to me': Fathers Helping Their Young Children Learn to Read. *Reading Horizons*, **38**, 108-115.

Palkovitz, R. and Palm, G. (1998) Fatherhood and faith in formation: The developmental effects of fathering on religiosity, morals, and values. *Journal of Men's Studies,* **7,** 33-51.

Paulson, S. and Sputa, C. (1996) Patterns of Parenting During Adolescence: Perceptions of Adolescents and Parents, *Adolescence*, **31(122)**, 369-381.

Pendleton, R. (2003) Involving Dads. *Teachers,* **May 2003**.

Pleck, J. and Masciadrelli, B. (2004) Paternal Involvement by U.S. Residential Fathers: Levels, Sources, and Consequences. In M. Lamb (Ed.) *The Role of the Father in Child Development* (4th Edition). New Jersey: John Wiley & Sons.

Radin, N. (1981) The role of the father in cognitive, academic and intellectual development. In M. Lamb (Ed.), *The Role of the Father in Child Development,* 2nd edition. New York: Wiley.

Raty, H., Snellman, L. and Vainikainen, A. (1999) Parents' assessments of their children's abilities. *European Journal of Psychology and Education,* **14(3)**, 423-437.

Raymond, C. and Benbow, C. (1986) Gender Differences in Mathematics: A Function of Parental Support and Student Sex Typing? *Developmental Psychology,* **22(6)**, 808-819.

Razwan, S. (2002) *Fathers' Involvement in Their Children's Upbringing and Education: A study of experiences of fathers and children in the Thornbury and Bradford Moor areas of Bradford.* Bradford: The Safestart Project, The Children's Society.

Reissman, R. (2001) The Dad Dimension. *New Good Apple Newspaper,* **28(5)**, 50-54.

Sharma, V. and Nairn, L. Dads only!: Ground Breaking SHARE Group at South Haringay Infants. *Haringey LEA Ethnic Minority Achievement Team Bulletin,* Issue 11.

Shumow, L. and Miller, J. (2001) Parents' At-Home and At-School Academic Involvement With Young Adolescents. *The Journal of Early Adolescence,* **21(1)**, 68-91.

Simpson, J. (2003) Mom Matters: Maternal Influence on the Choice of Academic Major. *Sex Roles,* **48(9-10)**, 447-460.

Singh, K., Bickley, P., Keith, T., Keith, P., Trivette, P. and Anderson, E. (1995) The effects of four components of parental involvement on eighth-grade achievement: structural analysis of NELS-88 data. *School Psychology Review.* 24 (2), 299-317.

Smithers, R. (2003) More men aim at primary teaching. *The Guardian,* 5 June 2003. Online at www.guardian.co.uk in July 2004.

Stewart, Susan D. (1999) Disneyland Dads, Disneyland Moms? How Nonresident Parents Spend Time With Absent Children. *Journal of Family Issues,* **20(4)**, 539-56.

Stile, S. and Ortiz, R. (1999) A Model for Involvement of Fathers in Literacy Development with Young At-Risk and Exceptional Children. *Early Childhood Education Journal,* **26(4)**, 221-224.

Teacher Training Agency (TTA) (2003a) *Teacher Training Agency headhunts men.* Press release, 24 October 2003. Online at www.tta.gov.uk in July 2004.

TTA (2003b) *Qualifying to Teach: Professional Standards for Qualified Teacher Status and Requirements for Initial Teacher Training.* London: TTA. Downloaded from ttp://www.tta.gov.uk/php in July 2004.

TTA (2003c*) Induction Standards: TTA guidance for newly qualified teachers.* London: TTA. Downloaded from http://www.teachernet.gov.uk in June 2004.

TTA (2004) *Qualifying to teach: Handbook of guidance: Spring 2004.* London: TTA. Downloaded from ttp://www.tta.gov.uk/php in July 2004.

Tenenbaum, H. and Leaper, C. (2003) Parent-Child Conversations About Science: The Socialization of Gender Inequities? *Developmental Psychology,* **39(1)**, 34-47.

The National Literacy Trust (2003) *The Primary Improvement Project.* London: The National Literacy Trust. Downloaded from www.literacytrust.org.uk on 16/6/03.

The Reading Agency (2003) *The Big Book Share: Libraries and Family Reading in Prisons: A Handbook.* St Albans: The Reading Agency.

Todd Jones, G. and Evans, M. (undated) *Developing Services for Fathers in a School Setting: Pen Pych Superdads Group.* Unpublished: Pen Pych Community Primary School.

Tranter, S. and Bright, K. (2004) *Fathers and Schools Together (FAST) Literacy Program Information Sheet* Newcastle, Australia: The Family Action Centre at the University of Newcastle. Downloaded from www.newcastle.edu.au/centre/fac/efathers on 5/9/03.

Trent, L., Cooney, G., Russell, G. and Warton, P. (1996) Significant others' contribution to early adolescents' perceptions of their competence. *British Journal of Educational Psychology,* **66(1)**, 95-107.

Trusty, J. and Pirtle, T. (1998) Parents' Transmission of Educational Goals to their Adolescent Children. *Journal of Research and Development in Education,* **32(1)**, 53-65.

Tucker, C., Barber, B. and Eccles, J. (2001) Advice about life plans from mothers, fathers, and siblings in always-married and divorced families during late adolescence. *Journal of Youth and Adolescence,* **30(6)**, 729-747.

Turbiville, V., Umbarger, G. and Guthrie, A. (2000) Fathers' Involvement in Programs for Young Children. *Young Children,* **55(4)**, 74-79.

Updegraff, K., McHale, S. and Crouter, A. (1996) Gender Roles in Marriage: What Do They Mean for Girls' and Boys' School Achievement? *Journal of Youth and Adolescence,* **25(1)**, 73-88.

Wallace, W. (2000) Pa for the course. *Times Educational Supplement,* 17/11/2000. Online at www.tes.co.uk.

Warin, J., Soloman, Y., Lewis, C. and Langford, W. (1999) *Fathers, work and family life.* London: Family Policy Studies Centre for Joseph Rowntree Foundation.

Waugh, G. and Redding, J. (2003) *Dads and Lads Programme Report 14th June – 2nd August 2003.* Bradford: City of Bradford YMCA.

Webster, P. (1999) Raising the status of design and technology through a family learning focus. In C. Benson and W. Till (Eds.) *Second international primary design and technology conference.* Birmingham: CRIPT at University of Central England.

West, A., Noden, P., Edge, A. and David, M. (1998) Parental Involvement in Education in and out of School. *British Education Research Journal,* **24(4)**, 461-484.

Williams, B., Williams, J. and Ullman, A. (2002) Parental Involvement in Education. *DfES Research Report* 332. London: DfES.

Women and Equality Unit (2004) *Equal Pay Questionnaire.* Online at www. womenandequalityunit.gov.uk/pay on 29/6/04.

Working Families (2003) *Factsheet: Shiftworking and Atypical Hours.* London: Working Families. Online at www.workingfamilies.org.uk/asp/family_zone on 29/6/04.

Working Families (2004) *Factsheet: Fathers rights. April 2004.* London: Working Families. Online at www.workingfamilies.org.uk/asp/family_zone on 29/6/04.

Working with Men (2001) *WWM Fathers Day Pack for primary schools.* London: Working with Men.

Working with Men (2004) *DIY Dads Project Report, 1999 to 2003.* London: Working with Men. Downloaded from www.workingwithmen.org on 15/12/03.

Yeung. J., Duncan, G. and Hill, M. (2000) Putting Fathers Back in the Picture: Parental Activities and Children's Adult Outcomes. *Marriage and Family Review,* **29(2/3)**, 97-113.

Zimmerman, M., Salem, D. and Maton, K. (1995) Family structure and psychosocial correlates among urban African American adolescent males. *Child Development,* **66**, 1598-1613.

Appendix: Research methods

A review of research evidence and other literature on fathers' involvement in their children's learning and education

Extensive searches of educational and psychological bibliographic databases were carried out in summer 2003 to find published research and other literature[1] which related to fathers' involvement in their school-aged children's learning and education (see Tables 1, 2 and 3 in Chapter 2) and the different research questions for this evidence review (see Chapter 1).

Relevant English-language research studies and other literature, published or carried out between 1997 and 2004 in the UK, USA, Australia, New Zealand, Canada and Europe, were identified by using a long list of keywords (see the list later in this appendix). To be eligible for inclusion, citations had to include both an educational keyword and one of the keywords 'father', 'dad' or 'paternal' in their title, summary (i.e. abstract) and/or bibliographic database keywords. The reports or papers had to relate to school-aged children aged 4-16 years.

The searches excluded literature on the overall father–child relationship, father's overall parenting role and parenting style, work in schools with teenage fathers (unless focused on their children's learning and education), and fatherhood education in schools for boys and young men. See later section of this appendix for a list of exclusions.

Additionally, in summer 2003, numerous UK websites[2] (and a few selected websites in other countries) were searched, and requests were made over various academic, research, practitioner and organisational networks, to locate other relevant research and literature (for example, ongoing research and unpublished project evaluations). A few journals (e.g. *Fatherwork,* published by Fathers Direct) were hand-searched.

All the chapters in this report except for Chapter 3 are based on a full review of all the relevant literature found in the searches. In Chapter 3, a more restricted range of literature is reported, as explained in that chapter.

A review of recent and current initiatives in England and Wales that engage fathers in family learning and/or in schools

Requests were made in summer 2003 over various organisational and practitioner networks for information on current or recent home–school and family learning programmes in England and Wales which aimed specifically to engage fathers and other male carers; or which were

---

1   For example, articles in journals, newspapers and magazines written by journalists, policymakers and practitioners.

2   Including the websites of major funders of educational research in the UK, and the websites of academics, other researchers and organisations leading in the fields of parental involvement in children's education, family learning and fatherhood.

for mothers, fathers and carers but attracted fathers in substantial numbers. Project managers of these initiatives were asked to send reports of any evaluation of their programme.

Additionally, numerous UK websites (and a few selected websites in other countries) were searched to identify further initiatives and resources (such as training and good practice recommendations) relevant to fathers' involvement in their children's learning and education. Further contacts were made at a number of conferences and seminars. A few journals (e.g. *Fatherwork,* published by Fathers Direct) were hand-searched.

Thirteen in-depth case studies of schools and family learning programmes in England and Wales which successfully engage fathers

From the review of recent and current initiatives in England and Wales that engage fathers in family learning and/or in schools, 13 programmes were selected for detailed case study. The selection process ensured that there was a range of projects on the following criteria:

- age-group of children

- target groups of fathers and children

- provider and venue

- curricular area and learning methods, for family learning programmes

- type of school involvement, for home–school programmes.

Beyond these criteria, priority was given to initiatives with evidence-based practice such as an evaluation.

In 2003-04, a semi-structured telephone interview was carried out with the project manager of each initiative. Additionally, project documentation and any evaluation reports were reviewed, and the internet was searched to identify any further information, including articles in the press. A written case study of each initiative was developed under common themes (see Chapter 6). Finally, the manager of each initiative was given an opportunity to comment on each written case study before it was finalised.

Further details on the searches of bibliographic databases

The databases searched were:

British Education Index (BEI)

Education Line

Education Resources Information Center (ERIC)

Educational Research Abstracts (ERA)

Scottish Council for Research in Education (SCRE)

Psych Info

EBSCO Sociological Collection

EBSCO Behavioural Sciences Collection

ESRC Regard

Current Educational Research in the UK (CERUK)

Library Catalogue of National Family and Parenting Institute

Library Catalogue of Department for Education and Skills

The following keywords were used for searches:

father* and school*

father* and educat*

father* and academic*

father* and learn*

father* and teach*

father* and classroom*

father* and kindergarten*

father* and nursery*

father* and pupil*

father* and student*

father* and homework

father* and leisure*

father and recreation*

father* and achieve*

father* and grade*

father* and curricul*

father* and play*

father* and numera* (numeracy)

father* and litera* (literacy)

father* and read*

dad* (and above keywords)

paternal* (and above keywords)

stepfather*

step-father*

"step father"

The following literature was excluded from the scope of this review:

- fathers' involvement with babies, infants and children younger than four years; or on fathers' involvement in ante-natal services, post-natal services, early years services, pre-school education, childcare and family support services for children under four years

- fathers' involvement with young people and adults older than 16 years

- role of fathers/fathering/fatherhood/father involvement, but no mention of children's learning or education

- overall father–child relationship/overall father–child interactions/overall parenting style/nurturing and attachment behaviours

- interventions with fathers (i.e. general parenting programmes) which aim to develop positive parenting style, father–child relationship and nurturing/attachment behaviours, but which do not focus on fathers' involvement in children's learning nor on fathers' involvement in schools

- fathers' involvement in care of children with disabilities or special needs, unless specifically concerned with children's learning and education or interaction with schools

- young fatherhood/programmes with teenage and young fathers (e.g. in schools) unless about involvement of these fathers with their own school-aged children's learning and education

- fatherhood education for children and young people in schools

- the impact of fathers' involvement in their children's learning and education on children's social or emotional outcomes which were not defined for the purposes of this research as 'educational outcomes' (see first footnote in Chapter 3), for example general well-being, overall self-esteem, overall confidence, overall self-efficacy, other aspects of psychological health, peer relationships, romantic relationships, relationships with family members, offending, conduct and behaviour outside school, sexual behaviour, teenage pregnancy, health outcomes and health behaviours.